Tourism Behaviour

Tourism Behaviour

Travellers' Decisions and Actions

Roger St George March

University of New South Wales, Australia

and

Arch G. Woodside

Boston College, USA

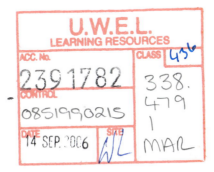
CABI Publishing

CABI Publishing is a division of CAB International

CABI Publishing
CAB International
Wallingford
Oxon OX10 8DE
UK

CABI Publishing
875 Massachusetts Avenue
7th Floor
Cambridge, MA 02139
USA

Tel: +44 (0)1491 832111
Fax: +44 (0)1491 833508
E-mail: cabi@cabi.org
Website: www.cabi-publishing.org

Tel: +1 617 395 4056
Fax: +1 617 354 6875
E-mail: cabi-nao@cabi.org

A catalogue record for this book is available from the British Library, London, UK.

Library of Congress Cataloging-in-Publication Data
March, Roger.
    Tourism behaviour : travellers' decisions and actions / Roger St. George March and Arch G. Woodside.
        p. cm.
    ISBN 0-85199-021-5 (alk. paper)
    1. Tourism--Psychological aspects. 2. Travelers--Psychology. 3. Consumer behaviour. I. Woodside, Arch G. II. Title.

    G155.A1M2655 2005
    910'.68'8--dc22

                                    2004026226

ISBN 0 85199 021 5

Typeset in 9pt Souvenir by Columns Design Ltd, Reading.
Printed and bound in the UK by Biddles Ltd, King's Lynn.

Contents

Preface

Tourism Behaviour focuses on deeply examining individuals' and households' thinking and behaviour relating to discretionary travel behaviour. The book comprises two parts. Part I includes three chapters covering new theories of tourism behaviour and examples of empirical examinations of these theories in three settings: Australia, Hawaii and Prince Edward Island (Canada). In eight chapters, Part II builds and examines a theory comparing leisure traveller plans and behaviour.

The book offers a theory and examination of the causes of why individuals do, versus do not, participate in leisure travel. Chapter 1 builds and examines an ecological system theory of how individuals make trade-offs among work, life maintenance, leisure and travel. The appendix to Chapter 1 includes an example of a complete survey instrument for probing the unconscious and conscious thinking regarding such work–leisure–travel trade-offs. Chapter 1 includes a step-by-step report of applying the theory to learn how the residents in one country (Australia) do, and do not, make travel-related decisions. The chapter includes tourism strategy implications for identifying and influencing (non)travellers through influencing their unconscious–conscious thought paths.

Chapter 2 presents the purchase–consumption system of the leisure travel framework, for examining how travel decisions interact in ways unanticipated by the traveller. As an example of how to apply the framework, Chapter 2 includes an empirical report of using the framework in a study of visitors to the Big Island of Hawaii. Chapter 2 closes by demonstrating tourism marketing implications from research results for the Big Island.

Chapter 3 extends the purchase–consumption system model to another field setting – Prince Edward Island. Chapter 3 thoroughly demonstrates the details on how to go about segmenting travellers by grouping alternative purchase–consumption systems of different visitors. Chapter 3 closes with answers to several key tourism strategists' issues raised when planning effective tourism marketing programmes.

While the three chapters in Part I focus on building theory from data using interpretative research methods, the eight chapters in Part II focus on uncovering and reporting the nitty-gritty details of how travellers' intended behaviours (their plans) match and differ from their actual travel behaviours. The chapters in Part II cover all four possibilities:

- planned behaviours that are done;
- planned behaviours that are not done;
- unplanned behaviours that are done; and
- unplanned behaviours that are not done (but available to do).

The eight chapters in Part II describe the method and compare the findings of two studies focusing on traveller planned versus done behaviour, respectively. Part II includes detailed recommendations for the tourism strategist on crafting messages, using communication media, designing trip experiences and identifying travellers who will, versus those who will never, return to a given destination.

The readers intended for Tourism Behaviour include tourism marketing strategists, researchers, scholars and students seeking a deep understanding and a rich description of consumers' thoughts and actions regarding their leisure and travel behaviour. The book consciously attempts to build bridges linking theory, research and management action that results in travellers satisfied with their trips, and successful tourism marketing strategies. Please contact each of us with your thoughts and suggestions for future editions of the book.

1 Ecological Systems in Lifestyle, Leisure and Travel Behaviour

Arch G. Woodside[1], Marylouise Caldwell[2] and Ray Spurr[3]
[1]Boston College, USA; [2]University of Sydney, Australia;
[3]University of New South Wales, Australia

Introduction

Ecological systems research focuses on describing and explaining the thoughts and actions of individuals and groups within specific contexts of their lives. This chapter applies ecological systems theory to examine the contextual facilitating and constraining factors in the thoughts and actions of individuals regarding work, leisure and travel alternatives. The chapter presents the results of a case research study of seven Australian households, with thought protocol data on these households' lived experiences in work, leisure and travel, and learning how they compare 'non-comparable' leisure expenditure options. The discussion leads to advancing macro- and micro-ecological systems theory in leisure travel behaviour. The chapter includes suggestions for future research and implications for tourism marketing strategy.

Ecological Systems Theory

Ecological systems theory (e.g. Bronfenbrenner, 1986, 1992; Raymore, 2002) states that an individual's thoughts and actions can be explained only by understanding the micro- and macrosystem of the person's environment. 'An ecological perspective of human development is concerned with understanding the contexts in which an individual exists, and incorporates the interactions between the indi-

vidual, other individuals, and the social structures of society to explain human development' (Raymore, 2002, pp. 41–42).

Microsystems include past and present roles, individuals and activities a person has experienced in his or her interactions, while a macrosystem includes belief systems regarding societal conceptions of ethnicity (i.e. a cultural mental model of correct behavioural practices for members of a particular society), socioeconomic status and gender, as well as best practices for structuring society and institutions.

This chapter advances ecological systems theory in examining individuals' lived experiences and choices in lifestyle, leisure and travel behaviours. The focus here is more limited than attempting to describe and understand 'turning points' in a person's path through life, from being with friends, marriage, career choice, job search and selection, decisions related to having and raising children, divorce, search for and selection of housing, and hundreds of additional major and minor thoughts and actions occurring in life. Rather, the focus here is on how travel and leisure pursuits occur, or do not occur, from an individual ecological systems perspective. This chapter confirms the usefulness of the facilitators–constraints interaction proposition (see Phillip, 1998; Raymore, 2002) for understanding and describing the combinations of factors resulting in travel, as well as non-travel, behaviours.

One of the objectives of conducting the study was to provide information and insights useful for planning effective marketing strategies by Australian national and regional government and near-government organizations (NGOs) to stimulate domestic leisure travel among Australians. Consequently, this chapter concludes with specific marketing strategy implications that follow from the case-study research data used for examining the ecological systems framework as applied to leisure behaviour.

The facilitators–constraints interaction proposition is that specific combinations of facilitating and constraining factors create paths leading to, versus preventing, certain outcomes (e.g. overnight travel or no travel during available leisure-time periods). The proposition matches with the comparative method perspective in sociology (see Ragin, 1987), that multiple paths of events occur that lead to one outcome versus its opposite (e.g. revolutions versus peaceful transformations). In defining facilitators Raymore (2002, p. 39) adapts Jackson's (1997) definition of constraints: 'Facilitators to leisure are factors that are assumed by researchers and perceived or experienced by individuals to enable or promote the formation of leisure preferences and to encourage or enhance participation'. For Jackson's constraints definition, substitute 'limit', 'inhibit' and 'prohibit' for 'enable', 'promote' and 'encourage or enhance' in the previous sentence.

Raymore (2002) crafts three levels of facilitator and constraint factors: intrapersonal (i.e. individual characteristics, traits and beliefs), interpersonal facilitators (i.e. other individuals and groups) and structural (i.e. social and physical institutions, organizations or belief systems of a society that operate external to the individual to promote or restrain leisure preferences and participation). The present chapter serves to examine how interactions across the three facilitator–constraint levels affect individuals' current thinking and behaviour.

Micro- and Macrosystems

Microsystems of individuals' lives include past and present roles and actions that often affect both subconscious and conscious thinking (cf. Wilson, 2002). This microsystem proposal rests on several tenets: (i) most thinking occurs unconsciously (for reviews, see Bargh, 2002; Zaltman, 2003); (ii) individuals and organizations make sense of their actions retrospectively (Weick, 1995); (iii) individuals tend to find themselves in contexts – situations in their lives – that they had not planned consciously to experience; (iv) in any one context, multiple facilitators and constraints interact to push, pull, block and prevent both thoughts and actions; and (v) individuals exhibit a volitional bias, that is, they tend to report that they decided to engage in a leisure behaviour, and planned actions required to complete such behaviour, without seeking information or help from others – they tend to become aware of the sequence of contextual facilitators and constraints affecting their thinking and actions only through guided self-examination and reflection (Woodside, 2005).

The following context illustrates the interaction of facilitators and constraints in one individual's microsystem and its impact on *not* engaging in a behaviour – that is, one more rewrite on a manuscript:

> Slowly an analysis takes shape and a paper develops. We may even reach a final delusional state where we think that with perhaps one more rewrite, the paper will rise from mere perfection to beatitude and the representation will at last correspond to the world out there. But because of some wicked editor's deadline, classes that must be taught, the demands of a new project, the family vacation, the illness of a child, the visit of out-of-state friends, or the five minutes we have left to catch a plane, the form and content of the paper freeze. We know that our analysis is not finished, only over.
> (Van Maanen, 1988, p. 120)

Macrosystem facilitating and constraining factors include money, ethnicity, gender, social class, institutions and culture (see Floyd et al., 1994; Raymore 2002). Rhoads (2002) provides several illustrations of macrosystem factors facilitating and constraining leisure, for example, in 2002 France extended its 3-year-old law reducing the work week to 35 hours from 39. 'The far-reaching measure now includes companies with fewer than 20 employees. Parents in Sweden just got another

30 days of parental leave, at 80% of their salary. That brings the total to 480 working days per couple for each child—almost a threefold increase since the 1970s' (Rhoads, 2002, p. 1).

In 1991 Juliet Schor found that Americans were overworked, working an average of 163 hours more per year in 1990 than they did in 1970. 'The result is less adult free time per family than before, hence more stress on each adult from juggling household duties, and jobs' (Beatty and Torbert, 2003, p. 240). Early in the 21st century the average German adult spends 1400 hours/year at work, versus 1800 for adult Americans.

> About 52% of Italians between the ages of 20 and 34 live at home with parents, an arrangement that provides not only warm meals and free laundry service but the opportunity not to work. That's a steady rise since the late 1980s ... The differing work habits of the two continents stem in part from a choice on how to use the gains from prosperity. Europeans opted for more free time; Americans for more money and consumption, surveys show. From the perspective of many Europeans, it's the hard working Americans who have it wrong, at a heavy price to society.
>
> (Rhoads, 2002, p. A6)

literature

Defining and Measuring Work and Leisure

Applying ecological systems theory to human behaviour research suggests the need for defining and measuring both work and leisure within the same research context. Beatty and Torbert (2003) inform this need in their essay, 'The False Duality of Work and Leisure'. In reviewing the literature, Beatty and Torbert report that work and leisure are commonly viewed as dichotomous and antithetical and argue that this conceptual duality is unreflective of reality and confounds the meaning of each concept. They report three common approaches for defining leisure: (i) the time-based approach (how much time are people not working?); (ii) the activity-based approach (what do people do when they are not working?); and (iii) the intention-based approach (what kind of intention is the intent to act in a

leisurely manner?). Beatty and Torbert (2003) 'support the third approach as primary and advocate a definition of leisure *as the experiential quality of our time when we engage voluntarily and intentionally in awareness-expanding inquiry, which in turn generates ongoing, transforming development throughout adulthood*' [original italics].

While sharing Beatty and Torbert's (2003) view that between the poles of pure work (e.g. assembly-line labour done for money and as the boss requires) and pure leisure (e.g. meditating by oneself or producing works of art for which there is no pre-existing market) are many hybrid states, we advocate the activity-based approach for defining and measuring work, leisure and additional behaviour. The activity-based approach is useful in particular because of the core tenets of analysing microsystems, especially the tenet that most thinking occurs unconsciously. Also, intention, volition, awareness-expanding enquiry and 'ongoing, transforming development throughout adulthood' are *not* necessary or sufficient for leisure experiences; an individual may engage in a leisure activity with little prior thought, no planning, with no freedom (e.g. required to perform the leisure activity by a spouse or medical doctor) and without committing to an awareness-expanding enquiry.

We advocate the view that leisure refers to an activity context (e.g. thinking, playing and socializing) unrelated to a job, employment, trade, profession or to maintaining life. Work represents an activity done in the context of a job, employment, a trade or profession, whether or not such activity is necessary for livelihood; this view of work is similar to, but distinct from, Ransome's definition that work 'is a purposeful expedient activity requiring mental and/or physical exertion, carried out in the public domain in exchange for wages' (Ransome, 1996, p. 23). Purpose, expediency, exertion, public domain and wages are not necessary or sufficient for work.

Beatty and Torbert (2003, p. 244) emphasize that 'distinguishing work from leisure is not easy. There are many examples of activities that conjoin both freedom and necessity [implying that leisure equals freedom and work equals necessity], muddying the distinction between pure work and leisure'. Work can transform into leisure and vice versa (cf. Stebbins, 1992, 1997). Daydreaming in the office about being on the beach is an example of conjoining leisure and work contexts.

Similarly, Cotte *et al.* (2004, p. 334) describe the difficulty in respondents' abilities to report only on their leisure behaviour, 'We initially set out to study the consumption of leisure, but our informants frequently shifted their thoughts from leisure per se to talk in detail about the role and meaning of time as they experienced it in everyday life'. Consequently, the results of their study contribute mostly within the time-based approach to examining leisure and timestyles (i.e. the customary ways in which people perceive and use time; see Feldman and Hornik, 1981; Lewis and Weigert, 1981; Zerubavel 1981; Hall, 1983; McGrath and Kelly, 1986; Hirschman, 1987; Bergadaà, 1990). Cotte *et al.* (2004) and Cotte and Ratneshwar (2001) describe 'four key dimensions of timestyle'.

1. Social orientation dimension: approaching and categorizing units of time as either 'time for me' or 'time with (or for) others'.
2. Temporal orientation dimension: focusing on the past, present or future.
3. Planning orientation dimension: how the individual approaches time management.
4. Polychronic orientation dimension: tendency toward monochronic or one-thing-at-a-time style to a polychronic, multitasking style.

From a grounded theory perspective, advancing an ecological systems theory of lifestyle, leisure and tourism benefits by identifying four conjoining activity contexts within present time, as well as identifying additional behaviours (e.g. planning activities and actions done that a consumer would undo if he or she could). The possible existence of four present activities and their combinations include work, leisure, life maintenance and resting/sleeping (see Exhibit 1.1). While resting/sleeping is part of life maintenance, Exhibit 1.1 illustrates this activity uniquely because of its ubiquitous nature and the substantial daily time commitment involved (e.g. for most humans, 6–12 hours of resting/ sleeping, depending on age and additional facilitating and constraining factors).

Life maintenance frequently includes such activities as eating, maintaining normal body temperature, urinating/defecating, doing the laundry, driving the kids to football practice, the dentist, and to/from school (nurturing), sexual intercourse, and taking actions to stay out of harm's way (e.g. buckling a safety belt before driving). Note that Exhibit 1.1 depicts some portion of life maintenance activities conjoining with work, leisure and resting/sleeping activities. For example, alternative life maintenance activities sometimes occur while travelling overseas by airline (e.g. eating, sleeping and urinating) on a combined vacation/ work-related trip (i.e. the ABCD space in Exhibit 1.1). Recognizing the possibilities in life contexts of conjoining two or more activities, Exhibit 1.1 includes all two-way, three-way, as well as four-way combinations of work, leisure, life maintenance and resting/sleeping.

Exhibit 1.1 includes three additional areas that relate to contexts in life: E, F and G. Area E indicates non-activity – life contexts that an individual does not engage in or plan to engage in but she or he sometimes thinks about, or activities confronting the individual from time to time in life, or a special area of interest by a researcher brought up for discussion with a respondent (e.g. learning why the individual does not engage in domestic travel). Area E recognizes the possibilities of unplanned and undone activities that sometimes occur in an individual's life space and asks the questions:

● What thoughts first come to mind about doing such an activity?
● What might you do in such a circumstance?
● What would be the likely outcome for you from such a behaviour?

See March and Woodside (2005) for further discussion on unplanned and undone behaviour.

Area F indicates intentions related to work, leisure, life maintenance and/or resting/ sleeping. Work and leisure researchers often focus on examining the contents and degrees of commitment of an individual's intentions toward activities such as leisure and planned travel behaviour, and on learning how current life activities influence the contents and degrees of commitment of an individual's

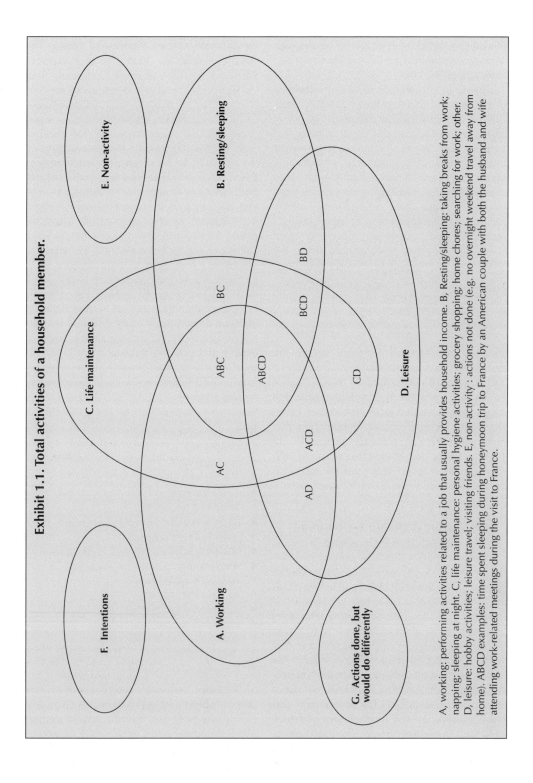

Exhibit 1.1. Total activities of a household member.

E. Non-activity

B. Resting/sleeping

F. Intentions

C. Life maintenance

A. Working

BC

BD

BCD

ABC

ABCD

CD

AC

ACD

AD

D. Leisure

G. Actions done, but would do differently

A, working: performing activities related to a job that usually provides household income. B, Resting/sleeping: taking breaks from work; napping; sleeping at night. C, life maintenance: personal hygiene activities; grocery shopping; home chores; searching for work; other. D, leisure: hobby activities; leisure travel; visiting friends. E, non-activity : actions not done (e.g. no overnight weekend travel away from home). ABCD examples: time spent sleeping during honeymoon trip to France by an American couple with both the husband and wife attending work-related meetings during the visit to France.

intended activities. Area F recognizes the planning orientation dimension and asks what thinking processes and facilitators versus constraints occur in informants' specific short- and long-term plans.

Area G reflects an individual's (unconscious and conscious) thinking about activities done that he or she would do differently, or not at all, regarding one or more single or conjoined areas of work, leisure, life maintenance and/or resting/sleeping. Some amount of reflection occurs naturally among humans as they attempt to make sense of recent or long-ago events in their lives (see Weick, 1995). Reflections about activities in prior contexts include several categories depending upon whether or not they were actually done, the recognition of alternative activities now or at the time of the prior context, the individual's beliefs about the causes of the done activity and evaluation of the outcome of the activity done versus likely outcomes of alternative foregone activities, and the individual's ability to retrieve and consciously think about the specific steps taken regarding the activity done. The contents of such reflections likely influence individuals' understanding of the activities that they engage in currently, as well as their intentions. Area G recognizes the temporal orientation dimension of timestyle and asks, in particular, how past experiences affect the individual's interpretation of the present and plans for the future.

Probing the Facilitators–Constraints Interaction Proposition

To probe how facilitator and constraint factors may combine to form contingency routes leading to engaging in some leisure activities, while preventing others from occurring, the long interview method (McCracken, 1988) was applied in a national study of Australian households. The long interview method includes the use of face-to-face 1–3-hour interviews, to permit interviewer probing for learning about informant reflections on the antecedents and consequences, as well as descriptions, associated with lived experiences. The main objective of the interviews was having the informants describe and explain behaviours

done: (i) today, yesterday evening; (ii) the most recent past weekend; and (iii) last summer, this autumn and coming winter and spring. The data were collected during the early autumn, 2000.

Survey instrument

A 44-page survey questionnaire was used; see the Appendix to this chapter for one version of this instrument. The questionnaire includes both open-ended and close-ended items. The first 26 pages of the questionnaire (Sections 1–3) include mostly open-ended questions, asking the respondent to describe the details of activities done, or being planned, as well as the antecedents leading up to these activities.

Section 3 asks the respondent to put 'a tick next to all that apply' among 240 possible leisure activities that she or he has done, or plans on doing in 2000. Section 3 also asks the respondent to 'please underline the activities in the list that you did three or more times this year'. The 240 listed activities were compiled from several sources and include the following, among others:

- reading a lightweight paperback;
- having a dinner party;
- playing golf;
- making love;
- playing with children;
- going camping;
- going to a sing-along;
- fixing a car;
- walking the dog;
- watching a TV sitcom;
- taking a nap;
- taking a bubble bath;
- going to the casino;
- going to the races/trots;
- surfing the Internet;
- dining at a casual restaurant;
- visiting friends;
- hanging out with mates.

Because the way choice problems are framed affects decision-makers' thinking and choice processes (e.g. Tversky and Kahneman, 1984; Woodside and Chebat, 2001), Section 4 asks the informant to consider activity options for two scenarios and to talk about each option as if he or she is thinking about different ways of spending time and money: 'Each scenario has several different options for you to consider. Please comment on each option presented in the scenario'. The first scenario included ten alternative options.

After commenting on each option and making a choice of an option for the first scenario, the informant was asked to consider a second scenario having 20 options. Each respondent was given one of two versions for the second scenario; the 20 options were identical for each of the two alternative versions of the second scenario. Thus, three scenarios were created for the survey but only two were covered per informant, to keep the interview time under 2 hours. The following stories describe each scenario:

- Scenario 1: You have a good bit of money set aside for paying for one or two big purchases that you are thinking about making within the next few months. Here are possibilities that you are thinking about, or someone has mentioned to you. [Ten options presented; see Exhibit 1.2.]

- Scenario 2a: You have the opportunity to sign up for a new credit card offering a low interest rate of any unpaid balance plus no interest charges on any balance during the first 6 months of purchase. You decide to sign up for the new credit card and consider using the new card to pay for one of the following options. You say to yourself, 'I might splurge for once in my life!' [Twenty options presented; see Exhibit 1.3. Note: some informants refused to consider any options; they reported that they would never sign up for another credit card.]

- Scenario 2b: You have set aside some 'mad money' to pay for something you always wanted to have or do even if some people say, 'it was a frivolous thing to do'. Here are some possibilities that you are thinking about or someone has mentioned to you. [Twenty options presented – the same options as used for scenario 2a; see Exhibit 1.3.]

All respondents were asked to provide comments on each option available for scenarios 1 and 2a or 2b. The set of options was created to

---

Exhibit 1.2. Framing of the first scenario and ten options.

Scenario 1. You have a good bit of money set aside for paying for one or two big purchases that you are thinking about making within the next few months. Here are some possibilities that you are thinking about or someone has mentioned to you.

- Option U: getting a used car to get to work easier than sharing one car with a family member, partner
- Option R: going to a really good hotel on the beach in South East Queensland with your spouse/partner for a few days; enjoying some great meals and the international ambience
- Option K: getting new kitchen cabinets because you hate the appearance of your current kitchen
- Option B: renovating your bathroom – the bathroom that is all pink and you hate pink bathrooms
- Option F: visiting and staying with family members (parent, child, uncle, aunt, or cousin) out-of-town; you really like these family members and you might visit theme parks, zoos, amusement parks, go to the beach, go shopping
- Option S: buying some shares of stock in a company that you think is going places
- Option H: using the money for a house payment or the down payment on a house mortgage
- Option D: buying a used car to have a second fun car to drive
- Option W: taking a wine tasting tour in South Australia with a family member/partner and maybe spend about half to two-thirds of the funds you have set aside
- Option G: spending a week in Adelaide going to art galleries, theatre, performing arts, dining out, shopping and maybe some wine tasting

---

Exhibit 1.3. The alternative two frames used for the second scenario and 20 options.

Scenario 2a. You have the opportunity to sign up for a new credit card offering a low interest rate on any unpaid balance plus no interest charges on any balance during the first 6 months of purchase. You decide to sign up for the new credit card and consider using the new card to pay for one of the following options. You say to yourself, 'I might splurge for once in my life!'

Scenario 2b. You have set aside some 'mad money' to pay for something you always wanted to have or do even if some people might say, 'it was a frivolous thing to do'. Here are some possibilities that you are thinking about or someone has mentioned to you.

- Option R: going to a really good hotel on the beach in South East Queensland with your spouse/ partner for a few days; enjoying some great meals and the international ambience
- Option W: taking a wine tasting tour in South Australia with a family member/partner and maybe spend about half to two-thirds of the funds you have set aside
- Option D: buying a used car to have a second, fun car to drive
- Option G: spending a week in Adelaide going to art galleries, theatre, performing arts, dining out, shopping and maybe some wine tasting
- Option C: buy new clothes just for you – a whole new wardrobe
- Option P: go to France and tour Paris, the wine region, and maybe French Riviera
- Option Y: go to the United States, visit friends and/or go to San Francisco; New York, or other cities or places
- Option J: go to Japan and really experience the local culture
- Option E: buy some new, really great, furniture for my home
- Option Q: have some second thoughts about opportunity [mad money] and end-up giving the money to my favourite charity, or a family member, or investing it for my retirement
- Option M: your own credit card [mad money] option, please describe briefly here: _____
- Option H: do things in Perth and maybe travel around Western Australia to see natural beauty
- Option I: do things I really want to do in Sydney and maybe attend some special events in and around Sydney
- Option B: do things I really want to do in Brisbane and maybe attend some special events in and around Brisbane
- Option N: do things I really want to do in Melbourne and maybe attend some special events in and around Melbourne
- Option A: go to Alice Springs, maybe Ayers Rock, and maybe tour central Northern Territory and see unspoiled natural beauty
- Option S: visit Cairns, coastal Queensland and Islands, maybe to do some snorkelling or scuba diving
- Option D: visit Darwin, do some four-wheel driving, and maybe some fishing and/or camping
- Option X: travel around Canberra and attend a great special event or educational/learning experience
- Option Z: visit Tasmania, including Hobart, see unspoiled beauty, enjoy peace and solitude

---

include both non-travel and domestic travel alternatives, to provide insights into informants' top-of-mind thoughts and decisions on how well domestic travel alternatives compete against other ways to spend available funds.

Scenario 2a was crafted to gain insights into the ways some informants might use a new, low-cost, line of credit presented to them. One aim of the study was to learn if such easy credit availability is likely to increase interest in domestic and/or overseas travel options. Scenario 2b was created to gain insights into ways some informants might spend money in situations framed to be high in personal freedom (i.e. spending 'mad money'); the aim here is to learn the nuances in evaluating options and making choices that include domestic and international trips versus non-travel options.

The study includes data collection on consumer analysis of scenarios for two reasons. First, the decision-making and consumer psychology literature reports that individuals tend to think, prefer and are more influenced by a narration (i.e. a story) compared to processing product descriptions (see Adaval and Wyer, 1998). Tversky and Kahneman (1984) report, 'The construction and evaluation of scenarios of future events are not only a favorite pastime of reporters, analysts, and news watchers ... It is of interest, then, to evaluate whether or not the forecasting or reconstruction of real-life events is subject to conjunction errors. Our analysis suggests that a scenario that includes a possible cause and an outcome could appear more probable than the outcome on its own.' A conjunctive error is predicting higher probability for the combination of two events (i.e. events A and B both occurring) than one of the two events occurring (i.e. B). For example, subjects in one study gave higher probability estimates to the first scenario given below, joining together earthquake and flood, than subjects gave to the second scenario (flood only).

- Scenario 1: An earthquake in California sometime in 1983, causing a flood in which more than 1000 people drown.
- Scenario 2: A massive flood somewhere in North America in 1983, in which more than 1000 people drown.

Thus, the scenarios frame story lines (i.e. contexts) that possibly legitimize the consideration of alternative use of time and money. Important issues here include the consumer's perception of the likelihood of each option in a given scenario, and the consumer's preferred option for the given scenario.

The second reason for crafting scenarios with several options was to learn individuals' thinking processes when 'comparing noncomparable alternatives' (Johnson, 1984); that is,

learning how individuals make comparisons and choices when evaluating products and services in different categories that cannot be compared on concrete attributes. Thus, the first scenario asks the informant to consider domestic travel options, renovating their bathroom, buying shares in a company and additional options (see Exhibit 1.2). The literature includes two relevant findings on making such non-comparable comparisons. First, subjects tend not to use the lowest level of comparison possible when making their choices; people focus their comparisons at the levels that are most relevant to their ultimate satisfaction with their choices. Subjects who are less interested tend to use more abstract comparisons – as more abstract comparisons are easier to make, this finding suggests that less interested subjects are less motivated to exert the effort necessary for more concrete comparisons (Johnson, 1988, 1989; Corfman, 1991).

Section 5 asked a number of demographic questions (e.g. age, gender, occupation, weekly and annual income using ten range categories), use of the Internet, frequent flyer club memberships, use of specific credit cards, and media behaviour.

Procedure

The service of a professional research firm was used to select households that were representative theoretically of most Australian households. An objective for the study was to include all combinations of the following factors in identifying households for inclusion in the study:

1. Marital status: single (never married adults), married, separated/divorced.
2. Age: <30; 30–50; >50.
3. City/state locations in proportion to populations of each, with a 20% oversampling of small towns and the Outback (15 areas in total, including: Brisbane, Queensland other than Brisbane, Sydney, New South Wales other than Sydney, Melbourne, Victoria other than Melbourne, Hobart, Tasmania other than Hobart, Adelaide, South Australia other than Adelaide, Perth, Western Australia other than Perth, Darwin, Northern Territory other than Darwin, Australian Capital Territory).

4. Equal shares of non-overnight travellers, domestic only, and domestic and overseas travellers.

Following a telephone screening procedure, each qualified informant agreeing to participate in the study was sent a letter confirming their participation, time, and place for the interview. More than 90% of the interviews were conducted in the informants' homes. Each informant was informed by telephone and letter that she or he would receive AUS$70 (AUD) payment for their participation. The AUS$70 payment was made by cheque at the close of each interview.

After extensive training, which included completing two practice interviews by each interviewer, seven interviewers collected the data for the study. Each interview was done primarily with one interviewer and one informant; however, pairs of informants participated in answering questions for 86 interviews. All interviews were completed in face-to-face settings. The field study includes complete data for interviews from 184 households.

To provide gestalt views of informants' reports of lived experiences and the interactions of facilitators and constraints regarding their leisure behaviour, the findings section of this chapter presents detailed results of an interpretive analysis of seven households. The choice of the seven households for this report was based on income, age, and current domestic and international leisure travel behaviour, with the aim of achieving substantial diversity. Where discussed, the general conclusions found across the seven households also apply for the total households in the sample.

Findings

The findings include descriptions of ecological micro- and macrosystems of seven households that succinctly and tellingly reflect the combinations of factors resulting in travel, as well as non-travel, behaviours. Two key points are worth noting here. First, the facilitators–constraints interaction proposition that specific combinations of facilitating and constraining factors create paths leading to, versus preventing, certain outcomes (e.g. overnight travel or

no travel during available leisure time periods) implies that no one 'main effect' (e.g. employment status) is necessary or sufficient in explaining a specific work/leisure/travel outcome. However, the combination of specific states or levels of a limited number (i.e. 3–6) variables is sufficient for explaining and describing the observed outcome – even if other possible combinations (paths) also exist for the same case study that are also sufficient for explaining the same behavioural outcome. Thus, the second point: the claim is not made that the following case study reports describe the only sufficient paths leading to the observed behavioural outcomes – the claim is made that the reported path of events for each case is starkly observable in the data and sufficient in leading to the reported behavioural outcome.

Andy Hill: Staying Home Despite the Money and Time Available for Leisure Travel

Exhibit 1.4 summarizes Andy Hill's very comfortable, home-centred, life. Note that Andy intends to travel both domestically and overseas, but that his lived experience includes infrequent leisure travel. Work, grandchildren, skill in fixing cars and in sports, parties with friends, and other local-area activities dominate his life.

Exhibit 1.5 illustrates a parsimonious path of work–grandchildren–coaching that is a dominating combination, resulting in facilitating and constraining his life toward a local-centred, non-travel lifestyle. Exhibit 1.6 summarizes Andy's responses to the first scenario exercise; note that Andy reports the beach on the ocean option (R) to be a 'possibility' but his comments about this option reflects its dormant unconscious state in Andy's mind. None of the travel-related options compete successfully for Andy's final selection in scenario 1.

Andy's comments about each option in the first scenario support the very abstract processing level for non-comparable alternatives that Corfman (1991) and Johnson (1984, 1988, 1989) describe in their studies. Andy's comments centre on mental processes that provide answers to two questions:

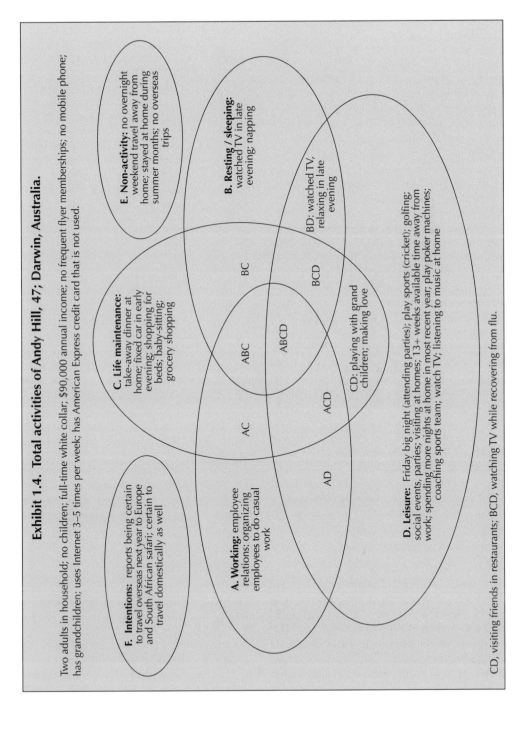

Exhibit 1.4. Total activities of Andy Hill, 47; Darwin, Australia.

Two adults in household; no children; full-time white collar; $90,000 annual income; no frequent flyer memberships; no mobile phone; has grandchildren; uses Internet 3–5 times per week; has American Express credit card that is not used.

E. Non-activity: no overnight weekend travel away from home; stayed at home during summer months; no overseas trips

B. Resting / sleeping: watched TV in late evening; napping

BD: watched TV, relaxing in late evening

C. Life maintenance: take-away dinner at home; fixed car in early evening; shopping for beds; baby-sitting; grocery shopping

BC

BCD

ABC

ABCD

CD: playing with grand children; making love

AC

ACD

F. Intentions: reports being certain to travel overseas next year to Europe and South African safari; certain to travel domestically as well

AD

A. Working: employee relations: organizing employees to do casual work

D. Leisure: Friday big night (attending parties); play sports (cricket); golfing; social events, parties; visiting at homes; 13+ weeks available time away from work; spending more nights at home in most recent year; play poker machines; coaching sports team; watch TV; listening to music at home

CD, visiting friends in restaurants; BCD, watching TV while recovering from flu.

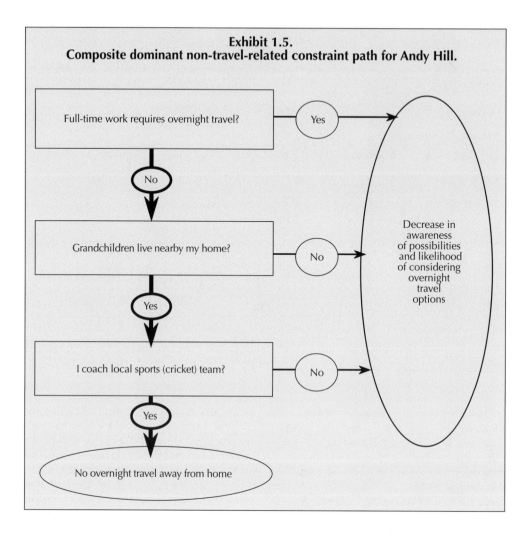

Exhibit 1.5.
Composite dominant non-travel-related constraint path for Andy Hill.

1. Is this option relevant in my life (an ecological issue)?
2. Do I like or dislike the option globally (an affect-referral simplifying heuristic, see Wright, 1975)?

The comment, 'It's not pink', regarding the bathroom remodelling option reflects relevancy. 'Not OK with me', reflects the global attitude strategy of 'affect referral' (Wright, 1975). Certainly, relevancy and affection are non-orthogonal issues that reflect a behavioural imprinting influence on affection. The following rule captures this influence: my behaviour indicates to me what I like to do, and by implication, I must not like the activities that I don't do.

Andy refused to participate in responding to scenario 2a, the new credit card opportunity, 'I am never going to have another credit card'. His statement reflects both a lack of relevancy and affection toward using credit cars. The lack of use of his only credit card (American Express) is further evidence of his anti-credit card stance.

Strategy implications

Andy Hill's lived experiences and thinking processes strongly reflect a home-centred lifestyle. The implication of such a lifestyle and household ecological system for

---

Exhibit 1.6. Responses of Andy Hill to first scenario and ten options.

Scenario 1. You have a good bit of money set aside for paying for one or two big purchases that you are thinking about making within the next few months. Here are some possibilities that you are thinking about or someone has mentioned to you.

Option:	Response:
• U: used car for work	Not OK. I just purchased a new car.
• R: hotel, beach, South East Queensland	Possible, have been thinking of this for some time.
• K: new kitchen cabinets	Possible, needs working on.
• B: renovating pink bathroom	It's not pink.
• F: visiting with family members	Don't do this too often. They only visit me.
• S: buying shares of stock	Possible. High on my priority list of things to do.
• H: a house payment	Not OK with me.
• D: used car for fun	Not OK; just bought a new car.
• W: wine-tasting tour in South Australia	Not OK.
• G: week in Adelaide	Not OK.

Final selection: S. I need to get money working for me so that I may reward myself with R and K.

Australian national marketing strategies to stimulate domestic travel might be to ask, what are the lifestyles alternative to Andy Hill's that indicate higher likelihood of a favourable response to such strategies – investing in marketing actions to stimulate Andy Hill to travel domestically is less likely to be influential than stimulating alternative focal consumers whose lives and thinking are more ready to accept domestic leisure travel opportunities.

Vera Kellie: Domestic Travel by a Low-income, Retired Older Person Living Alone

Exhibit 1.7 summarizes Vera Kellie's activities in her life. Note that Vera is retired from work and engages in no job-related activities; consequently, Exhibit 1.7 does not include an oval related to work.

Vera is separated from her husband, lives alone with a cat, and has a very limited annual income. Yet Vera's life is enriched by her bridge hobby and companionship with her bridge partner; this hobby affects her frequent domestic travel behaviour. Note that the path through the travel-facilitating variables in Exhibit 1.8 includes attending to a brochure promoting an event-specific leisure trip (e.g. a bridge tournament) as well as trip nurturing events by her bridge partner. This combination of domestic-travel facilitating factors supports the view that stimulating domestic travel effectively may need to include several lifestyle-specific marketing campaigns rather than a general image campaign.

For example, rather than spending AUS$5 million for a national image advertizing campaign to stimulate domestic travel, a national tourism NGO might test the strategy of providing relatively small grants (e.g. an average grant of AUS$50,000) to national hobby organizations, with the grants earmarked for promoting regional and national meetings and membership expansion programmes. Both the immediate and long-term (say, over 10 years) influence of such micro-marketing campaigns might be more influential in affecting actual travel behaviour than image-only advertizing.

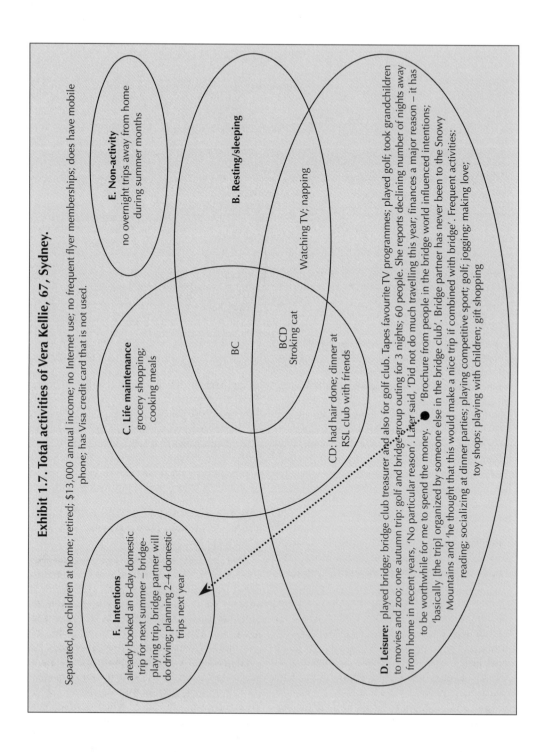

Exhibit 1.7. Total activities of Vera Kellie, 67, Sydney.

Separated, no children at home; retired; $13,000 annual income; no Internet use; no frequent flyer memberships; does have mobile phone; has Visa credit card that is not used.

E. Non-activity
no overnight trips away from home during summer months

B. Resting/sleeping

Watching TV; napping

C. Life maintenance
grocery shopping; cooking meals

BC

BCD
Stroking cat

CD: had hair done; dinner at RSL club with friends

F. Intentions
already booked an 8-day domestic trip for next summer – bridge-playing trip; bridge partner will do driving; planning 2–4 domestic trips next year

D. Leisure: played bridge; bridge club treasurer and also for golf club. Tapes favourite TV programmes; played golf; took grandchildren to movies and zoo; one autumn trip: golf and bridge group outing for 3 nights; 60 people. She reports declining number of nights away from home in recent years, 'No particular reason'. Later said, 'Did not do much travelling this year; finances a major reason – it has to be worthwhile for me to spend the money.' 'Brochure from people in the bridge world influenced intentions; 'basically [the trip] organized by someone else in the bridge club'. Bridge partner has never been to the Snowy Mountains and 'he thought that this would make a nice trip if combined with bridge'. Frequent activities: reading; socializing at dinner parties; playing competitive sport; golf; jogging; making love; toy shops; playing with children; gift shopping

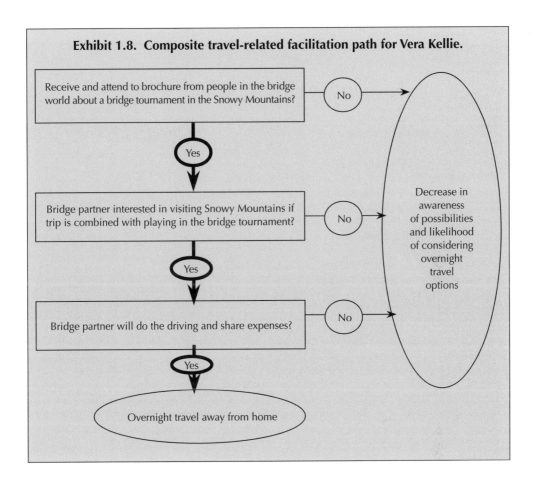

Exhibit 1.8. Composite travel-related facilitation path for Vera Kellie.

Receive and attend to brochure from people in the bridge world about a bridge tournament in the Snowy Mountains? — No

Yes

Bridge partner interested in visiting Snowy Mountains if trip is combined with playing in the bridge tournament? — No

Yes

Bridge partner will do the driving and share expenses? — No

Yes

Overnight travel away from home

Decrease in awareness of possibilities and likelihood of considering overnight travel options

Strategy implications

Exhibits 1.9 and 1.10 include Vera's responses to the two choice scenarios. Note that both sets of responses imply that Vera does like the idea of some of the travel options but this affection is unlikely to morph into high intention or actual behaviour – remodelling a bathroom or investing options dominate her preferences. Travel options must fit like a glove in Vera's ecological system to be considered and acted upon. The interaction of Vera's dedication to playing bridge and resulting bridge tournaments, coupled with her bridge companion relationship, represents a facilitating route for generating domestic travel.

Bonnie Moss: Combining Pleasure with Work-related Travel

Exhibit 1.11 summarizes the busy conflicted life of Bonnie Moss. Bonnie's work as a university academic/administrator requires frequent overnight domestic trips, as well as overseas trips annually; she tries to squeeze in some leisure-related activities on some of these trips. Bonnie is also a single parent of a teenager and her leisure-time lived experiences centre on localized activities (e.g. gardening, visiting friends and the local beach, local activities with child). When Bonnie does domestic leisure-only travel, she is a budget-oriented traveller: does long-haul travel by personal caravan vehicle, eats low-price junk

Exhibit 1.9. Responses of Vera Kellie to first scenario and ten options.

Scenario 1. You have a good bit of money set aside for paying for one or two big purchases that you are thinking about making within the next few months. Here are some possibilities that you are thinking about or someone has mentioned to you.

Option	Response
• U: used car for work	I would never buy a used car.
• R: hotel, beach, South East Queensland	Love to.
• K: new kitchen cabinets	No, I love my kitchen.
• B: renovating pink bathroom	That would be great.
• F: visiting with family members	I would love to visit but would not like to stay with them.
• S: buying shares of stock	Yes.
• H: a house payment	I have no mortgage so this would not interest me.
• D: used car for fun	I don't like used cars.
• W: wine-tasting tour in South Australia	No way …
• G: week in Adelaide	That would be nice.

Final selection: B. My bathroom is functional but I would like to update it if I had the money.

Exhibit 1.10. Vera Kellie's responses to 'mad money' second scenario.

Scenario 2b. You have set aside some 'mad money' to pay for something you always wanted to have or do even if some people might say 'it was a frivolous thing to do'. Here are some possibilities that you are thinking about or someone has mentioned to you.

Option	Response
• R: hotel, beach, South East Queensland	Love it!
• W: wine-tasting, South Australia	No.
• D: fun, used car	No. I don't like used cars.
• G: week in Adelaide	That would be interesting.
• C: buy new clothes just for you	I would love that.
• P: got to France, tour Paris, wine region	I've already been there. [No.]
• Y: United States, visit friends, cities	I've always wanted to go there.
• J: Japan, the local culture	My husband always wanted to go there.
• E: new, really great furniture	I am too old [for new furniture].
• Q: second thoughts, give or invest	Yes, investing in my retirement.
• M: own mad money option, describe here	Give it to my children.
• H: do things in Perth, Western Australia	Not interested.
• I: Sydney, special events	Yes, I would.
• B: Brisbane, some special events	I have been there. [No.]
• N: Melbourne, special events	Yes, I would.
• A: Alice Springs, Ayers Rock, tour	I did that. [Would not do again.]
• S: Cairns, coastal Queensland and Islands	I did that too. Loved it. [Would not do again.]
• D: Darwin, four-wheel driving, fishing, camping	Too hot. [No.]
• X: Canberra, educational/learning experience	Travelling in Canberra is a nightmare. [No.]
• Z: Tasmania, Hobart, unspoiled beauty	I did that many years ago. [No.]

Final selection: Q. I am a sensible person and having money in retirement is important.

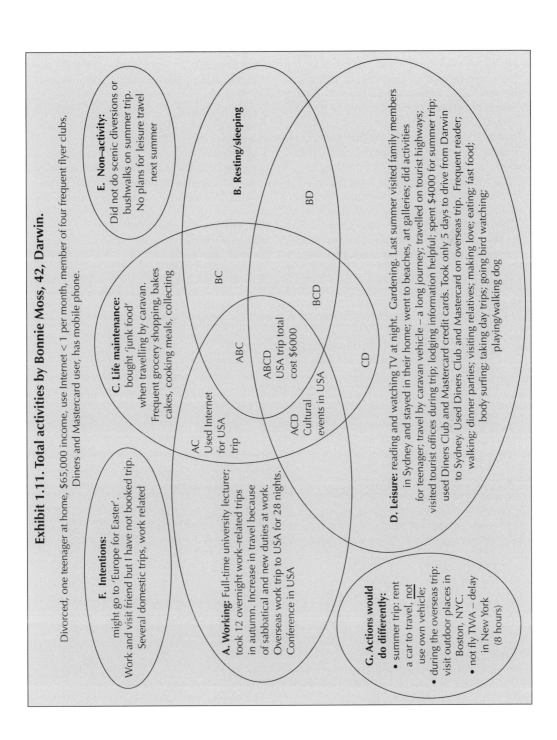

Exhibit 1.11. Total activities by Bonnie Moss, 42, Darwin.

Divorced, one teenager at home, $65,000 income, use Internet < 1 per month, member of four frequent flyer clubs, Diners and Mastercard user, has mobile phone.

E. Non-activity:
Did not do scenic diversions or bushwalks on summer trip. No plans for leisure travel next summer

B. Resting/sleeping

C. Life maintenance:
bought 'junk food' when travelling by caravan. Frequent grocery shopping, bakes cakes, cooking meals, collecting

BC

BD

BCD

ABC

ABCD
USA trip total
cost $6000

AC
Used Internet
for USA
trip

ACD
Cultural
events in USA

CD

F. Intentions:
might go to 'Europe for Easter'. Work and visit friend but I have not booked trip. Several domestic trips, work related

A. Working: Full-time university lecturer; took 12 overnight work–related trips in autumn. Increase in travel because of sabbatical and new duties at work. Overseas work trip to USA for 28 nights. Conference in USA

G. Actions would do differently:
• summer trip: rent a car to travel, not use own vehicle;
• during the overseas trip: visit outdoor places in Boston, NYC.
• not fly TWA – delay in New York (8 hours)

D. Leisure: reading and watching TV at night. Gardening. Last summer visited family members in Sydney and stayed in their home; went to beaches, art galleries; did activities for teenager; travel by caravan vehicle – a long journey; travelled on tourist highways; visited tourist offices during trip; lodging information helpful; spent $4000 for summer trip; used Diners Club and Mastercard credit cards. Took only 5 days to drive from Darwin to Sydney. Used Diners Club and Mastercard on overseas trip. Frequent reader; walking; dinner parties; visiting relatives; making love; eating; fast food; body surfing; taking day trips; going bird watching; playing/walking dog food along the way, and stays with relatives whenever possible.

Exhibit 1.12 displays a conflicted ecological micro-environment: Bonnie's lived-work reality requires trips away from home, but her single-parenting requirements, along with personal lived experience behaviours, lead to infrequent leisure travel. The resulting travel experiences are low in satisfaction for Bonnie and she does appear to be unable to combine work and leisure-related travel successfully.

While some individuals may be able to combine work with leisure travel, such persons are less likely to have ecological systems that include single-parent commitments with heavy additional commitments to home-centred activities (e.g. note the dog-walking

activity in Exhibit 1.11). Bonnie's life reflects Scitovsky's (1992) description of living in a 'joyless economy'.

Part of the solution of enabling more joy to enter Bonnie's life (and possibly increase her domestic leisure travel) may include suggesting that she reframe her work lifestyle to include *less* travel – a 'take time to smell the roses and really connect with loved ones' image campaign. However, Exhibits 1.13 and 1.14 include results that indicate that such a campaign is unlikely to be successful. Bonnie's choice of options indicates that for Bonnie, travel-related options cannot stand up to the attractions of non-comparable alternatives. Life maintenance requirements felt by Bonnie take precedence over her attraction toward domestic travel options.

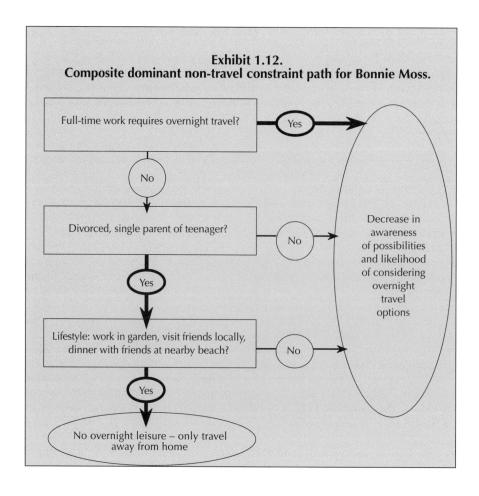

Exhibit 1.12.
Composite dominant non-travel constraint path for Bonnie Moss.

Full-time work requires overnight travel? — Yes →

No ↓

Divorced, single parent of teenager? — No →

Yes ↓

Lifestyle: work in garden, visit friends locally, dinner with friends at nearby beach? — No →

Yes ↓

No overnight leisure – only travel away from home

Decrease in awareness of possibilities and likelihood of considering overnight travel options

---

Exhibit 1.13. Responses of Bonnie Moss to first scenario and ten options.

Scenario 1. You have a good bit of money set aside for paying for one or two big purchases that you are thinking about making within the next few months. Here are some possibilities that you are thinking about or someone has mentioned to you.

Option:	Response:
• U: used car for work	No. Never share a car; it causes too many problems.
• R: hotel, beach, South East Queensland	I would have to be really selective – a boutique, not too large hotel only – maybe from Gourmet Traveller
• K: new kitchen cabinets	Quite in line with my priorities. I did it last year. [No.]
• B: renovating pink bathroom	Absolutely – give me $5,000 now. Our present one is old; has mould.
• F: visiting with family members	A good way to keep in towels but not too many activities. They make me exhausted.
• S: buying shares of stock	I would need advice to make a real sure buy.
• H: a house payment	Not for me. Too boring.
• D: used car for fun	As long as it's better than my $2000 one [20 years old].
• W: wine-tasting tour in South Australia	Not with the kids in the car.
• G: week in Adelaide	Great! I would love to stay at a small boutique hotel and do the festival.

Final selection: D. My family car is now on its last legs and we never buy new cars so I would use $5000 to $7000 for a second-hand one

---

Strategy implications

Bonnie's ecological (environment and thinking) profile indicates a low response to domestic-travel marketing campaigns attempting to increase trip frequency. However, Bonnie does rely on tourist offices while travelling. Supporting the work of tourist offices serves to facilitate domestic leisure travel by households similar to Bonnie's profile. Bonnie's domestic-leisure travel behaviour indicates the continuing need to offer information at tourist offices that such travellers find useful.

Richard Mills: High-income Guy Seeking a 'Good Deal' when Travelling

Richard Mills is retired from working and has a high annual income from investments. He is recently married. He often includes domestic and overseas travel in his life but seeks to get a 'good deal' for both trip categories. Exhibit 1.15 summarizes his leisure-oriented life.

Note in Exhibit 1.15 that his home life includes playing with grandchildren, a dog and a cat, along with going to sporting events and many other local activities. Still, Richard and his new wife are rich in time in comparison to other informants. Being retired with a comparably high annual income enables engaging in a wide variety of local and travel-related activities.

He often crafts a good deal into his domestic and overseas trips. He stays overnight in friends' homes and bought an airline–accommodations–breakfasts package for his recent overseas honeymoon trip. Richard is responsive to credit-card deals that enable him to acquire points on his frequent flyer airline memberships.

Exhibit 1.14. Bonnie Moss's responses to new credit card second scenario.

Scenario 2a. You have the opportunity to sign-up for a new credit card offering a low interest rate on any unpaid balance plus no interest charges on any balance during the first six months of purchase. You decide to sign-up for the new credit card and consider using the new card to pay for one of the following options. You say to yourself, 'I might splurge once in my life!'

Option:	Response:
• R: hotel, beach, South East Queensland	No way! Not for credit.
• W: wine-tasting, South Australia	Not my idea of fun.
• D: fun, used car	A good sound choice for me at this moment.
• G: week in Adelaide	Would not be bad; I would rationalize and do this.
• C: buy new clothes just for you	No way! Not on credit.
• P: go to France, tour Paris, wine region	If it maybe was lotto, not me paying; too expensive!
• Y: United States, visit friends, cities	If it was organized with work for a visit to another institution.
• J: Japan, the local culture	Would be loved by my son who is a martial arts zen person – would be fun.
• E: new, really great, furniture	Would make me feel better about being at home.
• Q: second thoughts, give or invest	A great idea, but which to choose? Maybe a friend who is really sick.
• M: own mad money option, describe here	Buy a reliable second hand car.
• H: do things in Perth, Western Australia	Needs too much time and we have gone to WA two years ago.
• I: Sydney, special events	Would be good but not unique enough.
• B: Brisbane, some special events	No way!
• N: Melbourne, special events	Would be good if I can stay with friends.
• A: Alice Springs, Ayers Rock, tour	Spent 12 years there already – couldn't recommend it more highly!
• S: Cairns, coastal Queensland and Islands	Great fun and especially if we had four weeks to go to the Cape and Capetown.
• D: Darwin, four-wheel driving, fishing, camping	[No response.]
• X: Canberra, educational/learning experience	I go every year; it is where I would move to if I left Darwin.
• Z: Tasmania, Hobart, unspoiled beauty	One of the most beautiful and uncluttered environments.

Final selection: M. I would want to make a sensible choice; no choice for me really. Scenario is not realistic for me; I am a single parent. I have to be real with money and try to keep down credit commitments or I will sink!

Exhibit 1.16 shows the combination of macro- and microsystem facilitating factors influencing Richard's travel decisions. The interaction of money, time and deal responsiveness stimulates domestic travel; lengthening the path to include a macrosystem development (i.e. honeymoon) stimulates overseas travel.

Exhibits 1.17 and 1.18 report Richard's responses to the two choice scenarios. Notice that the framing of the scenarios affects his final selections. The first scenario about money set aside for paying for one or two big purchases enables consideration of a wide variety of options, ranging from very sensible to highly frivolous; Richard chooses a very sensible, non-travel, option. In framing a 'mad money' context, the second scenario is more biased toward carefree options than the first scenario;

Exhibit 1.15. Total activities of Richard Mills, 57, Sydney.

Married, $150,000 annual income, retired, uses Internet daily, member of three frequent flyer clubs, Diners' Club and Mastercard, has mobile phone.

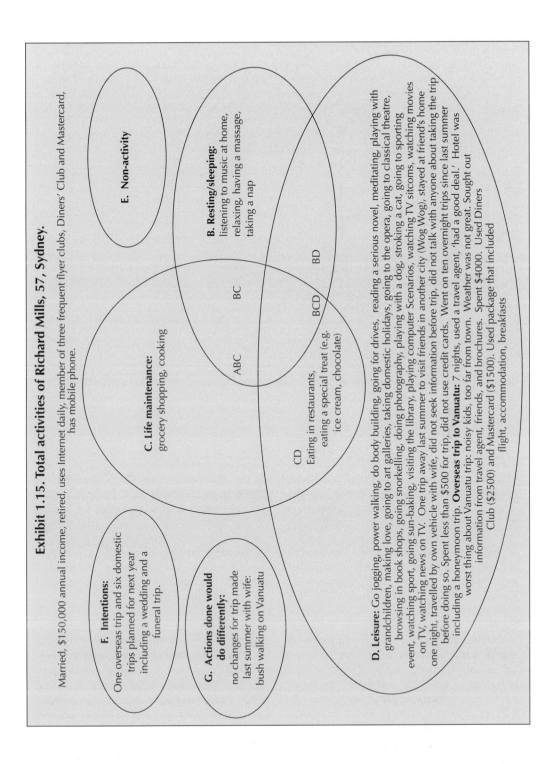

E. Non-activity

B. Resting/sleeping: listening to music at home, relaxing, having a massage, taking a nap

BD

BC

BCD

ABC

C. Life maintenance: grocery shopping, cooking

CD

Eating in restaurants, eating a special treat (e.g. ice cream, chocolate)

F. Intentions: One overseas trip and six domestic trips planned for next year including a wedding and a funeral trip.

G. Actions done would do differently: no changes for trip made last summer with wife: bush walking on Vanuatu

D. Leisure: Go jogging, power walking, do body building, going for drives, reading a serious novel, meditating, playing with grandchildren, making love, going to art galleries, taking domestic holidays, going to classical theatre, browsing in book shops, going snorkelling, doing photography, playing with a dog, stroking a cat, going to sporting event, watching sport, going sun-baking, visiting the library, playing computer Scenarios, watching TV sitcoms, watching movies on TV, watching news on TV. One trip away last summer to visit friends in another city (Wog Wog), stayed at friend's home one night, travelled by own vehicle with wife, did not seek information before trip, did not talk with anyone about taking the trip before doing so. Spent less than $500 for trip, did not use credit cards. Went on ten overnight trips since last summer including a honeymoon trip. **Overseas trip to Vanuatu:** 7 nights, used a travel agent, 'had a good deal.' Hotel was worst thing about Vanuatu trip: noisy kids, too far from town. Weather was not great. Sought out information from travel agent, friends, and brochures. Spent $4000. Used Diners Club ($2500) and Mastercard ($1500). Used package that included flight, accommodation, breakfasts

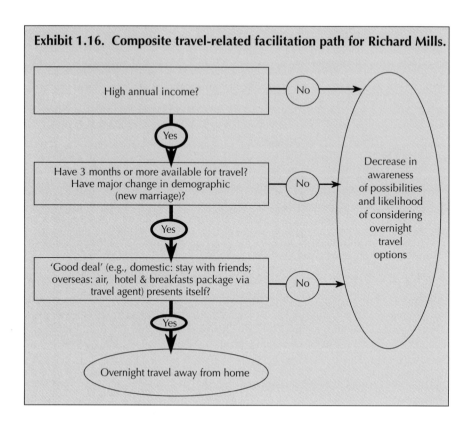

Exhibit 1.16. Composite travel-related facilitation path for Richard Mills.

Richard chooses an exotic option – a second visit to Japan. However, the note in Exhibit 1.18 indicates that Richard quickly reports second thoughts about such a trip; he is willing to consider his wife's preferences and substitute a cruise for the trip to Japan – again illustrating a complex combination of macro- and microsystem factors leading to behavioural outcomes.

With the exception of remarrying, Richard's lifestyle, leisure and tourism behaviour matches closely with Stanley and Danko's (1996) 'millionaire next door' (e.g. such millionaires live well below their means). Richard is ready to spend money on leisure activities but wants to save money while spending it.

Strategy implications

When thinking about who buys packaged travel deals, Richard might not represent most marketers' first-to-mind prototype. However,

Richard's ecological travel-related profile supports the view that offering upscale airline–accommodation–meal deals are likely to be effective in promoting domestic as well as overseas leisure trips. Designing travel packages that enable thoughts of saving money and achieving a good deal among wealthy households may be more effective in travel marketing than designing budget packages for middle- and low-income households – where non-comparable alternatives often have a dominating presence.

Lynn Hale: Domestic Travel by a Single, Low-income, House Cleaner

Exhibit 1.19 includes domestic travel in Lynn Hale's lived experience, but highly restricted plans for such travel. Lynn's lifestyle includes hard manual work and the expressed need for domestic 'resort' travel to rest and be pampered.

Exhibit 1.17. Responses of Richard Mills to first scenario and ten options.

Scenario 1. You have a good bit of money set aside for paying for one or two big purchases that you are thinking about making within the next few months. Here are some possibilities that you are thinking about or someone has mentioned to you.

Option:	Response:
• U: used car for work	Not an option.
• R: hotel, beach, South East Queensland	Sounds like a whole lot of fun.
• K: new kitchen cabinets	Definitely not.
• B: renovating pink bathroom	No.
• F: visiting with family members	Would always contemplate [doing].
• S: buying shares of stock	I don't think I need to.
• H: a house payment	Sounds like a good idea.
• D: used car for fun	No.
• W: wine-tasting tour in South Australia	My wife has connections in the Baroon Valley. I would definitely do it.
• G: week in Adelaide	My wife has connections there too – would do it.
	Final selection: H. Fundamental economic – get rid in one bump.

Note. Mr Mills moves from 'sounds like a whole lot of fun' to 'definitely would do it' when a destination includes 'connections' with the possibility of free accommodation; Mr Mills looks for a good deal occurring before increasing his intention to travel.

Lynn intends to decrease the frequency of her leisure travel next year, due to the combination of her self-awareness of 'getting older, having a cat, and limited finances'. Lynn's current leisure travel behaviour runs counter to intuitive thoughts that the poor cannot afford to stay in moderately priced resorts. The combination of sharing expenses with a friend and buying a travel package facilitates Lynn's felt need for 'resort' travel that includes sitting by the pool, being waited on and watching people.

Exhibit 1.20 summarizes the combination of facilitating factors enabling Lynn to attend Mardi Gras in Sydney. For such a distant trip from her hometown, Lynn requires free accommodation, and consequently she stays with friends in Sydney. Lynn's perception that she is time rich overcomes her felt financial constraint for such a trip. Visiting friends in Sydney alone is not sufficient to stimulate the trip; the Sydney Mardi Gras alone is not sufficient to stimulate the trip. However, the presence of both factors is necessary, along with Lynn's lifestyle orientation (i.e. felt time availability and desire to get away from her local area way-of-life), for the trip to Sydney.

Lynn's responses to the two scenarios are very enlightening. Lynn's way of life does not facilitate savings and encourages leisure travel. She rents and does not own a house; she has no need to buy a mortgage. She often uses public transportation and has no need to buy a used car. In Exhibits 1.21 and 1.22 her final selections in the two scenarios are leisure trips. Rest, relaxation and, by implication, reward and rejuvenation, are the end states achieved by Lynn via leisure travel.

Exhibit 1.18. Richard Mills' responses to 'mad money' second scenario.

Scenario 2b. You have set aside some 'mad money' to pay for something you always wanted to have or do even if some people might say, 'it was a frivolous thing to do'. Here are some possibilities that you are thinking about or someone has mentioned to you.

Option:	Response:
• R: hotel, beach, South East Queensland	Definitely.
• W: wine-tasting, South Australia	Yes.
• D: fun, used car	No. I would rather take a holiday [trip].
• G: week in Adelaide	Yes.
• C: buy new clothes just for you	Me? No.
• P: go to France, tour Paris, wine region	Always. It's great over there.
• Y: United States, visit friends, cities	Not interested in the US.
• J: Japan, the local culture	Definitely! But my wife wouldn't.
• E: new, really great, furniture	No.
• Q: second thoughts, give or invest	No.
• M: own mad money option, describe here	I would like to take a long cruise and travel in luxury.
• H: do things in Perth, Western Australia	Perth is too far [away].
• I: Sydney, special events	Always.
• B: Brisbane, some special events	Brisbane is not an exciting place.
• N: Melbourne, special events	Melbourne is not an exciting place.
• A: Alice Springs, Ayers Rock, tour	Yes, that would be interesting.
• S: Cairns, coastal Queensland and Islands	I love to snorkel; I've been there and it was great.
• D: Darwin, four-wheel driving, fishing, camping	No.
• X: Canberra, educational/learning experience	I lived in Canberra for five years – no thanks!
• Z: Tasmania, Hobart, unspoiled beauty	I'd like the hiking in the wilderness – not Hobart itself.

Final selection: J. Fascinating for 14 years. History, culture, language challenge, interesting. Went there in 1969; a great time. Art, religion.

Note. Based on responses to both scenarios, if 'good deals' come to Mr Mills' attention, travel is more likely than other options; overseas travel more likely than domestic; luxury cruise may be more likely than visit to Japan because his new wife 'wouldn't' [go to Japan] and no objection by wife was mentioned about the cruise option.

Strategy implications

The mistake in marketing domestic travel would be to ignore Lynn Hale and similar residents as a focal customer. Domestic travel packages designed to attract the working poor and fill their needs for rest and renewal are likely to be effective and profitable – and beneficial for these customers. Visual and word positioning messages that reflect the following benefits are likely to match the unconscious–conscious thoughts about travel generated by these customers' macro–micro-ecological system: 'Come to us – rest, relax and be pampered – you've earned it'.

Aiden Blechynden: the Good Life for Generation X Includes Travel

Exhibit 1.23 summarizes travel and local-area behaviour in Aiden Blechynden's life. His work as an accountant does not require overnight travel; he does engage extensively in domestic leisure. Aiden is 27, married, with limited financial obligations, and feels time-wealthy now that he has completed part-time postgraduate training in accounting. Aiden plans to reward himself and wife for completing his training with a trip to Europe – indicating that a travel destination

Exhibit 1.19. Total activities of Lynn Hale, 52, Cairns.

Female, single, works full-time: cleans houses, $12,000 annual income, has Visa credit card, member of one frequent flyer club, never uses the Internet, no mobile phone, no children at home

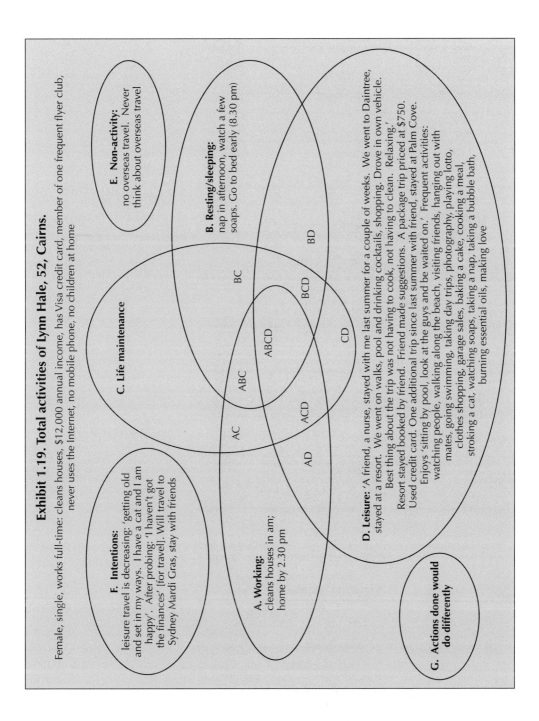

F. Intentions:
leisure travel is decreasing: 'getting old and set in my ways. I have a cat and I am happy'. After probing: 'I haven't got the finances' [for travel]. Will travel to Sydney Mardi Gras, stay with friends

A. Working:
cleans houses in am; home by 2.30 pm

C. Life maintenance

E. Non-activity:
no overseas travel. Never think about overseas travel

B. Resting/sleeping:
nap in afternoon, watch a few soaps. Go to bed early (8.30 pm)

AC   ABC   ABCD   BC

AD   ACD   CD   BCD   BD

D. Leisure: 'A friend, a nurse, stayed with me last summer for a couple of weeks. We went to Daintree, stayed at a resort. We went on walks, pool and drinking cocktails, shopping. Drove in own vehicle. Best thing about the trip was not having to cook, not having to clean. Relaxing.' Friend made suggestions. A package trip priced at $750. Resort stayed booked by friend. One additional trip since last summer with friend, stayed at Palm Cove. Used credit card. Frequent activities: Enjoys 'sitting by pool, look at the guys and be waited on.' watching people, walking along the beach, visiting friends, hanging out with mates, going swimming, taking day trips, photography, playing lotto, clothes shopping, garage sales, baking a cake, cooking a meal, stroking a cat, watching soaps, taking a nap, taking a bubble bath, burning essential oils, making love

G. Actions done would do differently

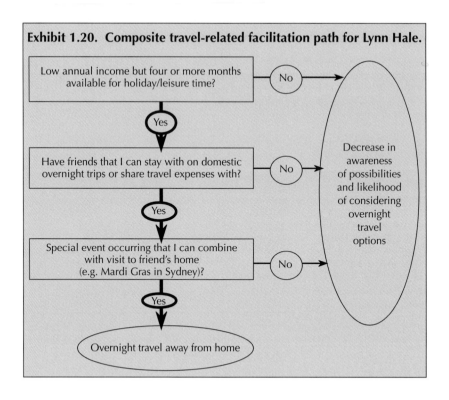

Exhibit 1.20. Composite travel-related facilitation path for Lynn Hale.

Low annual income but four or more months available for holiday/leisure time? — No →

Yes ↓

Have friends that I can stay with on domestic overnight trips or share travel expenses with? — No →

Yes ↓

Special event occurring that I can combine with visit to friend's home (e.g. Mardi Gras in Sydney)? — No →

Yes ↓

Overnight travel away from home

Decrease in awareness of possibilities and likelihood of considering overnight travel options

---

Exhibit 1.21. Responses of Lynn Hale to first scenario and ten options.

Scenario 1. You have a good bit of money set aside for paying for one or two big purchases that you are thinking about making within the next few months. Here are some possibilities that you are thinking about or someone has mentioned to you.

Option:	Response:
• U: used car for work	Got car. [No.]
• R: hotel, beach, South East Queensland	Great!
• K: new kitchen cabinets	Have new kitchen cabinets [now].
• B: renovating pink bathroom	No.
• F: visiting with family members	No.
• S: buying shares of stock	Good idea.
• H: a house payment	I'd rather rent.
• D: used car for fun	No.
• W: wine-tasting tour in South Australia	Great idea!
• G: week in Adelaide	Sounds nice.

Final selection: R. Restful holiday.

Exhibit 1.22. Lynn Hales' responses to new credit card second scenario.

Scenario 2a. You have the opportunity to sign-up for a new credit card offering a low interest rate on any unpaid balance plus no interest charges on any balance during the first six months of purchase. You decide to sign-up for the new credit card and consider using the new card to pay for one of the following options. You say to yourself, 'I might splurge once in my life!'

Option:	Response:
• R: hotel, beach, South East Queensland	Good idea.
• W: wine-tasting, South Australia	No.
• D: fun, used car	No.
• G: week in Adelaide	No.
• C: buy new clothes just for you	[Okay.] Why not.
• P: go to France, tour Paris, wine region	No.
• Y: United States, visit friends, cities	Yes.
• J: Japan, the local culture	No.
• E: new, really great, furniture	No.
• Q: second thoughts, give or invest	Not a good idea.
• M: own mad money option, describe here	Clear my credit card.
• H: do things in Perth, Western Australia	Yes.
• I: Sydney, special events	Yes.
• B: Brisbane, some special events	No.
• N: Melbourne, special events	No.
• A: Alice Springs, Ayers Rock, tour	No.
• S: Cairns, coastal Queensland and Islands	Live in Cairns.
• D: Darwin, four-wheel driving, fishing, camping	No.
• X: Canberra, educational/learning experience	No.
• Z: Tasmania, Hobart, unspoiled beauty	Would be nice.

Final selection: Y. To visit friends. Scenario 2 is realistic for me.

Note. Ms. Hale only travels domestically and shares expenses with a friend when she does travel. She does use her credit card to borrow money (pays monthly interest charges). She prefers to travel to a resort and sit by a pool and be waited on when travelling.

---

unique from destinations experienced on an annual basis may signify a major epiphany to oneself and others.

Aiden engages in automatic–habitual leisure travel annually; such travel includes his 10-day camping holiday with male friends, taken every year, as well as visits to his parents and to his wife's parents. Aiden also engages in two or more 'purely holiday trips' taken annually. Exhibit 1.24 reflects both types of holiday travel by Aiden.

Aiden's responses to the two scenarios show his preoccupation with his upcoming trip to Europe. Exhibits 1.25 and 1.26 indicate that domestic destinations *per se* do not moti-

vate Aiden's domestic travel behaviour. His domestic travel decisions focus on friends and family events in his life – promoting travel to see and experience a particular destination is not going to impact Aiden.

Strategy implications

Maintaining and nurturing camaraderie and family bonds reflect the lived experience outcomes of Aiden's travel behaviour. 'Seen that, done that' are not thoughts that are relevant for Aiden's domestic travel experiences. Similar to the experiences portrayed in the

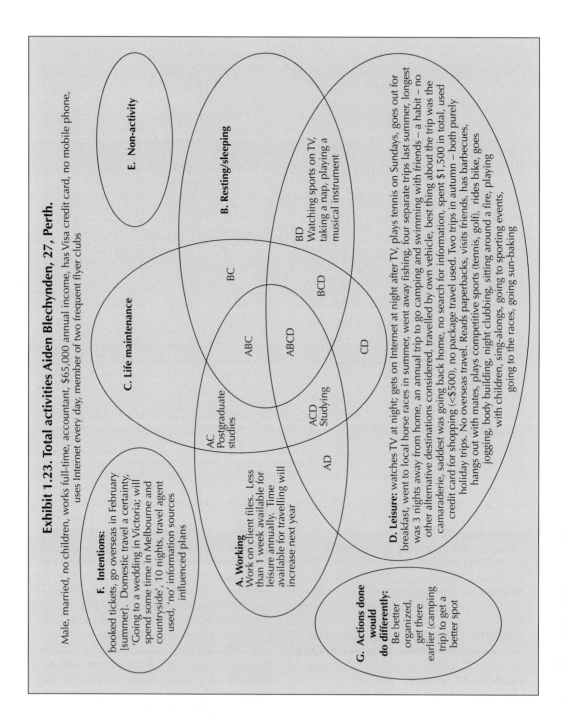

Exhibit 1.23. Total activities Aiden Blechynden, 27, Perth.

Male, married, no children, works full-time, accountant, $65,000 annual income, has Visa credit card, no mobile phone, uses Internet every day, member of two frequent flyer clubs

F. Intentions:
booked tickets, go overseas in February [summer]. Domestic travel a certainty, 'Going to a wedding in Victoria; will spend some time in Melbourne and countryside', 10 nights, travel agent used, 'no' information sources influenced plans

A. Working
Work on client files. Less than 1 week available for leisure annually. Time available for travelling will increase next year

G. Actions done would do differently:
Be better organized, get there earlier (camping trip) to get a better spot

C. Life maintenance

E. Non-activity

B. Resting/sleeping

AC
Postgraduate studies

AD

ACD
Studying

ABC

ABCD

BC

BCD

CD

BD
Watching sports on TV, taking a nap, playing a musical instrument

D. Leisure: watches TV at night; gets on Internet at night after TV, plays tennis on Sundays, goes out for breakfast, went to local horse races in summer, went away fishing, four separate trips last summer, longest was 3 nights away from home, an annual trip to go camping and swimming with friends – a habit – no other alternative destinations considered, travelled by own vehicle, best thing about the trip was the camaraderie, saddest was going back home, no search for information, spent $1,500 in total, used credit card for shopping (<$500), no package travel used. Two trips in autumn – both purely holiday trips. No overseas travel. Reads paperbacks, visits friends, has barbecues, hangs out with mates, plays competitive sports (tennis, golf), rides bike, goes jogging, body building, night clubbing, sitting around a fire, playing with children, sing-alongs, going to sporting events, going to the races, going sun-baking

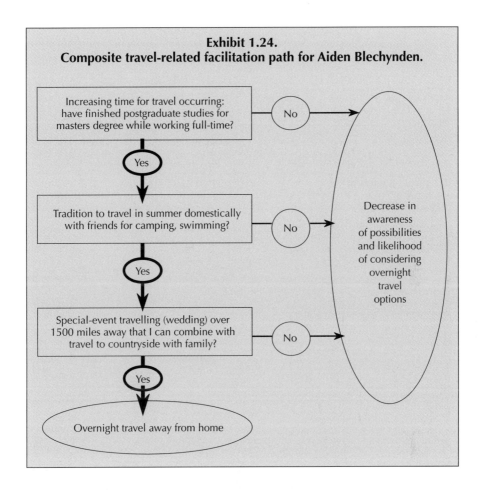

Exhibit 1.24.
Composite travel-related facilitation path for Aiden Blechynden.

Increasing time for travel occurring: have finished postgraduate studies for masters degree while working full-time? — No →

Yes ↓

Tradition to travel in summer domestically with friends for camping, swimming? — No →

Yes ↓

Special-event travelling (wedding) over 1500 miles away that I can combine with travel to countryside with family? — No →

Yes ↓

Decrease in awareness of possibilities and likelihood of considering overnight travel options

Overnight travel away from home

movie, *The Big Chill*, domestic travel for reunions, weddings and funerals, to be with close friends and family members, fit closely into Aiden's ecological system. Positional messages reinforcing the nurturing of close bonds with friends and family are more likely to be effective in promoting domestic travel among such Generation X members.

Michelle Ciccolella: Travel by a Middle-income Married Couple with Children

Exhibit 1.27 illustrates how young children can partially constrain domestic travel behaviour. Michelle reports that her children are now reaching a travel-friendly age (i.e. >7 years old) and that more frequent trips are likely, starting next year. Michelle and her husband own a house with a pool in the backyard and 'don't really go anywhere'. Still, they did manage to travel with the kids to Sydney (2 hours away by highway) twice last summer for 3 nights away from home each time.

Exhibit 1.28 indicates that Michelle and her husband are influenced by package travel offers when they can combine such travel with another couple. Overseas travel does not compete with domestic travel; Michelle reports never thinking about overseas travel, and her responses to the two scenarios back up her assessment. However, non-comparable alternatives do compete with domestic travel for Michelle. See her final selections in Exhibits 1.29 and 1.30.

Exhibit 1.25. Responses of Aiden Blechynden to first scenario and ten options.

Scenario 1. You have a good bit of money set aside for paying for one or two big purchases that you are thinking about making within the next few months. Here are some possibilities that you are thinking about or someone has mentioned to you.

Option:	**Response:**
• U: used car for work	No. Not practical for us to have two cars.
• R: hotel, beach, South East Queensland	No. Have plans to go to Europe.
• K: new kitchen cabinets	No. Don't own a house yet.
• B: renovating pink bathroom	No. Don't own a house.
• F: visiting with family members	No. Plans are set to go to Europe.
• S: buying shares of stock	Yes.
• H: a house payment	No, but if not going to Europe, would be an option.
• D: used car for fun	No.
• W: wine-tasting tour in South Australia	No – not that fanatical about wine.
• G: week in Adelaide	No.

Final selection: Europe [my real choice]. But of the options mentioned above: H is most appealing considering my present circumstances.

Michelle's choices of leisure activities are fluid and depend on ease of mental availability of competing options. When Michelle stops and thinks about comparing non-comparable alternatives, domestic travel options are not the ones finally selected. However, in real life, Michelle and her husband do not usually make such comparisons.

Strategy implications

Designing travel packages that include adult and child activities (e.g. casino and beach experiences) are likely to be attractive to middle-income married couples with children older than 6 years, as represented by Michelle and family. Such guests likely represent substantial total room sales and profits for hotels and casinos, even though such revenues and profits are below average per customer visit. Because of the substantial number of house-

holds in this population segment, and the segment's responsiveness to promotional offers, the failure to identify such families as a focal (i.e. target) customer segment, and the lack of creating special deals to facilitate their travel, would be a mistake.

Discussion, Limitations and Suggestions for Future Research

Exhibit 1.31 represents a composite generalized model of the facilitating and constraining factors described in one or more of the seven case studies. Exhibit 1.31 illustrates the central conclusion of the study: ecological systems theory is relevant and useful in explaining and describing the interactions of macro and micro facilitating and constraining factors affecting lifestyle, leisure and travel behaviour. For an individual, each of the issues in Exhibit 1.31 may occur uncon-

Exhibit 1.26. Aiden Blechynden's responses to 'mad money' second scenario.

Scenario 2b. You have set aside some 'mad money' to pay for something you always wanted to have or do even if some people might say, 'it was a frivolous thing to do'. Here are some possibilities that you are thinking about or someone has mentioned to you.

Option:	Response:
• R: hotel, beach, South East Queensland	I would be interested, perhaps concerned about cost.
• W: wine-tasting, South Australia	Not quite excited enough about wine. [No.]
• D: fun, used car	Not interested.
• G: week in Adelaide	Would not interest me.
• C: buy new clothes just for you	I am not overly interested in clothes.
• P: go to France, tour Paris, wine region	This option is quite appealing.
• Y: United States, visit friends, cities	Sounds great.
• J: Japan, the local culture	Would be interested.
• E: new, really great, furniture	Do not have a home.
• Q: second thoughts, give or invest	None of these options appeals to me.
• M: own mad money option, describe here	Go to Europe and tour for six months.
• H: do things in Perth, Western Australia	Would not be an option.
• I: Sydney, special events	Not that appealing.
• B: Brisbane, some special events	Not interested in Brisbane.
• N: Melbourne, special events	Would be interested because family is over there.
• A: Alice Springs, Ayers Rock, tour	Not at this stage in my life.
• S: Cairns, coastal Queensland and Islands	Scuba-diving sounds appealing.
• D: Darwin, four-wheel driving, fishing, camping	This would be great.
• X: Canberra, educational/learning experience	I've heard that Canberra is quite boring.
• Z: Tasmania, Hobart, unspoiled beauty	Maybe later in life.

Final selection: M. It was easy to make this choice as it was my own idea and not one of the generic options. Europe is the most appealing option at present.

Note. Domestic travel trigger includes a conjunction of friends or family times along with outdoor activities; cities are in the reject set of options; overseas, holiday/vacation, travel plans to Europe are completed.

sciously, consciously or with elements of both unconscious-automatic and conscious-strategic thinking (cf. Bargh, 2002; Wilson, 2002; Zaltman, 2003).

Note that the first issue (box 1) considers more than level of income related to leisure travel. The case studies of Andy Hill and Lynn Hale, respectively, illustrate how a high-income household may appear cash strapped and a low-income household cash enabled, depending on the interactions of macro- and microsystem factors in their lives.

For many individuals, passing through the contingency steps leading to box 7 occurs automatically, with little to no conscious thought, or occurs in combination with con-scious thoughts and trade-offs that occur over seconds rather than minutes, hours or days. The very limited relevancy and affect–referral responses of all the informants to each of the scenario options support and extend Tversky and Kahneman's discussion on the nature of thinking and making choices:

> People do not normally analyze daily events into exhaustive lists of possibilities or evaluate compound probabilities by aggregating elementary ones. Instead, they commonly use a limited number of heuristics, such as representativeness and availability (Kahneman *et al.*, 1982).
>
> (Tversky and Kahneman, 1984, p. 296)

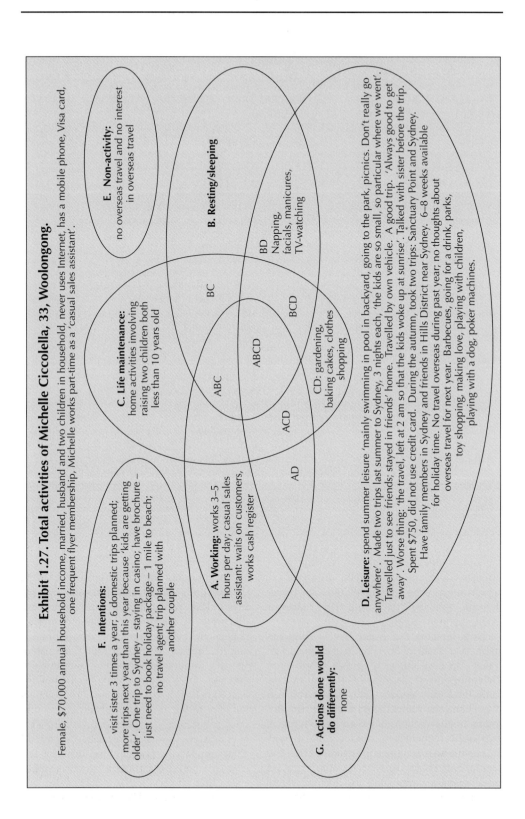

Exhibit 1.27. Total activities of Michelle Ciccolella, 33, Woolongong.

Female, $70,000 annual household income, married, husband and two children in household, never uses Internet, has a mobile phone, Visa card, one frequent flyer membership. Michelle works part-time as a 'casual sales assistant'.

E. Non-activity:
no overseas travel and no interest in overseas travel

B. Resting/sleeping

BD
Napping, facials, manicures, TV-watching

C. Life maintenance:
home activities involving raising two children both less than 10 years old

BC

ABC

ABCD

BCD

ACD

CD: gardening, baking cakes, clothes shopping

AD

F. Intentions:
visit sister 3 times a year; 6 domestic trips planned; more trips next year than this year because 'kids are getting older'. One trip to Sydney – staying in casino; have brochure – just need to book holiday package – 1 mile to beach; no travel agent; trip planned with another couple

A. Working: works 3–5 hours per day; casual sales assistant: waits on customers, works cash register

D. Leisure: spend summer leisure 'mainly swimming in pool in backyard, going to the park, picnics. Don't really go anywhere'. Made two trips last summer to Sydney, 3 nights each, 'the kids are so small, so particular where we went'. Travelled just to see friends; stayed in friends' home. Travelled by own vehicle. A good trip. 'Always good to get away'. Worse thing: 'the travel, left at 2 am so that the kids woke up at sunrise'. Talked with sister before the trip. Spent $750, did not use credit card. During the autumn, took two trips: Sanctuary Point and Sydney. Have family members in Sydney and friends in Hills District near Sydney. 6–8 weeks available for holiday time. No travel overseas during past year; no thoughts about overseas travel for next year. Barbecues, going for a drink, parks, toy shopping, making love, playing with children, playing with a dog, poker machines.

G. Actions done would do differently:
none

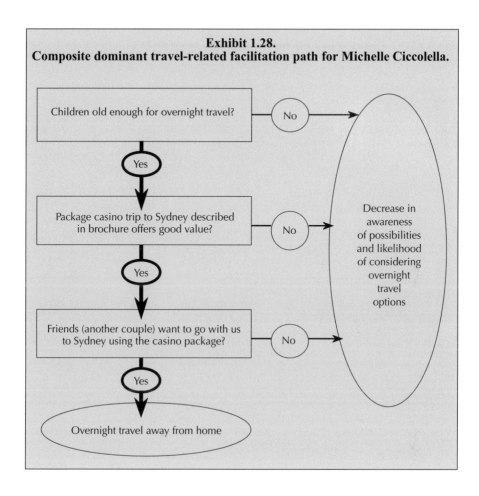

Exhibit 1.28.
Composite dominant travel-related facilitation path for Michelle Ciccolella.

Children old enough for overnight travel? — No →

Yes ↓

Package casino trip to Sydney described in brochure offers good value? — No →

Yes ↓

Friends (another couple) want to go with us to Sydney using the casino package? — No →

Yes ↓

Overnight travel away from home

Decrease in awareness of possibilities and likelihood of considering overnight travel options

Tversky and Kahneman's research focuses on how individuals make judgements about the probability of occurrence of events for which the probabilities are accurately known by the researcher. For personal choices in lived experiences, and in evaluating scenarios from an informant's perspective, the concept relevancy to her life is both analogous and more applicable than the concept of representativeness – because relevancy covers not only the idea, 'Yes, I've done that!' but also, 'Yes, I can see myself doing that', versus, 'No, that's not [for] me'. Affect–referral relates to availability (a mental process by the individual about her past, present or future life) of an event occurring; affect–referral (good versus bad for me) evaluations are likely to occur automatically with judgements regarding the personal availability of an event seen by the informant in her life.

Note that the path likely to occur with the greatest frequency (1–2–3–4–5–6–7 to 8 and 9) supports the main tenet of comparative analysis (e.g. Ragin, 1987) – multiple facilitating factors and constraining factors combine to result in a given event outcome. Such contingency path descriptions and explanations of behaviour are particularly useful for building inductive theories of leisure and travel behaviour. For testing deductive models of the influence of independent variables on respondents' intentions towards leisure activities, such modelling suggests the need for thorough examination of three-factor and more complex interaction effects – rather than focusing only on main and two-way interaction effects.

Exhibit 1.29. Responses of Michelle Ciccolella to first scenario and ten options.

Scenario 1. You have a good bit of money set aside for paying for one or two big purchases that you are thinking about making within the next few months. Here are some possibilities that you are thinking about or someone has mentioned to you.

Option:	Response:
• U: used car for work	I'd consider it.
• R: hotel, beach, South East Queensland	I'd consider it but not a strong possibility.
• K: new kitchen cabinets	I'd consider it but not pressing.
• B: renovating pink bathroom	Yeah, more likely.
• F: visiting with family members	Yep, an option [that I'd consider].
• S: buying shares of stock	Definitely!
• H: a house payment	Most definitely.
• D: used car for fun	No.
• W: wine-tasting tour in South Australia	Would be nice.
• G: week in Adelaide	I'd consider it.

Final selection: S. Shares hopefully [would] make me the most money.

Limitations

This chapter focuses on building and probing theory from the perspective of case-study research, rather than generalizing findings to a population. A substantial number of replications of the case studies are needed to confirm or refute the reported descriptions and explanations before concluding that the described paths and outcomes are accurate among samples of informants or populations.

The accuracy and value of future research using long interviews are likely to be increased by incorporating second interviews with the same informants. These second interviews might be planned for a few weeks to 1 year after the first interviews. Data on whether or not leisure and travel plans became reality could be collected during the second interviews. The researcher's interpretations (i.e. etic observations) from the data collected from the informant from the first interview could be discussed with the same informant during the second interview, and the informant's interpretations (i.e. emic observations) about the original findings could be collected – paradoxes in the data might be cleared up and additional insights gained. Also, conducting second interviews with the same informants recognizes the wisdom of Chris Rock's (an American comedian and philosopher) observation, 'When you meet someone for the first time, you are not meeting that person; you are meeting the person's representative.' Responses from a second interview are likely to uncover thoughts and knowledge usually held only unconsciously by informants – thoughts expressed only during the second interview due to unintended reflections from the first interview, as well as due to the greater familiarity and trust of the informant felt toward the researcher (cf. Bargh, 2002; Woodside, 2004).

Exhibit 1.30. Michelle Ciccolella's responses to 'mad money' second scenario.

Scenario 2b. You have set aside some 'mad money' to pay for something you always wanted to have or do even if some people might say, 'it was a frivolous thing to do'. Here are some possibilities that you are thinking about or someone has mentioned to you.

Option:	Response:
• R: hotel, beach, South East Queensland	Yep. I'd consider it.
• W: wine-tasting, South Australia	Love that!
• D: fun, used car	Yep, definitely.
• G: week in Adelaide	Yes/no?? [Can't decide].
• C: buy new clothes just for you	Most definitely in doubt. [Unlikely to consider].
• P: go to France, tour Paris, wine region	Yes.
• Y: United States, visit friends, cities	Of course. Like that.
• J: Japan, the local culture	Not when I haven't seen other places.
• E: new, really great, furniture	Definitely would consider.
• Q: second thoughts, give or invest	Probably.
• M: own mad money option, describe here	Would make family debt free if a lot [of money].
• H: do things in Perth,Western Australia	Definitely; sister-in-law in Perth.
• I: Sydney, special events	Yes.
• B: Brisbane, some special events	Yes.
• N: Melbourne, special events	Yes, nice shopping in metro area.
• A: Alice Springs, Ayers Rock, tour	Consider it.
• S: Cairns, coastal Queensland and Islands	Definitely would; haven't been to Queensland.
• D: Darwin, four-wheel driving, fishing, camping	No, not in others [consideration set].
• X: Canberra, educational/learning experience	Consider it.
• Z: Tasmania, Hobart, unspoiled beauty	Not first on my list.

Final selection: M. Just would – family debt free. Help family to be free to do what they like to be happy.

Note. First orientation to stay home but children getting older (all over 7 years old) and more capable of domestic travel but other facilitating factors must occur to trigger domestic trip (e.g. friends going and package trip available to casino in Sydney); Sydney is 75 miles north of Wollongong. Overseas travel: no experience, no plans, no substantial interest in overseas destinations.

Marketing Strategy Implications

Exhibit 1.32 considers marketing strategy implications designed to stimulate domestic leisure travel, based on the seven general facilitating/constraining factors in Exhibit 1.31. Exhibit 1.32 implies a global strategy recommendation: implementing multiple strategies focusing on enhancing travel facilitators and reducing constraints is more likely to be effective than executing a single national image-advertising campaign.

Exhibit 1.32 summarizes several strategy implications that involve cooperation across government marketing organizations (e.g. national, state and provincial government units), NGOs (non-governmental organizations) and sectors of the travel industry (e.g. airlines, coach firms, destination attractions, accommodation enterprises). While such strategies may be executed rather infrequently, examples of successfully implementing such cooperative marketing programmes are available in the literature (e.g. see Brennan and Woodside, 1982).

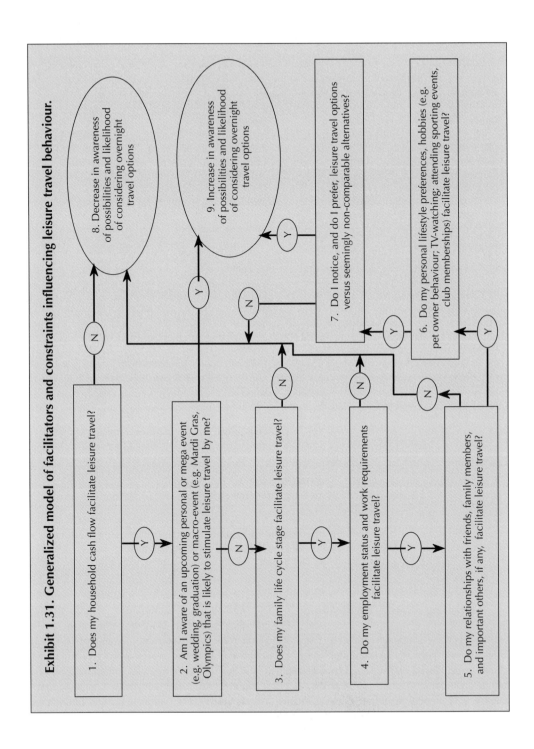

Exhibit 1.31. Generalized model of facilitators and constraints influencing leisure travel behaviour.

Exhibit 1.32. Marketing and positioning theme implications from generalized model.

Facilitator/constraint factor	Marketing and positioning theme implication
1. Does my household cash flow facilitate leisure travel?	1. Travel via credit card and debt is possible, legitimate and worthwhile.
2. Aware of upcoming personal or mega-event?	2. Seek/create mega-events; reinforce need to attend mega- and personal events.
3. Does my family life cycle stage facilitate leisure travel?	3. Create travel-friendly environments and events for young children.
4. Do my employment status and work facilitate travel?	4. Create life-changing epiphany (e.g. graduations) themes.
5. Relationships – friends, family members facilitate travel?	5. Create relationship-bonding travel products and themes.
6. My personal lifestyle, hobbies, facilitate travel?	6. Nurture/sponsor regional and national lifestyle, hobby meetings.
7. Do I notice and prefer leisure travel versus non-comparable options?	7. Create/nurture frequent traveller programmes and themes that a full, rich life includes travel and destination experiences.

Appendix

INTERVIEW PROTOCOL
(for use by interviewer only)

Survey of Household Activities
During the Day, Night, Weekends and Seasons

INTERVIEW DETAILS

Date (dd/mm/yr):   _____

Interviewer name (please print):   _____

Respondent's name (please print):   _____

Respondent's attitudinal segment
classification: _____

Respondent's city/location of
interview: _____

                                        Capital City? ( ) Yes ( ) No

Respondent's frequency of holidays **( ) Frequent**
                                        (5 or more holidays past 2 years)
                                        ( ) Less frequent
                                        (2 or less holidays past 2 years)
                                        ( ) Lapsed
                                        (no holidays past 2 years)

Introduction

Thank you very much for agreeing to participate in this research project that we are conducting as staff and students of the University of New South Wales. The purpose of the survey is to learn about activities by individuals and household members. The time to complete our meeting will be approximately 50–60 minutes. In appreciation of your participation in the study, you will receive a gift of $70.00. Before starting the interview, there are a few points I'd like to mention.

Respondent advice

- This interview consists of questions in a number of sections. All of the questions deal with situations that may be relevant to you. Hence there are no right or wrong answers. Please relax and respond freely.
- We realize that it is often difficult to accurately remember the past. So please take the time you need to recollect what happened. If you realize you have made an error, then correct it by letting me know.
- If you don't understand any aspect of what I say, please tell me and I will try to make it clear for you.
- During the interview if there is anything you have here at home that you think relates to what we are saying and you want to show me, please do, e.g. photos, programmes, awards.
- This may seem like a conversation between you and me, but actually you take centre stage here. So I will be interested in hearing what you think and feel rather than telling you my views.

Interviewer's instructions

- Allow the respondent sufficient time to recall and explain situations, experiences, etc. **PAUSE OFTEN AND DO NOT INTERRUPT RESPONDENT WHILE S/HE IS ANSWERING.**
- Make every effort to reduce distractions to a minimum during the interview, e.g. noise, people interrupting.
- Encourage the respondent to recall as much as possible.
- Vary the way you ask questions, especially when you are asking a respondent to discuss the same issue for an extended period of time.

SECTION 1
Recent Experiences

Question 1

1a. I'd like you to tell me about what you've recently been doing during your days and evenings. For example, are you currently working somewhere outside your home?

( ) Yes ( ) No ...**Go to Question 2 below** ( ) Other response: _____
1b. **If yes**, please describe your work [verbatim response]:

_____

1c. What is your job title? [verbatim response]:

_____

1d. Are you working full-time, half-time, less than half-time?
( ) Full ( ) Half ( ) Less than half-time

1e. Please describe your <u>most recent</u> day at work (today? yesterday? etc?):

- What time did you get to work?

_____
_____

- What activities did you do at work yesterday in the morning?

_____
_____

- What activities did you do at work yesterday in the afternoon?

_____
_____

Now go to Question 3 below

Question 2

2. If you are currently <u>not</u> working outside the home, please describe your day yesterday: what activities were you engaged in during the morning and afternoon yesterday?

- Morning activities:

_____
_____
_____

- Afternoon activities:

_____
_____
_____

Question 3

3a. Please describe your activities yesterday <u>evening</u>, beginning with dinner. Was dinner at home or did you eat out somewhere?
( ) dinner at home   ( ) ate out

3b. What activities did you engage in yesterday evening?

● Right after you had dinner?

_____

_____

3c. And for the rest of the evening before you went to bed?

● Early evening activities:

_____

_____

● Late evening activities:

_____

_____

Question 4

4a. Was what you did last night typical, somewhat unusual, or very unusual for your evening activities?

( ) typical   ( ) somewhat unusual   ( ) very unusual

4b. What are your reasons for saying that?

_____

_____

Question 5

5. Please describe your activities during the most recent weekend.
    [dates of weekend (dd/mm/yy): _____]

Did you mostly stay home, travel around the area where you live, or travel overnight away from home during this most recent weekend?

Tick in the space below

● ( ) at home mostly or entirely . . . . **Go to Question 6**

● ( ) travel around the area where I live . . . . **Go to Question 7**

● ( ) travel overnight somewhere away from home . . .**Go to Question 8**

Question 6

6. Please describe your activities on Saturday and Sunday this past weekend.

● Saturday activities:

_____

_____

● Sunday activities:

_____

_____

Now go to Question 9 below

Question 7

7. Please describe your recent weekend activities in travelling around the area where you live.

- Saturday activities:

_____

_____

- Sunday activities:

_____

_____

Now go to Question 9 below

Question 8

8a. Please describe your activities during your recent weekend overnight trip away from home.

_____

_____

8b. What were the triggers/reasons for this trip?

_____

_____

8c. What were the limitations or constraints, if any, that influenced your decision to take this trip?

_____

_____

8d. What town, city, or place did you stay in overnight?

_____

_____

8e. Did you consider any other destinations before choosing this destination? If yes, how many and what were they?

_____

_____

8f. What made you choose the destination you did?

_____

_____

8g. For this recent trip, did you stay at the home of friends or family, camp-out, or did you stay at a hotel, B&B, or other paid for accommodation?
( ) friend's home ( ) family member's home ( ) camp-out ( ) hotel ( ) B&B
( ) other, please describe: _____

8h. What activities did you do during this trip?

_____

_____

8i. What other activities did you do during this most recent trip?

_____

_____

8j. Did you travel alone, with other members of your household, and/or other persons? [verbatim response]:

_____

_____

8k. Did you travel using your own vehicle, rent a vehicle, go by bus, by train, plane or some other mode?
( ) own vehicle ( ) rental vehicle
( ) bus   ( ) train
( ) plane ( ) other, please describe: _____

8l. How did this particular trip turn out? Would you describe the trip as a 'bad trip', a 'just okay trip', or a 'good trip' experience?
( ) Bad trip   ( ) Just okay trip   ( ) Good trip

8m. What makes you say that? [verbatim response]:
_____
_____

8n. What was the best thing about this trip?
_____
_____

8o. What was the worst thing about this trip?
_____
_____

8p. If you could go back in time, is there anything you'd change about this trip?
_____
_____

8q. Thinking back before you went on this trip, did you talk with anyone about the taking the trip or possible destinations to visit – for example, did you discuss the trip with family members, friends, or other people?
( ) No   ( ) Yes   ( ) Not sure, do not remember or other response

If yes, what did you talk about? [verbatim response]:
_____
_____

8r. Again thinking back before you went on this trip, did you seek out some information about activities to do on the trip, or about destinations or attractions that you might visit?
( ) No   ( ) Yes   ( ) Not sure, do not remember or other response

If yes, what information did you seek out? [verbatim response]:
_____
_____

Where did you get this information from? [Probe: 'Did you ask a friend or family member, request brochures, look in magazines, newspapers, watch a TV programme, go on the Internet, read a travel guidebook, etc.?']
_____
_____

Did you get some information related to what you were looking for? Was it helpful for you?
_____
_____

How specifically was the information helpful for you?
_____
_____

8s. Considering all costs related to the trip, including lodging, petrol, food, gifts, ticket prices, and rental fees, about how much did this trip cost overall – the total costs for all persons going on the trip?
( ) Less than $500
( ) $500–$1000
( ) $1001–$2000
( ) $2001–$3000
( ) $3001–$5000
( ) Above $5000

8t. For this trip, did you make any payments using credit cards or charge cards?
( ) No – **Go to Question 8w**　　　( ) Yes, in part　　　( ) Yes, most to all of the expenses

8u. Which part or parts of the trip did you charge to credit or charge cards, if any?
[Circle all mentioned by respondent]
Travel 1
Accommodation 2
Meals – food and beverage 3
Shopping 4
Activities (including entry fees and equipment hire) 5
Rental car 6
Entertainment 7
Other 8

8v. Roughly how much did you charge to credit card(s) overall on your last holiday or break, and to which card or cards did you charge it? [Circle the appropriate number(s) for the relevant credit/charge card types]

TO AMERICAN EXPRESS
Less than $500 1
$500–$1000 2
$1001–$2000 3
$2001–$3000 4
$3001–$5000 5
$5001 and over 6

TO MASTERCARD
Less than $500 13
$500–$1000 14
$1001–$2000 15
$2001–$3000 16
$3001–$5000 17
$5001 and over 18

TO DINERS' CLUB
Less than $500 7
$500–$1000 8
$1001–$2000 9
$2001–$3000 10
$3001–$5000 11
$5001 and over 12

TO VISA
Less than $500 19
$500–$1000 20
$1001–$2000 21
$2001–$3000 22
$3001–$5000 23
$5001 and over 24

TO ANOTHER CARD 25
Please specify _____

8w. Was any part of your trip covered by a transport package? That is where your (airfare/coach/train/other major transport) and one or more of accommodation, food, car hire, activities or equipment were included in the price? [Circle the appropriate number]
Yes. . . . . 1　　　　　No . . . . 2　　　　　Don't know 3

8x. If yes, please describe what parts were covered by the transport package:

_____

_____

Question 9

9. Please think back and describe your activities during the months of last summer – from December 1999 to February 2000. Did you stay in the area where you live and work or did you travel overnight away from home sometimes during these three months?
( ) Stayed at home   ( ) Sometimes travelled   ( ) Other

Question 10

10. What activities <u>first come to mind</u> that you did at your home and in your home town area last summer? [Probe, ONLY IF necessary: 'Gardening, go on walks, housework, cooking, watching TV, quilting, reading, talking with neighbours, homework with children, etc.'] [verbatim response]:

_____

_____

Question 11

11. What other activities did you do last summer at home or in your home town area? [verbatim response]:

_____

_____

Question 12

12. Did you and/or persons in your household take some overnight trips away from home <u>last summer</u>?
( ) No ... **Go to Question 15**   ( ) Yes ... **Go to Question 13**

Question 13

13a. How many total separate trips were made away from home last summer?
( ) 1   ( ) 2   ( ) 3–5   ( ) 6–7   ( ) 8+

13b. For the <u>longest trip in nights away</u> from home <u>last summer</u>, how many days were spent away from home? [verbatim response, number of nights away from home on longest trip]:

_____

13c. What were the reasons for, or what triggered, this longest trip away from home last summer? [verbatim response]:

_____

_____

13d. What were the limitations and constraints, if any, that influenced your decision to take this trip? [verbatim response]:

_____

_____

13e. What towns, cities, or places did you stay overnight on this longest trip last summer? [Probe: 'Did you stay overnight at different locations or spend all your nights at one location? Please name each overnight location you stayed at and how many nights you stayed at each for the longest trip.] [verbatim detailed response]:

_____

_____

3f. Did you consider any other destinations before choosing this destination? If yes, how many and what were they? [verbatim response]:

_____

_____

13g. What made you choose the destination you did?

_____

_____

13h. For this trip last summer, did you stay at the home of friends or family, camp-out, or did you stay at a hotel, B&B, or other paid for accommodation?
( ) friend's home   ( ) family member's home
( ) camp-out   ( ) hotel
( ) B&B   ( ) other, please describe: _____

13i. What activities did you do during this longest trip last summer?

_____

_____

13j. What other activities did you do during this trip last summer?

_____

_____

13k. Did you travel alone, with other members of your household, and/or other persons? [verbatim response]:

_____

_____

13l. Did you travel using your own vehicle, rent a vehicle, go by bus, by train, plane or some other travel means – or did you use a combination of travel methods?
( ) own vehicle ( ) rental vehicle
( ) bus   ( ) train
( ) plane   ( ) other, please describe [verbatim response]: _____

13m. How did this particular trip turn out? Would you describe the trip as a 'bad trip', a 'just okay trip', or a 'good trip' experience?
( ) Bad trip   ( ) Just okay trip   ( ) Good trip

13n. What makes you say that? [verbatim response]:

_____

_____

13o. What was the best thing about this trip?

_____

_____

13p. What was the worst thing about this trip?

_____

_____

13q. If you could go back in time, is there anything you'd change about this trip?

13r. Thinking back before you went on this trip, did you talk with anyone about taking the trip or possible destinations to visit – for example, did you discuss the trip with family members, friends, or other people?
( ) No   ( ) Yes   ( ) Not sure, do not remember or other response

If yes, what did you talk about? [verbatim response]:

_____

_____

13s. Again, thinking back before you went on this trip, did you seek out some information about activities to do on the trip, or about destinations or attractions that you might visit?
( ) No   ( ) Yes   ( ) Not sure, do not remember or other response

If yes, what information did you seek out? [verbatim response]:

_____

_____

If yes, where did you get this information from? [Probe: 'Did you ask a friend or family member, request brochures, look in magazines, newspapers, watch a TV programme, go on the Internet, read a travel guidebook, etc.?']

_____

_____

If yes, did you get some information related to what you were looking for? Was it helpful for you?

_____

_____

If yes, how specifically was the information helpful for you?

_____

_____

13t. Considering all costs related to the trip, including lodging, petrol, food, gifts, ticket prices and rental fees, about how much did this trip cost overall – the total costs for all persons going on the trip?
( ) Less than $500
( ) $500–$1000
( ) $1001–$2000
( ) $2001–$3000
( ) $3001–$5000
( ) Above $5000

13u. For this trip, did you make any payments using credit cards or charge cards?
( ) No   ( ) Yes, in part   ( ) Yes, most to all of the expenses

13v. Which part or parts of the trip did you charge to credit or charge cards, if any?
[Circle all mentioned by respondent]
Travel 1
Accommodation 2
Meals – food and beverage 3
Shopping 4
Activities (including entry fees and equipment hire) 5
Rental car 6
Entertainment 7
Other 8

13w. Roughly how much did you charge to credit card(s) overall on your last holiday or break, and to which card or cards did you charge it? [Circle the appropriate number(s) for the relevant credit/charge card types]

TO AMERICAN EXPRESS		**TO MASTER CARD**	
Less than $500	1	Less than $500	13
$500–$1000	2	$500–$1000	14
$1001–$2000	3	$1001–$2000	15
$2001–$3000	4	$2001–$3000	16
$3001–$5000	5	$3001–$5000	17
$5001 and over	6	$5001 and over	18
TO DINERS' CLUB		**TO VISA**	
Less than $500	7	Less than $500	19
$500–$1000	8	$500–$1000	20
$1001–$2000	9	$1001–$2000	21
$2001–$3000	10	$2001–$3000	22
$3001–$5000.	11	$3001–$5000	23
$5001 and over	12	$5001 and over	24

TO ANOTHER CARD 25
Please specify _____

13x. Was any part of your trip covered by a transport package? That is where your (airfare/coach/train/other major transport) and one or more of accommodation, food, car hire, activities or equipment were included in the price? [Circle the appropriate number]:
Yes 1   No 2   Don't know 3

13y. **If yes**, please describe what parts were covered by the transport package:
_____
_____

Question 14

14. Thinking about your longest trip that you made last summer, if you could go back and change something about the trip, or even not make the trip, what would you do differently, if anything? [verbatim response]:
_____
_____

Question 15

15. What activities would you have liked to have done but did not get to do on this summer trip, if any? [verbatim response]:
_____
_____

Question 16

16. After last summer and up until last weekend (between March 1 and up until last weekend), how many overnight trips away from home, if any, did you take?
    ( ) None .... **Go to Section 2 below**
    ( ) 1   ( ) 2   ( ) 3–5   ( ) 6–10   ( ) 10+

Question 17

17. As much as you can recall, please describe the reasons for these trips? For example, how many of these overnight trips were primarily work related, if any? How many were purely holiday,

for pleasure, trips. How many were combinations of work and holiday travel? [verbatim response]:

SECTION 2
Holiday Time and Activities During This Calendar Year 2000

Question 1

1. How many total days or weeks <u>during this year, 2000,</u> have been available for you as holiday time – time for you to spend doing things at home and away by yourself or with friend and family members?

( ) None ( ) less than 1 week ( ) 1–3 weeks ( ) 4–5 weeks
( ) 6–8 weeks ( ) 9–12 weeks ( ) 13+ weeks

Question 2

2. During 2000 compared to the previous year, 1999, did you spend a greater number of nights at home or away from home, or about the same number of nights at home in both years?

( ) More nights at home in 2000 compared with 1999
( ) More nights at home in 1999 compared with 2000
( ) About the same number of nights at home in both years.

Question 3

3a. From 1998 to 2000, do you see a change in the total number of nights you spend away from home?

( ) No … **Go to Question 4 below** ( ) Yes

3b. **If yes**, are the total number of nights you spend away from home increasing or decreasing?

( ) Increasing ( ) Decreasing

3c. What are the reasons for this change in number of nights away from home? [verbatim response]:

3d. What additional reasons are behind this change in your number of nights at home and away from home? [Probe deeply]

Question 4

4. Even if you have already mentioned travelling overseas in 2000, I would like to ask you specifically, IF you have made any <u>overseas trips during this calendar year</u>?

( ) No…**Go to Question 15 below** ( ) Yes…. **Go to Question 5 below**
Other, please explain:

Question 5

5a. In 2000, what countries, cities, and places did you visit on your most recent overseas trip? [verbatim response]:

_____

_____

5b. What triggered this particular overseas trip? How did the trip come about? [verbatim response]:

_____

_____

5c. How many nights overseas, outside of Australia, did you spend on this particular trip?
( ) 1–3   ( ) 4–6   ( ) 6–9   ( ) 10–14   ( ) 15–21   ( ) 22+

5d. Before taking the trip, how did you go about booking travel arrangements for the trip? Did you book with an airline directly or did you use a travel agent?
( ) Booked directly   ( ) Used a travel agent
[Verbatim comments by respondent]:

_____

_____

5e. What activities did you do on this most recent overseas trip in 2000? [verbatim response]:

_____

_____

5f. What activities would you have liked to have done but did not get to do on this most recent overseas trip, if any? [verbatim response]:

_____

_____

5g. How did this particular trip turn out? Would you describe the trip as a 'bad trip', a 'just okay trip', or a 'good trip' experience?
( ) Bad trip   ( ) Just okay trip   ( ) Good trip

5h. What makes you say that? [verbatim response]:

_____

_____

5i. What was the best thing about this trip?

_____

_____

5j. What was the worst thing about this trip?

_____

_____

5k. If you could go back in time, is there anything you'd change about this trip?

_____

_____

5l. Thinking back before you went overseas on this trip, did you talk with anyone about taking the trip or possible destinations to visit – for example, did you discuss the trip with family members, friends, or other people?
( ) No   ( ) Yes   ( ) Not sure, do not remember or other response

If yes, what did you talk about? [verbatim response]:

_____

_____

5m. Again thinking back before you went on this overseas trip, did you <u>seek out some informa-</u><u>tion</u> about activities to do on the trip, or about destinations or attractions that you might visit?
( ) No   ( ) Yes   ( ) Not sure, do not remember or other response

If yes, what information did you seek out? [verbatim response]:

_____

_____

If yes, where did you get this information from? [Probe: 'Did you ask a friend or family member, request brochures, look in magazines, newspapers, watch a TV programme, go on the Internet, read a travel guidebook, etc.?']

_____

_____

If yes, did you get some information related to what you were looking for? Was it helpful for you?

_____

_____

If yes, how specifically was the information helpful for you?

_____

_____

5n. Thinking about this most recent overseas trip that you made in 2000, if you could go back and change something about the trip, or even not make the trip, what would you do differently, if anything? [verbatim response]:

_____

_____

5o. Considering all costs related to the overseas trip including lodging, petrol, food, gifts, ticket prices, and rental fees, about how much did this trip cost overall – the total costs for all persons going on the trip?

( ) Less than $500
( ) $500–$1000
( ) $1001–$2000
( ) $2001–$3000
( ) $3001–$5000
( ) Above $5000

5p For this trip, did you make any payments using credit cards or charge cards?
( ) No...**Go to Question 5w**   ( ) Yes, in part   ( ) Yes, most to all of the expenses

5q. Which part or parts of the trip did you charge to credit or charge cards, if any? [Circle all mentioned by respondent]:
Travel 1
Accommodation 2
Meals – food and beverage 3
Shopping 4
Activities (including entry fees and equipment hire) 5
Rental car 6
Entertainment 7
Other 8

5r. Roughly how much did you charge to credit card(s) overall on this overseas trip, and to which card or cards did you charge it? [Circle the appropriate number(s) for the relevant credit/charge card types]:

TO AMERICAN EXPRESS		TO MASTER CARD	
Less than $500	1	Less than $500	13
$500–$1000	2	$500–$1000	14
$1001–$2000	3	$1001–$2000	15
$2001–$3000	4	$2001–$3000	16
$3001–$5000	5	$3001–$5000	17
$5001 and over	6	$5001 and over	18

TO DINERS' CLUB		TO VISA	
Less than $500	7	Less than $500	19
$500–$1000	8	$500–$1000	20
$1001–$2000	9	$1001–$2000	21
$2001–$3000	10	$2001–$3000	22
$3001–$5000	11	$3001–$5000	23
$5001 and over	12	$5001 and over	24

TO ANOTHER CARD 25

5s. Was any part of your trip covered by a transport package? That is where your airfare/coach/ train/other major transport and one or more of accommodation, food, car hire, activities or equipment were included in the price? [circle the appropriate number]:

Yes 1
No 2   **Go to Question 6**
Don't know 3   **Go to Question 6**

If yes, please describe what parts were covered by the transport package:

_____

_____

Question 6

6. During this coming year, 2001, have you thought not at all, some, or a lot about travelling overseas?
( ) Not at all...**Go to Question 10**   ( ) Some   ( ) A lot

Question 7

7. Have you made definite plans to travel overseas some time in 2001?
( ) No   ( ) Maybe/somewhat   ( ) Yes

Question 8

8. On a scale of zero to ten, how likely are you to travel overseas in 2001 – with zero being absolutely certain that you will **not** travel overseas during 2001 and ten being absolutely certain that you will travel overseas? [Circle one]:

0   1   2   3   4   5   6   7   8   9   10

Question 9

9. What makes you say that? [verbatim response]:

_____

_____

Question 10

10. On a scale of zero to ten, how likely are you to travel domestically – <u>overnight away from home and in Australia in 2001</u> – with zero being absolutely certain that you will **not** travel domestically during 2001 and ten being absolutely certain that you will travel overseas? [Circle one]:

    0   1   2   3   4   5   6   7   8   9   10

Question 11

11. What makes you say that? [verbatim response]:

_____

_____

Question 12

12. How many <u>domestic trips</u> in Australia of one or more nights away from home do you think that you are most likely to take during 2001, if any?

    ( ) 0   ( ) 1   ( ) 2–4   ( ) 5–7   ( ) 9–11   ( ) 11+

Question 13

13. Do you expect that the total number of domestic trips that you take in Australia in 2001 will be about the same, less, or more compared to the number that you have taken in 2000?

    ( ) about the same   ( ) less   ( ) more

Question 14

14. What makes you say that? [verbatim response]:

_____

_____

Question 15

15. Have you made any specific plans for travelling domestically in Australia sometime this summer (during December 2000 to February 2001)?

    ( ) No   ( ) Not sure, a little, somewhat   ( ) Yes

Question 16

16. What are your thoughts about, or specific plans, about travelling in Australia this summer? [verbatim response]:

_____

_____

If no thoughts or plans, Go to Section 3.

Question 17

17. If you do have specific plans for travelling in Australia this summer, please provide some information about your upcoming trip?

17a. What thoughts or events triggered your plans?

_____

_____

17b.How many nights away from home do you plan to spend on this trip?
    ( ) 1   ( ) 2   ( ) 3–5   ( ) 6–8   ( ) 9–11   ( ) 12–14   ( ) 15+

17c. Do you have some specific destinations in mind for the trip? If yes, please describe:

_____

_____

17d. Please describe how you went about planning for the trip. Have you used some brochures, a travel agent, or information from friends to help you plan this trip?

_____

_____

17e. Will you go on this trip by yourself, or with family members or friends?
    ( ) Yourself   ( ) Family members   ( ) Friends
    ( ) Other, please describe: _____

17f. Did any information sources influence you in planning to make this trip? If yes, please describe the sources and how the sources influenced your trip.
    ( ) No   ( ) Yes
[Verbatim response]:

_____

_____

17g. Have you made trips similar to the one that you are planning?
    ( ) No   ( ) Not sure   ( ) Yes

17h. Is this trip likely to be a very unique experience for you or be a lot similar to previous trips?
    ( ) Very unique   ( ) Similar
[Verbatim response]:

_____

_____

17i. If you changed your mind or had to cancel the trip, what would you do with the time and money that you would have spent on this trip?
Time:

_____

_____

Money:

_____

_____

17j. Do you think that you will be travelling in Australia more often in the next few years compared to the last few years, or about the same?
    ( ) More   ( ) Less   ( ) About the same

17k. What makes you say that? [verbatim response]:

_____

_____

SECTION 3
Things that You Do or Did in 2000

[Hand the respondent the survey form for answering the following questions.]

Question 1

1. Which of the following activities did you do, or do you plan on doing, in 2000? Please put a **tick** next to all that apply.

Reading a lightweight paperback
Reading magazines
Reading the paper
Reading a serious novel
Watching people
Going for a drive
Walking along the beach
Going for a walk
Doing a crossword puzzle
Meditating
Writing stories/poetry, etc.
Writing/reading own correspondence
Having a dinner party
Throwing a party
Going to a birthday party
Going to a party
Socializing at a dinner party
Visiting friends
Visiting relatives
Having a barbecue
Dining at a casual restaurant
Having coffee with a friend/s
Going for a drink
Dining at an up-market restaurant
Hanging out with mates
Going disco dancing
Going to a dance party
Going night-clubbing
Going raging
Dancing at a social event
Going to a bush dance
Going to a buck's/hen's night
Going to a fast-food restaurant
Pigging out
Sitting around a fire
Toasting marshmallows
Playing Monopoly
Playing pool/billiards
Going to a food and/or wine festival
Tasting food/wine
Engaging in kinky sex

Going bush walking
Going to a zoo or animal park
Going to an aquarium
Going to a national park
Going to the botanical gardens
Playing hockey
Playing netball
Playing basketball
Playing competitive sport
Playing touch football
Playing cricket
Playing soccer
Participating in a triathlon
Going swimming
Riding a bike
Playing squash/racquetball
Playing tennis
Playing badminton
Playing golf
Doing tai chi
Doing yoga
Going jogging
Going power walking
Doing athletics
Doing body building
Doing weight lifting
Doing gymnastics
Doing martial arts
Doing aerobics
Going hang-gliding
Going sky diving
Flying a glider
Flying a plane
Going bungy jumping
Going car racing
Going go-carting
Going mountain climbing
Going rock climbing
Going abseiling
Going mountain biking
Going orienteering

Making love
Going snow mobiling
Engaging in flirting
Going snow skiing
Going to a puppet show
Going ice skating
Watching a magic show
Going roller-blading
Going to a laser show
Going horse riding
Watching a fireworks display
Going rock fishing
Going to a fun park
Going trout fishing
Going to the circus
Going deep-sea fishing
Going to the Royal Easter show
Going wharf fishing
Going to a toy shop
Going rowing
Playing with children
Going surf life-saving
Going to a children's birthday party
Going canoeing
Going to a children's party

Going body surfing
Taking children to sporting activities
Going boogie boarding
Throwing a children's party
Going surfboard riding
Touring historic sites
Going water skiing
Visiting a monument
Going wind-surfing
Going to a museum of history
Going aqua-jetting
Going to a science museum
Going scuba diving
Going to an art gallery
Going snorkelling
Going away for the weekend
Going power boating
Taking a domestic holiday
Sailing a boat
Taking a day trip
Going for a holiday overseas
Looking at nature
Going camping
Going picnicking

Question 2

2. Please go back over the list of activities that you just read and put a cross next the ones that you are very certain that you will do next year, in 2001.

Question 3

3. One final time, please underline the activities in the list that you did three or more times this year.

SECTION 4
Thinking About Spending Time and Money

In this section, you are asked to talk as you are thinking about different ways of spending your time and money. Three scenarios are described in this section. Each scenario has several different options for you to consider. Please comment on each option presented in each scenario.

Scenario 1: You have a good bit of money set aside for paying for one or two big purchases that you are thinking about making within the next few months. Here are possibilities that you are thinking about or someone has mentioned to you. After you read all the options, please mention the first thoughts that come to mind about each.

- **Option U:** getting a used car to get to work easier, rather than sharing one car with a family member, partner.
- **Option R:** going to a really good hotel on the beach in South East Queensland with your spouse/partner for a few days; enjoying some great meals and the international ambience.
- **Option K:** getting new kitchen cabinets because you hate the appearance of your current kitchen.
- **Option B:** renovating your bathroom – the bathroom that is all pink and you hate pink bathrooms.
- **Option F:** visiting and staying with family members (parent, child, uncle, aunt, or cousin) out of town; you really like these family members and you might visit theme parks, zoos, amusement parks, go to beach, go shopping.
- **Option S:** buying some shares of stock in a company that you think is going places.
- **Option H:** using the money for a house payment or to pay-down the principal on a house mortgage.
- **Option D:** buying a used car to have a second, fun car to drive.
- **Option W:** taking a wine-tasting tour in South Australia with a family member/partner and maybe spend about half to two-thirds of the funds you have set aside.
- **Option G:** spending a week in Adelaide going to art galleries, theatre, performing arts, dining out, shopping and maybe some wine tasting.

1. First thoughts about each option:

U: _____

R: _____

K: _____

B: _____

F: _____

S: _____

H: _____

D: _____

W: _____

G: _____

2. Given the description of Scenario 1, what are the two to three options that you would really consider doing? List in order of mention:

_____

_____

_____

3. Please make a final selection of one of the options and describe how you made your selection.
- Final selected option: _____
- Description of choice process:

_____

_____

Scenario 2a: You have the opportunity to sign up for a new credit card offering a low interest rate of any unpaid balance plus no interest charges on any balance during the first 6 months of purchase. You decide to sign up for the new credit card and consider using the new card to pay for one of the following options. You say to yourself, 'I might splurge for once in my life!'

- **Option R:** go to a really good hotel on the beach in South East Queensland with your spouse/partner for a few days; enjoy some great meals and the international ambience.
- **Option W:** take a wine-tasting tour in South Australia with a family member/partner and maybe spend about half to two-thirds of the funds you have set aside.
- **Option D:** buy a used car to have a second, fun car to drive.
- **Option G:** spend a week in Adelaide going to art galleries, theatre, performing arts, dining out, shopping and maybe some wine tasting.
- **Option C:** buy new clothes just for you – a whole new wardrobe.
- **Option P:** go to France and tour Paris, the wine region and maybe the French Riveria.
- **Option Y:** go to the United States, visit friends and/or go to San Francisco, New York or other cities or places.
- **Option J:** go to Japan and really experience the local culture.
- **Option E:** buy some new, really great, furniture for my home.
- **Option Q:** have some second thoughts about opportunity and end up giving the money to my favourite charity, or a family member, or investing it for my retirement.
- **Option M:** your own credit card option – please briefly describe here:

- **Option H:** do things in Perth and maybe travel around in Western Australia to see natural beauty.
- **Option I:** do things I really want to do in Sydney and maybe attend some special events in and around Sydney.
- **Option B:** do things I really want to do in Brisbane and maybe attend some special events in and around Brisbane.
- **Option N:** do things I really want to do in Melbourne and maybe attend some special events in and around Melbourne.
- **Option A:** go to Alice Springs, maybe Ayers Rock, and maybe tour central Northern Territory and see unspoiled natural beauty.
- **Option S:** visit Cairns, coastal Queensland and Islands, maybe do some snorkelling or scuba diving.
- **Option D:** visit Darwin, do some four-wheel driving, and maybe some fishing and/or camping.
- **Option X:** travel around and in Canberra and attend a great special event or educational/learning experience.
- **Option Z:** visit Tasmania including Hobart, see unspoiled beauty and enjoy peace and solitude.

1. Given Scenario 2a, your first thoughts about each option:

R: _____
W: _____
D: _____
G: _____
C: _____
P: _____
Y: _____
J: _____
E: _____
Q: _____
M: _____
H: _____
I: _____
B: _____

N: _____

A: _____

S: _____

D: _____

X: _____

Z: _____

2. Given the description of Scenario 2a, what are the two to three options that you would really consider doing? List in order of mention:

_____

_____

_____

3. Please make a final selection of one of the options and describe how you made your selection.

- Final selected option: _____
- Description of choice process:

_____

_____

4. Is Scenario 2a realistic for you? Please comment. For example, do you sometimes pay interest charges on a monthly basis on one or more credit cards?

( ) Yes   ( ) Rarely   ( ) Never

Comments:

_____

_____

Scenario 2b: You have set aside some 'mad money' to pay for something you always wanted to have or do even if some people might say 'it was a frivolous thing to do'. Here are some possibilities that you are thinking about or someone has mentioned to you. After you have read all of the options, please mention the first thought that comes to mind about each:

- **Option R:** go to a really good hotel on the beach in South East Queensland with your spouse/partner for a few days; enjoy some great meals and the international ambience.
- **Option W:** take a wine-tasting tour in South Australia with a family member/partner and maybe spend about half to two-thirds of the funds you have set aside.
- **Option D:** buy a used car to have a second, fun car to drive.
- **Option G:** spend a week in Adelaide going to art galleries, theatre, performing arts, dining out, shopping and maybe some wine tasting.
- **Option C:** buy new clothes just for you – a whole new wardrobe.
- **Option P:** go to France and tour Paris, the wine region and maybe the French Riveria.
- **Option Y:** go to the United States, visit friends and/or go to San Francisco, New York or other cities or places.
- **Option J:** go to Japan and really experience the local culture.
- **Option E:** buy some new, really great, furniture for my home.
- **Option Q:** have some second thoughts about 'mad money' and end up giving the money to my favourite charity, or a family member, or investing it for my retirement.
- **Option M:** your own 'mad money' option – please describe briefly here:

_____

- **Option H:** do things in Perth and maybe travel around in Western Australia to see natural beauty.

- **Option I:** do things I really want to do in Sydney and maybe attend some special events in and around Sydney.
- **Option B:** do things I really want to do in Brisbane and maybe attend some special events in and around Brisbane.
- **Option N:** do things I really want to do in Melbourne and maybe attend some special events in and around Melbourne.
- **Option A:** go to Alice Springs, maybe Ayers Rock, and maybe tour central Northern Territory and see unspoiled natural beauty.
- **Option S:** visit Cairns, coastal Queensland and Islands, maybe do some snorkelling or scuba diving.
- **Option D:** visit Darwin, do some four-wheel driving, and maybe some fishing and/or camping.
- **Option X:** travel around and in Canberra and attend a great special event or educational/learning experience.
- **Option Z:** visit Tasmania, including Hobart, see unspoiled beauty and enjoy peace and solitude.

1. Your first thoughts about each option:

R: _____
W: _____
D: _____
G: _____
C: _____
P: _____
Y: _____
J: _____
E: _____
Q: _____
M: _____
H: _____
I: _____
B: _____
N: _____
A: _____
S: _____
D: _____
X: _____
Z: _____

2. Given the description of Scenario 2b, what are the two to three options that you would really consider doing? List in order of mention:

_____
_____
_____

3. Please make a final selection of one of the options and describe how you made your selection.

- Final selected option: _____
- Description of choice process:

_____
_____

SECTION 5
Information That Describes You

These next few questions are now about you, to make sure we have spoken to a good cross section of people.

1. How many holidays and breaks away from home, of <u>3 days</u> or more, including weekends, have you taken in the last 12 months? [Circle the appropriate number]:

None 1
One 2
Two to four 3
Five to seven 4
Eight or more 5

2. Which of the following areas do you live in? [Circle the appropriate number]:

Brisbane 1
Queensland other than Brisbane 2
Sydney 3
New South Wales other than Sydney 4
Melbourne 5
Victoria other than Melbourne 6
Hobart 7
Tasmania other than Hobart 8
Adelaide 9
South Australia other than Adelaide 10
Perth 11
Western Australia other than Perth 12
Darwin 13
Northern Territory other than Darwin 14
Australian Capital Territory 15

3. How many people usually live in your household? (Don't forget to count yourself and any children) [Circle the appropriate number]:

One 1
Two 2
Three to five 3
Six or more 4

4. How many children aged up to 10 years live in your household? [Circle the appropriate number]:

None 1
One 2
Two 3
Three 4
Four 5
Five 6
Six or more 7

5. And how many children aged 11–15 years live in your household? [Circle the appropriate number]:

None 1
One 2
Two 3
Three 4
Four 5
Five 6
Six or more 7

6. And how many children aged 16–24 years live in your household? [Circle the appropriate number]:

None 1
One 2
Two 3
Three 4
Four 5
Five 6

7. What is your age group? [Circle <u>one</u> only]:

15–19 years 1
20–24 years 2
25–29 years 3
30–34 years 4
35–39 years 5
40–44 years 6
45–49 years 7
50–54 years. 8
55–59 years 9
60–64 years 10
65–69 years 11
70 or more years 12

8. What is your gender? [Circle the appropriate number]:

Male 1
Female 2

9. What is your marital status? (are you single or part of a couple?) [Circle the appropriate number]:

Single (never married, divorced, separated, widowed and not part of a couple) 1
Part of a couple (married, defacto, living together). 2

10. How would you describe the main income earner in your household? [Circle one only]:

Professional 1
White collar, employed by others 2
Blue collar, employed by others 3
White collar, self-employed 4
Blue collar, self-employed 5
Retired, white collar 6
Retired, blue collar 7

11. And which of these groups would contain the combined income of everyone in this household, before tax or anything else is taken out? Please include pensions and allowances from all sources. (Would it be more than $26,000 per year, that is, more than $500 per week? Would it be more than $52,000? etc.) [Circle the appropriate number]:

Weekly ($)		Annual equivalents ($)	
1–79	1	1–4199	1
80–159.	2	4200–8299	2
160–299	3	8300–15,599.	3
300–499	4	15,600–25,999	4
500–699	5	26,000–36,399	5
700–999	6	36,400–51,999	6
1000–1499	7	52,000–77,999	7
1500–1999	8	78,000–103,999	8
2000–2499	9	104,000–129,999	9
2500+	10	130,000+	10

12. How often do you use the Internet? [Circle the appropriate number]:
Every day or more than once a day 1
3–5 times per week 2
Once or twice a week 3
2–3 times per month 4
Once a month 5
Less than once a month 6
Never 7

13. And do you use it......? [Circle the appropriate number(s)]:
At home 1
At work 2
At university, college or TAFE 3
Via a PC owned by friends or family 4
Internet café 5
Local library 6
Other 7

14. Please indicate whether you are a member of any of the following: [Circle the appropriate number(s)]:
Qantas/One World Frequent Flyer 1
Ansett/Star Alliance Frequent Flyer 2
Fly Buys 3
A credit card which gives you Frequent Flyer points 4
A hotel chain club which gives you Frequent Flyer points or benefits like
      upgrades or discounts 5
A hire car card that gives you Frequent Flyer points or other benefits 6
Any other club/card that provides Frequent Flyer points 7

15. Which credit or charge cards do you hold? [Circle the appropriate number(s)]:
American Express 1
Diners' Club 2
Mastercard 3
Visa 4
Other 5

16. Do you have a mobile phone? [Circle the appropriate number]:
Yes 1
No 2

If no, Go to Question 18

17. Do you use it on holidays? [Circle the appropriate number]:
Yes 1
No 2

18. About how much annual leave (**not** including long service leave) do you currently have owing to you?
None 1
Less than 1 week 2
1 week 3
More than 1 week but less than 2 4
2 weeks 5
More than 2 weeks but less than 3 6
3 weeks 7
More than 3 weeks but less than 4 8
4 weeks 9
More than 4 weeks 10
I don't get annual leave 11

19. Please indicate which of the following media you watch/listen to/read on a regular basis. [Circle the appropriate number(s)]:
On TV, travel and holiday programmes 1
In the newspapers, travel and holiday features and articles 2
On the Internet, travel and holiday websites 3
On the radio, travel and holiday programmes 4
Travel magazines 5
Airline magazines 6
None of these 7

20. What type of radio do you listen to most often? [Circle the appropriate number(s)]:
Classic hits 1
Easy listening 2
Contemporary alternative 3
Top 40 4
Talk-back 5
News/continual news 6
Dance music/rave 7
Rhythm & blues 8
Soft rock 9
Classical music 10
National radio 11
None 2

21. On average about how many hours of TV (either Free to Air or PayTV) do you watch each day? [Circle the appropriate number]:
None 1
1–2 hours 2
3–4 hours 3
5 hours or more 4

22. Which TV channel/provider to you watch most frequently? [Circle the appropriate number]:
ABC 1
SBS 2
Channel 7/Southern Cross/Prime/WIN SA/GWN 3

Channel 9/Channel 8/Imparja/WIN/NBN 4
Channel 10/Nth 5
Channel 31 6
Foxtel 7
Optus 8
Other 9

23. What type of TV shows do you watch most often? [Circle the appropriate number(s)]:
Current affairs 1
News 2
Sitcoms 3
Soap operas 4
Talk-back shows 5
Children's TV shows 6
Music shows 7
Documentaries 8
Drama 9
Mystery shows 10
Comedies 11
Movies 12
Sports 13
Other 14

24. What type of magazines do you read regularly? [Circle the appropriate number(s)]:
Lifestyle 1
Fitness 2
Health 3
Women's magazines 4
Food/cooking 5
Home/décor 6
Gardening 7
Fashion 8
Beauty 9
Music and entertainment 10
Information technology 11
Travel 12
Other 13
None of these 14

25. Which newspapers do you read regularly? [Circle the appropriate number(s)]:
The Australian 1
Australian Financial Review 2
Sydney Morning Herald 3
Daily Telegraph-Mirror 4
The Age 5
Herald Sun 6
Courier Mail 7
Advertiser 8
West Australian 9
Mercury 10
Canberra Times 11
Northern Territory News 12
Any Sunday paper 13

A local paper 14
Other 15
None of these 16

26. About how often do you go to the cinema? [Circle the appropriate number]:
3 or more times a week 1
1–2 times a week 2
1–2 times a fortnight 3
Once a month 4
Once in a blue moon 5
Never 6

27. How often do you watch a video from a video store at home? [Circle the appropriate number]:
3 or more times a week 1
1–2 times a week 2
1–2 times a fortnight 3
Once a month 4
Once in a blue moon 5
Never 6

THANK YOU VERY MUCH – THIS IS THE END OF THE QUESTIONNAIRE!

2 Qualitative Comparative Analysis of Travel and Tourism Purchase–Consumption Systems

Arch G. Woodside[1] and Robert L. King[2]
[1]*Boston College, USA;* [2]*University of Hawaii, Hilo, Hawaii*

Introduction

A purchase–consumption system (PCS) is the sequence of mental and observable steps a consumer undertakes to buy and use several products, for which some of the products purchased lead to a purchase sequence involving other products. Becker (1998) and others (e.g. Ragin, 1987) recommend the use of qualitative comparative analysis (i.e. the use of Boolean algebra) to create possible typologies and then to compare these typologies to empirical realities. Possible types of streams of trip decisions from combinations of five destination options with six travel mode options and four accommodation categories, three accommodation brands, five within-area route options, and four in-destination area visit options result in 7200 possible decision paths. The central PCS proposition is that several decisions within a customer's PCS are dependent on prior purchases of products that trigger these later purchases. In this chapter, four additional propositions are presented for examination in future research. To examine the propositions and the usefulness of the PCS framework for tourism research, qualitative, long interviews of visitors to an island tourism destination (the Big Island of Hawaii) were conducted. The results include strong empirical support for the five propositions. Several suggestions for future research are offered.

Chapter Objectives

As with most consumer buying decisions, the leisure traveller collects and evaluates information, eventually decides and acts upon a set of complex and multiple travel decisions, and evaluates the satisfaction of individual experiences and the overall set of events. By better understanding how consumers use their information and sequence their travel-choice decisions, marketers would be in a better position to develop options that enhance the likelihood of improving travellers' experiences. Understanding the triggers initiating these processes is valuable as well.

The purpose of this chapter is: (i) to describe a general purchase–consumption systems (PCS) framework useful for mapping travellers' choice decisions before and during a trip, and to evaluate their actual experiences which may influence their future trip choices; (ii) to demonstrate that qualitative research observation and analytic techniques are useful for developing and validating complex and interactive models such as the PCS; and (iii) to show that conclusions using such qualitative techniques can improve government and business policy decision making processes.

©R. March and A.G. Woodside 2005. *Tourism Behaviour: Travellers' Decisions and Actions*
(R. March and A.G. Woodside)

Purchase–Consumption Systems

The examination of consumer behaviour related to buying and consuming a bundle, or set, of goods and services is not new (see Solomon, 1983; Solomon and Assael, 1988; Mittal *et al.*, 1999). A PCS is a related, but distinct, concept. PCS is the sequence of mental and observable steps a consumer undertakes to buy and use several related products, whereby some of the products purchased lead to a purchase sequence involving further purchases. For example, the study of PCSs in travel and tourism seeks to increase understanding of the relationships among the decisions to travel to one versus several destinations during a trip; to travel by plane, bus, or train with renting a car or using public transportation; to stay in a hotel or with friends overnight; to dine in restaurants; to buy gifts; and to travel extensively or only a little within destination areas.

Figure 2.1 summarizes a process framework that shows the complex dynamics of travellers' choice decisions. The framework indicates a total of 19 variables, in three principal boxes, that may be involved in travel and tourism-related PCSs. The first box contains the traveller's decision making process and potential predictors of the traveller's sets of choices.

Included are personal characteristics; the influence of family, friends and peer groups; as well as the effects of marketing activities. These variables influence thinking and decisions prior to and during travel.

The eight variables in Box 2 represent specific decisions/actions that comprise a trip. These choices interact and may affect immediate or future decisions. The three variables in Box 3 are event-specific and global evaluations and connotations that occur immediately following trip-specific experiences, near the end of the trip, and after the trip is completed. These outcomes and travellers' evaluations are predicted to impact future travel. Between and within each box, the variables may come into play sequentially and/or interactively.

Qualitative Research Methodology

The following described exploratory empirical study attempts to validate a complex process model and demonstrate its usefulness to policy decisions. The complexity of travellers' decision making is examined by employing qualitative research to capture and study the temporal effect of categories of travellers' choices. Data are collected using the long interview (see

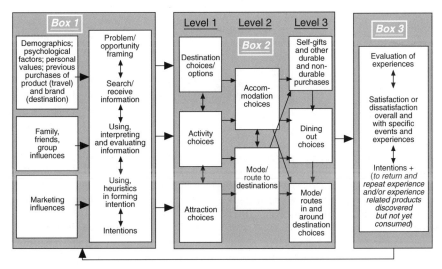

Fig. 2.1. Framework of purchase–consumption system applied to leisure travel behaviour.

McCracken, 1988; Woodside and Wilson, 1995) to portray the real-life mapping of travellers' choice processes.

The study of PCS in travel and tourism seeks to learn how different streams of behaviour influence the traveller's satisfaction with the destination and travel experience, as well as the traveller's intentions to return to the destination. From a theoretical perspective, the study of PCSs seeks to 'maximize the possibility of finding what you hadn't even thought to look for' (Becker, 1998, p. 164). Becker and others (e.g. Ragin, 1987) recommend the use of qualitative comparative analysis to create possible typologies, and then to compare these typologies to empirical outcomes. For example, there are 7200 possible streams of trip decisions from the combinations of five destination options, six travel mode options, four accommodation categories, three accommodation brands, five within-area route options and four in-destination-area visit options. The task is to identify those streams used by travellers and to determine whether the decision processes and/or travel outcomes differ.

Cognitive mapping using the long interview: the Big Island study

The long interview, guided by a ten-page questionnaire covering 48 topic areas, was designed to examine the 20 variables in the PCS framework. The questionnaire formed the basis of 68 face-to-face interviews administered by trained interviewers. Each interview, conducted in the waiting areas of the two major Hawaii Island airports, averaged 30 minutes each. Respondents were visitors (usually in groups of 2–6) about to depart from the Big Island. Techniques were used to ensure the reliability of the interview, recording and summarizing processes. The long interviews yielded 12–15 page 'thick descriptions' (see Geertz, 1973) in the travellers' own words about their decision processes and about their interactive decision making for trip choices. A value of the long interview was learning the triggering variables that activate current and future travel choices. Generalizations may be reached by categorizing travel decisions and processes of various visitor segments.

Data were further reduced and summarized by developing a map-shell with respect to the PCS framework. Figure 2.2 shows the mapping of one case study: a honeymoon couple from Colorado. A summary of this case is included in the full version of this paper. The mapping data from each case study were also placed into a SPSS data file.

Comparative analysis using combinatorics

Our analysis used combinatorics, a form of comparative analysis to better describe and understand configurations of travel-related phenomena. Figure 2.3 shows eight traveller

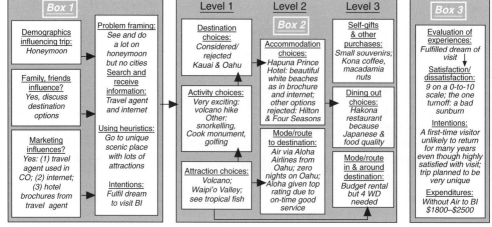

Fig. 2.2. Honeymoon couple from Colorado visiting Big Island for 6 nights.

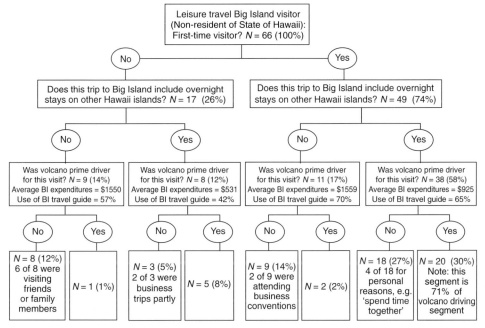

Fig. 2.3. Decision frame, decisions and behaviour streams among respondents.

segments resulting from cross-classifying respondents into three categories: (i) first-time versus repeat visitors; (ii) overnight stays on other islands in the State of Hawaii; and (iii) the Big Island volcano being a prime driver for the visit. It provides details of the principal and secondary visitor segments classified by decision-behaviour streams. For example, the majority of the respondents were first-time visitors to the Big Island (74%); the majority of the respondents were also staying overnight on two or more islands in Hawaii *and* were first-time visitors to the Big Island. Note after examining all possible combinations of just these three issues, no one stream includes more than 50% of the total respondents. Also notice in the third row of boxes that expenditures are higher among respondents reporting not staying overnight at other Hawaiian destinations besides the Big Island; this finding holds for both repeat and first-time visitors.

Visitors' expenditures on the Big Island increase dramatically as the number of nights spent on the Big Island increases. Visitors' expenditures on the Big Island also increase when they use travel guidebooks in planning and during their visits (see Fig. 2.4 for detailed

findings). Figure 2.4 illustrates the central point of this chapter: the interactions (i.e. the combinatorics) of travellers' decisions and behaviours dramatically influence additional decisions/behaviours, as well as trip outcomes.

Propositions

To test the validity of the PCS model, several propositions, based upon the results of past studies, are expressed as follows:

(P$_1$) The central proposition in this study is that several decisions within a customer's leisure travel PCS are dependent on prior purchases of products that trigger these later purchases.

(P$_2$) Some product purchases made subsequent to the destination choice are not planned before the start of the trip (see Belk, 1975; Woodside and Bearden, 1978).

(P$_3$) Two categories of choice decisions occur for many travellers within a leisure-travel PCS: (i) the generic product decision (e.g. should I plan a trip?); and (ii) the brand choice decision (e.g. which destination alternative should I select?). These two choice decisions are

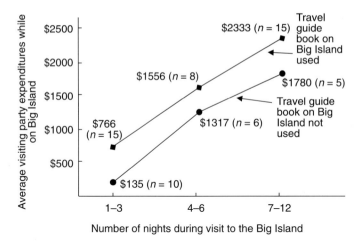

Fig. 2.4. Influence of using travel guide book and number of nights on the Big Island on expenditures on the Big Island (not including travel to/from Big Island). Parsimonious results of multiple regression analysis: adjusted $R^2 = 0.39$ ($P < 0.000$); df = 2,51; beta for nights = 0.443 ($P < 0.001$); beta for interaction of nights by use of guide = 0.287 ($P < 0.028$); beta for use of guide did not enter this stepwise model. The simple correlation of use of guide and visitor expenditures on the Big Island was $r = 0.24$, $P < 0.04$, one-tailed test.

labelled single-option accept/reject decisions and competing-option decisions, respectively. (P_4) Destination visitors who are high information users tend to participate more in activities, spend more money per day in an area, are more positive about their experiences and indicate higher intentions to return compared with low information users and non-users (see Woodside et al., 1997).

(P_5) The eight travel choices (Fig. 2.1, Box 2) affect the travellers' evaluations of their experiences, the satisfaction and dissatisfaction of these experiences, and the intention to repeat the visit to the same destination(s).

The analysis of the interview and mapping data collected provides support, in most cases strong support, for each of these propositions.

P_1 supported: many discretionary travel decisions trigger additional purchases

Extensive confirmations were found in the majority of the case interview studies in support of P_1. The majority of the travel parties interviewed reported that destination choices and activity/attraction choices interacted with each other and dominated early in the trip-planning process. These two decision areas are categorized as *Level 1* decisions in Box 2 of the PCS framework (Fig. 2.1). These *Level 1* decisions were then followed most often by accommodation and mode/route decisions to the destination area and labelled as *Level 2* decisions.

The mode/route and the accommodation decisions both appear to be made most often independently of each other, and were completed prior to visiting the Big Island. *Level 3* decisions/behaviours shown in the PCS occurred among all respondents after arriving on the Big Island, except car rental decisions. Car rental industry sales are not dependent on the alternative streams of visitors' decisions/behaviours examined here. Most respondents (72%) reported renting a private vehicle during their visits. The decision to rent a private vehicle may depend mainly on demographic variables (i.e. income and credit card availability or cultural values).

P_2 supported: a substantial number of purchases of travel-related products are not pre-planned before the start of the trip

The analysis of all case studies provided strong support for P_2. More than 85% of the leisure parties reported gift-purchases of products they planned to return home with but had no plans for buying on their arrival. Other *Level 3* decisions most often included local area route decisions, local transportation decisions and dining-out decisions; in more than half of the cases.

Many *Level 3* decisions, especially self-gift buying and other durable purchases, were not pre-planned decisions. Visitors rarely reported planning on durable and non-durable purchases before their visit. It is important to study unplanned purchases for two reasons: (i) a large share of monetary expenditures by travellers may be unplanned; and (ii) the travellers' overall satisfaction with their trips is likely to depend on these highly situation-influenced decisions.

P_3 supported: both single-option and multiple-option destinations occur in travellers' PCSs

In general, destination choices are multiple-option decisions for most travel parties; travellers make use of single-option choices for the greatest number of their purchases while in a destination area. Travellers are likely to use more complex heuristics when making the multiple-option decision compared to single-option decisions. The majority (60%) of respondents reported that they did *not* consider and reject alternative destinations when deciding on visiting the Big Island. Almost all respondents reporting the volcano to be the prime driver for their visit also reported *not* considering and rejecting other destinations. Thus, these findings are additional evidence of the strong magnetic power of the volcano in attracting visitors to the Big Island.

P_4 supported: high information users differ in their decisions and behaviours compared to low information users

Substantial support was found among respondents in support of P_4. Surprisingly, in this study, given the expenditures of several hundred to several thousands of dollars, close to one-third of the visitors to the Big Island arrived without undertaking a prior search for information from travel guides, government agencies or travel magazines. Substantial differences in average numbers of activities/sites visited, money spent (*see* also previous comparative analysis example), reported quality of the visit and intentions to return were found between low-search and high-search segments for visitors to the island. The evidence leads us to conclude that some leisure travellers may need training about the usefulness of information to increase the quality and enjoyment of their trips.

P_5 supported: the eight decision areas in the PCS framework influence traveller judgments of destination quality and overall satisfaction

Substantial intuitive support verifies the large impact of the eight decision areas on post-trip evaluations, satisfactions and intentions to return. Thus, P_5 was supported by the results. Almost all visitors could recall vividly two to four experiences that resulted in positive impacts on their trip summary evaluations. When pressed, nearly all could also identify at least one negative experience. 'Too much rain in Hilo' was mentioned most often as a turn-off, with nine mentions. Four respondents mentioned not actually seeing lava flowing into the Pacific Ocean as a turn-off. Both of these issues illustrate the need to inform visitors on what to expect when visiting natural attractions.

Conclusion and Recommendation for Additional Research

Our findings support the view that travellers' decision making behaviours are based on many variables, in relationships that are interactive rather than linear. The PCS framework may be operationalized using cognitive mapping to obtain a better understanding of the interactions of travellers' choices, their decisions for a complete trip and the potential impact on future trips.

Employing qualitative research techniques has several advantages for examining purchase–consumption systems in future leisure travel research. The long-interview method and qualitative comparative analysis employed in the study reveal the value of gaining deep knowledge of travellers in their own words and interpretations. Examining the thick descriptions provided in the long-interview technique, for example, enables a better understanding of the activations of choice processes. Qualitative comparative analysis assists in identifying possible decision streams, allows an examination of interactions among tourist decision variables and enhances the probability of discovering the unexpected.

Learning travellers' specific sequences of decisions and the triggers leading to selection/rejection of a firm's services can provide information important for increasing the effectiveness of strategies and policies. This type of in-depth research will provide knowledge and insights for effective and socially responsible tourism management.

3 Holistic Case-based Modelling of Customers' Thinking–Doing Destination Choice

Arch G. Woodside[1], Roberta MacDonald[2] and Marion Burford[3]

[1]Boston College, USA; [2]University of Prince Edward Island, Canada; [3]University of New South Wales, Australia

Introduction

Chapter 3 reviews grounded theory studies available in the literature that deepen understanding of holistic case-based modelling of customers' thinking–doing brand experiences. The chapter includes an empirical study to illustrate the method. The reported study includes applying the 'long-interview method' and 'theoretical sampling' in completing personal, face-to-face, interviews of travel parties when just ending their visits to a Canadian Province. The empirical analysis focuses on acquiring process data held in the minds of customers – that is, the analysis illustrates emic-based storytelling of what was planned and what actually happened, leading to what specific outcomes. Achieving such holistic, case-based, views of customer decisions and behaviour provides a rich, deep and nuance-filled understanding of the causes and consequences of such behaviours.

Emic versus Etic Interpretations of Thinking and Doing

Grounded theory development often includes 'thick descriptions' (Glazer and Strauss, 1967; Geertz, 1973) of behavioural processes from the perspectives of informants participating in these processes (i.e. emic interpretations) rather than only from the researcher's own per-spective (i.e. etic interpretations). Chapter 3 reviews grounded theory studies available in the literature that deepen understanding of leisure travel decisions and tourism behaviours. The chapter includes a set of core propositions that are examined empirically.

The reported empirical study includes applying the 'long-interview method' (McCracken, 1988) and 'theoretical sampling' (Ragin, 1987) in completing personal, face-to-face interviews of travel parties at the moment of just completing their visits to a Canadian Province. The study's findings support the core proposition in building grounded theory: a few (more than 2 but less than 40) major process paradigms arise inductively from the data that conjunctively (i.e. holistically) link: (i) antecedent-to-trip conditions, to (ii) trip-planning strategies, to (iii) destination activities, to (iv) participants' evaluations of outcomes. One aim of such grounded theory develop-ment is to provide a gestalt understanding of the unconscious and conscious thoughts and behaviours of specific travellers who are repre-sentative of each visitor segment of all the seg-ments relevant for a given destination.

Chapter 3 illustrates gestalt profiling for Canadian domestic and foreign tourists visiting Prince Edward Island (PEI), a Canadian Province. The data from long interviews (McCracken, 1988; Woodside and Wilson, 1995) were collected, for most cases, on the final day of the visitors' stays in PEI. The findings provide nuances on 'what makes the difference' for each of the travel parties in their selection of PEI and whether or not they perceive returning to PEI to be likely or not. Unlike etic reporting via participant observations and interviews collected by the researcher (e.g. see Arnould and Price, 1993; Belk and Costa, 1998), the aim here is to capture complexity in reporting the nuances and process details of complete purchase consumption systems for leisure-related trips – from the seemingly mundane to the extraordinary thoughts, actions and outcomes that reflect the emic views of processes planned and experienced.

Reasons for Holistic Case Studies in Leisure Research

Reports of holistic case studies may be valuable for several reasons. First, episodic memory dominates much of the conscious reporting and unconscious thinking of individuals – the metaphor of file drawers of stories in a human's memory is apt (see Shank, 1999). Frequently, humans catalogue and retrieve episodes (i.e. stories) that represent their lives. While useful for developing and testing theory, the dominating logic in travel research of variable-based empirical positivism (e.g. Woodside and Dubelaar, 2002) needs to be complemented by additional theory–research paradigms, such as holistic case-based empirical relativism, that focus on thick descriptions of an individual's thoughts and actions constituting the stories in their lived experiences.

Secondly, humans have limited cognitive access to most of the details of the stories stored in their memory file drawers (see Zaltman, 2003); most thinking occurs unconsciously (Wegner, 2002; Zaltman, 2003). Consequently, many details of the thoughts and behaviours that occur during an overnight destination visit are available only unconsciously to the tourist – especially as days turn into months and years after visiting a destination. The stories that individuals report weeks or months after visiting a destination are summaries of the minutiae of events and thoughts that occurred while experiencing the visit. The old saw, 'God is in the details', applies here: theory and research to capture as much detail

as possible of holistic stories may help to increase understanding of the unconscious thinking that supports individuals' summary conscious thoughts and evaluations about their destination visits.

Thirdly, consumers prefer narrative forms of events related to a destination visit rather than simply listings of features and benefits (Adaval and Wyer, 1998): using different travel brochures, the attractiveness of vacation trips was greater in the study of Adaval and Wyer when a story described visits, rather than the listing of features and benefits of visits. Given that consumers store and retrieve stories, and may prefer stories for processing communications, storytelling research may help tourism marketing strategists (TMSs) design-in destination experiences and communications that partially shape fondly held retrieved memories, as well as design-out experiences and communications that lead to a 'bad trip' summary evaluation. Thus, learning emic, holistic, stories of visits may have practical importance for offering products and services customers prefer – by providing deeper and broader information than found in variable-based (e.g. waiting time and customer satisfaction) reporting systems.

Theoretical Sampling in Holistic Case Studies

Note that if a destination identifies 20 distinct visitor segments by origins (e.g. ten domestic and ten foreign) and breaks visitors into two distinct length-of-stay groups (e.g. short- versus long-term); and into repeat versus first-time visitors, then a total of 80 potential profiles may occur (i.e. $20 \times 2 \times 2 = 80$ theoretical segments). About 10–20 of these segments are likely to be important strategically for the quality of life (e.g. economic and social well-being) of the destination (or hotel, car rental firm, or airline company), assuming that tourism is a major industry for the destination. For the study that this chapter reports, the quality of life for many PEI residents depends substantially on the success of its tourism industry – the Province's largest employer.

Empirical evidence from several studies often supports propositions that appear to be 'just common sense', such as, domestic visitors to a destination usually stay longer and manage to spend less than foreign visitors; domestic visitors more often represent repeat visits to a destination, compared to foreign visitors. However, the conjunction of the seemingly unexpected combinations of levels of different attributes among some visitors do occur frequently, and the examination of such unusual cases increases substantially our knowledge of causes, consequences and trends in the behaviours of visitors. As such, comparative analysis (see Ragin, 1987) advocates abandoning the concept of 'statistical outlier' and rejects the practice of discarding outlier cases. Thus, the 23-year-old domestic visitor who stays two nights and spends over $1000 during her visit becomes as intriguing in comparative analysis as the possibly more often appearing 23-year-old domestic visitor who stays 20 nights and spends $400 during her visit.

Theoretical sampling in comparative analysis does not attempt to plan for a representative sample of respondents from a population, but rather considers the theoretical possibilities of all unique combinations of case profiles typically across 4–7 attributes. For example, theoretical sampling might include recognizing the existence of domestic–foreign, short–long time, first–repeat, small–big expenditure visitors. After providing operational measures to the constructs, a quota sampling plan (assuming visitors can be found for all possible factor combinations) is implemented, to attempt to interview enough visitors representing each of the combinations (i.e. 16 combinations for the four constructs just listed). McCracken (1988) recommends 5–8 interviews per cell.

The objective of such research is to build and generalize to theory, rather than to test and generalize theory to a population (see Yin, 1994; Langley, 1999). Comparative analysis and process data from cases fit well with the wisdom that marketing strategists need to design product–service use experiences that satisfy the individual customer. The contents and levels of customer satisfaction and dissatisfaction may be learned from the stories that they tell when describing their travel experiences, and the 'good and bad memories' that they surface when describing these experiences.

The aim for comparative process case-based reports is to examine all theoretically identified customer samples that occur in real life, and provide thick descriptions for each multiple-attribute based conjunctive segment. Such reporting embraces an alternative paradigm from the positivistic view that some data cases should be discarded from analysis (and assigned the label 'statistical outliers') because they include extreme point values for one or more variables (i.e. unusually high expenditure spent in the destination area). Comparative analysis adopts an alternative paradigm that we should search for 'the tipping point' (Gladwell, 2000) of the seemingly unusual combination of events or levels (or the seemingly rare occurrence) of some antecedent attributes that result in the observed, seemingly extreme, behaviour.

Grounded Theory Construction of Tourism Behaviour

The concept of purchase–consumption systems (Woodside and King, 2001; Woodside and Dubelaar, 2002) is useful for grounded theory construction of tourism behaviour. A PCS is the sequence of mental and observable steps a consumer undertakes to buy and use several products, for which some of the products purchased lead to a purchase sequence involving other products. Becker (1998) and others (e.g. Ragin, 1987) recommend the use of qualitative comparative analysis (i.e. the use of Boolean algebra) to create possible typologies and then to compare these typologies to empirical realities. Possible types of streams of trip decisions from combinations of five destination options with six travel mode options and four accommodation categories, three accommodation brands, five within-area route options, and four in-destination area visit options result in 7200 possible decision paths.

The central PCS proposition is that several decisions within a customer's PCS are dependent on prior purchases of products that trigger these later purchases. While appearing to be intuitively obvious, empirical research for grounded theory construction is needed to verify how well emic views match etic mental models of how and what streams of tourism behaviour are implemented – and the causes and consequences of these streams.

Woodside and King (2001) describe category-level data relevant for grounded-theory construction among visitors to the Big Island of Hawaii; for example, the decision processes for selecting and the doing-behaviours while visiting the Big Island. Their research report is useful for answering several strategic policy issues; such as, can the Big Island be positioned as a brand standing alone from the State of Hawaii (the answer: not according to Woodside and King's report). However, their study does not include in-depth reporting at the individual visit-party level. The suggestion here is that grounded-theory construction needs to capture the emic holistic view of individual-level causes and consequences of processes in tourism behaviour. Thus, the stress of such theory construction is on applying Weick's (1995) wisdom to learn deeply by staying complex and providing thick descriptions of complete destination-related behaviours. Generalization to customer segments may then follow from building a collection of individual case studies of tourism behaviour processes.

While Woodside and Dubelaar's (2002) report is useful for describing how specific nuances in destination–area behaviours affect other behaviours, their empirical analysis does not actually include analysis of complete PCSs. The empirical report provides a variable-level-only analysis – two variables at a time – and not a deep understanding of complete decisions and flows at the individual level.

Figure 3.1 displays nine issues relevant for grounded theory construction of the flows of decisions and behaviours that focus particularly on destination choices – including antecedents and consequences of implementing these choices. Other tourism foci for grounded theory construction (not shown in Fig. 3.1) include mode/route to, and while visiting, decisions; accommodation decisions; dining-out choices; decisions and actual behaviours regarding the search for and use of information and advice of where to visit and what to do; and gift-buying decisions. For all these foci, decision topics that might be included focus on learning the alternatives that came to mind but were rejected in favour of what was done – and what made the difference in the choices made.

Grounded Theory Propositions

The arrows in Fig. 3.1 represent propositions relevant for grounded theory development and for guiding questions for thick descriptions of visitors' behaviours. While the propositions may imply a variable-based analysis, the research objective of Fig. 3.1 is to provide a template of topics to ensure coverage during long interviews in case studies – not to test statistically for generalizing to a population of visitors. The following discussion summarizes each proposition.

P_1 (Box 1 to 2 in Fig. 3.1): demographics and lifestyles of visitors influence how they frame leisure choices. For example, households with two teenage children will often consider only leisure trips that include 'things to do' for teenagers, but the same things to do are not found among visiting households travelling without teenagers.

P_2 (Box 3 to 2): unexpected or unplanned events occur (or might be available, but are not used) that influence (or do not affect) the framing of leisure choices. For example, a household may receive an unsolicited brochure about a destination that triggers initial thoughts of planning a visit. If such thoughts are triggered by such brochures, the brochures may represent a necessary, but not sufficient, condition resulting in a visit to the given destination.

P_3 (Box 4 to 2): external and internal personal influences affect the framing of leisure choices. For example, a comment made by a friend about the joyful experiences of visiting a destination might be retrieved and mentioned during the framing of leisure choices.

P_4 (Box 2 to 5): the features and benefits included in framing leisure alternatives affect the destination choices selected and rejected. For example, a specific activity-benefit resulting from visiting Destination X may tip the balance in favour of X versus alternative destinations considered by the visiting travel party.

P_5 (Box 3 to 5): information collected for framing and trip planning affects the process of selecting and rejecting destination alternatives.

P_6 (Box 4 to 5): friends' opinions and thoughts retrieved from memory influence the selection and rejection of destination alternatives.

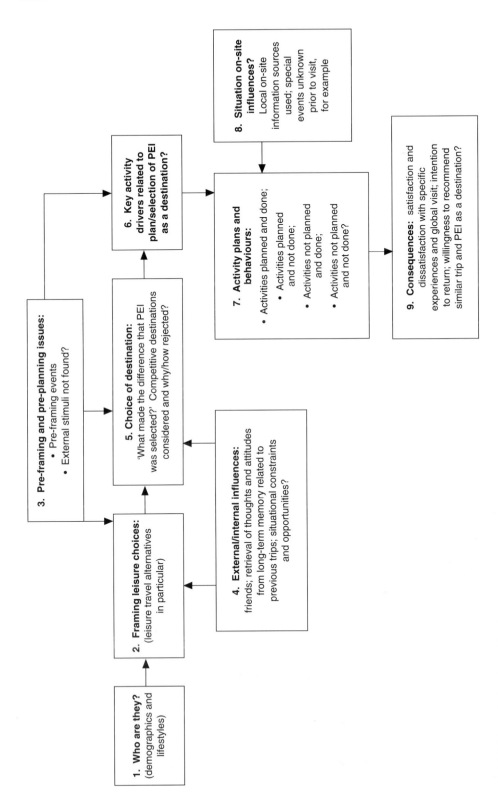

Fig. 3.1. Theoretical and empirical issues.

P$_7$ (Box 5 to 6): 'key activity' drivers solidify the decision to visit the destination selected – such drivers are concrete plans and pre-trip actions (e.g. bookings) regarding a specific visit to the destination selected.

P$_8$ (Box 6 to 7): key activity drivers affect what is planned and done in the destination area. Note in Box 7 that activities can be categorized into four quadrants: planned–done; planned–undone; unplanned–done; and unplanned–undone.

Activities planned and done are often key activity drivers related to deciding to visit a specific destination. Acquiring data on planned–done actions may provide information that is particularly helpful for designing destination attractions and positioning messages that match with activities important for some visitors.

Unplanned and done activities may represent destination features and benefits worthy of more attention by destination marketing strategists. Some unplanned and done actions may represent the largest share of leisure time pursuits done by many visitors – given that in-depth prior trip planning does not occur for many travellers (see Fodness and Murray, 1999).

Planned and undone activities may be the result of loss of interest, some unexpected situational contingency preventing the activity from being realized, or some on the scene trade-off/replacement of a planned action with some other action judged more desirable. Collecting data on planned and undone activities may prove particularly valuable for destination attractions receiving many customer enquiries but few customer visits.

Unplanned–undone activities are tourism-related activities that are possible to do but the visitor does not plan on doing and does not do. For example, from time-to-time a deep-sea fishing service-operation starts up in PEI, but soon fails because unplanned–undone deep-sea fishing behaviour occurs among PEI visitors during the 1–3 years such services operate. The visitor may be aware that deep-sea fishing sometimes exists on some ocean islands, but the activity never 'comes to mind' during her visit. Identifying such unplanned–undone activities relevant for specific destinations may be useful for designing experiences that visitors may find rewarding, and may serve as an early warning

system of what activities may not be implemented by visitors.

P$_9$ (Box 8 to 7): information and events learned by the visitors while visiting affects their plans and behaviours. To apply Weick's (1995) sensemaking wisdom, visitors sometimes only think about doing something after they see it being done.

P$_{10}$ (Box 7 to 9): the activities done (and not done) affect much of the attitude and intention consequences resulting from, and associating with, visiting a destination. Thus, 'what we saw' and 'what we did', that result in specific outcomes, are the antecedents to a 'good' or 'bad' trip (see Frazer, 1991).

A Decision-stages-by-trip-components (DSTC) Template

A decision-stages-by-trip-components template was designed before data were collected, to ensure that at least some information collected covered multiple components of visitors' purchase–consumption systems. The template includes four decision stages by seven trip components. The decision stages are:

1. Consideration set and choice made;
2. Motives and situational conditions affecting the choice;
3. Search and use of information in making the choice; and
4. A summary of the outcome of the experiences related to the choice.

Each of these four stages is considered across the seven trip components. The seven trip components include data on:

1. Destinations;
2. Route/mode to and in the principal destination;
3. Accommodation during the stay in the destination;
4. Activities done in the destination;
5. Regions visited in the destination;
6. Attractions visited including restaurants; and
7. Gifts and other purchases made in the destination area for taking away.

Exhibit 3.1 displays the template and provides summary data from one case study for the four decision stages across the seven trip components.

Exhibit 3.1. Summary of family, two children, visit to PEI (Case 21)

This family lives close to PEI and made a decision to go to PEI after a *This Week in PEI* was put in their letterbox. They had not been to the island for 'many, many years'. The son was the primary decision maker for the location. They had some trouble finding accommodation at short notice. They ended up in a motel with a pool that suited the children. Other activities were centred on the children. They were looking for a short family vacation, to relax and escape daily concerns. They enjoyed their stay and said they would be very likely to return. Key words: younger family, 3-day stay, local repeat visitors, mostly unplanned activities, drive, moderate involvement once on island, very short planning time frame.

Decision stages 2,2,CO3	Destinations	Route/mode to and in PEI	Accommodation during PEI stay	Activities in PEI	PEI regions visited	Attractions visited including restaurants	Gifts and purchases leaving PEI with
Consideration set and choices	PEI versus other Maritime tourist areas	Moncton–Borden Ferry–Charlottetown; Private vehicle	MacLaughlan's Motel–Charlottetown; Museum, Woodleigh could not get first choice Rodd's Cottages, Montague	Rainbow Valley (1st day) Wax Replica's, Ripley's – planned. Very pleased with RV	Cavendish area was the only region they planned to visit	Cavendish area; Rainbow Valley (planned). Museum, Woodleigh Replicas, Ripley's eating at Macdonald's and Pizza Delight	No gifts or other purchases and no intention to buy
Motives	Get-away leisure trip. Rest and relaxation	Shortest and fastest way to PEI	Love to swim in pool (children and parents), so looked only at places with pools	Children, particularly the son, wanted to visit Rainbow Valley and some other theme parks	To take the children to attractions and theme parks in that area	Fun and enjoyment particularly for children, relaxing for parents	No desire to purchase gifts on this trip
Information search and use	Read *This Week in PEI* to learn about attractions (mainly Cavendish area)	No assistance required en route	*This Week in PEI* helpful	Heard about RV from friends, found other attractions in *This Week in PEI*	Found their way on their own as had been to PEI before. Used small map in publication	*This Week in PEI* received prior to visit	None
Outcomes	As expected, both for attractions and destination. Pleased with accommodation particularly	Route and experiences as expected	As expected	Loved Rainbow Valley	Pleased with Rainbow Valley, very pleased with pool	As expected	None

Notes from interviews: From Moncton, New Brunswick. Stayed 3 nights at Charlottetown. Income range; not given. Expenditures; $655. Repeat visitors. Both parents in their 40s, boy aged 10, girl aged 5 years. Work status: father full-time. Visitor segment: near-distant, domestic, short get-away leisure, young family market. Primary destination: PEI.

One objective of the DSTC template is to briefly summarize key thoughts and actions across multiple components of a visitor's purchase–consumption system. A second objective is to use such a template to help to place each case easily into one category among 20 to 80 theoretically possible categories of visitors (e.g. domestic/foreign, regional area; short/long stay; new/repeat) and to consider the nuances in the decisions and behaviours within each of the real-life cases available per category. Thus, by examining several ($n > 5$) cases among repeat visitors to PEI from New England who stayed 7+ nights in PEI, the key drivers (in actions and thoughts) relevant particularly to such visitors, more than visitors in other categories, are identified.

Method

A field study was designed to examine the propositions and to explore the usefulness of writing reports of the holistic purchase–consumption systems of visitors at a time very close to their completing their visits to a given destination. The field study was designed to allow for 90–120 minute, *in situ* interviews using a 22-page questionnaire that permitted probes and follow-up questions (e.g. 'What makes you say that?') to issues raised by the respondent that were not thought about by the researchers in planning the study.

Informants and Procedure

The informants for the study were Canadian, American and overseas overnight visitors to PEI. All the data were collected 2–4 hours before the informants departed PEI. The data collection locations included ferry terminals, Charlottetown (PEI's capital city) Airport, and hotels and motels. The data were collected in 1993 – before the 'fixed link' (i.e. the bridge linking PEI to New Brunswick) was constructed. At the time of the study, nearly all overnight visitors to PEI entered and left the province via the ferry terminals and the Charlottetown Airport. The specific findings relevant for PEI visitors reported below may differ from data collected after the opening of

the fixed-link connection; however, such influence is unlikely to alter the findings related to the propositions in developing a grounded theory of leisure travel. Most often, to qualify for the study, a visiting party approached had to have completed two-thirds or more of their total time for their current visit in PEI.

Many interviews were conducted at the island's two ferry terminals. The occupants of personal vehicles with non-PEI licence plates were approached and asked to participate in a PEI Visitor Survey. A University of PEI t-shirt was offered as a gift for cooperating in answering the questions. The questions were asked by an interviewer, with the interviewer writing down the answers to the questions. Three interviewer training sessions and two-rounds of pre-tests of the questionnaires were completed before agreement was reached by the authors that the questionnaire was ready for use.

To reduce unknown self-selection biases at the ferry terminals, the fourth and twelfth vehicles in line were selected for the study. Similarly at the airport, the fourth person arriving at the departure gate was selected for participation for the study.

The questionnaire used includes questions asking for:

- a complete demographic description of the members of the travel party;
- total nights away from home, as well as total nights spent on PEI for this trip;
- details of the trip itinerary actually completed for the trip;
- amount and details of the planning done before the trip;
- use of travel professional help, if any;
- requesting and use of information (*PEI Visitor's Information Guide*, VIG) from government travel offices, if any;
- who was involved (and how) in deciding to visit PEI;
- use of the Province's official visitor's guide after arriving in PEI;
- destinations visited in PEI for this trip;
- overnight accommodation used in PEI and how/why selected;
- prime motives in visiting PEI;
- prior visit history to PEI;
- activities done and attractions/places visited in PEI for the current trip;

- whether or not the informant considered different modes of travel to PEI;
- whether or not the informant considered different routes of travel to PEI;
- visiting friends and/or relatives in PEI;
- evaluation of specific activities done, attractions experienced, accommodation used; and PEI as a leisure destination, and reasons for these evaluations;
- gift-buying behaviour: what was bought if anything; what was considered and not purchased; principal reasons for buying and not buying; where purchased; 'What "clinched the deal" for you?' for buying the highest-priced item purchased?
- expenditures related to travel to/from PEI, and while in PEI, including specific breakouts for accommodation, recreation/entertainment, food, gifts, within PEI travel;
- likelihood of returning to PEI within the next 2 years;
- detailed demographics: age, marital status, education, employment and income.

Analysis

A total of 34 interviews were completed; 27 were completed at the two ferry terminals and 7 at the airport. For each informant travel party, written thick descriptions were completed and the DSTC template was filled in by the interviewer. Each case-study report was read and revised following questions asked of the interviewer by the research team.

Findings

The origins, prior PEI visit experiences, and length-of-stays of the informants, reflect the core PEI total visitor data:

- the majority of visitors are from two domestic origin markets: other Maritime Provinces and the Province of Ontario;
- the majority of foreign visitors are Americans;
- nearly all maritime visitors to PEI are repeat visitors;
- most Ontario visitors to PEI are repeat visitors;
- most American visitors to PEI are first-time visitors.

Economically, three visitor segments are vital for the tourism as a PEI export industry: repeat visitors from other Maritime Provinces; repeat and new visitors from Ontario; and new visitors from the USA. The following discussion provides case-study holistic summaries of a travel party planning and visiting PEI for each of these three critical visitor segments, as well as two additional case studies from non-critical origin markets: western Canada and Europe.

A Young Family from New Brunswick Visits Prince Edward Island

Interview synopsis

This case study includes responses by a young family visiting PEI for pleasure, for 3 nights, in late July 1993. The family includes a husband, wife and two children, a boy aged 10 and a girl aged 5. A fun trip, primarily for the children, was the motive. No particular destination was considered until a copy of *This Week in PEI* appeared in the family's mailbox (not sent for), approximately 2 weeks before departure. The son was the primary decision maker in deciding where to spend this leisure time. Total expenditures for this trip were estimated to be $655.00. This total did not include any purchase of gifts or other items to take home, nor was there any plan to make such purchases before returning home. The family used primarily the publication *This Week in PEI* while they were visiting. They were unfamiliar with the *PEI Visitor's Information Guide* (VIG) and had never heard of this publication. The family reports being very likely to return to PEI in 1994.

The data in Exhibit 3.1 apply to this family's trip. Note that Exhibit 3.1 indicates the high impact of the publication, *This Week in PEI*, for triggering the visit, booking accommodation, and selecting activities to engage in. The publication was a necessary, but not sufficient, condition for the decision to visit PEI. Figure 3.2 includes external influences that influenced the decision to visit PEI, including the son's friends highly recommending going to PEI's Rainbow Valley theme park. Voicing this recommendation and desire by the son was a necessary, but not sufficient, condition for completing the decision to visit PEI.

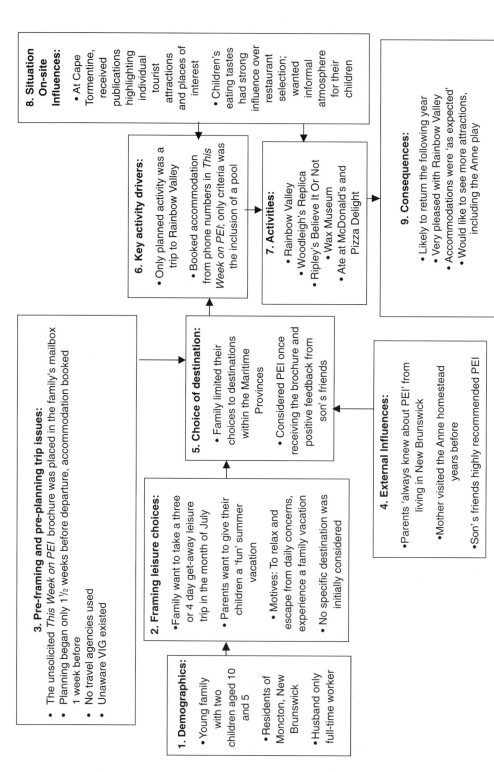

Fig. 3.2. Young family from Maritime Provinces.

Description of the family visiting PEI and interview site/day

Demographics

The travel party included Larry McKnight (LM), his wife Charlene (CM), and their two children, a girl and a boy aged 5 and 10 years, respectively. CM answered all the questions. CM and her husband are both in their forties. CM has some level of college/university education while her husband has a high school diploma. CM does not work outside the home; her husband is employed full-time. LM did not reveal his occupation. I was unable to determine the level of family income as CM declined to answer this question. They reside in Moncton, New Brunswick.

Interview site/day

The interview was conducted in the pool room at McLaughlin's Motel in Charlottetown. CM's two children were enjoying swimming in the pool while CM was watching them. The interviewer and the interviewee sat at a pool-side table in the pool room so that CM could have a good view of the children. LM was in the family's motel room, resting. It was a beautiful evening outside (19°C). The pool room was very hot. The family had just returned from a day trip to Rainbow Valley.

Trip decisions for the total trip

This trip to PEI for CM and her family was planned about 1.5 weeks prior to their departure for PEI. They planned a 3–4-day get-away leisure trip. Using the publication *This Week in PEI*, plans for accommodation were also made about 1 week before departure. At the same time, tentative plans were made to visit some attractions while on PEI. The only concrete plan was a one-day visit to Rainbow Valley. No other destinations were named in the planned trip, only 'somewhere in the Maritime Provinces'. Marketing Management Implication (MMI): if such customers represent an important target market for Maritime visitors to PEI, their planning time is very brief, thus advertising media schedules should include in-season advertising placements and messages to reach such customers.

Planning horizon

CM stated 'very little' planning time prior to making the trip to PEI. No other destinations outside the Maritimes were considered. MMI: Once on PEI, the family saw and read about many attractions of interest to them, through their travels about the island and from publications passed out to them in the compound at Cape Tormentine prior to driving on to the ferry. Note also that the arrival of the publication in their mailbox at their home in Moncton was the critical deciding factor or 'clinched the deal' (a publication at no cost to the consumer and one which they had not requested). As soon as the publication was looked at, the decision was made to come to PEI, as the son had heard his friends talk a lot about PEI, primarily Rainbow Valley as a fun place to visit.

Assistance by travel professionals

No assistance was considered or sought from travel professionals prior to the trip. Such assistance would likely have benefited the McKnights, as they had to make several phone calls prior to the trip to book accommodation.

Requesting information from travel offices before visiting

No information was requested prior to the visit, nor was any sought once the family arrived on PEI. They were, however, given handouts at the ferry terminal at Cape Tormentine. Other than a planned visit to Rainbow Valley, the rest of the visit was unplanned as they went along.

PEI planning issues

The family 'always knew about PEI' but had not visited for 'many, many years'. CM stated that she had once visited the homestead at *Anne of Green Gables* in Cavendish, but that her husband and children had not seen it. No one in the family had read the *Anne of Green Gables* book collection nor had they seen the play. [The play is presented in Charlottetown 6 days per week during the summer months.] They did state, however, that on a return visit they would like to see many more attractions, including the play.

The publication that was used was *This Week in PEI*. From this guide the family was able to make telephone calls to obtain reservations, as well as to decide on a number of other attractions that they might like to see, besides Rainbow Valley, during their visit, that is, Woodleigh Replicas, Wax Museum and Ripley's Believe It Or Not.

Decision making process for the trip

Although all family members took part in the decision making process in terms of where to go on this trip, no one person was really adamant as to where they should go. The son finally became very excited about a visit to PEI, but only after the publication *This Week in PEI* appeared in the mail and he then remembered comments made to him by his friends about the wonderful time they had had at Rainbow Valley. This conversation was the turning point in their decision on where to go on their leisure trip. The rest of the family also agreed that PEI would be a 'fun place to visit'.

PEI visit issues

Decision making process for accommodation

The family made reservations for accommodation on PEI only 1 week prior to leaving home. The publication *This Week in PEI* listed several possible accommodations which this travel party considered. Although they could not remember the names of the places which they called, they did express an interest in staying in the eastern part of the Island, around the Montague area, and had called Rodd's Brudenel Resort. Friends had recommended the area because of its beautiful scenery. However, they were unable to obtain a reservation in that area from those listed in the publication. They called three other places before they finally obtained a reservation at MacLaughlan's Motel. Once they found an opening here, they stopped looking. They planned to stay a total of 3 nights at MacLaughlan's Motel before heading back home. A pool in which the children could enjoy themselves was of major importance in the selection of accommodation. Those accommodations without an indoor pool were not considered.

Assessment of accommodation

The assessment of the accommodation was 'about as expected'. The motel was found to be 'reasonably priced' and there were no negative comments about the accommodation. The pool 'clinched the deal'. The McKnights also enjoyed the layout of the rooms, in that there was a separate room in which the children could sleep, apart from the main bedroom. Total amount spent on accommodation was $320.00.

Mode of transportation and route taken

This party travelled to PEI by car direct from Moncton, (a 1-hour drive to Cape Tormentine). No other route was considered as the family wanted to travel the most direct route possible. They were pleasantly surprised to be able to drive on to the ferry very shortly after coming into the ferry terminal, as they had expected to have to wait in a line-up at the compound. During the interview their plans were to return home by the same route.

Purchases of gifts and other items

Prior to visiting PEI, there were no plans to buy gifts or other items to take home. When interviewed, CM stated that they indeed had not purchased any gifts and had no plans to do so. MMI: This market segment tends to stay for shorter periods of time and spends less money on gifts/souvenirs.

Activities and attractions visited

Rainbow Valley was the only planned attraction. Rainbow Valley turned out to be as expected and CM commented that it was 'reasonably priced'. However, others that were considered were the Wax Museum, Woodleigh Replicas and Ripley's Believe It Or Not. The plan was to 'play it by ear and see what develops', while driving around the Cavendish area the next day. The beach area at Cavendish was also under consideration, but plans were very flexible. MMI: Little formal planning was completed by this travel party prior to the visit.

Eating places

The children in this travel party were the primary decision makers about where to eat while on the trip to PEI. On the trip they preferred to eat in places such as Pizza Delight and MacDonald's. The parents preferred these places for the children as they were not into formal dining rooms with children at these ages. Total food expenditure was around $200.00.

Motives for the trip

The motives for this trip were evenly distributed between a chance to experience a family vacation and a chance to relax and escape from daily concerns. MMI: This travel party appears to reflect a more relaxed, slower-paced experience in which recuperation may be more important than stimulation.

Summary

CM and her family plan to return to PEI in 1994. MMI: A significant number of near-home travellers predict that they will actually return to the site in the near future. Also, near-home travellers have a higher potential of being repeat customers if they are satisfied. These conclusions suggest important marketing implications for design of an offering and the way it should be promoted for the near-home traveller. The near-home market segment may spend only a brief time planning their trip, so advertising and media are important in reaching this market. Product positioning is as important a prerequisite to designing market strategies for this group as for the distance traveller.

How the propositions apply to such repeat Maritime Province visits to PEI

This first case study provides strong support for P_1, demographics and lifestyles of visitors influence how they frame leisure choices. Ensuring fun experiences for the children was the key driver behind the visit.

P_2 is strongly supported. An unexpected event occurred that influenced the framing of leisure choices: the arrival of *This Week in PEI*. While not a controlled experiment demonstrating influence (see Woodside, 1990), this case study provides strong investigative evidence that this publication is a necessary, if not a sufficient, condition for causing some share of repeat PEI visits from travel parties residing in other Maritime Provinces. P_3 receives strong support. Both external and internal personal influences affect the framing of the trip to PEI by this family.

P_4 receives modest support. Visiting a particular theme park, Rainbow Valley, is the specific PEI attribute that was mentioned by the son, who became a key driver in deciding to make this visit to PEI. However, this case report does not include thinking processes that reflect destination rejection or comparing PEI with alternative destinations. A key driver was also identified that influenced their choice of accommodation: the presence versus absence of a swimming pool.

P_5 receives strong support: information collected for framing and trip planning affected the process of selecting and rejecting destination alternatives. However, the principal information used was not sought – it just arrived in the mailbox. P_6 receives strong support: friends' opinions and thoughts retrieved from memory influenced the selection and rejection of destination alternatives. P_7 receives strong support: 'key activity' drivers solidified the decision to visit the destination selected – in this case the key driver was one theme park. P_8 receives strong support: one activity driver (the theme park visit) affected what was planned and done in the destination area.

P_9 receives support: information and events learned by the visitors while visiting affected their plans and behaviour. For example, where they ate meals was very much affected by travelling by fast food restaurants. P_{10} receives support: visiting Rainbow Valley was a successful experience – the activities done (and not done) affect much of the attitude and intention consequences resulting from, and associating with, visiting a destination. Not-done activities included visiting more attractions and seeing the *Anne of Green Gables* production in Charlottetown.

High-income Couple from Ontario Visit Prince Edward Island

Synopsis

This section provides a descriptive analysis of a middle-aged couple's recent pleasure trip to PEI for a total of 3 nights during the first week of August 1993. The couple had originally planned a week's stay on the island, but left because of unsuitable accommodation, and their inability to find appropriate accommodation. The couple described their visit to PEI as a 'complete disaster', as they spent the entire 3 days driving around the island in search of accommodation. The primary and sole motive of the married couple's visit to the island was to relax and escape in a 'quaint cottage close to the ocean'. There were no competing destinations for this trip to PEI, as the trip had been planned for 4 years in advance of the visit. Expenditure for the couple's 3-day stay amounted to $925.

The couple received the visitor's guide before arriving on PEI, and used it heavily to assist in locating accommodation and attractions. The couple was very unsatisfied with the trip to PEI, as they spent the entire 3 days searching for accommodation, and finally, became frustrated and cut their trip short to return to Ontario. Both the husband and the wife said they would most definitely not return to PEI in 1994, 1995, or any year after. Exhibit 3.2 and Fig. 3.3 summarize details of the planning, visit activities and trip evaluations by this couple.

Demographics of the family visiting PEI and interview site/day

The party that was interviewed consisted of Edward (EA) and Anita Ausborne (AA). Both actively participated in the interview and answered all directed questions. EA and AA were in their late 40s, both with postgraduate training, and working outside the home full time. EA works in an accounting firm, while AA works with the Province of Ontario. The couple's annual income before taxes ranges between $75,000 and $100,000. The Ausbornes currently reside in Ontario.

The interview was conducted in the Charlottetown Airport waiting area as the Ausbornes awaited their departing flight to Toronto. The time of the interview was at 12.30 p.m. and lasted until 1.15 p.m. At first the interviewer was reluctant to do the survey with them, as their flight departure impeded the amount of time required to talk with them. The Ausbornes said they would really like to talk about their trip because it had been such a horrible experience. The interviewer sat alongside the Ausbornes in the waiting area to conduct the interview. The day was sunny, warm and humid, with a temperature of 22°C.

The decision for the trip

The total trip included a 1 week's stay on Prince Edward Island, with no secondary destinations planned. The Ausbornes started planning this visit to PEI in 1989, as EA lived on PEI for a period of 4 months and had made plans to return for leisure purposes. The primary reason to return to PEI was the opportunity to escape and relax in a cottage atmosphere overlooking the ocean, and to enjoy fresh island seafood delicacies.

The couple had planned to stay on the island for a week in the St Peters area, but because of the quality of the accommodation, and their endless search to find respectable accommodation, they decided to return to Ontario 4 days earlier than planned.

When asked about the extent of planning involved in their trip to PEI, EA responded that the trip had been '4 years in the making', and as a result no other destinations were included in their destination choice set. Prior to arriving on PEI, EA made accommodation arrangements, car rental arrangements and telephoned the 1–800 number for information on PEI and to receive a visitor's guide. PEI was the sole Province contacted for travel information, but upon calling PEI, he was also sent visitor guides from the three other Atlantic Provinces. EA responded that this was useless information and was discarded because they had no intention to visit the other provinces. The Ausbornes indicated that if they had the time available, they might venture to Nova Scotia for a day. But this was uncertain, and would have been decided on during their stay on PEI.

Exhibit 3.2 Summary of visit by couple to PEI (Ex 26).

This middle-aged couple cut short their planned weeklong trip because of problems with the accommodation. The planning horizon for the trip was 4 years, ever since the husband had spent 4 months working on the island. They aimed to relax in a cottage by the sea. They had used the *Visitor's Guide* to locate the cottages they thought fitted their criteria. On arrival they found the cottages were substandard and had no view of water. This they considered to be false advertising. They then spent the rest of their time trying to find suitable accommodation. They stated that they would never consider returning to PEI.

Key words: middle-aged couple, medium to high income, 3-day stay, one first-timer, one repeat, planned activities but did none – disaster, fly/drive, involvement only in finding alternative accommodation, planning, long planning time frame.

Decision area 2,0,S07	Destinations	Route/mode to and in PEI	Accommodation during PEI stay	Activities in PEI	PEI regions visited	Attractions visited including restaurants	Gifts and purchases leaving PEI with
Consideration set and choices	PEI only	Flight to PEI Toronto to Halifax to Charlottetown	Shaw's Hotel. Rodd Royalty Inn, Rodd Charlottetown Hotel	Wanted to visit beaches. Lobster suppers /museums/ Anne of Green Gables House	None	No attractions visited	No gifts bought. Accommodation, meals, car rental gas.
Motives	Relax, escape daily concerns, tap into island offerings	Flew as time was a primary consideration	Wanted a cottage by the sea (booked Steadman's Cottages but not acceptable)	Could not do any, as all time was spent looking for alternative accommodation	Looking for accommodation	Looking for accommodation	These were necessity
Information search and use	VIG, from having lived on island for 4 months	VIG. Previous visit	Charlottetown VIC VIG	Visitor's Centre	None	Visitor's Centre	On the way
Outcomes	Negative impression of PEI	Negative impression	Grading system of VIG was only fair. Star system misleading, less than expected	Negative impression of PEI	Negative impression of PEI	Negative impression of PEI	Negative impression of PEI

Notes from interviews: From Ontario. Stayed 3 days (of planned 7 days) at Brackley and Charlottetown. Income range: $75,000–$100,000. Expenditures; $925. One repeat visitor (husband had worked on the island). Both aged in their late 40s. Work status: full-time with postgraduate training. Both responded. Visitor segment: medium–distant, domestic, touring, market. PEI was the primary destination.

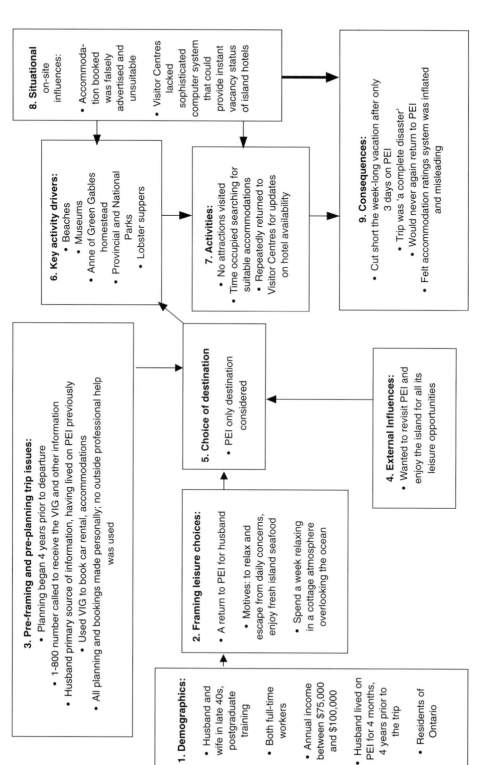

Fig. 3.3. High-income couple from Ontario.

Planning decisions

Both the Ausbornes were involved actively in the decision to visit PEI, but EA was the person who initiated the trip to PEI. He was more involved because he had lived here for a short period, and EA believes that he knows all of what PEI had to offer, specifically, fine beaches, a relaxing atmosphere and great seafood. He became aware of PEI when he had to move there to work for a short period, and had no recollection of anyone actually recommending a visit to the island.

PEI visit questions

The primary motive to visit PEI was to escape and relax. When asked to assign votes, in a constant sum question of ten votes, for nine alternative motives for visiting PEI, the Ausbornes both assigned relax and escape all ten votes. The fine beaches and seafood were also motives, but they accompanied the idea of relaxation and escape.

The Ausbornes chose to fly to PEI, as it was easier and occupied less leisure time. This would enable them to spend more time on PEI enjoying the attractions and relaxing. They flew Air Canada out of Toronto into Halifax and then on to Charlottetown. This was the only route debated, as the Ausbornes wanted to get here as quickly as possible. An automobile, as a means of travel, was not even discussed or considered.

Assistance by travel professionals

The Ausbornes took care of all their travel arrangements on their own, prior to leaving Ontario. They made reservations for their flight, accommodation and car rental without professional assistance.

After arriving on PEI and discovering that their accommodation had been falsely advertised, they visited the Charlottetown Visitor Centre to have the Centre assist in finding accommodation. Because PEI was highly booked at the time, they had to keep returning to the Visitor Information Centre to see if anything better had turned up: preferably an oceanside cottage.

The Ausbornes were relatively pleased with the travel counsellors at the centres and reported them to be very friendly and helpful. They did not hold them responsible for the lack of vacancies. The only criticism was the inability to get immediate responses. Because of this, the Ausbornes were required to constantly check in with the centres. Marketing management implication (MMI): PEI might consider upgrading the reservation system to be more technologically advanced, thus providing visitors with quicker responses through the use of computerized reservations. A system such as that in place in Nova Scotia, 'CHECK INS', is sophisticated and provides callers with an immediate response to accommodation enquiries. The system in place on PEI is not as modern as the one used in Nova Scotia.

Requesting information from travel offices before visiting

Prince Edward Island was the only destination contacted for information. The Ausbornes indicated that they called a 1–800 number for the information and specified that they only required information on PEI. When the information was received the Ausbornes found information on all the Atlantic Provinces. The Ausbornes did not appreciate this and quickly discarded the information they had not requested.

If and how the VIG was used during the PEI visit

Since the guide was received prior to arriving on PEI, the Ausbornes had the opportunity to go through it and see what attractions they wished to visit. Their reservations had already been made at this point, but they referred to the guide to see the grading of the property.

The Ausbornes took the guide on their trip, and used it heavily to find replacement accommodation. They did not use it for anything else because they spent the entire trip travelling around the island in search of accommodation. They evaluated the guide as very helpful, but thought the grading system to be only fair. They did not feel that standards were set very high and the star system was very misleading. MMI: PEI might consider enforcing stricter standards on the accommodation grading system so that visitors know exactly what to expect and are not upset after arrival.

Accommodation decisions and experiences

Initially, the Ausbornes had planned to spend their entire vacation at Steadman's Cottages in St Peters. They read about this property in the *Toronto Star* and it seemed to meet their expectations: a quiet oceanfront cottage with some amenities. Upon arriving at the cottages the first day, they were outraged at what they saw. Their description of the cottages included being in the middle of nowhere, poorly furnished, pre-1950 decor, no curtains, no amenities and no view of the water. This situation was unacceptable, and they refused to stay, thus losing their $100 deposit.

A visitor centre was contacted, and accommodation was found at Shaw's Hotel in Brackley. This night did not turn out very well as there were bugs throughout the room that kept them awake all night. The operators were very apologetic and did not charge them for the night.

The next 2 nights were spent at the Rodd Royalty Inn and the Rodd Charlottetown Hotel. The Ausbornes had to settle for something they did not want. These two facilities were rated as fair, as the couple had their mindset on a cottage atmosphere that was relaxing and secluded. Thus, their experience at these downtown hotels was less than expected.

When asked what they would like to see changed in their accommodation Mr Ausborne replied, 'updated facilities, amenities, cleanliness and proper advertisement of facilities'. MMI: these findings reinforce the need for a stricter grading system, as well as a greater need of supporting infrastructure. The summer demand for updated and better-quality accommodation facilities suggests that PEI may be discouraging visitors by not being able to accommodate this need.

Attraction Decisions and Experiences

Some of the attractions that the Ausbornes were interested in visiting included beaches, lobster suppers, museums, Anne of Green Gables House, and provincial and national parks across the island. Because they had to spend all their time searching for accommodation, they were unable to visit any attractions. Their first day included driving from the airport to St Peters, looking for new accommodation, and driving to Brackley for accommodation. Day two involved a search for new accommodation again. Day three also involved looking for accommodation and running to and from visitors' information centres, a 0.5 hour visit to the Charlottetown Mall, and finally a decision to return home.

Evidently, the low-quality accommodation caused the Ausbornes to be unable to enjoy their vacation. They did say that the VIG was very helpful in planning what attractions they would visit each day. MMI: ensure that visitors receive VIG prior to or after arriving the island, so they can learn about attractions and regions they would other wise be unaware of, and make plans in advance to visit them. This objective can be achieved by distributing the VIG to all incoming visitors at the airport and both ferry terminals.

Expenditures

Again the accommodation dilemma was so discomforting that the Ausbornes did not have the opportunity to shop for gifts for friends and relatives or themselves. They had intended to purchase some gifts to return home with.

Total expenditures came to $925: accommodation $300, meals in restaurants $200, car rental $350, and petrol $75. From this, it is easy to say that the Ausbornes spent money only on necessities, but had been willing to spend much more on attractions and gifts. Because of the accommodation, PEI lost money on shopping, attractions, and food, accommodation, and gas for the remaining 3 nights.

Conclusions and implications

This experience of the Ausbornes gives an example of how one sub-decision within a vacation can ruin an entire vacation. Because of the poor quality of accommodation, the Ausbornes spent less money, returned home 4 days early, and will most likely tell people about their horrible PEI vacation.

Instead of influencing the Ausbornes to return, their PEI experience created a negative impression that will produce bad word of mouth which could affect other potential visitors' intention to visit. PEI may have lost additional travel parties as a result of this one bad experience.

The Ausbornes' report focuses theoretical attention mostly on P_9 (Box 8 to 7 in Fig. 3.3), that is, information and events learned by the visitors while visiting affects their plans and behaviours. Note that high occupancy rates in alternative sought-after accommodation were a contributing condition to the couple's reports of misery in searching for suitable accommodation. Note in Fig. 3.3 that an additional association (thick arrow) is included to indicate the direct influence of situational conditions affecting this couple's overall evaluation of visiting PEI.

First-time Visitors from a Far-distant Domestic Origin

Synopsis

This case study focuses on the responses by both Shelley and Dave Ozinko who were visiting Prince Edward Island on a pleasure trip for 7 days and 6 nights during the first week of August. Exhibit 3.3 and Fig. 3.4 summarize the couple's decision process and purchase–consumption system.

This young couple resided in Calgary, Alberta. Their main motivation for coming to Prince Edward Island was to learn about another 'culture', PEI's art, history and cultural events. Accordingly, they chose bed and breakfasts as their main accommodation while on PEI. Other destinations considered and rejected included the New England States (for reasons of driving time and distance between attractions). Their primary travel destination, Prince Edward Island, along with Nova Scotia, provided them with enough to do in a 3-week period with little driving time – in comparison to travel to the New England region of the USA.

This trip was their first visit to Prince Edward Island. Total expenditure while on PEI amounted to approximately $1200. They had no criticisms of PEI and suggested that it exceeded their expectations. Information was sought out in April and accommodation/attractions booked upon receipt of the *Visitor's Information Guide*. They are very unlikely to return to PEI over the next 2 years but perhaps in 10 years' time.

Background data

The Ozinkos had never previously visited the Island. They had no friends or family on the island and, as a result, their primary intention for visiting eastern Canada was to see PEI and all that it had to offer. They learned of PEI from friends' recommendations, saying 'You'll love it'. Upon attending the 1992 Calgary Stampede (the theme was 'Provinces in Canada') they visited the Prince Edward Island booth with literature displays and agents from the island promoting the area as a vacation destination. Information was available for their perusal and plans were made. As their flight arrived in Halifax airport, they chose to tour Nova Scotia first. This provided close approximation to PEI if they were well planned in their itinerary. Shelley was the organizer of the whole expedition, and as a result, plans had proceeded smoothly – they had completed just over half of their vacation when interviewed. Their trip would conclude in Halifax, then they would depart back to Calgary to continue the savings plan that will take them on another voyage in the forthcoming year.

Demographic and psychographic information

The Ozinkos were in their early thirties. They had no children. They both have post-secondary education. Dave is a college graduate while Shelley graduated from university. They both hold full-time jobs. As a result of their double income, they are categorized in the upper income bracket, earning $75,001–$100,000 per annum. This couple seeks out new cultures with a focus on the historical aspect of a travel destination. PEI provided them with much more enjoyable experiences than they had anticipated.

Exhibit 3.3. Summary of a far distant domestic Canadian couple's visit to PEI (Case 15).

PEI and Nova Scotia were the primary destinations for this young couple from Calgary, Alberta. A 3-week vacation planned with 6 nights being spent on PEI. The strongest influence on their choice was friends and knowledge of *Anne of Green Gables*. They stayed in bed and breakfast accommodation. Booking of accommodation, travel and the various attractions was done without the assistance of a travel agent. They visited a lot of the tourist attractions and areas, covering most of the areas on the island. Key words: younger married couple, medium–high income, 7-day stay, first-timers, fly/drive, high involvement, 'experience', knew of *Anne of Green Gables*, long planning time frame.

Decision area 2,0,SO4	Destinations	Route/mode to and in PEI	Accommodation during PEI stay	Activities in PEI	PEI regions visited	Attractions visited including restaurants	Gifts and purchases leaving PEI with
Consideration set and choices	PEI, Nova Scotia and New England. Choice was PEI and NS	Air from Calgary to Halifax, rental car to PEI	See whole island starting at Cornwall then go west, north and east.	*Anne of Green Gables* play; Olde Dublin movie, Charlottetown walking tour, St Ann's Lobster Supper, Victory-by-the-Sea, Potato Museum, Woodleigh replicas, Anne House,	Charlottetown, South Shore, West Prince, North Shore – Cavendish, East Kings	Olde Dublin Confederate Centre, City Hall, Chocolate Factory, Woodleigh, Anne House, Anchor & Oar, Dunes House	Anne doll and poster
Motives	Places of interest close. Experience 'culture'	See NS for 1 week then go to PEI by shortest route possible	Have 1 week to see all of PEI. Read VIG and planned and booked the things of interest	Crafts shopping, wanted to experience whole culture of PEI, learn all about PEI	Reach attractions throughout PEI	Experience island way of life and attractions representative of it	Read Anne books, likes unique crafts
Information search and use	Recommended by friends, Calgary Stampede information booth. 1-800#. Direct calls to PEI operators	Follow map totally and stop at places according to VIG	Extensive use of VIG to chose B&Bs and country inns. Clean homey atmosphere	Read about attractions in VIG and brochures from VIC	Read about accessing places by certain routes and used map	VIG and brochures	VIG for New London to purchase Anne doll
Outcomes	Enjoying PEI far more than expected. Accommodation B&B and *Anne of Green Gables* play good	PEI map makes PEI bigger than it really is. It takes no time to go from one area to another on PEI	Very pleased thus far. Not one complaint. Much better than NS	Enjoyed play and Irish pub immensely	Very beautiful. More than expected	Great portions (food). Great prices and atmosphere	Pleased

Notes from interviews: From Calgary, Alberta. Stayed 6 nights at various B&B. Income range; $75,000–$100,000. Expenditures: $1195. First-time visitors. Both in their early 30s. Work status: both full-time and had post secondary education. Visitor segment: far-distant, domestic, touring 'experience' market. Both Nova Scotia and PEI were primary destinations.

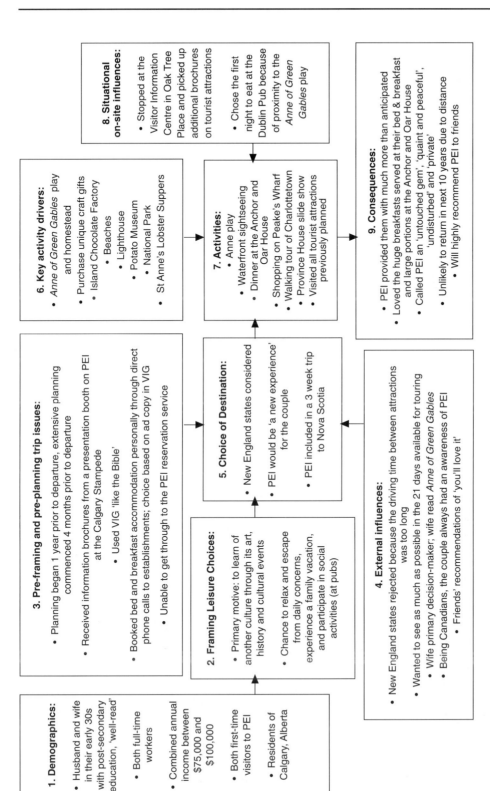

1. Demographics:

- Husband and wife in their early 30s with post-secondary education, 'well-read'
- Both full-time workers
- Combined annual income between $75,000 and $100,000
- Both first-time visitors to PEI
- Residents of Calgary, Alberta

2. Framing Leisure Choices:

- Primary motive: to learn of another culture through its art, history and cultural events
- Chance to relax and escape from daily concerns, experience a family vacation, and participate in social activities (at pubs)

3. Pre-framing and pre-planning trip issues:

- Planning began 1 year prior to departure, extensive planning commenced 4 months prior to departure
- Received information brochures from a presentation booth on PEI at the Calgary Stampede
  - Used VIG 'like the Bible'
- Booked bed and breakfast accommodation personally through direct phone calls to establishments; choice based on ad copy in VIG
  - Unable to get through to the PEI reservation service

4. External influences:

- New England states rejected because the driving time between attractions was too long
- Wanted to see as much as possible in the 21 days available for touring
  - Wife primary decision-maker; wife read Anne of Green Gables
  - Being Canadians, the couple always had an awareness of PEI
  - Friends' recommendations of 'you'll love it'

5. Choice of Destination:

- New England states considered
- PEI would be 'a new experience' for the couple
- PEI included in a 3 week trip to Nova Scotia

6. Key activity drivers:

- Anne of Green Gables play and homestead
- Purchase unique craft gifts
- Island Chocolate Factory
  - Beaches
  - Lighthouse
  - Potato Museum
  - National Park
- St Anne's Lobster Suppers

7. Activities:

- Anne play
- Waterfront sightseeing
- Dinner at the Anchor and Oar House
- Shopping on Peake's Wharf
- Walking tour of Charlottetown
- Province House slide show
- Visited all tourist attractions previously planned

8. Situational on-site influences:

- Stopped at the Visitor Information Centre in Oak Tree Place and picked up additional brochures on tourist attractions
- Chose the first night to eat at the Dublin Pub because of proximity to the Anne of Green Gables play

9. Consequences:

- PEI provided them with much more than anticipated
- Loved the huge breakfasts served at their bed & breakfast and large portions served at the Anchor and Oar House
- Called PEI an 'untouched gem', 'quaint and peaceful', 'undisturbed' and 'private'
- Unlikely to return in next 10 years due to distance
  - Will highly recommend PEI to friends

Fig. 3.4. Couple in early 30s from Alberta.

Interview site and day

The interview was completed at Chez-Nous Bed & Breakfast, located in Cornwall. An appointment was set up with the owner of the establishment (Sandi Gallant) and the interview took place at 9.30 a.m., 4 August 1993. The interview took 1 full hour to complete, with discussion and suggestions as to where to visit while on PEI. It was a very hot, sunny day with no interruptions during the course of the interview.

Planning decisions for the total trip

The planning process for this trip began, technically, during the previous year at the Calgary Stampede. The actual 'extensive' planning of when they were coming, and requesting the information, began in early April. Upon receipt of all requested information, Shelley proceeded to highlight the accommodation and attractions that appealed to her taste. (Note that her main focus was on B&Bs and country inns as they provided her with more of a personal touch, allowing them to experience the culture to a greater degree during their short visit.) The descriptions in the ad copy 'clinched the deal' on booking the chosen accommodation. Upon review of the highlighted portions of the guide, she proceeded to call the reservation service on PEI. She was unable to get through to the reservation service, so direct calls were made to the local establishments for bookings. Shelley mentioned that she did not mind dealing directly with the local operators, as this was a chance to briefly establish a 'feeble relationship' and obtain a feel for the place through conversing with the owners. Brochures were then sent to her, but by this time her mind was made up that she and her husband would stay in the sites that were sending her the literature.

For attractions such as organized tours and theatre (*Anne of Green Gables*), reservations were also made, so the whole itinerary was planned 4 months in advance of departure. At no time was a travel agent consulted. MMI: if this couple is representative of the typical younger couple, any advertising or booth displays at major events throughout the country

might be targeted towards females in early April. The reservation system should also be more accessible for convenience purposes.

Travel route

The modes of travel included air and rented vehicle. The Ozinkos flew out of Calgary on 25 July 1993 heading for Halifax, NS. Upon arrival, they proceeded to rent a car (which they took over to PEI). Over the next 7 days, they toured the south-western portion of Nova Scotia, before proceeding to PEI via Caribou Ferry Terminal. Their wait was expected and lasted 2 hours. They had accommodation booked for 6 nights and 7 days of entertainment on PEI. The conclusion of their trip was intended to entail 7 more nights in Nova Scotia before flying out of Halifax, back to Calgary.

PEI planning issues: PEI versus NS

Shelley was the main decision maker and planner of this trip, as was previously mentioned, although it was a joint decision between her and Dave to actually come to PEI and Nova Scotia.

Being Canadians, they had an awareness of PEI, although it may not have been in their consideration set of possible destinations to visit if it had not been for the *Anne of Green Gables* book that Shelley had previously read, or the recommendations from friends to visit the island. As a result of the prompting from friends and prior readings and promotional displays (Calgary Stampede), all things were pointing to a visit to PEI.

Other destinations under consideration included the New England region. This idea was ruled out due to the distance involved in travelling from state to state. The Ozinkos wanted to see as much as possible in the 21 days available for touring. Since PEI was the main destination considered, they chose this area along with Nova Scotia. Prince Edward Island was allocated 6 nights while Nova Scotia garnered 15 nights. Nova Scotia was allocated more time due to its larger size and the appeal of Cape Breton for its scenery and culture. MMI: to persuade tourists to visit PEI over Cape Breton, management might focus on PEI's competitive advantage over Cape Breton through the promoting of more things to do and experience while on PEI (i.e. festivals, amusement parks, beaches). While both destinations have beautiful scenery, Cape Breton does not have as much to see or do for the younger market, outside of viewing the landscape. PEI may be 'a little bit above and beyond Cape Breton' in this respect, as mentioned by Shelley.

Motivational drivers

Being young and well-read, this couple came to learn about another culture, PEI's art, history and cultural events. This objective was their primary motive for including PEI on their vacation. This trip was also their first visit to PEI, so all that there was to experience would be new to them. This view may account for the heavy weight that was placed on cultural experiences motivating their visit.

Secondary motives were numerous including: a chance to relax and escape from daily concerns, experience a family vacation, participation in social activities (pubs) and a chance to see nature on PEI.

Daily itinerary

Day 1

Upon arrival on Prince Edward Island, they visited Point Prim's Chowder House and Art Gallery for dinner. They were very impressed by the food and service provided. Next, they departed for Charlottetown to the Visitor Information Centre located in Oak Tree Place. While conversing with one of the tourism officers, they picked up additional brochures on local attractions and advice on particular sites to visit. Next, they proceeded to Chez-Nous to check in and get ready for an eventful evening in Charlottetown. Dinner was enjoyed at the Olde Dublin Pub. Their choice of this location was for its casual atmosphere and reasonably offered prices. The proximity of this location also allowed for them to spend more time over a relaxed meal before a short walk to the *Anne*

of Green Gables main stage production at the Confederation Centre of the Arts. The play was a highlight for Shelley as she had read the book and cried at the conclusion of the performance! 'I bawled' were her words. Finally, they retired back to Chez-Nous to recuperate from their exhausting day.

Day 2

They enjoyed a huge breakfast at Chez-Nous, which Dave remarked was uncharacteristic of B&Bs in Nova Scotia, where they would serve themselves a meagre continental breakfast. MMI: management should educate the local operators on servicing the customer more effectively in small details. These are the things that are remembered during recall when conversing with friends. As these small operators do not have the budgets for advertising, they rely heavily on word of mouth advertising.

The Ozinkos then departed for Charlottetown to participate in an educational walking tour of the capital city. While on the tour, Dave had an uninvited guest attend. A mosquito lodged in his ear and was buzzing. It was driving him to the point of annoyance, so, upon completion of the walking tour, they made a detour to the Queen Elizabeth Hospital for flushing of the intruder (after a 2 hour wait).

After the mishap, they ventured to Province House for participation in the slide presentation and guided tour throughout the building. They found the actor portraying the keeper of the house during that time period to be quite amusing. As they were close to the waterfront, they proceeded to view the crafts available at Peake's wharf. (Shelley's intentions on PEI are to purchase unique crafts that were typical of the culture and reflective of the heritage of islanders.) Next, they visited Cow's for a $2.54 single ice-cream cone. The waterfront was, yet again, frequented later that afternoon for dinner at the Anchor and Oar House located just behind the CP Prince Edward Hotel. There they enjoyed an Italian meal at a reasonable price in the outdoor seating area. Dave remarked that the 'portions were huge' at a reasonable price. Shelley had not made any purchases on Peake's Wharf that day, other than a picture of PEI, so they left

Charlottetown for the Stoneware Pottery shop in Winsloe. While there she made a purchase of spice holders. Their uniqueness appealed to her taste and for $20 she could not refuse. To end the day, they proceeded to the Charlottetown Cinemas to view *The Firm*. Upon its completion, they departed for Chez-Nous to end the day in conversation with Sandi Gallant (owner).

Day 3

As the interview was conducted at the beginning of the third day, they proceeded to tell me their plans which included a visit to: Island Chocolate Factory, Victoria-by-the-Sea (beach); Summerside/Spinnaker's Landing (waterfront); West Point Lighthouse (beach and B&B); PEI Potato Museum (possibly).

Days 4 and 5

These days were to be spent touring the Cavendish area, including planned visits to: New London (purchase of Anne of Green Gables doll); Anne of Green Gables House; Shining Water's Country Inn and Cottages; St Ann's Lobster Suppers, National Park beaches.

Days 6 and 7

These days were to be spent touring the eastern portion of PEI in the Kings County region. They planned to visit Beasin Head, which is just north of Souris. This beach area supplies relaxation for mainly locals. They were to spend 1 night in a B&B in Murray Harbour before departing via the Wood Islands Ferry Terminal.

Expenditure

Some costs are based on projections, while others are based on receipts thus far in the tour. Below is the breakdown of expenditure:

Accommodation	$400
Recreation/entertainment	$100
Meals in restaurants	$180
Food purchased in stores	$15
Handcraft purchases	$500
Total	$1195

Conclusions

This couple represents ideal tourists, who spend 7 days on PEI and see and do all there is to experience. They used the VIG as a bible on the trip and referred to it, along with the map, when approaching different craft shops or attractions. MMI: ensure that this type of traveller leaves with a positive affection for PEI, so they will become repeat visitors, even if a few years later. As destinations are sought out largely through recommendations from friends, there is no better way of advertising than through the provision of excellent service while travellers are visiting the island. (The *Visitor's Information Guide* is a closure on the sale to visit local establishments. It plays a major role in the short-listing decision process.)

The majority of the attractions that the Ozinkos visited were read about in the *Visitor's Information Guide*. When queried about their current experience of PEI and what adjectives came to mind to describe the island, the following statements were mentioned by one or both of them: 'undisturbed'; 'so quaint and peaceful'; 'untouched gem'; 'privacy/seclusion'; 'natural beauty'; and 'friendliness'.

Note that Fig. 3.4 includes important details affecting the Ozinko's trip to PEI. These details include the wife reading the *Anne of Green Gables* book in her youth, attending and receiving literature at the PEI booth while at the Calgary Stampede, friends' recommendations to visit PEI, and the availability to make travel plans that combined visits to both Nova Scotia and PEI. Each of the four factors appears to represent necessary, but not sufficient, conditions leading to the decision for leisure travel to PEI.

The main conclusions for theory are that: (i) each of the ten propositions receives strong support in this case study; and (ii) conjunctive occurrences of unplanned and planned events and thoughts are antecedents leading to first-time leisure visits. Consider how encouraging the reading of *Anne of Green Gables*, at least among Canadian schoolchildren, likely influences leisure travel some 10–20 years later in their lives – given that the reading is enriched by additional information collected at such events as the Calgary Stampede. Such case-study evidence supports the marketing value of participating in distant special-attraction events.

First-Time Visit by an Older American Couple

Synopsis

This interview report includes responses by an American couple visiting PEI for pleasure for 7 nights in August 1993. The travel party is a senior American couple – first-time visitors to PEI. A chance to relax and escape from daily concerns was the principal motive of the trip, with additional motives being a chance to learn about another culture, and to observe and experience nature. PEI was the primary destination, with the secondary destination being Iles-de-la-Madeleine. Exhibit 3.4 and Fig. 3.5 summarize this couple's decision process and purchase–consumption system with respect to visiting PEI.

The couple spent their 9 days touring PEI from west to east, exploring beaches and hitting every lobster dinner they could find. 'We love lobster' they were reported as saying. Total expenditures at the time of the interview were $955. PEI criticism: 'We were Anned to death'. They also did not like the fact that the National Park charges a $5.00 entrance fee just for driving through, and therefore did not make the drive. They found the Cavendish area overcrowded and over commercialized.

They used the PEI *Visitor's Information Guide* (VIG) to plan their itinerary and found it very useful. When asked what first comes to mind when thinking of PEI, Mr Dougherty said, 'The gorgeous coastline and lush growth on the island'. Mr Dougherty reported an unlikelihood of returning to PEI in 1994, 1995 due to his age, although being frequent travellers there are still many other places to visit while he is still able.

Interview procedure

The questionnaire was completed over a 1–2-hour period, in a face-to-face and telephone interview. The final portion of the interview was conducted over the telephone, the day following departure due to the Doughertys' desire to enter the boarding gate 20 minutes prior to plane departure. Data on the visiting party's intentions and actual actions were gathered. A

1-hour interview was conducted in a tense environment in a limited time-frame, where the visiting party communicated their decisions and activities related to their visit to PEI.

Description of the party visiting PEI and interview site/day

Demographics

The travel party interviewed consisted of a wife Mary Dougherty (MD) and her husband Donald (DD). MD answered all the questions at the airport and DD answered the questions asked over the telephone. MD and her husband are over sixty. Both have postgraduate training and work full time. The couple's annual income before taxes is between $35,000 and $50,000 (US dollars). They live in Cedar Grove, New Jersey, just outside of Newark.

Interview site and day

The interview took place at the Charlottetown Airport at noon on 3 August 1993, 1 hour prior to their flight departure. The interview was completed by MD while her husband was trying to retrieve a lost credit card. The temperature outside was in the high 20s°C, while the air conditioning was working on overtime.

Trip decisions for the total trip

PEI was the main destination of this visit, with a 2-night, 3-day excursion to Iles-de-la-Madeleine. They had planned their visit to PEI within the past year. The party flew from Newark, New Jersey, to Halifax, where they caught a connecting flight to PEI.

Planning horizon

MD reported extensive planning for this trip due to the fact that they had to contact the majority of the B&Bs in advance to make reservations. Very few of the reservations could be made through a 1–800 number. MMI: B&B enterprises may want to use the 1–800 number service to ease bookings from distant clients and possibly increase their revenues.

Exhibit 3.4. Summary of senior American couple's visit to PEI (Ex 16).

This couple travels frequently and this is their first trip to PEI. They had been planning for a year. They used an agent for their travel arrangements. They booked their bed and breakfast accommodation, during their 7-night stay, themselves. They made extensive use of the *Visitor's Guide*, both prior to their visit and once they were on the island. They felt the Cavendish area was ruined and that 'Anne' had been overdone. Key words: older couple, medium income, 7-day stay, first-timers, fly/drive, high involvement once on island, lobster, extensive arrangements (accommodation), travel agent, long planning time frame

Decision area 2,0,S05	Destinations	Route/mode to and in PEI	Accommodation during PEI stay	Activities in PEI	PEI Regions Visited	Attractions visited including restaurants	Gifts and purchases leaving PEI with
Consideration set and choices	PEI with added excursion to Iles-de-la-Madeleine, PQ	Driving too far and time consuming. Flew Newark–Halifax–Charlottetown. Rental car	B&Bs; a different one each night	Beaches, museums, boat tour, lobster suppers, pubs, restaurants and crafts store	Queens County, Kings County, Prince County. Followed the shore west to east	Dublin Pub, St Anne's, St Margaret's, Northumberland lobster suppers, Miscouche Acadian museum, Orwell Museum, seal watching, lighthouses	Books and tape (A. of G.G.). Earrings, multiple small gifts
Motives	Explore a new area, escape daily concerns, relax. Learn about another culture. Economical	Car 'more freedom'. Ferry for off island trip	Wanted to explore the whole island with a limited time span	Nature interest, educational learning experience	Nature lovers, wanted to stay away from 'commercialized areas'	They 'love lobster'. Wanted to observe nature. Educational experience for museums. Irish music	Books requested. Earrings (native work) wanted for wife. Gifts of local work
Information search and use	Read VIG prior to coming to PEI. Arranged B&B	Based their routes on VIG	Used B&B brochures provided by travel agent and VIG. 1-800# for bookings	Promotional literature. VIG, word of mouth	VIG the routes went through each region	Used VIG. Some word of mouth. Some discovered on their own	Other than A. of G.G. paraphernalia found by chance
Outcomes	Very pleased. Incredible coast line, the VIG is 'worn out'. Felt 'Anned to death'	Route and mode gorgeous and as expected, 'lush growth'	Very pleased, no complaints	Did not like Cavendish! Museums 'were great'. 'We love lobster!' Avoided most craft shops.	Enjoyed the coastline. Felt some areas were ruined	Lobster dinners great	Loved local (native) work – very unique

Notes from interviews: From Cedar Grove, New Jersey. Stayed 7 nights at various B&B. Income range; $35,000–50,000 (US). Expenditure: $955. First-time visitors. Both over 60 years of age. Work status: both work full-time and have postgraduate training. Respondent: Elizabeth. Visitor segment: medium–distant, foreign, touring (fly/drive), senior market. PEI was primary destination.

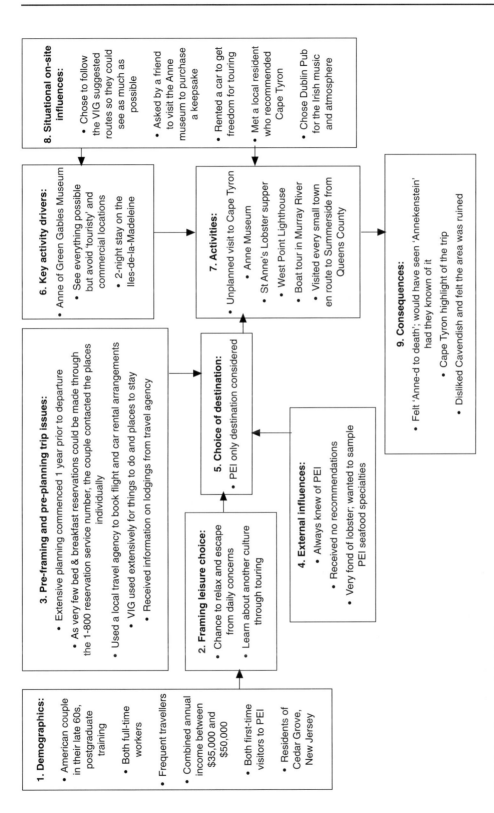

1. Demographics:
- American couple in their late 60s, postgraduate training
- Both full-time workers
- Frequent travellers
- Combined annual income between $35,000 and $50,000
- Both first-time visitors to PEI
- Residents of Cedar Grove, New Jersey

2. Framing leisure choice:
- Chance to relax and escape from daily concerns
- Learn about another culture through touring

3. Pre-framing and pre-planning trip issues:
- Extensive planning commenced 1 year prior to departure
- As very few bed & breakfast reservations could be made through the 1-800 reservation service number, the couple contacted the places individually
- Used a local travel agency to book flight and car rental arrangements
- VIG used extensively for things to do and places to stay
- Received information on lodgings from travel agency

4. External influences:
- Always knew of PEI
- Received no recommendations
- Very fond of lobster; wanted to sample PEI seafood specialties

5. Choice of destination:
- PEI only destination considered

6. Key activity drivers:
- Anne of Green Gables Museum
- See everything possible but avoid 'touristy' and commercial locations
- 2-night stay on the Iles-de-la-Madeleine

7. Activities:
- Unplanned visit to Cape Tyron
- Anne Museum
- St Anne's Lobster supper
- West Point Lighthouse
- Boat tour in Murray River
- Visited every small town en route to Summerside from Queens County

8. Situational on-site influences:
- Chose to follow the VIG suggested routes so they could see as much as possible
- Asked by a friend to visit the Anne museum to purchase a keepsake
- Rented a car to get freedom for touring
- Met a local resident who recommended Cape Tyron
- Chose Dublin Pub for the Irish music and atmosphere

9. Consequences:
- Felt 'Anne-d to death'; would have seen 'Annekenstein' had they known of it
- Cape Tyron highlight of the trip
- Disliked Cavendish and felt the area was ruined

Fig. 3.5. American couple in late 60s.

Assistance by travel professionals

MD used a travel agent (Cedar Grove Travel) to book their flight and arrange their rental car (a Ford Escort) through Budget Rental. Bed and breakfast information was given to MD by the travel agent and they, in turn, booked their own accommodation as they wanted to travel across PEI and would be staying in different places for each night.

Requesting Information from Travel Offices Before Visiting

No information was requested from any Canadian Provincial travel office. They received the VIG before beginning their visit and, with this, continued making bookings and doing further research and planning for their visit. They did find the VIG very helpful.

PEI planning questions

First learning about PEI

MD did not recall how she had learned of PEI and reported always knowing about it, 'through Geography I guess'. MD had read the book *Anne of Green Gables*; however, this was not a conscious factor in their decision-making to come to PEI. MD, as already stated, said 'I felt "Anned" to death'.

When asked if they had seen *Annekenstein* (a parody production of the *Anne of Green Gables* musical; *Annekenstein* is held in Charlottetown), MD responded, 'We would have loved to have seen it had we known about the play'. MMI: although 'Anne' is a traditional tourist attraction in PEI, some individuals feel this theme has been overdone. Possibly more promotion of a satirical view of 'Anne' could complement attendance at the regular musical.

PEI recommended for this trip?

MD reported no one recommended PEI as a vacation destination to them. They had never been to PEI before and felt it was an economical choice for a vacation destination. The main reason for the trip was to get away from daily concerns, while learning of another culture and observing and experiencing nature.

Using the VIG

MD reported extensive use of the VIG prior to arriving on PEI. 'The book is worn out', MD stated. The VIG was used prior to arrival to plan their travel route and decide where to stay and what to do.

PEI competitor considered but rejected

No other destination was considered as a principal destination.

Involvement in PEI destination choice

MD and her husband reported that they had equal shares in the decision of PEI as a destination choice. As well as being equally involved in the destination choice, MD and her husband were equally involved in the planning of their visit to PEI. They made use of a travel agent to plan getting to PEI and arrange their rental car. However, the travel agent in no way influenced their destination choice. Although they received the VIG prior to arriving on PEI, it also in no way influenced their destination choice. The VIG did, however, 'clinch the deal' for the activities and attractions they would do and see once on PEI.

PEI visit questions

MD and husband spent 7 nights on PEI, with 2 nights being spent on Iles-de-la-Madeleine. Being on PEI was the primary motivation leading to the add-on visit to Iles-de-la-Madeleine.

Main motives for PEI visit

MD reported three motives for their visit. MD assigned five votes to the chance to relax and escape from daily concerns. She assigned three votes to a chance to learn through touring about another 'culture', its art, history and cultural events, and two votes to a chance to observe and experience nature.

PEI trip route and destinations

MD and husband had no principal destination for their PEI visit. They had planned on seeing as much of PEI as they could in their stay, therefore choosing to follow the VIG recommended routes. They began their visit in Queens County and explored this county extensively, hitting Rocky Point, Canoe Cove and every small town and shore en route to Summerside, where they stayed their second night. Their third day was spent in the Evangeline area of Prince County, where they visited museums, other attractions and the West Point Lighthouse, spending the night in O'Leary at the Thomas B&B. The fourth day they returned to Queens County where they visited 'Anne of Green Gables Museum' (which they had been asked to visit and purchase a keepsake for a family member). An unplanned visit to Cape Tyron (recommended by a local) was the highlight of this day. 'It was the most beautiful place we saw on PEI' MD reported. After dining at St Ann's Lobster Dinners they spent the night in Darnley, once again at a B&B. The following (fifth day) was spent in Queens County and then their sixth day brought them into Kings County. MMI: the routes set out in the VIG were used by this visiting party; PEI may want to continue to recommend the routes as used in the VIG to parties who wish to see as much of PEI as possible in a limited time span, such as MD and husband.

Trip mode and route

MD chose to rent a car to allow them their freedom, although they would have taken a bus trip for the off-island excursion to Iles-de-la-Madeleine. 'The ferry is very expensive ($100.00 per car)' and upon return to PEI they needed a car to return them to the airport before departure. MMI: PEI tourism could consider a shuttle service to and from the airport for frequently visited PEI destinations. This particularly helps those who make off-island excursions while visiting PEI, as the Dougherty's did. MD reported only fleetingly considering alternative ways of getting to PEI, and the decision was made to fly, based on the distance and time required to drive to PEI. MMI: market PEI as a 'fly/drive' vacation destination for the American seniors market. The car rental agencies and airlines could work together to arrange a package best suited for this target, example: reduced rates on car rental when flying with local carriers. There was no choice offered to

enter and exit the Iles-de-la-Madeleine, as there is no alternative ferry service.

PEI activities and attractions visited

MD said, 'We had planned to see the island and whatever we could do we'd do.' They did such activities with aid of the VIG. MD mentioned they also found things to do/visit on their own. MD reported going to many beaches; however, she could not remember the names, other than Cavendish, which they did not enjoy. 'They've ruined that area', MD reported.

They visited several museums, educational/learning experience being the motive, and 'They were great', MD said. MD reported taking one boat tour on the Murray River, a 'Mussel Farm/Seal Watching Tour'. MD said the tour was, 'Enjoyable, but the only tour we knew of'. MD reported trying to avoid 'commercial, touristy places'. MMI: PEI might improve marketing the Provinces' outdoor activities and natural vistas for a target market such as the Doughertys. The VIG could have a section dedicated to nature lovers.

Evening restaurant dining

MD reported having all their meals in restaurants; due to fondness for lobster, they visited three lobster suppers. MD reported having chose 'Dublin Pub' to dine, for the Irish music. Otherwise they ate at local restaurants while en route to specific destinations. MMI: research the possibility of tours specifically designed for those who 'love lobster', by means of travelling to differing lobster suppers, in conjunction with lobster-fishing tours. In this manner two industries might complement each other and a greater awareness of each might be achieved.

Activities not engaged in

Available activities not engaged in by MD and her husband include deep-sea fishing, golfing, farmers' markets, art galleries and live theatre. The two latter-mentioned activities MD reported not seeing advertisements for and therefore not being aware of. They tried to avoid all craft shops. MMI: this particular market would have participated in some of the above-mentioned activities had they been more aware of these activities. Although this party was not at all interested in craft shops, there are other market segments that are more responsive target markets. PEI might consider ensuring that arts and crafts segments and arts and theatre segments are separate entities within the VIG.

The accommodation decision and experiences

MD and husband made their accommodation choices in advance using B&B promotional brochures and the VIG. They had no main accommodation and reported choosing their accommodation 'just by chance', selecting them out of the book coordinating their accommodation with their chosen route. MMI: the PEI VIG should continue listing accommodation with routes as this is an effective marketing tool for this particular target market.

Gifts and other purchases for returning home with

DD reported leaving PEI with three purchases, *Anne of Green Gables* books and tape valued at $43, earrings valued at $15 and a collection of small gifts valued at $90. DD reported having intended to return home with gifts; however, they had no specific gifts in mind other than *Anne of Green Gables* paraphernalia for a sister who is unable to travel and was raised on *Anne of Green Gables*. 'Just like the Japanese', DD was quoted as saying. The other purchases were bought by chance while browsing; DD could not remember the names of the shops. DD particularly liked the earrings and wanted them for his wife. DD stated 'male supremacy' clinched the deal on the purchase of the earrings.

Expenditure breakdown

DD reported their total expenditure to include the following: $240.00 on accommodation; $80.00 recreation/entertainment; $250.00

meals in restaurants; $10.00 food and alcohol purchases in PEI stores; $150.00 gifts (golf shirt) anticipating another purchase; $240.00 rental car; and $85.00 gasoline purchase on PEI. Thus their total expenditure was estimated to equal $955 for their 7-night stay on PEI. This amount does not include their airfare to and from PEI, or costs incurred involving their off-island excursion to Iles-de-le-Madeleine. MMI: if PEI implements specialized tour packages marketed in the USA, geared towards specific interests of seniors, increased awareness of what PEI has to offer visitors may be necessary. The result of such awareness building may be placing PEI in these seniors' consideration sets, which would, in turn, lead to PEI as a preferred destination.

Observations about customer choice processes

The decision to visit PEI by this party was made prior to receiving any promotional literature about PEI. Plans were made after receiving the B&B brochure and VIG. The Dougherty's eliminated the alternative of driving to PEI, due to time and distance involved. They then allowed a travel agent to make route decisions regarding getting to PEI. The accommodation decisions were made by chance, using promotional literature, including the VIG. The choices of restaurants were made due to their food preferences, and choice of activities due to their interests. Their purchases were spontaneous other than the one gift purchase requested by a family member. In this case, the location of shops is important in key areas to draw customers who have no specific purchases in mind prior to arrival.

Economic reasons and 'never having been there' were key decisions in coming to PEI. The availability of bed and breakfasts on PEI is a key marketing item in this case, whereas higher-priced accommodation would not attract this market.

Although their decision was made without the aid of literature, the VIG determined their routes once on PEI and, therefore, sending the VIG to visitors in advance could encourage travel to rural areas on PEI, and thus increase revenues in these areas.

This case study points to a market disinterested in Cavendish and 'Anne'. This visiting party could also be influenced to purchase package tours. Nature tours and lobster supper tours, or a combination of the two themes, are options in attracting this market. This visiting party was highly interested in understanding another culture and nature, therefore information on regional agriculture/fishery festivals (example, Blueberry Festival, Oyster Festival, Potato Blossom Festival) may have increased their awareness, and thus encouraged them to visit these areas.

PEI as a primary destination choice with off-island excursions

The fact that this PEI visit had included an off-island excursion should be emphasized. The number of visiting seniors from the USA interested in touring the Maritime Provinces is likely to be substantial. Thus, marketing PEI as a primary destination with easily accessible off-island excursions may be a successful strategy for reaching this target market. This strategy might also attract visitors residing in the Province of Quebec.

The VIG and PEI map as marketing tools

MD reported use of the VIG extensively before arriving on PEI. It was not mentioned if it was used often once on PEI, although it was stated 'the book is worn out'. The VIG did serve the function of drawing the visiting party to different rural areas. It created awareness of areas and attractions otherwise unknown to the visiting party. The description of the coastline on the visitor's map of PEI could be found as being partially responsible for DD's positive opinion of the coastline, expressed over the telephone interview. Offering such descriptions may be beneficial, resulting in positive association with the coastline and thus PEI.

Grounded theory conclusions

This older American couple, most likely visiting PEI for one-time only in their lifetimes, is repre-

sentative (and likely more typical than atypical) of a substantial market target segment for the Province. The data on this case provide substantial support for all ten propositions, especially P_2 concerning the influence of the VIG on planning activities and places to stay. Such data indicate a likely double impact of the VIG in: (i) influencing the decision to visit PEI (although this couple did not verbally state such an influence); and (ii) influencing what they did and where they spent their nights on PEI (the couple used the VIG extensively for guiding their days in PEI). Using the VIG appears to have been a necessary and sufficient attribution of several specific behaviours related to this couple's visit to PEI.

First-Time Visit by a Young European (Austrian) Couple

Synopsis

This interview reports the responses of two Austrian tourists travelling around the world, who spent 3 nights on PEI. Brigitte Binder (BB) and Gerti Lindmoser (GL) wanted to visit Halifax, but there was no flight to Halifax by their airline. They chose PEI because 'it is the closest stop to Halifax', said BB. They used the VIG to choose the places they wanted to see and they described the VIG as 'helpful'. Although they had no expectations for PEI, they described the trip as 'it was OK. [We] enjoyed everything'. The total expenditure of their 3-night stay at PEI was $474. When asked their intention to return to PEI in the near future, they reported that they are very unlikely to return because '[We] liked it very much but it is too far [from Austria]'. Exhibit 3.5 and Fig. 3.6 summarize this couple's decision process and purchase–consumption system with respect to visiting PEI.

Description of the travel party and the interview site/day

Demographics

The travel party included Brigitte Binder (BB) and her friend Gerti Lindmoser (GL). They

Exhibit 3.5. Summary of a European couple's visit to PEI (Case study 10).

Both travellers are from Austria, although they live in different cities. They visited PEI on their way to Halifax. They spent 3 days of their 30-day trip on the island. Both were in their 20s, employed on a low to medium income. There was little or no preparation for their PEI visit, although they used the VIG to select the places to see on the island. They saw a range of places: National Park, North Rustico beach, the chocolate factory, Rocky Point Indian Village, and the Borshaw Car Museum. They stayed in a B&B. The main aim of the trip was to see some of PEI as they were going to go near it to visit Halifax. They were unlikely to return in the near future as they felt it was a long way from Europe. Key words: foreign couple (not living together), low to medium income, 3-day stay as part of a month-long trip, first-time visitors, unlikely to return, both from Austria, unplanned activities, short planning time frame, low involvement once on island

Decision Area 2,0,S02	Destinations	Route/mode to and in PEI	Accommodation during PEI stay	Activities in PEI	PEI regions visited	Attractions visited including restaurants	Gifts and purchases leaving PEI with
Consideration set and choices	Austria, Munich, New York, Ottawa, Montreal, Ottawa, Toronto, Niagara Falls, Boston, New Brunswick, PEI, New Orleans, Vancouver, New York, Europe	Fly to Charlottetown from Boston, drive to PEI, New Brunswick, Borden terminal to exit PEI	Smallman's B&B, Tiachnabruaich, airport	National Park, Car Museum, Indian Village, Craft Studio	Charlottetown, Summerside, Stanley Bridge, North Rustico, New Brunswick, Victoria, Rocky Point	National Park, North Rustico Beach, Car Museum, Craft Studio, Indian Village, Rocky Point, Victoria Chocolate Factory	Nothing
Motives	PEI was used as a means to get to Halifax; 'We have friends on the east and west coast'	It is best to move around by car	Found as needed; airport, as very early flight	Beach fascinating; Weather good; National Park: looked interesting; car museum, Indian village	Waited to drive to Halifax by bridge	Wanted to see National Park, weather good; looked interesting (car museum and Indian village)	Not planned to buy anything
Information search and use	Oekista Travel Agency for PEI, book; 'We learn about this place when we arrive here'	VIG for maps	Saw both inns on the route	VIG	VIG for maps	VIG	N/A
Outcomes	No expectations but we like it very much OK	No expectations for ferry but it was OK	Better than expected. Stallman's: friendly and clean, good food. Tiachnabruaich: OK though no paved drive	No expectations, but enjoyed everything	No expectations, 'enjoyed everything'	No expectations, but enjoyed everything	N/A

Notes from interviews: From Austria. Stayed 3 nights at various locations. Income range for each was between $35,000–$50,000. First-time visitors. Both are in their 20s and single. Work status: both full-time employed. Visitor segment: far-distant, foreign, touring (world), young market.

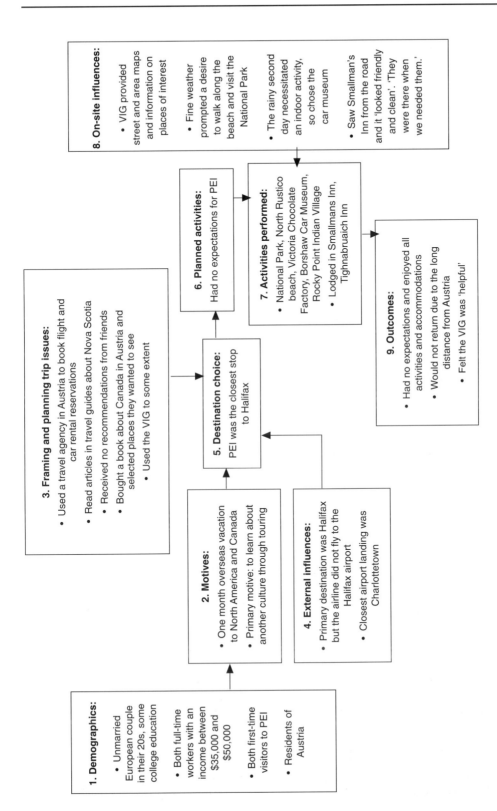

Fig. 3.6. Young Austrian couple.

were both in their 20s and single. They both have some college-level formal education. They were employed full-time and their annual income each, before taxes, was between $35,001 and $50,000. They lived in Austria.

Interview site/day

The interview was conducted at Charlottetown Airport when BB and GL were waiting for their plane to Boston. It was a Thursday and the interview started at 4.30 p.m.

Trip decision for the total trip

This trip for the two friends included a total of 30 days away from their Austrian home. They flew from Austria to Munich, Germany and then flew to New York. In New York, they rented a car and drove to Ottawa and stayed there with their friends for 3 nights. From Ottawa, they drove to Montreal and stayed there for 1 day. They then drove back to Ottawa, stayed there 1 night, and drove to Toronto. From Toronto, they drove to Niagara Falls and stayed there for 1 day. They then drove to Boston. From Boston, they flew to Charlottetown. They stayed there for 1 day and then rented a car and drove to New Brunswick. They stayed there for 2 days and visited Shediac and Moncton. From New Brunswick, they drove to PEI and stayed for 3 nights. After their 2-day visit to PEI, they planned to fly back to Boston and fly to New Orleans for the weekend. From New Orleans, they were to fly to Vancouver and stay there for 1 or 2 weeks with relatives. They then planned to fly to New York. From New York, they were to fly to Europe.

Planning horizon

They reported engaging in some planning before they made the trip. BB said, 'We live in different cities and didn't have time to meet. So we phoned each other to organize and rest a rough plan'. They wanted to visit Halifax but the airline they took did not land in Halifax. So they chose PEI because it is the closest stop to Halifax. Halifax was their primary destination and they arrived at PEI by chance.

Assistance by travel professionals

BB reported visiting the OEKISTA travel agency in Salzburg, Austria before their trip. 'They arranged for our trans-Atlantic flights and car reservation for [our] first car rental', reported BB.

Requesting information from travel offices before visiting

BB and GL did not contact any travel offices before they visited PEI. GL said, 'Brigitte bought a book about Canada before we came here (PEI). We read it and picked out places we want to see'.

PEI planning questions

First learning about PEI

BB reported that they read articles in travellers' guides and wanted to go to Nova Scotia. 'We learned about this place when we arrived here', she said.

PEI recommended for this trip? Why PEI included?

BB and GL reported that no one recommended PEI for their trip. The only reason for them to choose PEI was, 'It is closest to Halifax'.

Using the VIG

BB reported using the VIG to some extent. '[VIG has] map of the streets, accommodations, and sites.[It is] helpful', said BB. Note that Halifax was their primary destination and their PEI visit was because 'no flight [to Halifax] with this airline', said BB.

Involvement in the PEI destination decision

BB and GL both reported that they were equally involved in making the decision.

PEI visit

BB and GL stayed for 3 nights at PEI. They reported that their major destination was not

PEI. BB said, 'We plan to spend two weeks on the east coast and two weeks on the west coast'. For the reason of this choice, she said, 'It is most interesting. We have friends on east and west coasts.'

Main motives for the trip

Out of ten votes, BB and GL assigned five votes to a chance to learn through touring about another culture. They assigned two votes to a chance to visit friends and relatives. They assigned one vote each to a chance to relax and escape from daily concerns and a chance to observe and experience nature.

PEI trip route and destinations

On day 1 of their stay at PEI, BB and GL drove from Charlottetown to the National Park. They walked on the beach of North Rustico. They stayed at a bed and breakfast inn at Stanley Bridge. On day two, they drove to Summerside and exited PEI from Borden terminal to New Brunswick. On day three, they drove back from New Brunswick and entered PEI from the Borden terminal. They drove to Victoria. They visited the Chocolate Factory and the Borshaw Car Museum. They then drove to Charlottetown and stayed in a bed and breakfast inn in Meadowbank. On day four, they visited the Rock Point Indian Village and drove back to Charlottetown. They then stayed in the airport overnight to catch the 5.45 a.m. flight.

Trip route and mode

BB and GL chose a fly-and-drive mode for their trip. They reported to have not considered other alternatives because, they said, 'It is best to move around by car'. They picked PEI as their destination because, 'We thought this was closest to Halifax and we planned to go by "bridge" to Halifax', said BB. Both BB and GL were involved in making this decision. As for the ferry, they chose the closest terminal because there was a kilometre limit for the car (4 days = 800 km). BB said, 'We had no expectations for the ferry service but it was OK'.

PEI activities and attractions visited

Prior to their trip, BB and GL did not plan on any particular activities. They visited the national park beach because BB reported, 'The weather was fine and we wanted to exercise. The beach has fascinations. And we wanted to go to the National Park'. They picked the car museum because, 'It was raining and [the museum] looked interesting', said BB. They visited the Indian Village also because, 'It looked interesting', as GL put it. They went to a craft studio called the House of Dolls near the Indian Village. They described their experience with these places visited as, 'We had no expectations. But we really enjoyed everything'.

Evening restaurant dining

BB and GL did not dine out in the evenings during their stay at PEI. They did spend about $60 on meals in fast food restaurants.

Activities not engaged in

BB and GL did not visit any art galleries and farmers' markets. They did not engage in golfing, boat tours or deep-sea fishing. They did not attend any theatres. They did not dine out in the evenings and did not have a lobster supper. They did not visit any bars, either.

The accommodation decision and experience

They stayed 2 nights in bed and breakfast inns at PEI and 1 night at the Charlottetown Airport. They stayed one night in the 'Stallman's Inn' at Stanley Bridge and another night in the 'Tiachnabruaich Inn' at Meadowbank. They chose the Stallman's because, 'We saw another one in the guide but couldn't find it. And we saw this one on the road', said BB. Their experience with this inn was better than expected. 'They were very friendly. It was clean and the food is good', reported BB. For the other inn at Meadowbank, BB said, 'The first impression wasn't terrific. There is no paved drive. But it was very nice'. 'They were there when we need them and we didn't book any hotels [before we came here]', GL added. When asked about the things they would like to see changed at the inns, they said 'nothing'. Both BB and GL were involved in making the accommodation decision.

Gifts and other purchases returning home with

BB and GL did not plan to buy anything at PEI, and they bought nothing.

Expenditure breakdown

BB and GL reported their total expenditure to include the following: $65 on accommodation; $30 for recreation/entertainment; $60 for meals in restaurants; $20 for food and alcohol purchases in PEI stores; $31 ferry tickets; $45 gasoline; $223 car rental. The total expenditure of BB and GL during their 3 nights' stay at PEI was approximately $474.

Grounded theory conclusions from the European visit case study

At least two observations deserve emphasis. First, the impact of external situational influences is sometimes greater than the framing of leisure choices. These European visitors represent 'accidental tourists' in the truest sense of the concept – they had severely limited knowledge and no interest in visiting PEI during their trip to North America. The PEI visit was a glitch in their purchase–consumption system that included a desire and plan to visit Nova Scotia.

Secondly, such accidental tourism can sometimes result in rather extensive overnight stays and trip activities. Thus, the seemingly unlikely theoretical conjunction of travellers not planning on visiting or staying overnight, but who stay 4 nights or longer, sometimes occur. Studying such cases empirically enriches the development of a grounded theory, as well as providing important clues for developing effective destination marketing strategies. For the latter, the data from other European visitors, similar to that provided by these two

Austrian informants, suggest that PEI may be unable to stand alone as a core destination for such markets. Planning joint marketing programmes among the Canadian Maritime Provinces may benefit the smaller populated – and out of the way – Provinces in particular. Designing visit packages and promoting joint visits to two or more Maritime Provinces during a single trip is likely to be appealing for such customer segments more than others.

Limitations and Suggestions for Further Research

The case studies presented provide investigative evidence for the value of systems thinking (Senge, 1990), in examining purchase–consumption systems of leisure travel decision processes and behaviours. While such research provides data useful for building grounded theories of what is happening and why in the thinking and doing processes of customers, certain large-scale surveys and field experiments of the impact of marketing and measured variables (e.g. demographic variables) are necessary to generalize the resulting theory to populations.

The case studies reported do go beyond the implicit models of destination marketing executives in indicating the immediate and 'downstream' impacts of marketing tools, such as the impacts of *This Week in PEI* and the PEI VIG. The findings suggest that the biggest impact of the VIG is not in attracting visits, but in expanding the scope of visit behaviours. This conclusion is *not* meant to suggest that the marketing investment in the VIG was unprofitable in causing visits to occur that would not have otherwise have occurred; however, a substantial portion of the total VIG impact likely due to its influence on increasing the range of behaviours – including length of stays – of visitors using the VIG versus not using the VIG.

Contributions to Theory and Practice

Grounded theory serves to 'put people back into marketing research' (Zaltman, 1997). Certainly, collecting and mapping consumers' emic views of their planning and doing processes helps to revise and deepen the etic (i.e. researcher's) views of reality.

The main contribution to grounded theory from emic storytelling research in leisure travel may be the observation that no one dependent variable alone is both necessary and sufficient in influencing travellers' thoughts or actions. Even when a travel party reports experiences including bad accommodation, that alone is not sufficient to cause the entire trip to be judged a disaster; the conjunction of two bad accommodation experiences in a row and the lack of available alternative accommodation, resulted in days of frustration and the final judgement that PEI is a bad place to visit.

Similarly, receiving the copy of *This Week in PEI*, by itself, was necessary but not enough to cause the leisure trip to PEI reported by the New Brunswick family. In reviewing Fig. 3.2, several factors contribute to the family members reaching the unanimous decision to visit PEI – one or two of these factors appear neither necessary nor sufficient, such as the mother's remembering a visit to the Anne homestead years ago.

Figure 3.7 provides some summary information, based in part on the findings in the case studies presented as well as large-scale survey research findings (details available in Woodside *et al.*, 1997). Figure 3.7 indicates the need to ensure the design of effective PEI marketing strategies for three principal origin markets: residents in other Maritime Provinces; Ontario and the USA (especially New England and the mid-Atlantic states). Focusing on such an exhibit raises interesting marketing strategy issues – such as, what would happen if PEI placed the VIG in the hands of residents living in the other Maritime Provinces? Would the number of behaviours, including their length of stays in PEI, increase dramatically for these nearby consumers? Such an issue can be answered scientifically – with treatment and control groups, and such a study is suggested for future research.

Most likely three to five unique and valuable customer segments exist within each of the 'Big 3' origin markets for PEI. Certainly, not all PEI visitors from New Brunswick are young families and not all American visitors are seniors. The proposal here is that in-depth

case studies employing the long interview method of about five travel parties (see McCracken, 1988), of each of three customer segments, from each of the Big 3 markets, will provide both confirmatory evidence and additional nuances about visitors, critical for achieving success in PEI's tourism export industry (i.e. about 45 in-depth case studies). Such a research approach is useful for building grounded theories of leisure travel for other destinations as well.

Storytelling Theory and Strategy Applications

Given that a substantial share of unconscious thinking and learning occurs in stories (see Weick, 1995; Shank, 1999), in-depth reporting of real-life stories and advancing grounded theory of story-based thoughts and behaviour is worthy of scholarly attention. Also, consider Shank's (1999, p. 96) conclusion, 'When confronted with new problems, people almost inevitably search their memories for similar problems they have already solved (Johnson and Seifert, 1992; Gholson *et al.*, 1996). They are, in essence, recalling their own prior problem-solving stories'. People make sense of their worlds, and who they are, from the stories of their lived experiences that they tell to themselves and others. Research on emic sense-making is largely research to collect introspective stories (cf. Wallendorf and Brucks, 1993).

The application findings reported by Adaval and Wyer (1998) provide a very practical justification for thick descriptions of emic interpretations in whole stories. Whole-story based advertisements may have greater impact in building preference and action than simply listing benefits for a visiting a destination. Thus, destination marketers may want to ground their advertising campaigns in real-life stories of successful visits – successful as illustrated by the emic stories learned from storytelling research. Can such ads be designed effectively without deep emic knowing? Probably not.

Consequently, advertising creative work and storytelling ads may be more effective if they build from emic knowledge (i.e. empirical, case-based, introspective thick

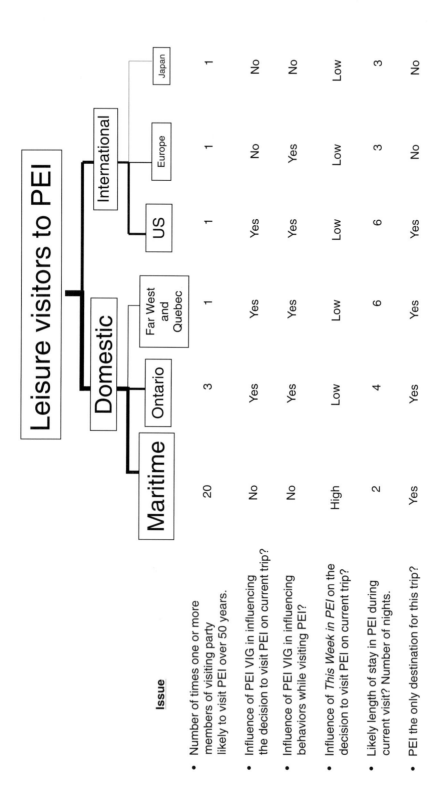

| Issue | Maritime | Domestic | | International | | |
		Ontario	Far West and Quebec	US	Europe	Japan
• Number of times one or more members of visiting party likely to visit PEI over 50 years.	20	3	1	1	1	1
• Influence of PEI VIG in influencing the decision to visit PEI on current trip?	No	Yes	Yes	Yes	No	No
• Influence of PEI VIG in influencing behaviors while visiting PEI?	No	Yes	Yes	Yes	Yes	No
• Influence of *This Week in PEI* on the decision to visit PEI on current trip?	High	Low	Low	Low	Low	Low
• Likely length of stay in PEI during current visit? Number of nights.	2	4	6	6	3	3
• PEI the only destination for this trip?	Yes	Yes	Yes	Yes	No	No

Fig. 3.7. Summary of findings. Different font sizes and chart lines for customer segments reflect the total export revenues for Prince Edward Island (PEI) contributed by tourism expenditures (see Tufte, 2003).

descriptions) rather than building using only the implicit etic views held by copywriters, or from variable-based, empirical-positivistic, sample-based studies. How do seniors from America go about planning and doing their once-in-their-lifetimes visits to PEI? How do repeat visitors to PEI from New Brunswick go about planning and doing their 18th visit? Thick descriptions of real-life stories told by participant-informants are likely to answer such questions well and provide information useful for effective storytelling ad copywriting and visualizations.

Emic storytelling research is likely to include reports of bad visits, such as the one described by the Ontario couple visiting PEI. The nuances reported in such bad visit stories suggest necessary design improvements in product and service offerings. Consequently, the practical value of emic storytelling research goes beyond creating advertisements effective in delivering visitors – such research helps identify specific product features that need to be redesigned, refurbished, quickly, before customers' negative evaluations snowball into permanent customer loss and bad publicity.

4 Introduction to the Theory and Investigation of Planned and Realized Consumer Behaviour

Explaining Gaps in Consumers' Plans and Behaviours

This chapter addresses a fundamental question in consumer behaviour: What explains the difference between what consumers plan to consume versus what they actually consume? The question is explored from three perspectives. First, the influence of product information on both planned and realized consumption behaviours is tested by grouping respondents into users and non-users of product information and investigating for differences in consumption patterns.

Secondly, changes that occur between planned and realized behaviours are exam-ined in the context of customer characteristics, such as product experience, income and geographical origin. These two areas of enquiry represent the major managerial contributions of the chapter.

Thirdly, the chapter probes theory by applying Henry Mintzberg's 1978 model of planned and unplanned organizational strategy to consumer strategies for the purchases of products and services (see Fig. 4.1). Heretofore, Mintzberg's (1978) model has been untested in the consumer behaviour academic literature. The model has two advantages for consumer behaviour researchers: it offers a new technique for matching intentions to actual behaviours, and, by extension, enables the

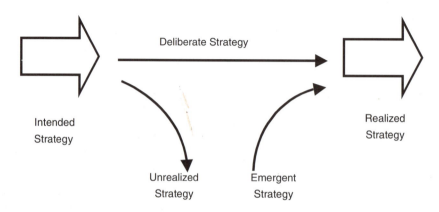

Fig. 4.1. Types of strategies (source: Mintzberg, 1978, p. 945).

identification of products whose actual consumption levels have failed to match the intended consumption levels. Most importantly, it offers a rich interpretation of how people behave.

The factors underlying consumers' planned and actual consumption behaviours are explored across six variables: spending, length of stay, attractions, destinations, accommodation and activities. Two data sets – derived from surveys administered upon entry to, and upon exit from, the research setting – are compared using ratio analyses. The research setting is the Canadian island province of Prince Edward Island, a popular summer holiday destination for North American and overseas visitors. The chapter generates and tests a series of hypotheses that relate to the influence of product information and demographics on realized and planned behaviours of visitors to Prince Edward Island. 'Product information' refers to the glossy, visitors' information guide that is produced and widely distributed for visitors to tourist destinations, in this case Prince Edward Island.

Why examine planned consumption versus actual consumption?

Personal experience tells us that what we plan is not always what we eventually do; conversely, what we do, we do not always intend. The same axiom holds true for consumption behaviour. First, we form intentions to purchase goods or services, or to consume experiences. Then we either actuate them, not actuate them or we consume something unplanned for. An unplanned behaviour may be the result of either an unpremeditated and spontaneous action (impulse purchase) or a previous intention that has been postponed or forgotten. Research, in mostly retail settings, has confirmed the remarkable prevalence of unplanned purchases, which account for one-half or more of total purchases (Kollat and Willett, 1967; Point-of-Purchase Institute, 1995, cited by Wood, 1998).

This study explores the nexus between planned and actual behaviours by examining the influences upon intentions and actual behaviour, whether they be planned,

unplanned or, in fact, not done at all. We offer fresh theoretical insights into consumer decision behaviour and provide strategic insights into how managers can segment their market more efficiently and communicate information more effectively to more customers.

This area of study is not the conventional approach to planned and actual behaviours. Previous research into intentions and consumption has overwhelmingly focused on planned behaviours, or intentions, and specifically with two aims: to improve the use of intention measurement to improve the predictive power of future behaviour, and to influence purchase behaviour. Although a multitude of factors and situations interfere or constrain an individual's ability to act upon his or her intentions (e.g. Belk, 1974, 1975; Filiatrault and Ritchie, 1988), intention is still an important construct found to be significantly related to actual behaviour.

Models of consumer behaviour typically treat intention (or purchase decision) as the immediate antecedent of purchase (e.g. Howard and Sheth, 1969; Engel et al., 1993; Peter and Olson, 1999). Intention and the subsequent consumption behaviour are regarded as fundamentally indistinguishable. Howard and Sheth (1969) state this explicitly: 'We may characterize intention to buy as a response short of actual purchase behaviour'. Other disciplines reflect a similar approach. Communication theory, for example, focuses extensively on planning, but does not account for changes in plans prior to actuation (e.g. Berger and Dibattista, 1999). Despite the existence of situational and individual-specific factors that often arise and, in many cases, cause shifts in intentions (cf. Belk, 1975), behaviours that are not planned or intentions that are not actuated have not been conceptualized in consumer behaviour models. Foxall (2000, p. 93) labels marketing theory's aversion to the study of unplanned and impulsive behaviour as 'pathological'.

Mintzberg (1978) used his typology to explore beyond the conventional interpretation of the concept of strategy which, he argued, had focused too heavily on the formation of intentions and too little on the process leading up to the enactment of the behaviour. In his words:

[C]onceiving strategy in terms of intentions means restricting research to the study of perceptions of what those who, it is believed, make strategy intend to do. And that kind of research – of intentions devoid of behaviour – simply is not very interesting or productive.

(Mintzberg, 1978, p. 465)

For Mintzberg, 'strategy' is more complex than a simple course of action adopted for the purpose of carrying out intentions. To achieve a deeper understanding of how organizations exhibit the strategic behaviours that they do, Mintzberg argues, we must examine the influences prior to the behaviour, and not simply intentions at the beginning of the process that may, or may not, result in the fulfilment of the original aim. Mintzberg follows the path of behavioural change from formation to implementation of organizational strategies. Underlying Mintzberg's research is his observation that 'strategies become consistencies in the behavior of organizations' (Mintzberg, 1978, p. 466). His related research involved the search for consistencies in decision making behaviour, the investigation of their appearance and disappearance, and the analysis of the relationships between intended and realized strategies (Mintzberg, 1973, 1978, 1987; Mintzberg and Waters, 1982, 1985).

Mintzberg categorized behavioural decisions and outcomes into three 'strategies': emergent, unrealized and deliberate. This chapter proposes a fourth category, a hitherto neglected element of consumer decision making, and what we refer to as 'unplanned/ unrealized' strategies (see Fig. 4.2). This fourth

cell can result from one of two thought processes: the consumption activity could have been considered and then rejected, or not considered and not done. Four possibilities exist to explain this final cell: (i) available to do, considered but not selected; (ii) available but not considered; (iii) unavailable but sought and learned to be unavailable; and (iv) unavailable and not considered. The last possibility is an empty set but not nonsense: new consumption activities often convert unavailability and not considered into available and considered; for example, prior to their creation, Disney World in Florida and in France were unavailable and not considered.

Testing Mintzberg's concepts of emergent (unplanned but done), realized and unrealized strategies, and by adding a fourth, unplanned and not realized behaviour, has the potential of generating fresh insights into a neglected area of consumer research. The research is the first time known that the discrepancies and similarities between consumers' plans and actual behaviour are measured and interpreted for major consumer services.

The classification of consumption outcomes according to the four 'strategies' represents a useful theoretical contribution to the understanding of what influences consumers in the actualization of their behavioural plans. Similarly, the discrepancies and similarities across a variety of consumption experiences that the research identifies are likely to assist public and private sector tourism marketers to craft more effective marketing communication strategies by more efficiently allocating scarce resources.

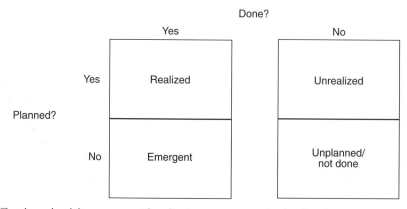

Fig. 4.2. The planned and done strategy grid: realized, emergent, unrealized and unplanned/not done strategies.

Points of theoretical interest

Investigations into the relationship between intentions and consumption behaviours in consumer behaviour can be classified in two ways: research to improve the predictability of purchases based on expressed intentions and research that quantifies (and occasionally seeks to explain) the degree of unplanned, mostly impulse, purchases. This chapter seeks to extend our understanding of the relationship between intention and consumption behaviour by investigating the factors that explain the shifts in consumption behaviour that consumers make between their planned and actual consumption acts.

This work contributes to the study of consumer behaviour in two ways. First, the influences of key variables – product information and consumer characteristics (in this research, demographics and product experience) – on the relationship between planned and actual consumption behaviours are examined and identified. While marketing research is used routinely to explore the predictive accuracy of intentions, there have been few empirical examinations of the influences that cause individuals to initiate an unplanned behaviour or to abandon a planned behaviour. A major reason has been the validity issues associated with the research instruments that measure intentions and subsequent behaviour, an issue addressed in this chapter.

Research into the dichotomy of planned–unplanned consumption behaviour has concentrated largely on the influences on unplanned purchasing. In seeking explanations, empirical researchers have examined such variables as the level of expenditure and characteristics of the shopping party (Kollat and Willett, 1967), personality traits (Raju, 1980) and proclivity to visit stores (Granbois, 1968). In the late 1980s the psychological dimensions of the compulsive type of unplanned purchases drew the attention of scholars in the fields of psychology and economic psychology (cf. Faber and O'Guinn, 1989; O'Guinn and Faber, 1989). Yet the results of these studies were mixed. Both Kollat and Willett (1967) and Prasad (1975) found that socio-economic characteristics were not a significant factor in shoppers performing

unplanned buying behaviour. All these studies quantified the degree of unplanned purchases in retail settings. With three exceptions, studies have tended neither to compare planned with realized purchases, nor to identify the factors that explain the differences between planned and actual behaviours (both these areas of planned and unplanned behaviour will be examined in this chapter). In a discussion paper, Earl and Potts (2000) argue that unplanned purchases arise as a result of browsing that diverts consumers from their planned information search or purchase intentions. The authors define browsing behaviour as the situation when 'people go shopping without any plans to search for particular items or any intention to purchase particular items from particular stores without even engaging in search activity' (p. 112). Although they point out that browsing behaviour need not necessarily result in unplanned purchases, they argue that browsing is often associated with such purchases because of the discovery of goods congruent with underlying latent demands that were not the basis of the shopping activities. Consumers shift from browsing to searching and back again, often due to stimuli they receive from the consumption environment in which they find themselves. For example, in the case of a shopping mall, the stimuli may include advertising signage, promotional activities and overall mall layout.

What are the exceptions? Pickering (1977) found that certain respondents, whose purchases deviated significantly from their intentions, were 'especially distinguishable in terms of their age and socio-economic status' and, interestingly, that they were 'overconfident or unduly cautious in their initial expectations' (p. 175). Iyer (1989) concluded that the degree of similarity between a shopper's 'encoded' and 'actual' purchasing sequence is a function of knowledge of the shopping environment (i.e. store layout) and time pressure (either absent or present).

The third exception is a qualitative study undertaken in the economic psychology field. Based on their qualitative examination of planned and impulse buying, Dittmar and Drury (2000) drew two conclusions about planned buying. First, it is based on a definite decision and intention to purchase (and often involves shopping around), and it can entail quite an extensive information search and careful price and quality comparisons. Secondly, planned buying is mostly for goods needed (although treats were mentioned a few times), it is functional and it has to be budgeted for.

Marketing studies examining the relationship of consumer plans and behaviours have primarily relied on the analysis of survey data to determine the accuracy of purchase intentions (e.g. Kalwani and Silk, 1982; Morwitz and Schmittlein, 1992). In these studies, intentions are measured in a survey and the same respondents are contacted at a later time to determine their realized consumption behaviours. These studies have a high degree of external validity because they are conducted over long-enough time horizons to examine the dynamics of actual purchasing. However, as Morwitz (1997a) points out, studies are typically descriptive, and do not experimentally or quasi-experimentally test the effect of factors that moderate the intention–behaviour relationship.

The major contribution of this chapter examines the influence of two moderating variables – product information and consumer characteristics – on consumer behaviour in a tourism and leisure setting. The second contribution is the conceptualized matrix of four behavioural outcomes that result from the interaction between planned and realized behaviours, shown earlier in Fig. 4.2.

Points of managerial interest

Marketing practitioners have long accepted the assumption that high correlations exist between intentions and behaviour. The argument can be viewed as circular: they believe that intentions are, more or less, likely to be manifested in consumption behaviours; and, by the same logic, they assume that behavioural outcomes are, more or less, manifestations of intentions. Yet sufficient empirical research has been undertaken to cast serious doubts on these propositions. Only under the strictest of conditions – such as when a behavioural intention is measured immediately prior to the behaviour to which it refers occurring – could strong correla-

tions likely be achieved. In the words of Foxall (1983, p. 234), 'investigations which attempt to predict behaviour from attitudes/intentions frequently fall drastically short'.

This study adds to the knowledge of marketing strategy practice through an examination of the critical variables that explain planned and unplanned behaviours. Because the research quantifies the extent to which certain demographic and situational variables influence particular consumption behaviours, it allows marketing strategists to formulate more effective marketing communications, particularly with regard to the provision of visitor information guides that can stimulate consumer demand and influence consumer choice. Destinational tourism bodies typically attempt to be 'all things to all people', a weakness in their marketing approach that has been recognized by marketers themselves (Alford, 1998). Researchers have also found that by studying the benefits that vacationers realize rather than the benefits they seek, marketers could have an improved understanding of the relationship between travel motivations and actual behaviours (Shoemaker, 1994). Also, within the tourism literature, research into the nature and context of the purchase decision has been neglected (Ritchie, 1994).

Planned Versus Realized Behaviour

We begin this section by defining what we mean by planned behaviour, intentions and realized behaviour. When consumers identify, evaluate and choose among alternatives during problem solving, they produce a decision plan. This plan comprises one or more behavioural intentions, depending on the specificity and complexity of the plan (Park and Lutz, 1982). Specific decision plans concern intentions to perform particular behaviours in highly defined situations: 'This weekend Peter intends to go to the mountains, stay in his favourite bed and breakfast and attend the annual antique fair'. Other decision plans involve more general intentions: 'Mathew intends to shop for a new winter jacket soon'. Some decision plans contain a single intention to perform a single behaviour: 'Angela intends to buy a Coke as soon as the lecture is over'. In contrast, some plans involve a series of intentions to perform a series of behaviours: 'The Robertsons intend to collect travel brochures from a couple of travel agents, browse through their tours to Europe and make a decision about a trip during summer'.

While we would expect a decision plan to increase the likelihood that the intended behaviours will be performed, we know from our everyday experiences that behavioural intentions are not always carried out.

The most thorough examination of the relationship between intentions and actual behaviour is found in the field of social psychology. Here, the traditional view is that human behaviour is goal-directed (Lewin, 1951; Heider, 1958) and that actions implemented to achieve these goals are controlled by intentions (Ajzen, 1985). Routine activities such as cleaning one's teeth before bedtime or typing a letter on one's computer are so habitual that they are performed automatically; they require no conscious formulation of a decision plan.

Two theories seeking to explain the relationship between planned and actual behaviour have developed over the years: the theory of reasoned action and the theory of planned behaviour. These will now be explained.

The theory of reasoned action

The theory of reasoned action (TRA) models the relationship between attitude and intentions. Its proponents (Fishbein and Ajzen, 1975; Ajzen and Fishbein, 1980) argue that human social behaviour is controlled not by unconscious motives or overpowering desires, but rather that people consider the implications of their actions before they decide whether or not to engage in a particular behaviour. Individuals are assumed to form attitudes towards engaging in behaviour (such as product purchase) and to consider subjective norms about whether their significant others would approve or disapprove of the consumer engaging in the behaviour. Based on these attitudes and norms, individuals form an intention to participate or not in the behaviour. Given this model, the accuracy of purchase intentions will depend on the accuracy of measuring attitudes towards the product, as well as the subjective norms. Intention in TRA is thus regarded as the immediate antecedent of behaviour. Attitude and intentions research inspired by Fishbein and Ajzen's (1975) theory adopted the following theoretical underpinning. (The reference to the use of information is of particular relevance to the aims of this chapter, as we shall learn later.)

> Human beings are usually quite rational, and make systematic use of the information available to them. We do not subscribe to the view that human social behavior is controlled by unconscious motives ... nor do we believe that it can be described as capricious or thoughtless.
> (Ajzen and Fishbein, 1980, p. 5)

Although Fishbein and Ajzen displayed confidence in the predictive and explicative powers of their model, their assurance of a causal relationship sequence in the decision process was questioned, and the limitations in the model and the implications for research practice and managerial decision making have been discussed in the consumer marketing literature. For example, Foxall's (1983) criticism is particularly trenchant, arguing that TRA 'can make only *trivial* [my emphasis] contributions to the understanding and prediction of managerially-relevant aspects of consumer choice' (p. 232).

Peter and Olson (1999) identify six main factors that reduce or weaken the relationship between intentions and behaviours:

- intervening time (between measurement of intentions and observation or measurement of behaviours) (see also Conner and Armitage, 1998);
- different levels of specificity (e.g. whereby the specific environment in which the behaviour is performed is the same as the one forecast when the intention was formed) (see also Fishbein and Ajzen, 1975);
- unforeseen environmental event (e.g. when an intended purchase is not possible due to the store having sold out of the product);
- degree of voluntary control (e.g. when a mother intended to buy a particular breakfast cereal only to be dissuaded by her son);

- stability of intentions (while some intentions are stable, others may be founded on weakly held beliefs that are easily changed);
- new information (new information could change a consumer's beliefs and attitudes towards a product which, in turn, change the intention).

Many elements of human behaviour defy prediction, and particularly so when they are influenced by factors over which people have only a degree of limited control. Some intentions are abandoned altogether, while others are revised to suit changing circumstances. From the viewpoint of the social science investigator, eventual behaviour will only match intention if two conditions are met. First, the measure of intention must reflect the respondent's intention as close to the point of actual behaviour as possible. Secondly, the behaviour must be under volitional control. Consistent with this, Sheppard *et al.* (1988) found that the correlation between intent and behaviour was greater for behaviours that are completely under an individual's volitional control, than for goals that are at least partly determined by factors beyond an individual's volitional control. In another test of TRA, Mullen *et al.* (1987) found that past behaviour was the best predictor of future behaviour. Particularly relevant to this study is the work of Young and Kent (1985), who tested the predictive power of TRA by examining intentions and behaviour in the leisure context of camping. They concluded that TRA can increase the understanding of the inter-relationships of influences of leisure activity participation and may aid in the predicting of behaviour.

Intentions will change even in a short space of time and the situational influences on intentions are varied and profound. Meta-analyses have shown that intentions, at least in the context of TRA, account for only 38% of the variance in behaviour (van den Putte, reported by Conner and Armitage, 1998, p. 1450).

Theory of planned behaviour

To address some of the issues, Ajzen (1985) extended the theory of reasoned action with his development of the theory of planned behaviour (TPB). This latter theory was designed to provide a more parsimonious explanation of informational and motivational influences on behaviour. In the theory of planned behaviour, Ajzen defined a behavioural intention as an intention to 'try' to perform a certain behaviour. Intention predicts whether an individual will attempt to perform a particular behaviour; if it does not predict attainment of the goal, then factors lying beyond the control of the actor prevented the person from carrying out the intention. In other words, the actualization of the intended behaviour is contingent on the individual's perception of control over the various factors that may prevent it, as well as the individual's perception of his or her ability to carry out the action successfully. (Also, the greater control one presumably has over the impeding factors, or indeed, the fewer the barriers that exist, the more likely that the resultant behaviour would approximate the intended action.) Ajzen reasons that intentions predict only a person's 'attempt' to perform a particular behaviour, and not necessarily the actual performance of the behaviour. East (1997) reviews the large number of studies undertaken on planned behaviour and concludes that the theory of planned behaviour provides more reliable predictions than reasoned action theory that 'it has now largely displaced' (p. 140). The theory of planned behaviour is shown in Fig. 4.3 and an expanded version, based on the concepts of unplanned and planned to be examined in this chapter, is shown in Fig. 4.4.

The greater conceptual complexity of the theory of planned behaviour offers deeper insights into the differentials that occur between planned and actual behaviours, by depicting behaviour as a function of behavioural intentions *and* perceived behavioural control (Conner and Armitage, 1998). Perceived behavioural control is the individual's perception of the extent to which performance of the behaviour is easy or difficult (Ajzen, 1991). It therefore became the third determinant of intentions, along with attitudes and subjective norms, which had been identified in the theory of reasoned action.

Control is seen as a continuum with easily executed behaviours at one end (e.g. buying milk at the local store) and behavioural goals

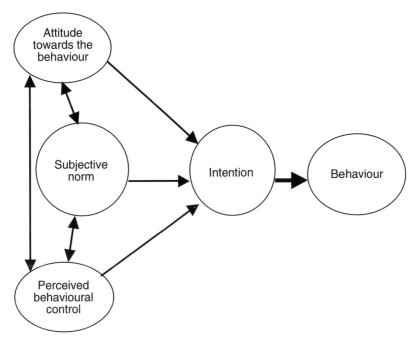

Fig. 4.3. Theory of planned behaviour (source: Ajzen and Driver, 1992).

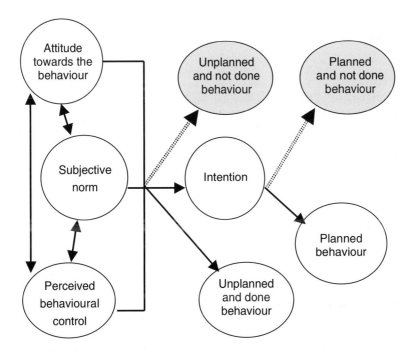

Fig. 4.4. Adapted theory of planned behaviour.

demanding resources, opportunities and specialized skills (e.g. becoming a professional share-market investor) at the other end.

The link between perceived behavioural control (PBC) and behaviour is more complex than the relation between PBC and intentions, however. We are more likely to engage in (attractive/desirable) behaviours we have control over, and less likely to carry out behaviours over which we have no control. In his early discussions on the theory of planned behaviour, Ajzen (1985) suggested that intentions would become stronger predictors of behaviour as PBC increased; the stronger perceived ease of performing the behaviour, the more likely the behaviour would be carried out. [Yet even the TPB fails to adequately explain variations between intentions and actual behaviour. Meta-analyses of the theory of planned behaviour indicate that intentions and PBC account for only 34% of behaviour (Sutton, 1998).]

Theory of planned behaviour provides a richer acknowledgement of the complexities associated with planned behaviours. The notion of control beliefs, for example, embodies the factors likely to facilitate or inhibit the performance of the intended behaviour. They are categorized as either internal control factors (e.g. information, personal deficiencies, skills, abilities, emotions) or external control factors (e.g. opportunities, dependence on others, logistic barriers such as time or distance). People who perceive that they have access to the necessary resources and that there are the opportunities (or lack of obstacles and barriers) to perform the behaviour are likely to have a high degree of PBC (Ajzen, 1991).

The influence of past behaviour and habit on future behaviour needs to be considered. Many behaviours are influenced by one's past behaviour, rather than by cognitions such as those described in the theory of reasoned action or the theory of planned behaviour. Indeed, a number of consumer studies have shown that past behaviour is the best predictor of future behaviour. One of the most notable is the study by Mullen *et al.* (1987) that used the theory of reasoned action to examine changes in the consumption of sweet and fried foods, smoking and exercise over an 8-month period. For each behaviour, initial behaviour was the strongest predictor of later behaviour. Clearly,

this does not mean that past behaviour *causes* future behaviour. What can be said is that frequent performance of a behaviour may bring subsequent behaviour under the control of habitual processes, although a behaviour does not necessarily become habitual just because it has been performed many times (Conner and Armitage, 1998).

The theory of planned behaviour states that the considerations that enter into the determination of a behavioural attempt include beliefs about the consequences of success and failure, the probabilities of successfully performing the behaviour, normative beliefs regarding important referents and motivations to comply with these referents (Ajzen, 1985). An individual will attempt to perform a behaviour if he or she believes that the advantages of success outweigh the disadvantages of failure, and if he or she believes that referents with whom he or she is motivated to comply think he or she should try to perform the behaviour. However, individuals often may not compare advantages of success versus disadvantages of failure; s/he may apply very simple heuristics in deciding to do/not do a behaviour, for example, recognition awareness alone may trigger attraction/avoidance to an activity.

Like the theory of reasoned action, the theory of planned behaviour has been criticized. Bagozzi and Nataraajan (2000) cite three shortcomings. First, they argue that while attitudes, subjective norms and perceived behavioural control provide reasons for acting, they lack the motivational impetus for 'energizing' actions. Secondly, because the theory focuses only on action as target referents, variables in the theory neglect the role of goals in decision-making completely. The authors mention (but neglect to cite) 'new' research that shows that consumers take into account anticipated positive and negative emotions towards possible goal attainment and goal failure, and that these emotions influence desires to perform certain goals. Thirdly, other research has shown that, in addition to desires and emotions, recency and frequency of performance of the consumption or experiential act are useful predictors of intentions and behaviour.

Gollwitzer (1993) and Heckhausen (1991) have explored how intentions *guide* the performance of behaviour. Various factors have been found to influence effort, continued commitment to a behavioural goal, and persistence in the face of obstacles. For example, individual differences according to whether a person possesses an action versus state orientation can affect persistence with a course of action (Beckman and Kuhl, 1984). Action-oriented individuals focus on a fully developed plan of action (intention) and are more likely to persist. State-oriented individuals are more likely to focus attention on internal or external states that are not related to the target behaviour and are thus likely to followed rather than an intention (see Kendzierski, 1990).

Warshaw et al. (1986) sought a middle ground by introducing the concept of behavioural expectation. This term refers to the distinction between what a person intends to do and what he expects he actually will do. Behavioural expectation refers to a person's estimate of the likelihood that he will actually perform a certain behaviour. According to their view, behavioural expectations are likely to predict actual behaviour more accurately than behavioural intentions. A similar distinction is that made between making a decision (forming an intention) and implementing a decision (for example, see Ajzen, 1996). The former is regarded as a motivational process, while the latter is primarily a volitional process.

Gollwitzer (1990) has argued that carrying out goal intentions is a two-stage process. The first stage is a motivational one and largely echoes Ajzen's (1996) definition. The second is a volitional or implemental cognitive stage. At the first stage, the individual weighs up the costs and benefits of pursuing a goal and then finally forms a goal intention or decision about whether to perform the behaviour. In the second stage, plans are formed about how to ensure that one's intention is acted upon. These plans are referred to as implementation intentions and specify what one will do and where one will do it in order to achieve the goal intention (i.e. 'I intend to initiate the goal-directed Behaviour X when Situation Y is encountered'). Importantly, implementation intentions commit the individual to a specific course of action when certain environmental conditions are met. In this way they translate goal intentions into action. Gollwitzer (1990) argues that by making implementation inten-

tions, individuals render control to the environment. The environment acts as a clue to action, such that when certain conditions are met, the performance of the intended act occurs.

Aarts et al. (1998) suggest that habit or past behaviour may act as a moderator of the relationship between the theory of planned behaviour (including intentions and planned behavioural control) and actual behaviour. Interestingly, they argue that habit or past behaviour are assumed to be related only for infrequently performed (or non-habitual, however that term is defined) behaviours.

A contrasting view to the theory of planned behaviour, and indeed to most theories that examine the connection between plans and behavioural outcomes, is that which argues that behaviour is not goal-directed but goal-interpreted. Preferences are constructed, rather than retrieved from memory. According to Weick (1998, p. 195), 'effect precedes the cause [of human action], the response precedes the stimulus, the output precedes the input'.

Behavioural decisions follow outcomes, rather than the other way around. The basic premise of this school of thought is that few actions are premeditated and few are the result of choosing one behaviour among a set of alternative possible courses of actions. When individuals plan, they seek to control and manipulate the future, they do not simply 'think' about it, make reasoned decisions and work towards the realization of those decisions. In essence, individuals create plans after the event (Weick, 1995). Weick (1995) uses the 'evolution' of careers to support his argument; our careers usually turn out to be a set of actions that are career-interpreted after the fact, rather than career-planned before the fact.

Weick argues persuasively that individuals are more vivid – and imaginative when asked to be so – in their descriptions of events after they occur than before. An individual's understanding of his action originates in reflection and looking backward (Weick, 1998). It is only when the action has been completed that the individual is able reasonably to comprehend the reasons that led to him, or her, choosing the enacted behaviour. We shall return to Weick's work in Chapter 8.

Marketing studies into planned and actual purchases

Substantial empirical research has been undertaken into the relationship between planned purchases and actual consumption. Typically, the aim of these studies was to measure intentions for the purpose of predicting future consumption behaviour. The US government conducted studies and experiments concerning purchase intentions between the 1940s and 1970s (cited by Young *et al.*, 1998). In many of these studies, significant relationships between intentions to buy durable goods and subsequent purchases were found using various econometric models on panel data (Tobin, 1959; Juster, 1966). Two decades ago, Kalwani and Silk (1982) showed that the intention–behaviour link is affected by factors such as type of product, type of measurement scale, time from measurement of intent until actual behaviour, and recency of the previous purchase. Many studies examined the relationship between purchase intentions and purchase behaviour for durable goods (e.g. Ferber and Piskie, 1965; Clawson, 1971) and non-durable goods (e.g. Tauber, 1975; Warshaw, 1980). Young *et al.* (1998) suggest that:

> Overall, based on empirical evidence, intentions appear to almost always provide biased measures of purchase propensity, sometimes underestimating actual purchasing and other times overestimating actual purchasing.
> (Young *et al.*, 1998, p. 189)

Most of these studies focus on the predictive powers and accuracy of intentions. This reflects most models of consumer behaviour, which incorporate intentions as an important predictor variable to forecast sales (Kalwani and Silk, 1982; Infosino, 1986; Morwitz and Schmittlein, 1992). Few distinctions are made between buyer intentions and buyer actions. Any divergences between intentions and behaviour are explained in terms of situational variables. In the words of Juster (1964), 'purchases (actions) are directly related to (or predicted by) intentions, modified by the incidence of unforeseen circumstances'.

Srull (1982) offers one reason why there is this apparent lack of investigation into the 'final stage' in the consumer consumption process. In his view, consumer research is primarily phenomenon driven, as opposed to theory driven. For marketing practitioners, particularly in advertising-related fields, the predictive power of intentions to forecast future consumption behaviour has obvious commercial appeal.

One dimension of the issue regarding the relationship between intentions and actual behaviour that has been examined in marketing is the concept of 'unplanned' behaviour. Stern's (1962) seminal article proposed four categories of unplanned purchases: 'pure' impulse buying, characterized by a total lack of preplanning; reminder impulse buying, whereby purchases are sparked by previous personal experience or recall; suggestion impulse buying, where the purchaser sees the purchased product for the first time and buys it; and planned impulse buying, typified by a shopper entering a store with some specific purchase in mind, but with the expectation and intention of making other purchases dependent on such things as price and coupon specials. Early marketing studies typically used the terms 'unplanned behaviour' and 'impulse buying' interchangeably, with the research settings confined mainly to the consumer goods/retailing sector (Kollat and Willett, 1967; Bellenger *et al.*, 1978; Deshpande and Krishnan, 1980; Cobb and Hoyer, 1986). Exceptions include a study that examined the relationship between decision plans and choice behaviours in a real-estate setting (Park *et al.*, 1981) and work into customer retention and unplanned purchases on the World-wide Web.

By the mid-1980s, scholars began to deconstruct the unplanned concept, and focus on its impulse dimension (cf. Rook and Hoch, 1985; Rook and Gardner, 1993). Although an impulse purchase is unplanned, it is also much more, argued researchers. The findings of Dittmar and Drury (2000) are particularly interesting:

> Impulse buying is characterised by little deliberation, and by psychological motivations – desire, wanting, treat, thrill – overtaking financial considerations. Women emphasise emotional aspects of impulse buying more than men, and the lack of regard for financial consequences becomes extreme for excessive shoppers who find the urge to buy irresistible. This is clearly a far cry from the definitions of planned buying, suggesting that it is meaningful to conceptualise

pure impulse buying as compared to pure planned buying as opposite extreme of buying behaviour, which are governed by different processes and motivations.

(Dittmar and Drury, 2000, p. 17)

While all impulse buying is unplanned, not all unplanned behaviour could be described as impulse purchases (Iyer, 1989; Beatty and Ferrell, 1998). Rook (1987) defines impulse buying as when 'a consumer experiences a sudden, often powerful and persistent urge to buy something immediately' (p. 191). Bayley and Nancarrow (1998) identified types of unplanned purchases that are non-impulsive by nature [here we use Dittmar and Drury's (2000) definition of 'impulse' purchase as a spur of the moment purchase, with no prior desire to purchase]. They are as follows:

- the 'oversight': not on a mental or written shopping list, but needed; shop display reminds the shopper and activates the need state;
- the 'deferred decision': decide to wait until in-store, where a more informed decision can be made;
- the 'shop as prompt': no need to plan, a well-oiled routine allowing shops to act as shopping prompt list;
- the 'unplanned is demanded': certain categories of products sometimes require an unplanned purchase, for example, when a shopper does not want to buy the same souvenirs or gifts as before.

While an increasing number of scholars have developed an interest in impulse buying since the 1980s (Gardner and Rook, 1988; Rook and Fisher, 1995; Dittmar et al., 1996; Beatty and Ferrell, 1998; Weun et al., 1998; Agee and Martin, 2001), the characteristics and antecedents of unplanned behaviour in the broader sense remain unexplored and unknown. (Indeed, some scholars neglect to mention the subject altogether. East, for example, in his 1997 book on consumer behaviour, makes no mention of the concept, although he briefly outlines compulsive shopping, a variation of the term.) Table 4.1 summarizes the empirical research undertaken into unplanned and impulse purchase behaviour.

One of the reasons for this lack of interest may be the complexity of the 'unplanned' concept. Behaviour can be unplanned yet done, either in the form of impulse buying (e.g. purchase of a chocolate bar at the supermarket check-out counter) or (for the want of a better term) 'unplanned purchases' (when knowledge of and interaction with the task environment and time pressure combine to force a decision that otherwise would have been forgone; Bettman, 1979).

To complicate matters more, not all impulse buying may be totally unplanned. Rook and Hoch (1985, p. 25) found that some people 'plan on being impulsive' [my emphasis] as a shopping strategy. Cobb and Hoyer (1986) draw an interesting distinction between impulse planners and partial planners. While both cohorts appear to be impulse purchasers, because they delay brand decisions until entering the consumption environment, impulse planners act almost entirely in a spontaneous manner, while partial planners exhibited careful in-site purchase behaviour, engaged in detailed search and were price sensitive.

Unplanned behaviour may also be unplanned and not done, as conceptualized in the Mintzberg matrix. Three scenarios are possible: the product may have been considered and rejected; it may have not been considered and rejected; or it may have not entered the consumer's awareness set. Reflecting Weick's approach to the intention–behaviour dichotomy, Bettman et al. (1998) highlight a growing belief among consumer-decision researchers that preferences for options of any complexity or novelty are often constructed and not simply revealed in making a decision. They cite the analogy used by Gregory et al. (1993, p. 181), whereby consumer preference formation is 'more like architecture, building some defensible set of values, rather than archaeology, uncovering values that are already there'. Little wonder, therefore, that Rook and Gardner (1993) concluded that impulse buying is still in a relatively immature state, especially compared to other areas of consumer research, such as attitude research (Beatty and Ferrell, 1998).

As Table 4.1 indicates, previous research into the nature of planned, unplanned and actual consumption has happened mainly in the supermarket setting. Key findings are summarized below:

Table 4.1. Summary of empirical research on unplanned and impulse purchasing.

Investigator(s)	Unplanned purchases (%)	Research setting	Tested for Influence of		Identified precursor variables of unplanned or impulse behaviour
			Product information	Demographics	
Clover (1950)	60–15	19 store types	No	No	
Cox (1964)	n.a.	Supermarket	No	No	Shelf space
Kelly (1965)	n.a.	Supermarket	No	No	Display location
Kollat and Willett (1967)	50.5	Supermarket	No	Income/education/occupation	Unplanned purchases increased with money spent and size of shopping list
Williams and Dardis (1972)	33/37/31	Speciality/department/variety	No	Income/gender	Low level of brand awareness indicates propensity for unplanned purchases
Prasad (1975)	39.3/62.4	Department/discount stores	No	Income/education	The greater the transaction size, the more likely are unplanned purchases
Bellenger et al. (1978)	38.7	Supermarket	No	Age/race/gender	Age and race were significant for certain product lines
McGoldrick (1982)	7	Pharmacies	No	No	In-store displays
Cobb and Hoyer (1986)	12	Supermarket	No	Age/sex/household size	Gender (males more likely to make unplanned purchases)
Rook and Fisher (1995)	n.a.	CD retail store purchases	No	No	Normative evaluations influence subsequent impulse buying behaviour
Dittmar et al. (1996)	n.a.	Survey of shopping habits	No	Yes	Attitudes to shops and gender were key variables
Beatty and Ferrell (1998)	n.a.	Recall of recent shopping trip	No	No	Time in store; enjoyment of shopping; 'impulse buying tendency'
Bayley and Nancarrow (1998)	n.a.	Survey of product items	No	No	Socio-psychological models developed to explain impulse purchase behaviour
Weun et al. (1998)	n.a.	Develop and test an instrument to predict impulse purchases	No	No	Antecedents of impulse behaviour were not investigated
Agee and Martin (2001)	n.a.	Purchasing from infomercials	Yes	Yes	Exposure to advertising increases likelihood of purchase; only demographic to influence purchase was age of children

n.a., not available.

- Despite the 'large' number of items that customers usually intend buying in supermarkets, Peterson (1987) found that just 30% of shoppers made shopping lists (cited by Shapiro and Krishnan, 1999, p.70).
- The incidence of unplanned purchases rises with the size of the shopping bill and the numbers of items purchased (Kollatt and Willett, 1967; Prasad, 1975).
- Since supermarkets often require a high degree of searching and scanning for desired items, the likelihood of the customer being distracted and engaging in unplanned purchase behaviour is increased. Most of this scanning is done completely subconsciously by the peripheral vision, which sifts out those items that are worthy of closer scrutiny (Bruce and Green, 1991).

The choice of supermarkets as the main research setting limits our insights into unplanned purchases. Supermarkets are, arguably, unique shopping environments, due to the large number of relatively inexpensive items on offer. While the choice is understandable, given the high prevalence of unplanned purchases, we need to broaden the variety of purchase settings to achieve a deeper understanding of the phenomenon. Until we do that, we will not fully understand the phenomenon of unplanned purchases.

Unplanned, and particularly impulse, purchases may happen with greater frequency in supermarkets, and thus the relevance to strategy of unplanned purchase behaviour is stronger for supermarket managers, than in other purchase environments. For example, McGoldrick (1982) found that in a pharmacy setting, just 7% of purchases were totally unplanned (as opposed to 13% attributed to reminders of needed items triggered by in-store influences). However, until these propositions are tested, we need to test for the behaviour in other settings.

The degree of unplanned purchases also differs according to product categories (see Table 4.1 and Dittmar et al., 1996). Simonson (1993) and Bemmaor (1995) also argue that while intentions predict behaviour for existing consumer products, they do not predict behaviour for new products and products targeted to business markets. In a similar finding, Morwitz

et al. (1996) found a significantly higher correlation between intentions and market performance for existing products than for new products. This research setting will therefore extend our understanding of planned and unplanned purchases.

As a first step towards an improved understanding of planned and actual behaviours, a conceptual framework that categorizes the behavioural outcomes of planned versus unplanned consumption is offered. For that, we turn to the management literature and a parsimonious model that has lain untested for over 20 years.

Towards a Richer Understanding of Planned and Unplanned Behaviour

Henry Mintzberg is a leading scholar in the field of organizational strategy. Over two decades ago he proposed a model to illustrate the relationship between planned behaviour and behavioural outcomes (Mintzberg, 1978) (see Fig 4.1). Mintzberg explored planning and outcomes as they related to organizations in pursuit of strategic goals. Although he never subsequently attempted to verify his parsimonious model empirically, Mintzberg's conceptual contribution is useful, if untested. He was the first to illustrate the variety of outcomes – planned and unplanned – that arise from intended and unintended actions. This chapter will be the first application of Mintzberg's theory to consumer behaviour.

Mintzberg identified three main types of strategies: *deliberate* strategies, which are planned and enacted; *emergent* strategies, which occur even though they were not intended (both of these he termed 'realized' strategies); and *unrealized* strategies, which are planned but not enacted. Of these, Mintzberg suggests deliberate strategies are the most commonly examined in the management planning literature (Mintzberg, 1994). His third case, *emergent* strategy, where a realized 'pattern' was not intended, has been of less interest to researchers and practitioners.

For the purpose of this chapter, 'deliberate' strategies will be called 'realized' hereinafter. We believe that the term better embodies the twin notions of both planning and completion.

According to *The Australian Oxford Dictionary* (p. 349), 'deliberate' is defined as 'intentional', a term that focuses more on the cognitive decision to act and less on the process that culminates in the act being carried out. 'Realized' more appropriately emphasizes an end result rather than 'deliberate' which, notwithstanding Mintzberg's own views, focuses more on the initial act rather than the culmination of behavioural actions.

We now add a fourth behavioural category. Termed 'unplanned/not done' behaviour, it refers to, as the name suggests, outcomes that are neither planned nor done; these four possible outcomes are illustrated in Fig. 4.2. The importance of this fourth 'outcome' lies in the implications it has for organizations when their marketing communications elicit such non-response from consumers. The need for management to identify and understand behaviours that are both unplanned and not realized is, arguably, as important as that for purchases that are planned and carried out. Put another way, the customer that an organization does not have may be its most important (Drucker, 2001). But even this hitherto ignored outcome of 'unplanned/not done' has a further dimension: consumers may have considered the product but rejected it, or they may have not considered it and therefore rejected it. Clearly, a firm's understanding of its existing and potential customers would be enhanced by insights into the factors underlying rejection of its product at the planning and the actual consumption stage.

Let us consider Mintzberg's three strategies in the marketing context. Deliberate strategies are self-explanatory and need little comment. Every day we decide upon, and then enact, a range of consumption behaviours: from buying a morning coffee to filling the tank with petrol on the way home from work. Similarly, unrealized strategies are not uncommon. We plan to go shopping at lunchtime, only for an urgent job at work to intervene and cause postponement of the action. Or a decision to buy a new Sony stereo system is changed after finding information about a less expensive and seemingly equally good system from Panasonic. (For the present purposes, it is does not matter whether the unrealized action relates to a product category or brand.)

'Emergent strategies', which occur when unplanned behaviours are enacted, most commonly take the form of impulse purchasing in consumer shopping situations. As was discussed earlier, no empirical research has been undertaken beyond this research setting.

To summarize, therefore, Mintzberg's work offers both conceptual and managerial insights for the marketing discipline. In terms of theoretical development, his typology can be applied to individual consumer behaviour as well as to its original context, organizational behaviours. Just as he extended the conceptualization of strategy in the management domain, marketers can generate deeper insights into consumer planning and implementation of consumption intentions by teasing out the influences that explain the shifts that occur between the expression of intention and the performance of the consumption behaviour (cf. Howard and Sheth, 1969; Engel *et al.*, 1993; Peter and Olson, 1999). Logic suggests that it is conceivable for individuals not to succeed in pursuing the strategies they intended. Equally, it is probable that individuals end up pursuing strategies they *never* envisaged. What it adds is the notion that an intention is a preliminary stage of a process that may, or may not, culminate in a consumption behaviour.

Managerially, the model provides marketing strategists a strategic tool that facilitates a richer understanding of reasons for a product's lack of appeal in the marketplace. The Mintzberg grid can be used to classify products of an organization's product mix by comparing the amount of intended consumption of each product with the amount that was actually consumed; then generating an arithmetic measure for each product to represent that difference; and finally using that measure to allocate each product to one of the four consumption behavioural outcomes.

Scholarly research into consumer purchasing behaviour has traditionally focused on pre-purchase settings in the form of consumer choice. This is managerially critical since advertisers need to understand customer intentions. Yet outcomes are the behaviours that consumers exhibit and that executives benchmark success against. Greater understanding of the influences exerted upon outcomes will deepen our theoretical understanding of consumption behaviour and provide richer insights for the marketing executive. This is particularly the case with the development of the concepts of emergent and unplanned/not realized strategies.

The differences between intentions and actual consumption behaviour require greater attention for several reasons. First, there is a need to more accurately identify and quantify the intervening and unforeseen factors that divert intentions away from the eventual behavioural outcomes. Lilien et al. (1992), in a review of marketing models, argue that there is a lack of exploration into the mechanisms that underlie the link between intentions and behaviour. More recently, Shapiro and Krishnan (1999) argue that memory represents an intervening variable between intention formation and behaviour, and not only one antecedent of intentions.

Secondly, given differences in the intention–behaviour link between durables and low-involvement products (Kalwani and Silk, 1982), the typical consumer behaviour model may not capture the dynamics of consumption behaviours in, for example, a services context (cf. Hawkins and Hoch, 1992). Morwitz (1997a), for example, has shown that the intention–behaviour relationship will differ across product types.

Thirdly, Morwitz (1997a) has urged further research into factors that moderate the relationship between intention and behaviour in consumption environments that entail a sequence of transactions or a bundle of products.

Fourthly, limiting research to prepurchase settings (as often occurs) can understate the amount and influence of information that customers have at their disposal at the time of actual purchase (Bloch et al., 1986). Fifthly, an increasingly prominent theme in recent behavioural decision research is that preferences are – rather than retrieved from memory and real experience – often constructed when consumers need to choose one alternative from a set of alternative products, services or courses of action (Kardes, 1994; Bettman et al. 1998).

Sixthly, there is a need to improve our understanding of the influence of information on consumer behaviour (Bettman and Park, 1980). Prior information is obviously very useful in narrowing the scope of the choice task

early in the decision process by allowing the consumer to focus on certain brands and attributes. Finally, unforeseen situational opportunities and constraints arise which are extremely difficult to predict (Belk, 1975).

Planned, unplanned and realized behaviour in leisure and tourism

Since the research focus for this project is consumption (and non-consumption) undertaken by tourists in a tourism destination, we turn to the tourism and leisure literature for further theoretical or empirical insights. Unfortunately, work carried out in these academic domains reveals a similar scarcity in identifying the influences upon either unplanned or planned behaviours. In an exhaustive review of research in leisure and tourism, Ritchie (1994) laments the lack of attention paid to the context of decision making in consumer behaviour, while Otto and Ritchie (1996) highlight the challenge of examining consumer behaviour in the tourism setting:

> Perhaps more than any other service industry, tourism holds the potential to elicit strong emotional and experiential reactions from consumers … utilitarian and rational information processing schemes which focus on functional or purely attribute-based elements are incommensurate with leisure and tourism.
> (Otto and Ritchie, 1996, p. 168)

Young and Kent (1985) examined planned and actual behaviours related to leisure campers, and found that intentions were slightly more influenced by the respondents' motivations than by the composition of the social group they were travelling with. Crotts and Reid (1993) found that most visitors to Alachuca County in Florida had decided upon recreational activities prior to arrival. Those travellers who made 'activity decisions' after arrival were typically long-haul, international visitors. In Tsang's (1993) survey of information search and travel planning behaviour of international visitors to New Zealand, over 40% of respondents indicated they pre-planned no vacation activities (cited by Hyde, 2000). Only a minority of visitors had pre-planned their length of stay in each sub-destination within New Zealand.

Jeng (1997) asked respondents to imagine a 2–4 day domestic vacation trip, and consider what elements they might plan before departure. He identified a set of core sub-decisions made *before* departure, including date of trip, primary destination, location of overnight stay, and travel route. He went on to identify a set of secondary sub-decisions, made before departure but considered to be flexible, including choice of attractions and activities. This subset made way for a third set of *en route* decisions, including where to dine, where to shop, and where to stop and rest. The one important caveat in this study was that dependents were asked to consider a short domestic trip, not an overseas one.

Stewart and Vogt (1999) adopted a case-based decision theory to understand how consumers plan for, and actuate, vacation travel. This approach assumes that consumers deal with uncertainty by basing their judgements of the current situation (or alternatives) on similar cases they have encountered previously; in other words, on past experience. The tourist plans for a series of activities and experiences for a future trip, but while s/he is on-site, a cycle of actuation–failure–revision–actuation occurs. Intuitively, this scenario approximates the complex process by which many of us decide upon plans, and then alter, abandon or implement the said plans.

Perdue (1986) touched upon the subject in a modest investigation that sought to verify empirically the proposition that unplanned yet realized behaviour yielded higher spending than unplanned and unrealized behaviour. He found that consumers who purchase a product that they had not planned for are likely to express satisfaction with the product as a means of justifying the purchase to themselves and other members of their travelling party.

Ajzen and Driver (1992) used leisure activities as the research setting for testing the theory of planned behaviour. They found that the theory was useful in predicting influences upon intentions and actual behaviours from intentions. The research had the limitation of being confined to college students and only five leisure activities were studied. As the authors concluded, future research needed to examine other recreation activities and to use more accurate and valid reporting means. Here

again, this chapter builds upon previous work by examining influences in a real tourist/leisure setting, with a large number of respondents and across a range of leisure activities and experiences.

In this context, it is worth remembering that existing models of decision behaviour, such as TPB, have been developed for tangible products, rather than intangible services such as tourism. The tourism product is an experiential product with emotional undertones, for which the decision process differs vastly from the rational, problem-solving scenario applied to many tangible products. Majo and Jarvis (1990) argue that 'travel is a special form of consumption behaviour involving an intangible, heterogeneous purchase of an experiential product' (cited in Gilbert, 1991, p. 98). As a consequence, existing models omit important realities of tourist behaviour. To cite Um and Crompton (1990, p. 437):

> It should be noted that perceptions of alternative destinations' physical attributes in the awareness set … are susceptible to change during the period of active solicitation of information stimulated by an intention to select a travel destination.

Finally, several writers have argued that the benefits *realized* from a consumption experience may be more useful to understand than the benefits that consumers say they intend to seek (Dann, 1981; Pearce and Caltabiano, 1983; Woodside and Jacobs, 1985; Shoemaker, 1994). This chapter adopts this imperative. Research that investigates the process by which intentions are actualized into actual behaviours, and elucidates the influences that result in unplanned as well as planned behaviours, has a valuable contribution to make to the marketing discipline.

Introducing the Research Setting

The research setting for this project is the tourism destination of Prince Edward Island, off the east coast of Canada, a destination that competes with other holiday destinations in the eastern region of North America for the lucrative summer holiday market. The July–August period, during which entry and exit surveys were administered, accounts for 90% of visitors (Woodside et al., 1997). Until 1995, when a bridge was built linking the island to the mainland province of New Brunswick, the main access to the island was by car ferry. Over 90% of visitors used the car ferry to access and exit the island (PEI Tourism Department). Surveys were administered on the car ferry as visitors were travelling to and leaving the island. Over 2000 respondents were interviewed in each survey.

This study is the first time that a tourism and leisure research setting has been utilized to examine planned and unplanned consumption. The benefits are twofold: first, our understanding of such behaviour is likely to be extended, since previous such studies have focused almost exclusively on supermarket shopping behaviour; secondly, the complex characteristics of tourism products are explored and considered.

This last point is important. We know that the vacation space (or any leisure environment), by its very nature, encourages the consumer to engage in spontaneous consumption behaviours. The decision task environment in the tourist consumption system is complex, and the decision process that tourists initiate can be highly arbitrary (Zajonc and Markus, 1982). Society's norms embodying rational behaviour are weakened, to be replaced by stimulus-seeking behaviour; and the imperatives on fiscal rectitude fewer. So irrational is much of touristic behaviour that some scholars portray it as 'play' (Berlyne, 1960, cited by Godbey and Graefe, 1991; Graburn, 1977), while others have conceptualized it as novelty seeking (Cohen, 1972; Plog, 1974; Crompton, 1979; Dann, 1981) and sought empirical testing of the concept (see, for example, Snepenger, 1987; Yiannakis and Gibson, 1992; Mo et al., 1993; Basala and Klenosky, 2001).

Parr (1989) sums it up: 'some [travellers] had little idea of what they wanted to see and do … Some people enjoyed the element of the unknown … they felt they were on an adventure, full of surprises and spontaneity'. In short, impulsiveness is OK when you're having fun. This premeditated 'irrational' dimension of the tourist/leisure experience contrasts starkly with the supermarket or shopping mall environment investigated by Rook and Fisher (1995), where consumers are more likely to experience, monitor and evaluate buying impulses. While the prevalence of unplanned behaviours, regardless of dimension, may be greater in these environments, the usefulness and strategic importance of better understanding the nature of unplanned consumption activities in tourist and leisure environments is without question.

Introduction to Hypotheses

This study investigates: (i) the differences between planned and realized consumption behaviours; (ii) the influence of product information on planned and realized consumption behaviours; and (iii) the influence of customer characteristics on planned and realized consumption behaviours.

In generating the hypotheses, the author is mindful of the gathering debate among marketing scientists regarding the validity of the so-called dominant hypothesis approach to research in the marketing field. Armstrong et al. (2001) point out the contradictory situation in which, on the one hand, the majority of articles that appear in scholarly marketing journals contain dominant hypotheses and, on the other, the majority of marketing scientists surveyed believe that the competing hypotheses approach produces 'deeper' information than an exploratory- or dominant-hypothesis approach. However, the exploratory nature of this chapter, in terms of methodology and research aims, renders a single model and dominant-hypothesis approach as appropriate.

Relationship between planned and realized consumption behaviours

The investigation into the discrepancies between planned and realized consumption activities is the core research focus of this chapter. Six consumption behaviours common to the tourism and leisure experience are used as dependent variables: spending (planned budget versus actual money spent); length of stay in the destination (planned number of days versus actual days stayed); attractions (planned to visit and actually visited); destinations (planned to visit and actually visited); accommodation (planned to use and actually used); and activities (planned to do and actually done).

A starting point for our investigation is whether consumers will, overall, consume or spend more or less than they plan. An obvious-enough question perhaps, but few studies have sought an answer. In a pioneering study, Kollat and Willett (1967) concluded 'there is a strong tendency for actual expenditure to approximate spending intentions' (p. 29) and that shoppers are 'more likely to spend less than they anticipated than they are to spend more than planned' (p. 30). They surmised 'that measured purchase intentions should correspond more closely to actual purchase intentions when the customers' time and effort are minimized' (p. 29).

Taken at face value, this early finding is puzzling. How could consumers engage in unplanned purchases and adhere to their intended budget – unless they abandon some planned purchases? In the absence of evidence that people abandon significant amounts of purchases to compensate for their unplanned purchase behaviour, it would seem likely that spending intentions are exceeded, to varying degrees, by actual expenditures. Indeed, the work of Abratt and Goodey (1990) confirms this logic. In their study of supermarket shopping behaviour, 41% of respondents reported that they had spent more than their expressed spending intention, which suggests, 'the proposition that consumers tend to spend more than they planned may hold' (p. 119).

Pertinent to this present chapter's research setting is the vacation planning study of Hyde (2000), and for that reason it will be considered at length. Hitherto, Hyde's work was the only longitudinal study examining the differences between travellers' plans and their eventual behaviours. He reported several interesting findings related to the present investigation: (i) respondents had fewer than seven specific planned elements in their planning, and almost half were sub-destinations (and this despite the fact that travellers' vacations had a mean of 33 elements); (ii) few attractions or activities had been planned; and (iii) a minority of travel parties had a pre-planned travel route. He found that of the vacation elements that travellers had specifically planned, a large proportion – a mean of 72.9% – was put into action. (It should be noted that a limitation of his work was the small qualitative sample of 20 travel

parties; all respondents were first-time visitors, none of whom were visiting friends or relatives.) Based on the preceding discussion, the following hypothesis is now formally stated:

H₁: Realized consumption behaviours are greater than planned for most specific services related to a purchased service system (see Fig. 4.5, panels A–D).

Numerous studies in the marketing field have examined the relationship between planned purchases and actual purchase behaviour (Warshaw, 1980; Manski, 1990; Young *et al.*, 1998). While the observed relationships are generally positive, the strength of the relationship has differed from study to study, depending on the contingencies inherent in the research setting. Three contingencies critical in tourist behaviour and consumption plans are: product experience, motivation and, in the tourist consumption system, composition of the travel party.

It is well documented that consumers' plans are affected by past experience (Fazio and Zanna, 1981; Morwitz and Schmittlein, 1992). Product experience is critical when studying the dynamic choice processes of consumers new to a market (Heilman *et al.*, 2000). Experience teaches people how to plan and that the actual behaviour of consumers with product experience will more closely approximate their plans than that of consumers with no or little product knowledge (Stewart and Vogt, 1999). Routine and habitual buyer behaviour allows for purposive and intelligent behaviour without deliberation (Katona, 1975). Visitors who vacation at the same place regularly are likely to engage in little pre-arrival planning, relying instead on their accumulated knowledge and experience from previous visits (Fodness and Murray, 1999). The relationships between experience and planned and realized behaviours are illustrated in Fig. 4.6.

Underlying motivations have a significant influence on the traveller's behaviour (Morrison, 1996). Travellers visiting friends or relatives (VFR) are more likely to rely on the advice of their hosts, less likely to use product information and therefore more likely to deviate between planned and eventual behaviours (Gitelson and Crompton, 1983). Leisure travellers, on the other hand, are more likely to

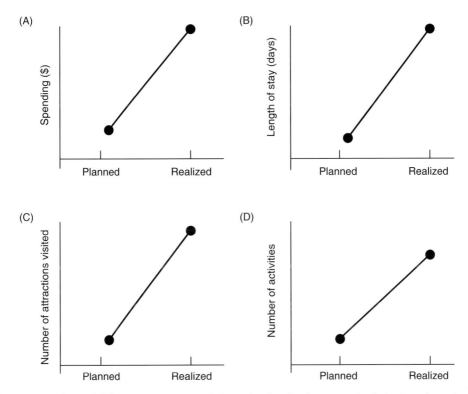

Fig. 4.5. Hypothesized differences in consumers' planned and realized consumption behaviours for main variables: (A) between planned and realized spending; (B) between planned and realized length of stay; (C) between planned and realized attractions; and (D) between planned and realized activities.

engage in pre-arrival planning by obtaining information, particularly if they are first-time visitors. Novelty seekers, operationalized in this study as seekers of new culture, tend to seek more information, undertake more activities but also engage in more unplanned activities (Gitelson and Crompton, 1983), in contrast to visitors seeking familiarity in the destination, whose plans are more likely to approximate their eventual behaviours.

In the general marketing environment, the social setting (presence or absence of others) that characterizes the consumption of a product or service influences both planned and actual behaviours, as it does other consumer behaviour (Stayman and Deshplande, 1989). Fisher (2001) found that greater collaboration led to higher decision quality and smaller deviations between consumers' planned and actual expenditures. In leisure settings, the behaviour of travellers is heavily influenced by the com-

position of the travel party (McIntosh and Goeldner, 1990). Leisure travel is a product that is jointly consumed, and leisure travel activities reflect the influence – direct and indirect – of all those travelling together (Chadwick, 1987). This phenomenon is particularly noticeable when children are present (or absent). It is safe to assume that travelling with children in a tourist destination requires greater planning and forethought than is required by couples or tourists travelling alone. Therefore, groups with children are likely to plan their trip itinerary prior to, rather than after, arrival in the destination (Fodness and Murray, 1999). Also, large travel parties comprising friends will require greater coordination in order to meet differential needs than will couples or individuals travelling alone.

In the context of contingencies, the following hypothesis is now formally stated, based on the foregoing discussion:

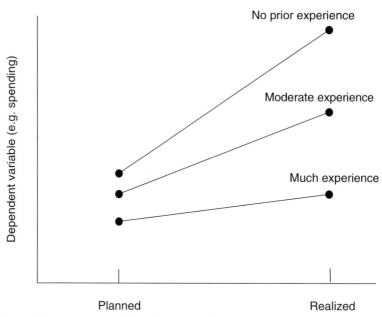

Fig. 4.6. Theory of how experience reduces the impact of planned versus realized strategies.

H₂: The level of matching between planned and realized actions varies as a function of contingency factors: composition of travel party, product experience and motivations. (i) For product experience, the greater the experience the more likely will planned behaviours match actual behaviours. (ii) For composition of travel party, the fewer the number of members, the more likely will planned behaviours match actual behaviours. (iii) For motivation, the planned behaviours of novelty-seeking individuals less likely match their actual behaviours, while the planned behaviours of familiarity-seeking individuals more likely match their actual behaviours.

The third proposition related to this section examines the relationship between shifts in planned and realized behaviours according to increases in the time spent in the consumption system. While research into time pressure effects has a long and deep history in both economics (Stigler, 1961) and psychology (Hendrick et al., 1968; Bishop and Witt, 1970; Wright, 1974), consumer researchers arrived late to the topic (Feldman and Hornik, 1981; Hornik, 1982; Iyer, 1989; Gross, 1994; Leclerc et al., 1994). Howard and Sheth (1969) included time pressure as an exogenous variable in their classic *The Theory of Buyer Behavior*, and commented that little was known about it. Writing in the

marketing literature, Jacoby et al. (1976) produced an excellent synthesis of work in the field, but were compelled to sub-title their paper 'An interdisciplinary overview' due to the 'scant attention' (p. 320) the topic had received in the marketing field. In a conference paper, Payne et al. (1987, cited by Iyer, 1989) alluded to, but did not examine, the time variable. Time has been shown to constrain unplanned purchases (Iyer, 1989), while time availability was linked to search activity in a retail setting (Beatty and Smith, 1987). Iyer (1989) found that time pressure, and the lack thereof, reduced unplanned purchases. In the tourism literature, determinants of planning time have been investigated (Zalatan, 1996), but the interaction between time in the consumption system and consumption behaviours has not. In this study, time is operationalized as length of stay and categorized as a contingency influence.

All other things being equal, we may assume that the longer the length of stay, the greater is the likelihood that individuals will engage in unplanned behaviours. In one study, Beatty and Ferrell (1998) treated time available as an external exogenous variable (along with budget available). In this study, however, since our main focus is to identify the characteristics of individuals engaged in planned, unplanned and actual consumption, time is defined as length of stay in the destination and treated as a dependent variable.

Kollat and Willett's (1967) research suggested that unplanned purchases were more likely to occur on a large shopping (grocery) trip than on a small one to buy just a few items. (This finding was confirmed years later by Inman and Winer, 1998.) Prasad (1975) found that the level of unplanned purchases increased with the size of the shopper's total transaction. Beatty and Ferrell (1998) found that time available, an exogenous variable, was particularly influential in the length of time devoted to browsing and purchasing. Based on the preceding discussion, the following hypothesis is now formally stated:

> **H₃**: Increases in length of stay in a destination region for planned and realized behaviours are associated with increases in the number of destination-area consumption activities, although the increase in the number of activities by length of stay will be greater for realized rather than planned behaviours (see Fig. 4.7).

Effects of product information on planned and realized consumption behaviours

The ability of individuals to anticipate outcomes is related to the availability of information, as well as to the individual's cognitive abilities. If information is available in the consumption environment, *ceteris paribus*, individuals should be able to anticipate their future outcomes more accurately; conversely, the absence of information heightens uncertainty and makes decision making more difficult and the outcomes less predictable.

While marketing communications are widely assumed to have a positive impact on consumption behaviour, the extent of the influence has long been debated. An important contribution of this chapter will be the examination of the impact of product information on consumer plans and consumption behaviour.

The supply of tourist information, typically in the form of a visitor information guide (VIG), is a critical element of the communication strategy of tourism marketing organizations. The VIG is important for three reasons: first, since a leisure trip is a high-risk purchase, involving the use of discretionary dollars, a VIG serves to reassure the consumer that his/her decision is the correct one; secondly, the intangibility of the tourism product means that the consumer is heavily reliant on information, whether it be printed, word-of-mouth, or electronic; and thirdly, since the majority of holiday makers visiting a particular place are likely to be first-time visitors, information about the destination is essential (Wicks and Schuett, 1991).

Despite this importance, little research has been undertaken in the tourism field to substantiate the widespread belief that visitors who use printed information will, all other things being equal, consume more than those visitors who do not. Ritchie (1994, p. 10) lamented

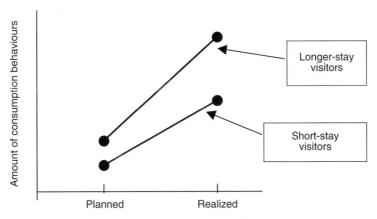

Fig. 4.7. Hypothesized differences between planned and realized consumption behaviours by length of stay.

that: '[W]e are still far from a clear understanding of the effectiveness of the various forms of advertising and promotion which are used so extensively by tourism marketers'. For example, although the investigation of trip-planning behaviour was a main objective of the authors' research into travel preferences of the US outbound travel market, Rao *et al.* (1992) did not ask respondents the degree to which different information sources influenced their trip decisions. Fesenmaier *et al.* (1993) examined the influence of information on future travel plans (defined as trip purpose, travel route, and information search strategies), and although the impact of information upon the actual behaviour was neglected, general support was found for their propositions. In a related study, Fodness and Murray (1999) identified a strong correlation between the number of information sources accessed and the length of stay, and the number of information sources accessed and overall spending. Little wonder, therefore, that in his study of VIGs produced by regional tourism bodies (RTBs) in the UK, Alford (1998) concluded that though the guides 'represent a major slice of the RTB marketing budget, [the RTBs] have little means of gauging the effectiveness of this publication, other than receiving general feedback from suppliers, distributors, and information gathered through surveys' (p.

67). Co-authors of one of the most recent studies of tourist information search and usage drew the conclusion that '[a]dditional research on tourist information search is needed in many areas' (Fodness and Murray, 1999, p. 229).

As the above discussion shows, destination marketing organizations need to better understand the extent to which printed information influences consumer choices and consumption outcomes. As studies have shown, the more activities and opportunities an individual is aware of at the intended destination, the greater is the individual's likely level of consumption (Chadwick, 1987; Moutinho, 1987; McIntosh and Goeldner, 1990). In addition, Etzel and Wahlers (1985) found a positive relationship between increasing levels of information search and increasing travel expenditures.

One of the core propositions in this chapter is that product information significantly increases the level of consumption behaviours undertaken by consumers, relative to those individuals who do not receive product information. When this assumption is applied to the hypothesis generated earlier, that realized behaviours will exceed planned behaviours, we can postulate that the consumers who have received the VIG and who have completed their visit to the destination will record higher consumption behaviours. This proposition is illustrated in Fig. 4.8.

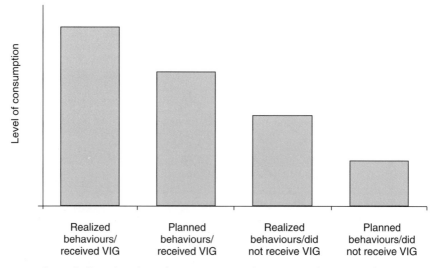

Fig. 4.8. Hypothesized effect of product information (visitor information guide, VIG) on planned and realized consumption behaviours.

Based on the foregoing discussion, the following hypotheses have been generated:

H$_4$: Consumers use product information more while in the consumption site than prior to entering the consumption site (Fig. 4.9B).

H$_5$: Consumers with product information are more likely to both plan and engage in more tourist consumption behaviours than those without product information (Fig. 4.9A).

H$_6$: Consumers who use product information are likely to plan and report higher consumption behaviours (such as spending and length of stay) than consumers who do not use product information (Fig. 4.9C).

Studies have shown that experience of the destination plays a significant role in various aspects of travel planning and activities, including information use (Etzel and Wahlers, 1985),

time spent planning (Zalatan, 1996) and destination attractiveness (Hu and Ritchie, 1993).

While conventional wisdom suggests that consumers with little or no product experience are likely to require and seek more information than experienced consumers, Bettman and Park (1980) have argued that consumers with little prior knowledge will engage in less information search if the nature of the search task appears overwhelming. Individuals in the exit survey who received the VIG are likely to record the highest number of (realized) activities, while their counterparts in the entry survey who did not receive the VIG will register the smallest number of (planned) activities. Finally, our hypothesis regarding the effect of destination experience on the use or non-use of the VIG is illustrated in Fig. 4.10.

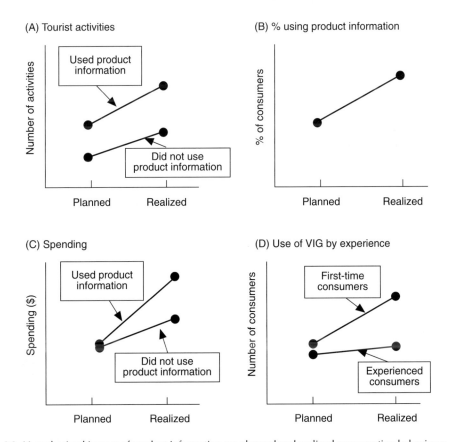

Fig. 4.9. Hypothesized impact of product information on planned and realized consumption behaviours. Hypothesized differences between (A) planned and realized consumption behaviours; (B) planned and realized use of information; (C) planned and realized spending according to use of information; (D) planned and realized use of information according to product experience.

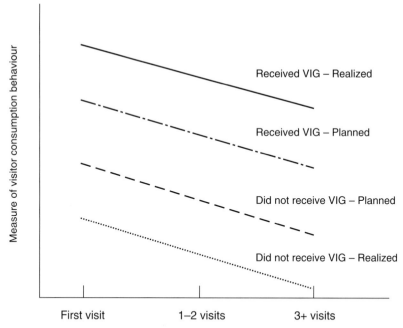

Fig. 4.10. Theorized impact of destination experience and use and non-use of visitor information guide (VIG) on planned and realized consumption behaviours.

Based on the foregoing discussion, the following hypothesis has been generated.

H₇: Within a given time period (period the consumer is in the tourism destination), first-time consumers planning and actually doing the trip will use product information more than experienced consumers (Fig. 4.9D).

Famous destinations and major tourist attractions benefit, by definition, from high brand awareness. Iconic attractions are 'pull factors' or motivators that influence tourists to visit. Information plays a minor role in prompting purchase or visit. For visitors to Prince Edward Island, the home of *Anne of Green Gables*, Charlottetown, is the island province's major (and probably only) icon. Conversely, unknown destinations require information to generate visitation. For that reason, consumers exposed to product information are more likely to visit unknown places than consumers not exposed to such information.

H₈: The more unknown an attraction is, the greater will be the influence of product information about that attraction on planning and actual consumption of the experience (Fig. 4.11).

Influence of customer characteristics on planned and unplanned consumption behaviours

This study informs our understanding of how customer characteristics shape both planned and unplanned consumption behaviours. One of the main shortcomings in research on unplanned consumption has been the inadequate consideration of consumer characteristics. As Table 4.1 reveals, only five empirical studies on the subject of planned and unplanned behaviours incorporate demographics or other consumer characteristics. Cobb and Hoyer (1986) felt sufficiently concerned about the neglect of research into customer characteristics associated with unplanned and impulse purchasing that they labelled it a 'shortcoming' (p. 389). From a strategic marketing viewpoint, understanding the characteristics of target segments is fundamental in creating an effective communication mix.

The relationship between distance travelled and behaviours is especially pertinent in the tourism context. There are a number of perspectives. First, the distance travelled to a con-

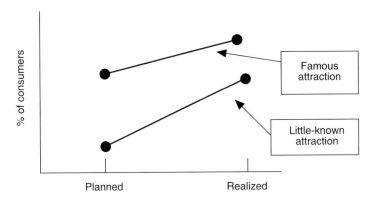

Fig. 4.11. Hypothesized differences between planned and realized visits to attractions.

sumption site has been used as a surrogate for risk in previous marketing studies; namely, Newman and Staelin's (1972) study of information-seeking behaviour related to new cars and household durables, and the tourism-related study by Fesenmaier and Johnson (1989) into involvement in the vacation planning process. These investigations suggest that individuals travelling long distances will plan more, due to higher perceived risk associated with the distance involved. Schul and Crompton (1983, p. 25) confirmed as such: 'information search [is] likely to be greater for major (that is long-distance travel) rather than minor (short-distance) investments'. Greater planning may suggest that eventual behaviours will more likely match intended behaviours. On the other hand, the very fact that long distances are required is likely to compel consumers to purchase low-risk package tours, rather than attempt to make their own travel arrangements.

> **H$_9$**: The greater the distance that consumers travel to engage in destination-specific consumption activities, the greater the difference in expenditures between planned and realized activities (Fig. 4.12).

The influence of experience on planned and actual behaviour is a fascinating area of our study. Research shows that intention formation is affected by past experience (Fazio and Zanna, 1981; Morwitz and Schmittlein, 1992). Product experience is critical when studying the dynamic choice processes of consumers new to a market (Heilman et al., 2000).

Since experience teaches people how to plan, the consumption actions of experienced consumers will more closely approximate their plans than consumers with little or no product knowledge (Stewart and Vogt, 1999). Routine and habitual buyer behaviour allows for purposive and intelligent behaviour without deliberation (Katona, 1975). Experienced consumers should be better able than less experienced consumers to assess the risks associated with engaging in particular behaviours and to understand the factors that will influence the decision. For example, how long it takes to drive to particular destinations on an island, which route offers the best scenery, which attractions are worth spending time and money on, and what accommodation is value for money are all questions more readily answered by the experienced rather than the inexperienced visitor. Consequently, hypothesis **H$_{10}$** states that experienced consumers differ from inexperienced consumers in two ways: they plan fewer consumption activities; and the difference between planned and realized consumption activities will be less for experienced consumers than for inexperienced consumers.

Product experience in this study relates to the number of times a respondent has visited Prince Edward Island. Consumers with previous experience should have more accurate predictions of whether or not they will engage in particular future behaviours than consumers with little or no experience. Again, experienced consumers should be better able to assess the risks associated with engaging in particular

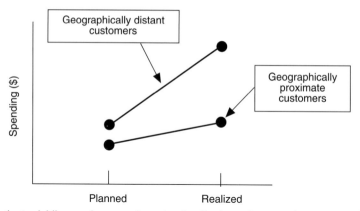

Fig. 4.12. Hypothesized differences between planned and realized spending according to geographical location.

behaviours and to understand the factors that will influence the decision than less experienced consumers.

Experienced shoppers in a supermarket environment, for instance, were found to repeat the same choice as the previous consumption experience and to have well-articulated preferences when they are familiar with the preference object (Bettman *et al.*, 1998). Morwitz and Schmittlein (1992) found that past usage of a durable good moderated the accuracy of future purchase intentions. Among individuals who stated an intention to purchase a personal computer (PC) in the following 6 months, 48% of those with experience of a PC fulfilled their intentions, while only 29% with no experience fulfilled their intentions. Similarly, Vernplanken *et al.* (1997) found that respondents who frequently performed a certain behaviour (a particular mode of transport) searched for less information about which travel mode to use and were more likely to focus on information about the habitual choice than alternative choices, compared to those who less frequently performed the behaviour. Past behaviour therefore acts as an internal source of information. And as consumers' experience with a product increases, consideration sets are likely to be increasingly stable over time (Klenosky and Rethans, 1988; Mitra, 1995). This would suggest that first-time customers would display less consistency that will, in return, be reflected in greater discrepancies between planned and actual behaviour. Aarts *et al.* (1998) argue that habitual

behaviours become capable of being automatically activated by features of the situation and context in which the behaviour occurs.

Much of the consumer research in this area has dealt with product brands rather than product categories. Brand loyalty and awareness become, therefore, critical issues for the researcher to understand. But what of product categories that lack powerful brands – or in situations when the powerful brands are simply not available? If we consider the variety of typical leisure consumption activities in a destination such as Prince Edward Island, few involve products with which travellers register any brand recognition whatsoever. There are no international hotel chains such as Hilton and Sheraton, no famous natural or man-made attractions such as the Canadian Rockies or Disneyland and no famous restaurants. The only study adopting this perspective found that preference reversals are less prevalent for familiar product categories (Coupey *et al.*, 1996). Given the large amount of consumption occurring in product categories in which brands are not important, this finding needs to be verified.

As discussed earlier, the influences upon unplanned purchasing that have been identified include characteristics of the shopping party (Kollat and Willett, 1967), personality traits (Raju, 1980) and proclivity to visit stores (Granbois, 1968). Neither Kollat and Willett (1967) nor Prasad (1975) found that socio-economic characteristics were a significant explanatory factor in shoppers performing unplanned buying behaviour.

Supporting the argument that inexperience and information-seeking behaviour are positively related is the finding by Bloch *et al.* (1986) who, in investigating consumer search procedures for clothing and personal computers, found that heavy searchers were heavy spenders within the product class. Higher spending was associated with higher product awareness and frequent contact with information providers and retailers. (They also identified two types of searchers: ongoing/hedonistic searchers and prepurchase searchers. Hedonistic searchers enjoyed the activity of seeking out information, perhaps even more than any actual consumption experience.)

Within the tourism literature, customer experience is commonly defined as whether the visitor is a first-time or repeat traveller. Similar to other consumption systems, it is assumed that first-time visitors to a destination have little product knowledge and will likely therefore spend more than their experienced counterparts. Woodside *et al.* (1997), for instance, support findings in other fields that experienced consumers undertake fewer consumption activities than inexperienced ones. Etzel and Wahlers (1985) sought to identify the characteristics of people who request travel information and those who do not. Several interesting findings emerged: first, information seekers tend to spend more than consumers who do not seek out information; secondly, the greater the frequency in product consumption, the less likely that consumers would seek information; and thirdly, experienced travellers

were less likely to request information. However, a major weakness in the study was the assumption that request for information equated with information used and, ultimately, actual behaviour.

The influence of experience upon consumption behaviour in the travel context is well documented. Studies show product experience of the destination plays a significant role in various aspects of travel planning and activities, including information use (Etzel and Wahlers, 1985); time spent planning (Zalatan, 1996); risk perception (Roehl and Fesenmaier, 1992); site choice (McFarlane *et al.*, 1998); destination attractiveness (Hu and Ritchie, 1993); and satisfaction with a destination (Mazursky, 1989b).

H_{10}: Experienced consumers will plan fewer consumption activities and are less likely to engage in unplanned activities than inexperienced consumers (see Fig. 4.13).

Attitudes towards planning differ between individuals. For some individuals, the planning of holidays, including the collection of vast amounts of information, is an integral part of the whole experience; for others, a holiday is a spontaneous experience, in which predetermined activities and time allocations are an anathema; and there are many individuals who fit somewhere in between. Greater planning of a holiday would, arguably, reflect greater involvement and commitment in the destination, which would then be reflected in higher expenditures. Vacation behaviours have been shown to differ according to specific socio-demographic variables (Gitelson and

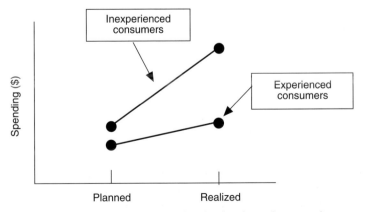

Fig. 4.13. Hypothesized differences between planned and realized spending according to experience.

Kerstetter, 1990). Morwitz and Schmittlein (1992) suggest that economic factors, such as wealth, will increase the likelihood of intentions matching actual behaviour. On the other hand, individuals with greater discretionary income would presumably be capable of engaging in a greater degree of unplanned, impulsive consumption.

> **H₁₁**: The higher the income level, and therefore the greater ability to undertake consumption behaviour, the greater the likelihood of unplanned consumption activity (see Fig. 4.14).

According to the theory of planned behaviour (Ajzen, 1985), a behavioural intention is defined as an intention to *try* to perform a certain behaviour. Intention predicts whether an individual will attempt to perform a particular behaviour; if it does not predict attainment of the goal, then factors lying beyond the control of the actor prevented the person from carrying out the intention. In other words, the actualization of the intended behaviour is contingent on the individual's control over the various factors that may prevent it. In a group travel situation, we might expect that the greater the number of individuals involved in, and/or affected by, a decision, the more unlikely it will be for the original plan to be actualized.

Early research in the tourism and leisure field flagged the association between social context and the individual's decision process. Burch (1969) was one of the first to discuss the importance of the social group in relation to recreation and tourist behaviour. His personal community hypothesis suggested that such behaviour is seldom an isolated individual decision. Christensen and Yoesting (1973) confirmed his thesis, and argued that the choice and use of recreational facilities are related to the social context in which the individual is located.

Leisure travel is a product that often is jointly consumed, and tourist activities reflect the influence (both direct and indirect) of all those travelling together (Chadwick, 1987). The behaviour of tourists is heavily influenced by the composition of the travel party (McIntosh and Goeldner, 1990). Travel party size can influence behaviour in several ways. First, a group of travel companions, whether extended family, friends or colleagues, requires more time for planning, and a stronger need for information, than do couples or singles (Fesenmaier and Lieber, 1988, cited in Stewart and Vogt, 1999). Conversely, independent travellers are more likely to engage in unplanned behaviours. According to Hyde (2000, p. 188), 'the [independent] tourist avoids vacation planning because flexibility of action and experiencing the unknown are key amongst the hedonic experiences they seeking'. Secondly, groups comprising children require greater planning efforts to coordinate schedules and differential needs than groups without children (Fodness and Murray, 1999). Thirdly, Fisher (2001) found that collaboration led to higher decision quality and smaller deviations between consumers' planned and actual

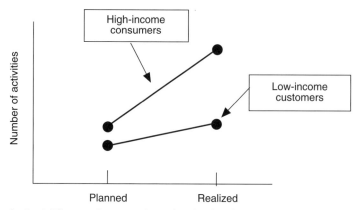

Fig. 4.14. Hypothesized differences between planned and realized activities according to income.

expenditures. Fourthly, a respondent travelling alone has more flexibility in changing plans than a respondent travelling with children or with a group of friends. Morwitz (1997b) posits that the intent–behaviour relationship for *durable products* might actually be weaker when the approval of more than one person is required, than products involving a single decision maker. Fifthly, preferences for travel experiences can differ according to travel party composition (Basala and Klenosky, 2001). Here the role of the family members is highly influential (Moutinho, 1987; Dimanche and Havitz, 1994).

H_{12}: The smaller the travel party size, the less will be the difference between planned and realized behaviours (Fig. 4.15).

Summary

This chapter introduces the main area of academic enquiry of Part II of this book, namely, the influences on consumers' planned and unplanned strategies in the purchases of products and services in a tourist consumption system. The rationale underlying this research area was explained. This relates to the need to better understand some of the determinants of consumption behaviours, particularly when they differ significantly from planned behaviours. Two critical determinants examined in this chapter are product information and demographics, such as income, age, and geographical location.

The main points of academic and managerial interest springing from the chapter were highlighted. From an academic perspective, our understanding of the influence of product information and demographics upon actual consumption behaviours will be enhanced. Also, the application of the Mintzberg strategy matrix offers a useful conceptual tool for future examinations of divergences between planned, unplanned and actual behaviours. Managerially, the chapter highlights the importance of product information as a means of positively influencing consumer demand for products and services.

Theory related to planned and unplanned behaviour was examined. Beginning with empirical and conceptual research in the field of social psychology, the discussion then summarized the contributions made in the marketing and tourism fields in the area of intentions and behaviour. A listing of marketing-related empirical research carried out in the topic area was provided to contextualize the significance of this chapter.

The research setting, the holiday destination of Prince Edward Island, is introduced. The size and robustness of the data sets, generated from entry and exit surveys, was explained. The hypotheses and their justifications are then detailed. The hypotheses are classified according to three categories: first, the relationship between planned and realized consumption

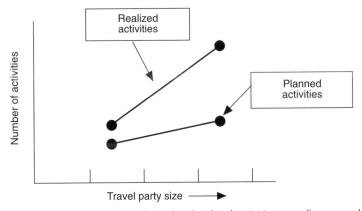

Fig. 4.15. Hypothesized differences between planned and realized activities according to travel party size.

behaviours; secondly, the effects of product information on planned and realized consumption behaviours; and thirdly, the influence of customer characteristics on planned and unplanned consumption behaviours. These relationships are detailed in Fig. 4.16.

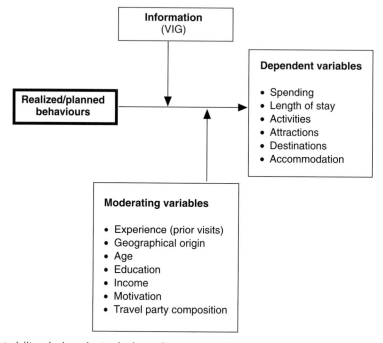

Fig. 4.16. Modelling the hypothesized relationships examined in this study (VIG, visitor information guide).

5 Summary of Findings

Introduction

This chapter provides a summary of the findings related to the hypotheses and research objectives outlined in Chapter 4. A thorough discussion of these findings and data analysis is found in Chapter 8 (Variations Between Planned and Realized Behaviours), Chapter 9 (Influence of Product Information on Planned and Realized Consumption Activities) and Chapter 10 (Influence of Consumer Characteristics on Planned and Realized Behaviours). These chapters also mention key conceptual and managerial implications arising from the analysis, although a deeper discussion is given in Chapter 11 (Strategic Implications and Discussion).

The analysis involves six dependent variables: spending, length of stay, attractions, activities, destinations and accommodation; seven independent or moderating variables: geographic origin, income, product experience, motivation, education, travel party size; and one other independent variable, product information (namely, visitor's information guide, or VIG). Aggregation of some variables was necessary to facilitate tests for associations among the criterion and predictor variables (for example, responses for the variables 'Attractions' and 'Activities' were aggregated into ratio-scale variables, ranging from 0 to 6 and 0 to 13, respectively). The tested relationships are shown in Fig. 5.1.

The structure of the chapter is as follows. First, the results of hypothesis testing are shown. The hypotheses are grouped under three headings, which represent the three sets of relationship being examined in this study. They are:

- relationship between planned and realized consumption behaviours;
- effects of product information on planned and realized consumption behaviours; and
- influence of customer characteristics on planned and unplanned consumption behaviours.

Secondly, the main and interaction effects are examined and discussed briefly. Thirdly, two models are offered and explained: the original model detailing the theoretical assumptions underpinning the research, and a revised model based on the research findings that extend our understanding of consumer behaviour. Fourthly, the application of Mintzberg's strategy model to the planned and realized behaviours of consumers, a key objective of this study, is undertaken.

Hypothesis Test Results

Planned versus realized behaviours

H_1: Realized consumption behaviours are greater than planned for most specific services related to a purchased service system.

© R. March and A.G. Woodside 2005. *Tourism Behaviour: Travellers' Decisions and Actions* (R. March and A.G. Woodside)

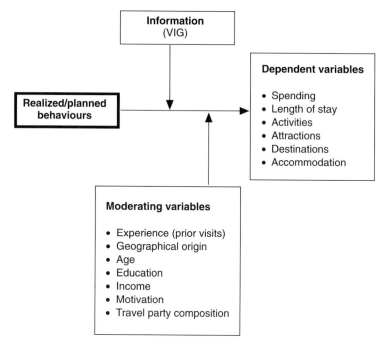

Fig. 5.1. Main relationships examined in this study.

Statistically significant differences between planned and realized behaviours were identified for spending, length of stay, total number of activities undertaken and total number of attractions visited. At the individual attraction level, overall realized visits to attractions were greater than planned visits to attractions for all six attractions, except Ardgowan and Green Gables. Similarly, overall realized activities were greater than planned activities for all 12 activities, except golf.

The following results refer to the difference between planned and realized main behaviours (spending, length of stay, activities and attractions) at the individual unit level for each independent variable. All results were statistically significant ($P < 0.05$). Where there was no statistical difference for all units of the independent variable – for example, planned and realized spending were not different for all education categories – the independent variable is not mentioned. This approach has been adopted for two purposes: first, it simplifies an already complex set of inter-relationships, and secondly, from a managerial perspective, it

serves to identify the most important customer variables that could be incorporated into future marketing communication strategies.

The results were as follows:

1. Realized spending exceeded planned spending for:
- *all* geographic origins
- *all* age categories
- *all* motivation categories
- *all* experience categories.

2. Realized length of stay exceeded planned length of stay for:
- *all* geographic origins
- *all* age categories
- *all* experience categories.

3. Realized activities were greater than planned activities for:
- *all* geographical origins
- *all* income groups
- *all* product experience categories
- *all* motivation types
- *all* educational categories
- *all* travel party types
- *all* age categories.

4. Realized number of attractions was greater than planned number of visits for:

- *all* geographic origins
- *all* income groups
- *all* product experience categories
- *all* educational categories
- *all* age categories.

H₂: The level of matching between planned and realized actions varies as a function of contingency factors: composition of travel party, product experience and motivations. (i) For product experience, the greater the experience the more likely will planned behaviours match actual behaviours. (ii) For composition of travel party, the fewer the number of members, the more likely will planned behaviours match actual behaviours. (iii) For motivation, the planned behaviours of novelty-seeking individuals less likely match their actual behaviours, while the planned behaviours of familiarity-seeking individuals more likely match their actual behaviours.

Neither higher experience nor smaller travel party were reflected in significantly smaller differences between planned and realized consumption behaviours. Planned and realized spending and length of stay for the different levels of experience and size of travel party are shown in Tables 5.1 and 5.2, respectively.

H₃: Increases in length of stay in a destination region for planned and realized behaviours are associated with increases in the number of destination-area consumption activities, although the increase in the number of activities by length of stay will be greater for realized rather than planned behaviours.

This hypothesis was supported. Changes in the number of planned and realized activities and spending for increases in the length of stay are tabulated in Tables 5.3 and 5.4. Linear regression analysis was undertaken to test the differences for the number of planned and realized activities for length of stay. The r-square value for planned activities by increasing length of stay was 0.06, whereas the r-square value for realized activities by increasing length of stay was 0.214 (both significant at 0.001). This supported **H₃**.

Differences for the number of planned and realized spending for length of stay were also plotted and the 'r' values calculated. The r-square value for planned spending by increasing length of stay was 0.43, whereas the equivalent value for realized activities by increasing length of stay was 0.47 (both significant at 0.001). This finding also supported **H₃**.

Table 5.1. Planned and realized consumption behaviours by degree of experience.

	Planned			Realized		
	First-timers ($n = 1236$)	Moderately experienced ($n = 489$)	Much experienced ($n = 637$)	First-timers ($n = 1184$)	Moderately experienced ($n = 397$)	Much experienced ($n = 524$)
Spending	$394	$432	$352	$518	$532	$453
Length of stay (nights)	3.0	3.8	4.8	3.5	4.6	5.5

Table 5.2. Planned and realized consumption behaviours by size of travel party.

	Planned				Realized			
	Alone ($n = 157$)	One couple ($n = 1076$)	One family ($n = 502$)	2 or more families ($n = 200$)	Alone ($n = 182$)	One couple ($n = 957$)	One family ($n = 467$)	2 or more families ($n = 139$)
Spending	$263	$370	$474	$390	$343	$475	$638	$520
Length of stay (nights)	5.4	3.5	4.2	3.1	6.0	4.2	4.5	3.8

Table 5.3. Average number of planned and realized activities by length of stay.

	Planned		Realized	
	Mean	SD	Mean	SD
0–3 days	2.5 (n = 1655)	1.68	5.6 (n = 1230)	2.31
4+ days	3.0 (n = 686)	2.07	7.0 (n = 813)	2.36
Total	2.7 (n = 2341)	1.81	6.2 (n = 2043)	2.43

Table 5.4. Average planned and realized spending by length of stay.

	Planned		Realized	
	Mean	SD	Mean	SD
0–3 days	$287 (n = 855)	255	$334 (n = 1222)	337
4+ days	$626 (n = 367)	572	$779 (n = 789)	715
Total	$389 (n = 1222)	409	$509 (n = 2011)	562

Effects of product information on planned and realized consumption behaviours

This section summarizes the results of the tested hypotheses relating to the effects of product information on planned and realized consumption behaviours. To provide an interpretative illustration the effects of the VIG on planned and realized activities, group-level analysis was undertaken, as shown in Fig. 5.2. To explain, the five columns on the far left of the diagram correspond to the five income levels (from lowest to highest) for planned behaviours by respondents who did not receive a VIG. Conversely, the five columns on the far right correspond to the five income levels (from lowest to highest) for planned behaviours by respondents who did receive a VIG. Although no causal inferences can be drawn, these results suggest a relationship between planned and realized consumption behaviours and the use or non-use of production information (and in this case, the independent variables 'income').

The same approach was used to illustrate the trend in consumption behaviour for two independent variables: income and home origin (see Fig. 5.3). Again, an interesting trend is revealed, although the same caveats apply as in the previous example.

H_4: Consumers use product information more while in the consumption site than prior to entering the consumption site.

This hypothesis was not supported. It was assumed that visitors avail themselves of product information more after arriving at a destination than prior to arrival. Certainly, the number of respondents reporting having received the VIG increased markedly between the entry and exit surveys; 22% of respondents in the entry survey reported receiving and using the VIG, compared to 65% in the exit survey. This is not surprising. Much more remarkable is the finding that the proportions of respondents reporting having used the VIG 'completely' or 'some' were almost identical, as Table 5.5 shows.

H_5: Consumers with product information are likely to both plan and engage in more consumption activities than those without product information.

Testing the three dependent variables of length of stay, activities and attractions revealed partial confirmation for this hypothesis. For planned consumption behaviours, respondents who received the VIG reported statistically higher consumption intentions for attractions only ($P < 0.001$). For realized consumption behaviours on the other hand, the behaviours of both activities and attractions were statistically significant at the $P < 0.001$ level. Length of stay was the exception, a finding confirmed in other sections of this study. This limitation on the number of nights suggests that while respondents with the VIG have the time and financial capacities to increase the

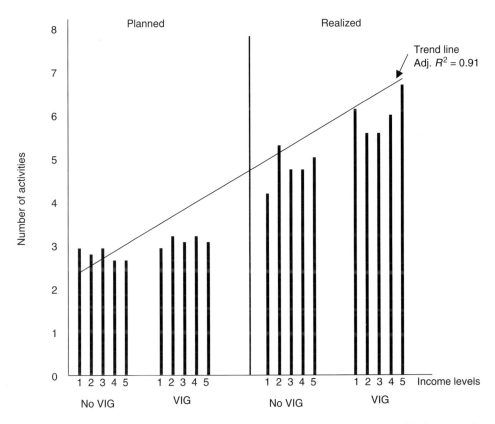

Fig. 5.2. Trend indicating that the number of activities increases as income rises, visitors shift from not using to using the visitor information guide (VIG), and strategy shifts from planned to realized.

amount of consumption activities during their planned stay, they are unable or unwilling to extend the number of days on the island.

> **H$_6$**: Consumers who use product information more often plan and report higher expenditures than consumers who do not use product information.

The test results reflect the findings of **H$_5$**. For planned spending, no statistical significant difference was found between respondents who received the VIG and those who did not. Significance ($P < 0.001$) was identified for realized spending, however. As such, the hypothesis is partially supported.

Spending by tourists may be regarded as the result of increased consumption of specific tourist services, such as accommodation, activities, visits to attractions, amount of shopping and so on. Spending is a macro-indicator and outcome of consumption activity, and (gener-

ally) not a consumption activity in itself (unless, of course, a consumer wants to, for example, 'shop for shopping's sake'). From the perspective of a marketing strategist in the tourism industry, spending levels offer few insights into the travel and consumption patterns of tourists.

Knowledge of spending levels nevertheless serves two useful purposes. Spending is both an indicator of the relative attractiveness of particular customer segments and a quantifiable measure to justify marketing budgets allocated to destination marketing organizations by government financial authorities. Of utmost relevance to this study, if increased spending can be shown to be the result of exposure to tourist information, then the costs incurred in the production and distribution of the information can be justified. For that reason, it was appropriate in this study to test for the effect of the VIG on spending.

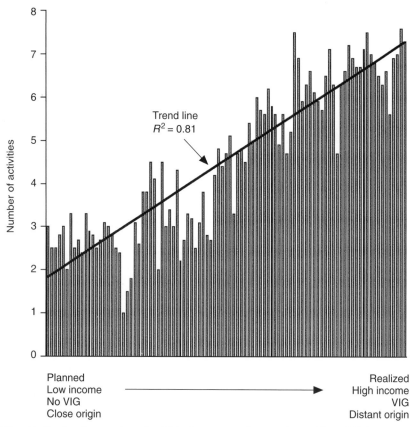

Fig. 5.3. Trend indicating that number of activities increases as income rises, visitors shift from not using to using the visitor information guide (VIG), visitors reside further from the destination, and strategy shifts from planned to realized.

Table 5.5. Use and non-use of VIG (visitor information guide) reported in entry and exit surveys.

	Entry (%)	Exit (%)
Received VIG	22	65
Did not receive VIG	78	35
VIG use by respondents who received VIG	$n = 517$	$n = 1313$
Used completely	27	30
Used somewhat	51	50
Used very little	10	9
Received and not used	10	9

A summary of the results of *t*-tests related to planned and realized behaviours and hypotheses **H₅** and **H₆** is shown in Table 5.6.

H₇: Within a given time period (period the consumer is in the tourism consumption system),

first-time consumers planning and actually doing the trip will use product information more than experienced consumers.

This hypothesis was not supported. The results challenge the assumption that first-time

Table 5.6. Planned and realized consumption behaviours by exposure to visitor information guide (VIG).

	Planned		Realized	
	VIG versus no VIG[a]	Sig.	VIG versus no VIG	Sig.
Spending	$512–$441	ns[b]	$605–$354	0.001
Number of nights	3.9–3.2	ns	4.3–4.1	ns
Number of activities	3.2–2.8	ns	6.8–5.1	0.001
Number of attractions	1.3–1.0	0.000	2.3–1.4	0.001

[a]VIG versus no VIG shows the mean values for each dependent variable for two groups: those who received the VIG and those who did not.
[b]ns, not significant.

visitors are much more likely to use product information than their more experienced counterparts. As analyses outlined in Chapter 7 will reveal, the effect of experience on tourist behaviour is complex indeed.

One of the assumptions concerning tourist behaviour is that first-time visitors to a destination will utilize product information more than experienced visitors. The logic underlying this assumption is self-evident: experienced consumers rely on memory and past behaviours to make consumption decisions, while new consumers require information on which to base and justify consumption decisions. This axiom underpins the activities of many marketing organizations that target first-time visitors with information, in the belief that: (i) they will be in the greatest need of such information; and (ii) they are more likely to generate higher spending activities than more experienced visitors, whose activities have been planned before arrival.

Our results indicate that extent of information usage by moderate repeaters (those reporting 1–4 previous visits) differs little from that of first-time visitors. In fact, in the exit survey, the percentage of moderate repeaters using the VIG 'somewhat' or 'completely' was greater than the percentage of first-timers using the VIG in the same manner. An explanation for this latter finding may be found in the argument put forward by Bettman and Park in their seminal paper (1980). The authors assert that novice consumers do not search because search is too difficult and complex, and highly experienced consumers do not search because they do not need to do so. According to this scenario, it is the somewhat experienced/knowledgeable consumer who searches the most. A summary of the relationship between use and non-use of the VIG and experience is shown in Table 5.7. As the figures suggest, no significant difference between the three levels of experience and level of VIG usage was identified.

Table 5.7. Relationship between planned and realized use of visitor information guide (VIG) and experience.

	Planned			Realized		
	First-timers	Moderately experienced	Highly experienced	First-timers	Moderately experienced	Highly experienced
Used completely or somewhat	277 (79%)	87 (75%)	133 (76%)	694 (83%)	224 (85%)	134 (63%)
Used a little or not at all	62 (18%)	29 (25%)	42 (23%)	136 (16%)	39 (15%)	75 (37%)
TOTAL	336 (100%)	116 (100%)	175 (100%)	830 (100%)	263 (100%)	466 (100%)

'Moderately experienced' refers to respondents with 1–4 visits and 'Highly experienced' refers to respondents with more than 4 visits.

H$_8$: The more unknown an attraction is, the greater the influence of product information about that attraction on planning and actual consumption of the experience.

The hypothesis is only partially supported. Many visitors are drawn to a destination because of the destination's famous icons. Sydney, for example, is well known for its harbour, Opera House and Harbour Bridge. Over 85% of visitors to Sydney report having visited one or all of these attractions (Bureau of Tourism Research, 2000); we could assume that few visitors to Sydney would require product information such as a VIG to trigger a visit. By extension, exposure to information about such icons is unlikely to substantially increase visitation or consumption of the 'experience'.

The reverse logic can be applied to lesser known attractions in Sydney. The Museum of Sydney (MoS) in Sydney's central business district is, for example, a relatively new facility, located underneath an office building, and relatively unknown even among Sydneysiders. For an attraction like MoS, print advertising is essential. Without it, low levels of visitation are inevitable.

The forgoing proposition is embodied in this hypothesis; namely, that the influence of the VIG in generating visitation will be far greater for little-known activities and attractions.

Let us first make a number of observations about the influence of the VIG. First, for the majority of activities and attractions (and certainly for all *major* activities and attractions), the proportion of respondents reporting planned or actual visitation was greater for those who received the VIG than for those who did not. For example, 53% of respondents who did not receive a VIG planned to visit Green Gables House, while this figure rose to 64% for respondents who did receive a VIG. Secondly, some activities and attractions generate so little planned or actual visitation that the small sample prevented analysis. For example, of respondents who received a VIG, 1.2% ($n = 4$) planned to visit Ardgowan, while 0.8% ($n = 10$) of those who did not receive a VIG planned to visit the seaside town. Obviously, some tourist places are so lacking in appeal that much more sophisticated marketing activity than inclusion of information in a VIG is required to spark consumer interest.

The test for this hypothesis was both subjective and inconclusive. The definition used for a lesser known or less popular attraction was one in which planned or realized visitation levels were less than 25%. The attraction of Province House fitted this definition. Planned visitation to Province House by respondents receiving a VIG was 19% ($n = 117$), compared to just 9% ($n = 63$) among those who did not receive a VIG – a comparative increase of 119%. In contrast, the increase for the popular destination of Cavendish Beach was 34% and for Green Gables, arguably Prince Edward Island's most famous attraction, the increase was 17%.

The figures for realized visitation complicate the situation. All attractions register large increases in actual visitation between respondents who received and those who did not receive the VIG. For example, the increase in visitation to Cavendish Beach was 78%, while the increase in visitation to Province House was less (62%). Even visitation to Green Gables House rose by 42% when respondents received the VIG.

The situation related to activities was markedly different. For realized activities, there were large differences in consumption between respondents who used and did not use the VIG – even for a popular activity such as 'Go to the beach'. Half the respondents (50%) without a VIG reported going to the beach, while over three-quarters (77%) with a VIG went to the beach; this represents an increase in percentage terms of 54%. A less popular activity, such as 'Attend live theatre', registered a much smaller increase (26%).

What phenomenon of tourist behaviour is at work here? Our conclusion is that man-made or natural attractions possess iconic drawing power, and activities (except in the case of an adventure tourism destination such as Queenstown, New Zealand) do not. Attractions serve as motivational pull factors for destinations. Activities available in the destination are, in general, of secondary importance and relatively less known (with the exception being, of course, sports-related holidays such as skiing or those activities that fit the umbrella term of 'adventure' tourism). Consider the massive increase in the consumption of the activity 'Antique or handcraft shopping' between the entry and exit surveys: in contrast to the 9% of respondents in the entry survey who intended undertaking this activity, 54% in the exit survey reported undertaking this activity. (This phenomenon is explained partly by the ubiquitous nature of antique and handcraft outlets on Prince Edward Island. The sheer number of such shops may encourage many tourists to visit them, even though few planned to do so.)

What conclusion can we draw overall? In the case of attractions, the most obvious pattern is that the VIG is more influential for lesser-known attractions in the planning stage, rather than while visitors are in the destination. In the case of activities, however, no clear pattern emerges.

Influence of customer characteristics on planned and unplanned consumption behaviours

H_9: Increases in the distance that consumers travel to engage in destination-specific consumption activities increases the differences in expenditures between planned and realized consumption activities.

The hypothesis is not confirmed. This hypothesis focuses on the effect of distance on the consumption behaviour of spending. It assumes that the further tourists travel, the higher will be their overall spending and the less accurately will they estimate their eventual level of spending. The geographical origins of respondents were divided into five categories: Maritime Canada, East Coast, Mid Atlantic, Other US, and International. Planned and realized spending amounts and their differentials are shown in Table 5.8. The 'Other US' segment is an outlier; otherwise the hypothesis would have been supported.

H_{10}: Experienced consumers will plan fewer consumption activities and are less likely to engage in unplanned activities than inexperienced consumers.

Let us consider the first proposition, that experienced consumers plan fewer activities, by comparing the planned behaviours of first-time visitors with those of visitors with at least three visits. The hypothesis is supported for spending, activities, attractions, but not length of stay. [Longer length of stay can perhaps be explained by the large number of respondents citing 'Visiting friends or relatives' (VFR) as their motivation for travelling to Prince Edward Island – 303 respondents or 77% of all respondents citing VFR.]

The second proposition is summarized in Table 5.9. As shown, the difference between planned and realized behaviours for inexperienced consumers is greater than for experienced consumers for all variables. As such, the hypothesis is supported.

H_{11}: The higher the income level and therefore the greater ability to undertake consumption behaviour, the greater the likelihood of unplanned consumption activity.

The proposition that higher-income groups, more than lower-income counterparts, will report greater differences between planned and realized behaviours was not supported by the immediate evidence. Table 5.10 summarizes the differences for consumption behaviours for each income level.

Intriguingly, the income group $35–50K appears as an outlier. Compared to the $20–35K group, it reports lower realized spending and fewer realized activities; and realized length of stay and realized number of attractions visited for the two groups are identical. Due to this anomaly, further analysis

Table 5.8. Planned and realized spending, by distance from Prince Edward Island.

		Planned	Realized	Difference	
Maritime Canada	(756–595)[a]	$350	$366	$16	+5%
East Coast	(288–285)	$497	$569	$72	+14%
Mid Atlantic	(568–576)	$392	$587	$195	+50%
Other US	(574–536)	$380	$456	$76	+20%
International	(145–213)	$470	$723	$263	+58%

[a] Entry and exit survey sample sizes.

Table 5.9. Planned and realized consumption behaviours by degree of experience.

	Planned			Realized		
	First-timers (n = 1236)	Moderately experienced (n = 489)	Highly experienced (n = 637)	First-timers (n = 1184)	Moderately experienced (n = 397)	Highly experienced (n = 524)
Spending	$394	$432	$352	$518	$532	$453
Length of stay	3.0	3.8	4.8	3.5	4.6	5.5
Activities	2.7	2.8	2.6	6.4	6.2	5.1
Attractions	0.9	0.7	0.3	2.5	1.9	0.9

'Moderately experienced' refers to respondents with 1–4 visits and 'Highly experienced' refers to respondents with more than 4 visits.

Table 5.10. Average planned and realized consumption behaviours by income group.

Variables	Planned	Realized	Difference
<$20K (124–108)[a]			
Spending	$293	$332	$39
Number of nights	3.7	4.2	0.5
Number of activities	2.9	5.1	2.2
Number of attractions	1.0	1.6	0.6
$20–35K (272–250)			
Spending	$298	$376	$78
Number of nights	3.6	3.9	0.3
Number of activities	2.7	5.9	3.2
Number of attractions	1.1	1.8	0.7
$35–50K (460–379)			
Spending	$359	$361	$2
Number of nights	3.6	3.9	0.3
Number of activities	2.9	5.7	2.8
Number of attractions	1.0	1.8	0.8
$50–75K (527–416)			
Spending	$401	$475	$74
Number of nights	3.9	4.0	0.1
Number of activities	2.8	6.1	3.3
Number of attractions	1.0	2.0	1.0
$75K+ (416–372)			
Spending	$503	$626	$123
Number of nights	3.8	4.1	0.3
Number of activities	2.8	6.5	3.7
Number of attractions	1.1	2.1	1.0

[a] Sample size for entry and exit surveys.

was undertaken. This income group was omitted, the two lower income groups combined as a new variable, 'Low income', and the two highest income groups combined as a new variable, 'High income'. The results of the new analysis are shown in Table 5.11. This analysis renders a clearer distinction between income groups. As indicated, the differential for each consumption behaviour between planned and realized behaviour is greater for the high-income group, except for number of nights.

H_{12}: The smaller the travel party size, the less the difference between planned and realized behaviours.

Table 5.11. Average planned and realized consumption behaviours by low- and high-income groups.

Variables	Planned	Realized	Difference
Low income (256–345)[a]			
Spending	$296	$373	$77
Number of nights	3.5	4.1	0.6
Number of activities	2.8	5.7	3.2
Number of attractions	0.71	1.7	0.6
High income (527–765)			
Spending	$445	$560	$115
Number of nights	3.7	4.0	0.3
Number of activities	2.8	6.3	3.5
Number of attractions	0.7	2.0	1.3

[a]Sample size for entry and exit surveys.

The assumption underlying this hypothesis is that individuals have more control over their planned tasks than, say, a group of friends or a family with demanding children. The average differences between planned and realized behaviours are shown in Table 5.12. The 'Organized tour' category has the lowest score in spending and number of nights, while 'Alone' has the lowest scores for differences in activities and attractions. The 'Organized tour' category result is unsurprising, since, by definition, the itinerary is typically fixed and free time is minimal.

Overall, the assumption that visitors travelling alone will have the least amount of variability between planned and realized behaviours is confirmed. However, there is no linear relationship between groups in terms of size. Thus the hypothesis is not supported.

Main and Interaction Effects in Planned/Realized Behaviours

The previous section detailed the results of hypotheses testing. This section builds on these results by examining the main and moderating effects of VIG use and customer characteristics on planned and realized behaviours.

Regression analysis applied to the seven independent variables on the four main dependent variables of activities, attractions, length of stay and spending produced the results shown in Tables 5.13, 5.14, 5.15 and 5.16. For all four dependent variables,

whether the respondents received or did not receive a VIG, significantly influenced the level of consumption behaviour between planned and realized behaviours. Apart from VIG use, 'age' had a significant effect on all four dependent variables. (Please note that in these tables, the independent variable 'Motivation' has been removed since it is not an ordinal variable.)

The influence of the VIG on behaviour is further confirmed when we examine the main effects for planned and realized behaviours. The main effects of the independent variables on four main dependent variables – activities, attractions, length of stay and spending – are detailed in Table 5.13 for planned behaviours and in Table 5.14 for realized behaviours.

For planned behaviours, the independent variable VIG better explains the level of spending and activities than any other such variable. VIG is also the second largest explanatory factor for the number of attractions. No other independent variable contributes as much to our understanding of the four consumption behaviours being investigated. For realized behaviours, the same pattern emerges. The VIG offers the best explanation for the spending and number of activities undertaken.

Correlations for planned and realized behaviours are shown in Tables 5.15 and 5.16, respectively. As expected, income and education are highly correlated, as are experience and home origin (i.e. geographical proximity to Prince Edward Island).

Table 5.12. Average planned and realized consumption behaviours by travel party size.

Variables	Planned	Realized	Difference
Alone (159–190)[a]			
Spending	$204	$336	$132
Number of nights	5.4	6.0	0.6
Number of activities	2.8	5.2	2.2
Number of attractions	0.8	1.6	0.8
One couple (1089–1000)			
Spending	$230	$456	$226
Number of nights	3.5	4.2	0.7
Number of activities	2.7	5.9	3.2
Number of attractions	0.9	1.8	0.9
One family (503–486)			
Spending	$318	$608	$290
Number of nights	4.2	4.5	0.3
Number of activities	3.0	6.6	3.6
Number of attractions	1.2	2.0	0.8
Two or more couples/families (58–141)			
Spending	$222	$497	$275
Number of nights	3.1	3.8	0.7
Number of activities	2.6	6.0	3.4
Number of attractions	1.0	2.0	1.0
Group of friends (215–205)			
Spending	$248	$531	$283
Number of nights	3.1	3.8	0.7
Number of activities	2.7	6.2	3.5
Number of attractions	1.1	2.2	1.1
Organized tour (94–117)			
Spending	$237	$227	−$10
Number of nights	2.3	2.7	0.4
Number of activities	3.4	6.5	3.1
Number of attractions	0.9	2.0	1.1

[a]Sample size for entry and exit surveys.

Table 5.13. Correlations of main effects of customer characteristics on planned consumption behaviour.

Moderating variables	Dependent variables			
	Spending	Length of stay	Attractions	Activities
Experience	ns	0.137	−0.292	ns
Age	ns	0.043	−0.112	−0.069
Origin	ns	ns	0.266	−0.074
Education	0.078	ns	0.099	0.123
Party size	ns	−0.053	0.154	0.099
Income	ns	ns	ns	−0.008
VIG	0.175	ns	0.165	0.155

ns, not significant at $P = 0.05$.

Table 5.14. Correlations of main effects of customer characteristics on realized consumption behaviour.

Independent variables	Dependent variables			
	Spending	Length of stay	Attractions	Activities
Experience	ns	0.176	−0.405	−0.178
Age	ns	ns	−0.048	ns
Origin	0.127	ns	0.344	0.188
Education	0.128	ns	0.133	0.154
Party size	ns	−0.065	0.099	0.046
Income	0.197	ns	0.083	0.132
VIG	0.241	ns	0.327	0.328

ns, not significant at $P = 0.05$.

Table 5.15. Kendall's tau-b correlations among main ordinal variables (entry survey).

Variable	1	2	3	4	5	6
Home origin	−					
Education	0.13**	−				
Experience	−0.56**	−0.11**	−			
Travel party	0.04**	−0.05**	−0.04*	−		
Age	0.14**	−0.05**	−0.05**	−0.04**	−	
Income	0.15**	0.28**	−0.12**	−0.01	0.12**	−

**, correlation at the 0.01 level (two-tailed).

Table 5.16. Kendall's tau-b correlations among main ordinal variables (exit survey)

Variable	1	2	3	4	5	6
Home origin	−					
Education	0.12**	−				
Experience	−0.537**	−0.13**	−			
Travel party	0.05**	−0.02	−0.06**	−		
Age	0.07**	−0.12**	−0.03	−0.05**	−	
Income	0.16**	0.27**	−0.11**	−0.02	0.09**	−

**, Correlation at the 0.01 level (two-tailed).

The two data sets were then combined and ANOVA tests were run to identify moderating variables. The result is the hypothesized set of relationships illustrated in Fig. 5.4 that show the relationship between 'Planned and realized strategies' and activities. The key moderating variables are VIG, experience and distance. At the same time, education and income are moderated by VIG.

Application of Mintzberg's Model

Mintzberg's model of planned and unplanned strategy was applied to the planned and actualized behaviours of consumers in Prince Edward Island. The Mintzberg typology is an innovative means of understanding and evaluating the shifts in behaviours between planned and actual consumption. The

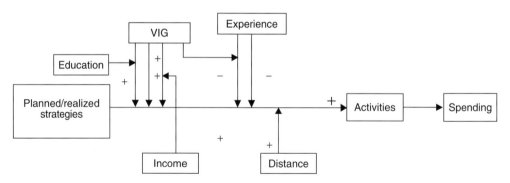

Fig. 5.4. Planned and realized consumer strategies, and moderating effects of consumer characteristics, on tourist consumption behaviours and spending.

Mintzberg matrix can be applied according to the three types of differences and effects being examined: (i) differences in planned and realized behaviours; (ii) influence of information on planned and realized behaviours; and (iii) the influence of customer characteristics on planned and realized behaviours.

Differences in planned and realized behaviours were examined for the dependent variables of attractions, activities, destinations and accommodation (Figs 5.5–5.8).

The Mintzberg model was also utilized to depict the shift between planned and realized behaviours according to whether the VIG (Fig.

5.9) or experience (Fig. 5.10) induced a significant influence on consumption.

Mintzberg's main conceptual contribution to marketing lies in the concept of the 'unplanned and undone' product; in other words, quadrant 4. As Drucker (2000) has stated, the organization's most critical potential customer may be the one who neither plans nor actually purchases the product or service. Classifying behavioural outcomes in a manner similar to the matrices generated above affords organizations (or destinations in this research setting) to better understand the strengths and weaknesses of their bundle of product offerings.

Fig. 5.5. The planned and realized strategy grid applied to planned and realized attractions.

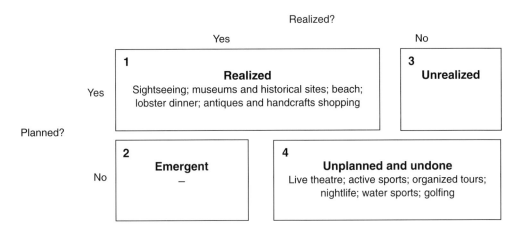

Fig. 5.6. The planned and done strategy grid applied to planned and realized activities.

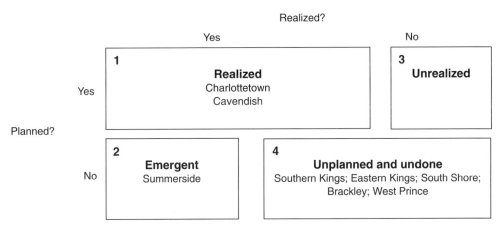

Fig. 5.7. The planned and done strategy grid applied to planned and realized destinations.

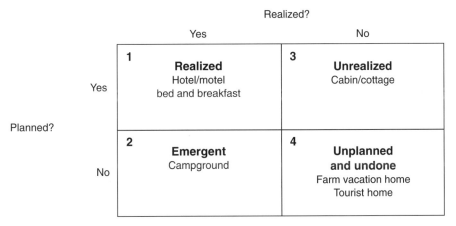

Fig. 5.8. The planned and done strategy grid applied to planned and realized accommodation.

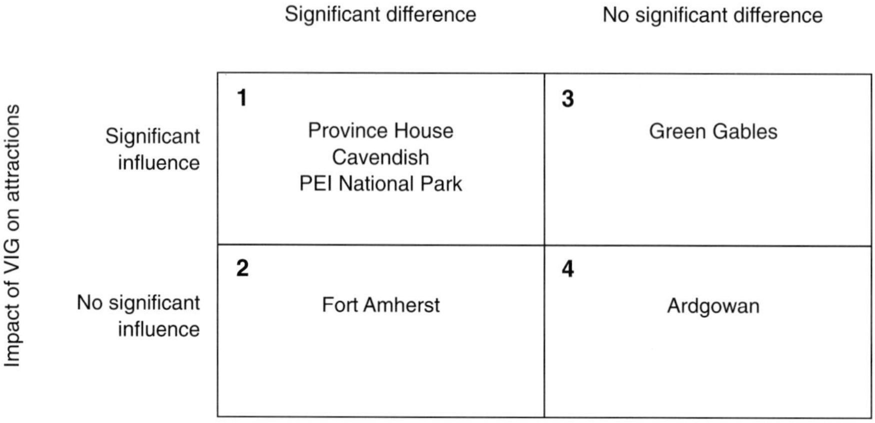

	Significant difference	No significant difference
Significant influence	**1** Province House Cavendish PEI National Park	**3** Green Gables
No significant influence	**2** Fort Amherst	**4** Ardgowan

Impact of VIG on attractions

Fig. 5.9. Increase between planned and realized attractions.

	Significant difference	No significant difference
Significant influence	**1** Cavendish Beach Province House Green Gables	**3** PEI National Park
No significant influence	**2**	**4** Ardgowan Fort Amherst

Impact of experience on attractions

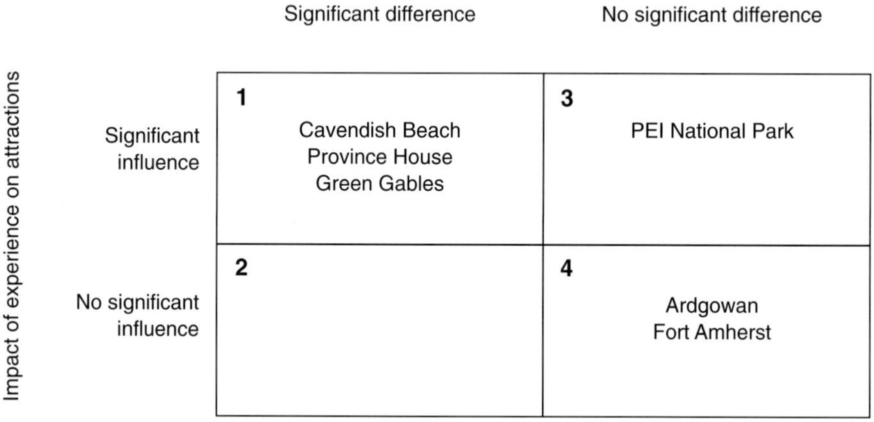

Fig. 5.10. Increase between planned and realized attractions.

6 Research Objectives and Theoretical Framework

Introduction

This chapter introduces the main research objectives and the theoretical framework used to guide the research agenda. The empirical analysis uses two data sets: entry and exit surveys of large population samples. These data enable a rare investigation of a hitherto methodological minefield for consumer researchers, namely, the evaluation of the discrepancies between, and influences on, planned and realized consumption activities.

Research Objectives

There are four main research objectives of this study, as follows.

Evaluate the differences between planned and realized behaviours

The first objective is to quantify and evaluate the differences between planned and actual consumption behaviours. Although research into planned and actual behaviours is substantial, when undertaken it typically seeks to develop a predictive method for determining behavioural outcomes derived from intentions. Rarely is the research focused on an improved understanding of the influences that act upon planned and actual behaviours.

Six consumption behaviours common to the tourism and leisure experience are used as variables to examine the extent to which individuals' plans are consistent or inconsistent with their actual behaviours. The variables are spending (planned budget versus actual money spent), length of stay in the destination (planned number of days versus actual days stayed), attractions (planned to visit and actually visited), destinations (planned to visit and actually visited), accommodation (planned to use and actually used), and activities (planned to do and actually done). The results of analysis and discussion related to this objective are detailed in Chapter 8.

Examine influence of product information and customer demographics on planned and realized behaviours

The second aim of this study is to empirically examine the twin effects of product information and customer demographics on planned and actual consumption behaviours. Product information is manifested in the visitor's information guide, or VIG, produced by the local destination marketing authority of the research setting (Prince Edward Island). The research compares the planned and actual (or realized) consumption behaviour of those visitors who used the VIG and those who did not. Six independent variables – income, age, travel party composition, geographical origin, education and motivation – are the demographic characteristics used to further explore the nature of planned and realized behaviours.

Application and testing of Mintzberg's model

The ambitions of this study extend beyond achieving an enriched understanding of consumers' plans and eventual behaviours. While the above objectives represent the core of the study's quantitative investigation, the unique data sets afford probing conceptual insights into consumer plans and behaviours. Toward this end, the third objective of this study is the application of Mintzberg's (1978) typology of organizational strategy outcomes to the context of consumers' planned and actual consumption behaviours. The graphical representation of the Mintzberg model is shown in Fig. 6.1, with four tourism activities – Water sports, Going to the beach, Antique and handcraft shopping and Attending live theatre – included as examples. The four quadrants are more or less self-explanatory (a full explanation of this matrix is detailed in Chapter 7, Research Method). An activity that is planned and undertaken is a 'deliberate' consumer strategy,

while one that is planned but not undertaken is 'unrealized'. Similarly, an activity that is not planned but undertaken is an 'emergent' consumer strategy, while an activity that is not planned and not undertaken is 'Unplanned and not done'.

Mintzberg's work offers both conceptual and managerial insights for the marketing discipline. Just as Mintzberg extended the conceptualization of strategy in the management domain, marketers can generate deeper insights into consumer planning and implementation of consumption intentions by exploring beyond the typical paradigm found in most consumer behaviour models, where intention is often regarded as the immediate antecedent of purchase (cf. Howard and Sheth, 1969; Engel *et al.*, 1993; Peter and Olson, 1999). Individuals may not succeed in pursuing the strategies they intended. Equally, individuals may enact strategies they never envisaged.

Develop a conceptual model of consumer plans and behaviours through time

Mintzberg's work reminds us that intention formation is just one stage in an often complex process that includes the planning, deciding

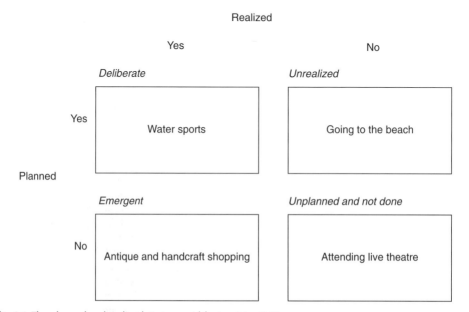

Fig. 6.1. The planned and realized strategy grid for tourist activities.

and implementing of consumption behaviours. The insights derived from this study will allow us to develop a conceptual model that illustrates the process by which consumption behaviours are formulated, adapted, completed and self-interpreted over time. As argued in Chapter 4, investigations in consumer behaviour have neglected to place consumption planning, the forming of intentions, and the articulation of those intentions and subsequent behaviours, in a temporal dimension.

A model that incorporates this view of consumer plans is shown in Fig. 6.2. The sensemaking dimension was first conceived by Weick (1998), and refers to the way that individuals construct meaning and comprehend information, essentially by shuffling it around within their memory systems until it is understandable to them. As Cohen and March (1974, cited in Weick, 1998) first pointed out, plans are symbols, advertisements, games and excuses for interaction (between individuals in organizations) and, in the context of consumer behaviour, action or non-action. Some consumers plan and some do not. According to Weick, consumer plans – when they do exist – become excuses for action in the sense that they induce awareness among consumers of products and services that hitherto they were either unaware of, or had forgotten. In the process of undertaking marketing research, the cognitive process of planning by an individual can be triggered by the asking of questions using brand names attached to products or services that the individual had previously no intention of consuming.

Although Weick anchors his treatise on sense-making in the organizational environment, the principles of sense-making could arguably be applied to consumption systems defined geographically. For example, in the consumption system delineated by Woodside and Dubelaar (2002), the geographical space where consumption behaviours occur is defined as the 'destination area'. According to Weick, consumers can only quantify and justify their intended behaviours, or plans, once they have entered and interacted with this space. If we apply the insights that Weick offers into organizational theory to a consumption system with specific geographical boundaries (just as organizations have psychological and physical boundaries), useful lessons may be generated into the ways that individuals adapt to existing planned behaviours and/or adopt new behaviours in response to the stimuli of that space.

Research Framework

A model outlining the theoretical framework to be tested in this study is now explained (Fig. 6.3). 'Customer characteristics', 'Contingency

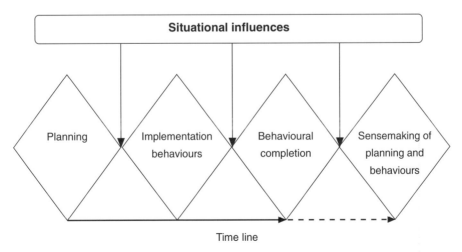

Fig. 6.2. Temporal flow of consumption planning, behaviours and sensemaking interpretation.

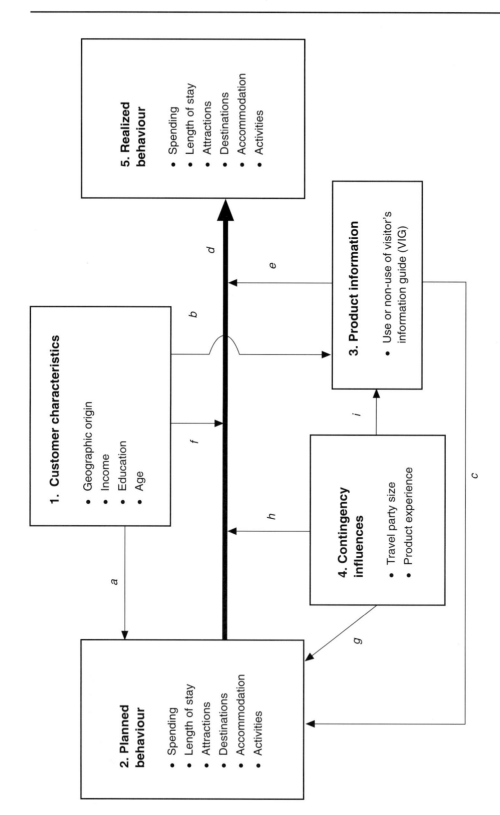

Fig. 6.3. Model of influences of customer characteristics, situational influences and product information on planned and realized behaviours.

influences' and 'Product information' are moderating variables that influence the impact of the planned and realized dependent variables of spending, length of stay, attractions, destinations, accommodations and activities. 'Planned behaviour' comprises the six dependent variables measured in the pre-consumption stage and 'Realized behaviour' refers to the same variables measured in the post-consumption stage. 'Product information' refers to the use or non-use of the visitor's information guide (VIG).

The proposed relationships are described as follows:

a: 'Customer characteristics' influence the extent and type of consumption behaviours planned by consumers.
b: 'Customer characteristics' influence, to some extent, whether consumers use or do not use product information.

c: 'Product information' influences the extent and type of consumption behaviours planned by consumers.
d: Realized consumption behaviours reflect, to varying degrees, planned behaviours.
e: 'Product information' moderates the extent of matching between planned behaviours and realized behaviours.
f: 'Customer characteristics' moderate the extent of matching between planned behaviours and realized behaviours.
g: 'Contingency influences' influence the extent and type of consumption behaviours planned by consumers.
h: 'Contingency influences' moderate the extent of matching between planned behaviours and realized behaviours.
i: 'Contingency influences' influence, to some extent, the consumers use or non-use of product information.

7 Research Method

Research Setting

The research setting was the Canadian eastern seaboard province of Prince Edward Island (PEI). The island covers 5660 km² (approximately 225 km long and ranges 3–65 km in width), making it the smallest province in Canada. PEI's capital, Charlottetown, located in the southern central region of the island, commemorates the wife of King George III. The island is most famous as the location of the novel *Anne of Green Gables*, by Canadian regional romantic novelist Lucy Maud Montgomery. First published in 1908, it is a sentimentalized, but often charming, story of a spirited, unconventional orphan girl who finds a home with an elderly couple. The book drew on the author's own girlhood experiences and on the rural life and traditions of Prince Edward Island. Green Gables House is one of the province's major tourist attractions; and 'Anne's Land' is a tourism-designated region of the island covering one-sixth of PEI.

Prior to 1995, no bridge connected PEI with the mainland. The majority of visitors to the island (over 90%) travelled by car ferry, and the remainder by aeroplane or cruise ship. Due to the limited access to PEI at the time of the survey, the island provided a unique social and natural laboratory for the investigation of consumption behaviours. In particular, the limited-access nature of the setting removed the problems of representativeness and sample size typically associated with data collection in tourism destinations (Ritchie, 1994).

Since a major research aim of this study was the investigation of the influence of product information upon purchase behaviour, the communication medium needs also to be introduced. The primary medium was the *Visitor's Information Guide* (VIG). It consisted of a 170-page glossy, soft-covered book in magazine format. For the 1992 marketing campaign, a total of 280,000 VIGs were printed: 250,000 in English and 30,000 in French. A total of 96% of the VIGs were distributed during 1992. Of these, 84% (267,860) were mailed to customers (and potential visitors) who requested the guide in response to the advertised free offer. The remaining 16% were distributed at PEI provincial information centres.

Data Sets

A secondary database was used to examine the hypotheses and propositions generated in this study. Two large-scale data files, from the 1992 face-to-face entry and exit surveys to PEI, were used. The entry survey consisted of 2239 individual interviews and the exit survey comprised 2362 persons interviewed; the long-interview method (McCracken, 1988) was employed. The surveys were undertaken by the Marketing Agency (a PEI government-sponsored organization) and Professor Roberta

MacDonald, University of Prince Edward Island. The two data sets have never been used in a single research project. The only previous use of the data was a government descriptive report profiling visitors' demographics, attitudes and behaviours (Marketing Agency, 1993) and a study on the impact of PEI's 1992 advertising campaign on attitudes, behaviours and traveller expenditures (see Woodside *et al.*, 1997). The data were collected using a 13-page entry questionnaire and a 12-page exit questionnaire.

Administration of Questionnaire and Response Rate

The interviews were completed during the peak tourism season (22 May to 5 October 1992), a period when over 95% of leisure travellers visit PEI. The questionnaire was administered at all points of and entry to and exit from PEI (ferry, airports and cruise ships) in matching proportions to total trip visits for each travel mode. Over 93% of all visitors to PEI arrived by one of two ferries; 6% via the airport and 1% via cruise ships. The interviews were conducted at ferry wharves prior to boarding, at the province's major airport near Charlottetown, and on board selected cruise ships. A team of nine interviewers worked on three-day-on, two-day-off schedules to ensure that weekdays and weekends were covered adequately. Respondents in the exit interviews were screened so as not to interview for a second time persons who participated in the entry interviews.

A quota sampling procedure was used to ensure that the proportions of Canadian, US and European respondents matched the population of visitors from these three origins: 65% of completed interviews were with Canadians; 31% were respondents from the US (two-thirds of PEI leisure visitors were estimated previously to be Canadian and about 30% were estimated previous to the study to be Americans).

The only exception to the quota-sampling plan involved Japanese visitors. Because profiles of Japanese visitors were an objective of the study, nearly 1% of the total respondents was Japanese, even though Japanese were estimated to represent less than 0.2% of total leisure visitors. To ensure a high cooperation rate (88% was achieved), the interviews with Japanese respondents were conducted in Japanese by native Japanese interviewers.

The overall cooperation/completion rate for the exit questionnaire was 94%. Due mainly to some non-responses to some of the questions, the useable number of responses to test the propositions was close to 88% of the completed interviews.

Data Analysis

The analytical approach was exploratory and empirical. Group-level (Bass *et al.*, 1968) and ratio analyses were performed on data from the two surveys. A between-groups research design was made possible from the use of the two data sets; this procedure ensures that the same respondents being asked earlier planning questions do not sensitize responses in the second data set. Interviewing the same respondents twice (at the start and end of their visits to PEI) likely would have increased such respondents' awareness, intentions and behaviours towards PEI attractions, activities and destinations.

The two data sets allowed quantification of planned and unplanned behaviour by visitors entering the site (PEI) and actual or unrealized behaviour by visitors leaving the site. (The results of the ratio analysis were then used to segment consumption decisions into realized, emergent strategies, and unplanned and unrealized strategies. These data will be used to quantify three types of strategies: realized, unrealized and deliberate, as well as unplanned/unrealized strategies.)

The analyses included two stages. First, the generalized behavioural intentions and outcomes for each of the six consumption behaviours – activities, destinations, attractions, accommodation used, expenditure and length of stay – were calculated. Secondly, ratio analysis was used to compare the planned/realized shares for each one:

- a ratio between 0.85 and 1.15 was defined to represent a realized strategy;
- when the ratio was less than 0.85 for an activity, the strategy was regarded as unrealized for any visitors;
- when greater than 1.15, the behaviour was regarded as emergent for many visitors; and,

- when only a small share of visitors planned an action and only a small portion did the action, say less than 10% in both instances, we defined the activity as unplanned and undone by most visitors.

Table 7.1 contains findings that hypothesized examples of each of these four strategies for attractions on Prince Edward Island.

Group-level analyses were performed to investigate relationships between the three sets of independent variables – planned and realized consumer strategies, the use or non-use of product information (the *Visitor's Information Guide*, VIG) and the socio-demographic characteristics of travellers – and the dependent variables of attractions, activities, spending and length of stay. Bass *et al.* (1968) argued persuasively for applications of group-level analysis in market segmentation studies.

Methodological Issues

Three methodological issues need to be addressed. These are:

1. The influence upon actual behaviour of respondents being asked their behavioural intentions;
2. The application of the intercept method for the entry and exit surveys; and
3. The use of different samples for entry and exit questionnaires.

Measuring intent

The measuring of intent affects actual behaviour. In recent times, research by Morwitz and her colleagues (Morwitz *et al.*, 1993; Fitzsimons and Morwitz, 1996) have demonstrated that merely asking consumers purchase questions has a significant impact on both their actual purchase incidence in their brand category and their brand choice. Asking intent questions increases the accessibility of respondents' preferences, which in turn increases the likelihood that behaviour is consistent with these preferences. Also, in the process of undertaking marketing research, the cognitive process of planning by an individual can be triggered by the asking of questions using brand names attached to products or services that the individual had previously no attention of consuming.

Perhaps even more critically, research on the constructive nature of preferences has shown that measures of preference, such as intentions, are often constructed in response to a request such as a survey question (Payne *et al.*, 1992).

Although this creates the problem of self-generated validity, this methodological conundrum cannot be easily avoided. Feldman and Lynch (1988) offer researchers suggestions about avoiding the distorting effects of measurement, but they admit the steps are 'likely to be costly and time consuming to implement' (Feldman and Lynch, 1988, p. 432). In their view, all real-world experiences that involve an object have the potential of shaping subsequent behaviours. The perspective of Gertrude Stein perhaps best summarizes the argument. Cited by Getzels (1982, p. 48), Stein was speaking in connection with problem formulation in social behaviour: 'Suppose no one asked a question? What would be the answer be?'.

Again, different variants of questions typically used to assess intentions have been found to give rise to different preferences (Morwitz, 1997a). Preferences have been shown to depend on such factors as the person's current state of mind (Gibbs, 1997), task complexity,

Table 7.1. Hypothesized examples of four consumer strategies for attractions on Prince Edward Island.

Strategy	Ratio	Attractions
Realized	0.85–1.15	Green Gables, Cavendish, Province House
Unrealized	<0.85	None
Emergent	>1.15	PEI National Park
Unplanned and not done	<10% of cases	Fort Amherst, Ardgowan

response mode, information display, agenda affects, similarity of alternatives and the consideration set (Payne, 1982).

Foxall (1984) has pointed out that proponents of the predictive power of intentions argue that if samples are large enough, the problems associated with the prediction of individuals' behaviour will disappear. By this line of reasoning, research that involves large samples is concerned with the aggregate level, thereby allowing the problem of the non-predictability of human behaviour to be ignored. Ajzen and Fishbein (1980) claim that the events that intervene between intentions and behaviour, rendering them inconsistent, can be expected to 'balance out', so that group behaviour can be predicted accurately over time, even if that of individuals cannot.

In the words of Rook and Fisher (1995), 'some (consumption) arenas emphatically promote spontaneous consumption behaviours – for example, amusement parks, vacation venues'. The authors make the comment that 'these situations, however, tend to be exceptional circumstances' (Rook and Fisher, 1995). This is an odd statement, given the frequency of holiday and leisure activity undertaken by individuals in today's world.

For the current research, the impact of measuring intent on actual behaviour is not part of the study; it focuses on plans that visitors report having made regarding the hours, and possibly, days immediately ahead, compared with the things other visitors reported that they had done.

Intercept surveys

The intercept methods employed in the entry and exit surveys offered several advantages. First, in the exit survey, for example, the 92% cooperation rate and 88% useable rate are considerably higher than reported in 'inquiry conversion' studies, which average less than 60% [for example, Messmer and Johnson (1993) reported a 67% response rate in a telephone study] (see also Woodside and Dubelaar, 2003).

Secondly, intercept interviews are likely to minimize memory problems in retrieving details of either the planning for the trip or for the mostly completed trip. The consumer behaviour literature suggests that when consumers are asked their intentions for purchase that is imminent, their behaviours are more likely to match their intentions than when the purchase is a distant event. Wright and Kriewall (1980) found that when consumers imagine that a purchase decision is imminent, as opposed to occurring further out in time, and when they deliberate in advance of preference measurement, their preferences more accurately reflect their actual behaviour.

Unlike mail and telephone procedures, the intercept method requires all respondents to answer the questions at the same time during their trip; thus confounding of responses caused by varying lengths of time since the trip and completing the questionnaire is eliminated.

Intercept surveys serve to minimize the problem of 'telescoping', whereby respondents over- or underestimate the length of time since they last purchased a product (for a thorough discussion on telescoping, see Morwitz, 1997b). Telescoping may occur in some instances because a respondent wants to be helpful and s/he enjoys telling about a trip or other purchase/use behaviours completed in a time period before the focus of the study. Also, if respondents were asked about their consumption behaviours after returning home, they may confuse behaviours not related to Prince Edward Island with those that were PEI-specific.

Thirdly, Shapiro and Krishnan (1999) found that certain consumers forget intentions after they have been asked to articulate them. Measuring intent as close to the time of actual consumption as possible would therefore reduce the likelihood of stated intentions being forgotten. Research has also shown that time has an impact on intentions (e.g. Mazursky and Geva, 1989).

Fourthly, the intercept method has the advantage of allowing comparison of responses by acquirers of advertising information (i.e. the VIG) with those of non-acquirers of such information. As Woodside et al. (1997, p. 221) have pointed out, the 'most important advantage of the exit-intercept method may be the opportunity to compare buying behaviour of visitors acquiring linkage-advertising [e.g. the VIG], with that of visitors not acquiring the linkage-advertising'.

Use of different samples

The use of different samples overcomes the potential for social desirability bias (Cobb and Hoyer, 1986); it is possible that the incidence of impulse or unplanned purchasing would be understated in a person's effort to appear rational and goal oriented. Rook and Fisher (1995) also pointed out that individuals make normative evaluations regarding the social acceptability of admitting to impulsive or unplanned behaviours in most consumption situations. Also, most individuals may be unable to describe potential impulse behaviours other than retrospectively.

A tabular comparison of the two data sets is offered. It reveals sufficiently strong similarities to suggest that inferences drawn and comparisons made between the two groups are useful and valid. Three examples that illustrate the relationship of geographical origin with three demographic variables, are offered. The relationships, expressed in percentage terms for the entry and exit surveys, are as follows:

1. Age groups and geographical origin (Table 7.2);
2. Income levels and geographical origin (Table 7.3); and
3. Traveller party composition and geographical origin (Table 7.4).

Application of Mintzberg's Model

One aim of this study is to apply Mintzberg's model of planned and unplanned strategy to the planning and actualized behaviours of consumers. The Mintzberg typology offers a new technique for evaluating consumers' behaviour towards certain consumption behaviours. The generic model is shown in Fig. 7.1.

The most appropriate technique for the measurement of planned versus unplanned and realized versus unrealized behaviour was carefully considered. For example, Lazarsfeld and Rosenberg (1965) proposed a formula for assessing the 'real' change between separate sample measures of two individual groups:

$$R = O\triangle/P\triangle$$

where $O\triangle$ = observed change and $P\triangle$ = possible change.

While the logic in Lazarsfeld's approach was attractive, the method was unwieldy when there were large discrepancies between the two samples, or when the first sample was a very small amount compared to the size in the second sample. Accordingly a second approach was adopted.

For planned behaviours, the first step in this approach is deriving the mean percentage of respondents reporting intention to consume a particular activity. The activities where means fall below the overall mean are classified as 'unplanned', and vice versa. For realized behaviours, the overall mean is again calculated. All activities above the overall mean are regarded as realized behaviours. In addition, a behaviour with a planned mean below the average overall mean, but a realized mean that at least matches the overall planned mean, will also be regarded as a realized behaviour.

Summary

The contribution of this study to the understanding of consumer behaviour within a marketing environment lies in the rigour of its methodology and the 'power of numbers'. Prince Edward Island has provided a remarkable social laboratory for an investigation into consumers' planned and actual consumption behaviours. The large samples, of over 2000 visitors in each of the entry and exit surveys, and the high degree of sample representativeness, combine to enable deep investigation of the influences that affect shifts in consumption behaviours between the pre-consumption and immediate post-consumption stages.

The methodology has three distinct advantages over conventional approaches to the study of the relationship between intention and consumption. First, the research setting, the type of consumption being investigated and the timing of the surveys minimized the likely influence of respondent bias in the reporting of their behaviours.

Secondly, the temporal proximity of the exit survey to consumption (remembering that most respondents visited the island for less than 5 nights) and the use of a separate sample – combined with high participation rate and representativeness of the sample –

Table 7.2. Proportion of respondents in entry and exit surveys, according to home origin and age (%).

	Mar. Can.	Quebec	Ont.	Prairie P.	Brit. Col.	New Eng.	Mid-Atlan	S.E.	S.W.	Mid-W.	W.	UK	Eur.	Japan	Aust.
Entry	33	5	18	5	3	8	6	6	1	5	4	1	1	4	0.3
Exit	28	5	20	6	3	7	7	4	1	5	4	1	1	7	0.5
<19 years	2	3	1	0	3	0	0	0	0	0	0	0	5	6	0
	3	2	1	2	1	2	1	1	3	2	0	0	5	3	0
20–29 years	21	14	14	16	15	6	10	3	0	3	9	17	11	75	14
	21	13	17	5	9	6	9	4	3	4	5	12	32	60	40
30–39 years	26	28	28	17	15	17	14	14	3	6	6	4	26	9	0
	28	25	24	24	20	18	16	6	7	11	14	12	21	17	10
45–54 years	31	34	34	33	21	36	28	16	31	22	22	30	32	7	57
	25	31	29	31	25	30	24	21	17	26	31	18	11	15	0
55+ years	20	19	19	33	45	40	48	68	63	67	60	48	26	2	29
	22	27	29	39	45	42	50	67	69	55	51	59	32	2	50

For each age category, upper figures are entry percentages and lower figures are exit percentages of respondents for each home origin.

Table 7.3. Proportion of respondents in entry and exit surveys, according to home origin and income (% and numbers).

	Mar. Can.	Quebec	Ont.	Prairie P.	Brit. Col.	New Eng.	Mid-Atlan	S.E.	S.W.	Mid-W.	W.	UK	Eur.	Japan	Aust.
Entry (N)	593	84	344	87	50	139	107	106	24	103	65	12	10	46	6
Exit (N)	472	82	295	81	47	100	100	63	18	73	72	12	5	87	3
<20K	11	4	5	10	14	2	3	4	4	4	2	17	0	7	0
	11	10	5	6	6	5	6	3	0	1	0	0	0	8	0
20–35K	21	8	11	15	12	11	7	11	4	15	14	8	10	41	17
	21	15	13	10	17	11	19	11	6	14	8	0	0	32	67
35–50K	29	31	23	29	20	27	26	21	21	23	25	8	0	26	17
	31	27	19	28	17	29	21	25	17	15	17	42	20	25	0
50–75K	28	33	30	16	24	40	31	36	21	34	29	33	10	13	50
	25	22	34	35	28	33	22	22	39	33	29	25	0	13	0
75K+	12	24	32	30	30	19	34	28	50	24	31	33	80	13	17
	12	27	28	21	32	22	32	38	39	37	46	33	80	22	33

For each age category, upper figures are entry percentages and lower figures are exit percentages of respondents for each home origin.

Table 7.4. Proportion of respondents in entry and exit surveys, according to home origin and size of travel party (% and numbers).

	Mar. Can.	Quebec	Ont.	Prairie P.	Brit. Col.	New Eng.	Mid-Atlan.	S.E.	S.W.	Mid-W.	W.	UK	Eur.	Japan	Aust.
Entry (N)	752	103	423	111	80	182	140	137	32	126	85	23	19	95	7
Exit (N)	590	126	428	120	70	159	146	94	29	115	103	33	19	148	10
Alone	11	6	4	4	3	3	4	2	–	2	4	13	11	14	14
	12	5	6	7	6	7	7	5	7	4	5	12	16	14	30
2 persons	46	56	54	59	61	65	62	57	78	64	69	35	74	53	43
	46	56	58	58	59	57	58	63	59	57	67	52	53	49	50
3 persons	15	12	11	8	11	4	9	5	9	6	6	4	–	16	14
	15	12	8	8	7	13	8	9	3	9	6	9	–	15	10
4 persons	16	18	19	15	13	18	12	15	3	17	5	26	3	5	29
	20	20	16	10	10	14	12	9	14	15	11	15	16	7	–
5 or more	13	9	12	14	13	11	13	21	3	11	17	22	–	13	–
	8	8	12	17	19	11	15	15	17	16	12	12	15	15	10

For each age category, upper figures are entry percentages and lower figures are exit percentages of respondents for each home origin.

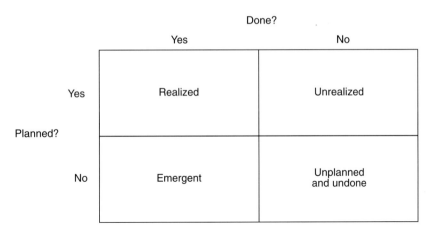

Fig. 7.1. The planned and realized strategy grid applied to planned and realized attractions.

maximized the likelihood of capturing actual consumption. The inherent problems of retrieving distant behaviours from memory, or bias created by self-generated validity, are removed.

Perhaps most significantly of all, the large samples enabled the in-depth analysis at the individual variable level of a wide variety of customer segments – such as geographical origin, product experience, income and so on – as well as the analysis of the consumption of individual products, such as activities, attractions and destinations. Smaller sample sizes would preclude analysis at the individual level, thereby diluting the richness of the insights able to be generated.

8   Variations between Planned and Realized Behaviours

This chapter compares the consumption behaviours that respondents planned to undertake, as reported in the entry survey, with the behaviours undertaken, as reported in the exit survey. We also tested for the effect of contingency influences – travel party composition, and product experience and motivations – on the differences between planned and realized behaviours. The findings here relate to the overall samples. This chapter closes with a detailed summary of conceptual and managerial implications arising from the empirical results.

As discussed earlier in this research (see Chapter 4), studies in the retailing sector (mainly supermarkets and shopping malls) have consistently shown that a significant proportion of what consumers actually purchase was not planned. Moreover, in findings of particular relevance to our leisure-destination research setting, the extent of unplanned consumption behaviour increased under the following conditions:

- the more that the consumption environment is unknown to the consumer (Bettman et al., 1998);
- when consumption outcomes are regarded as positive (Bagozzi and Nataraajan, 2000);
- when fewer constraints exist on consumers' time and effort (Kollat and Willett, 1967);
- when multiple items are purchased, rather than just a few (Inman and Winer, 1998; Kollat and Willett, 1967); and

- when the overall transaction involves a large, rather than a small, amount of money (Prasad, 1975).

A large number of studies into unplanned behaviour and impulse behaviour have quantified the extent of unplanned purchases. In contrast, few studies have sought to quantify the differences in what consumers planned and what they actually purchased. One that we identified was carried out by Abratt and Goodey (1990), in which 41% of respondents reported that they had spent more than their expressed spending intention, which suggests, 'the proposition that consumers tend to spend more than they planned may hold' (Abratt and Goodey, 1990, p. 119).

The tourism literature reveals a similar dearth of such studies. Stewart and Vogt (1999) surveyed the same visitors prior to and during a vacation trip for a number of measures, including length of stay, activities, accommodation and travel party composition. While they found that people tended to plan more activities than they actuated, plans regarding length of stay, travel party and transport mode were 'carried out as planned' (p. 91). The results of this study must be treated with caution, however. First, significance tests were not applied. Secondly, the same respondents were interviewed, thus creating two methodological problems: self-generated validity, whereby respondents attempt to justify their earlier expressed intentions (Feldman and Lynch, 1988) and social desirability bias (Cobb and Hoyer, 1986), in which impulse or unplanned purchasing would be underestimated in a person's effort to appear rational and goal oriented.

For the benefit of the reader, the three hypotheses (as well as their rationales) related to the relationship between planned and actual behaviours are repeated below. (For a full explanation of these hypotheses, please see Chapter 4.)

> **H₁**: Realized consumption behaviours are greater than planned for most specific services related to a purchased service system.

Three contingencies common in consumer behaviour and consumption plans are product experience, motivation and, in the tourist consumption system, composition of the travel party. These were incorporated into our model as moderating variables acting upon planned and realized behaviours.

Product experience is critical when studying the dynamic choice processes of consumers new to a market (Heilman et al., 2000). Experience teaches people how to plan, and the actual behaviour of consumers with product experience will more closely approximate their plans than in the case of consumers with no or little product knowledge (Stewart and Vogt, 1999). Experience, which is the accumulation of routine and habitual buyer behaviour, allows for purposive and intelligent behaviour without deliberation (Katona, 1975). Visitors who vacation at the same place regularly are likely to engage in little pre-arrival planning, relying instead on their accumulated knowledge and experience from previous visits (Fodness and Murray, 1999).

Motivations underlying a leisure trip will have a significant influence on the traveller's behaviour (Morrison, 1996). Travellers visiting friends or relatives (VFR) are more likely to rely on the advice of their hosts, less likely to use product information and therefore more likely to deviate between planned and eventual behaviours (Gitelson and Crompton, 1983). Leisure travellers, on the other hand, are more likely to engage in pre-arrival planning by obtaining information, particularly if they are first-time visitors. Excitement and adventure

seekers tended to seek more information and undertake more activities (Gitelson and Crompton, 1983). Their planned behaviours are therefore more likely to approximate their eventual behaviours.

In the general marketing environment, the social setting (presence or absence of others) that characterizes the consumption of a product or service influences both planned and actual behaviours, as it does other consumer behaviour (Stayman and Deshplande, 1989). Fisher (2001) found that greater collaboration led to higher decision quality and smaller deviations between consumers' planned and actual expenditures. In leisure settings, the behaviour of travellers is heavily influenced by the composition of the travelling party (McIntosh and Goeldner, 1990). Leisure travel is a product that is jointly consumed, and leisure travel activities reflect the influence – direct and indirect – of all those travelling together (Chadwick, 1987). This phenomenon is particularly noticeable when children are present (or absent). It is safe to assume that travelling with children in a tourist destination requires greater planning and forethought than is required by couples or tourists travelling alone. Therefore, groups with children are likely to plan their trip itinerary prior to, rather than after, arrival in the destination (Fodness and Murray, 1999). Also, large travel parties comprising friends will require greater coordination in order to meet differential needs than will couples or individuals travelling alone.

> **H₂**: The level of matching between planned and realized actions varies as a function of contingency factors: composition of travel party, product experience and motivations. (i) For product experience, the greater the experience the more likely will planned behaviours match actual behaviours. (ii) For composition of travel party, the fewer the number of members, the more likely will planned behaviours match actual behaviours. (iii) For motivation, the planned behaviours of novelty-seeking individuals less likely match their actual behaviours, while the planned behaviours of familiarity-seeking individuals more likely match their actual behaviours.

The third proposition related to this section examines the relationship between shifts in planned and realized behaviours according to increases in the time spent in the consumption system. All other things being equal, we may assume that the longer the length of stay, the greater is the likelihood that individuals will engage in unplanned behaviours. Time pressures have been shown to constrain unplanned purchases (Iyer, 1989) while time availability was linked to search activity in a retail setting (Beatty and Smith, 1987). Kollat and Willett (1967) suggested that unplanned purchases were more likely to occur on a large shopping (grocery) trip than on a small one to buy just a few items. (This finding was confirmed years later by Inman and Winer, 1998.) Prasad (1975) found that the level of unplanned purchases increased with the size of the shopper's total transaction. Beatty and Ferrell (1998) found that time available, an exogenous variable, was particularly influential in the length of time devoted to browsing and purchasing.

> **H₃**: Increases in length of stay in a destination region between planned and actual behaviours are associated with increases in the number of destination-area consumption activities, although the increase in the number of activities by length of stay will be greater for realized rather than planned behaviours.

Planned and Reported Spending

The great majority of travel decisions are made on the basis of temporal and financial affordability: Can we afford to take time off? How much can we afford to spend? While the time we can allocate to a vacation is generally fixed (as indeed we will learn below), consumers have more flexibility in the amount of money they set aside for vacation purposes. Or put another way, while most vacationers have a predetermined number of days they will or can be away from home, the number of consumers with a specific monetary amount (say, $1500 for discretionary spending on non-essential items) will be much smaller. As we found in the entry survey, more than one in three (37%) vacationers did not state a specific budget for their trip to PEI. And it is unlikely that all the respondents who provided a monetary figure had that exact figure in mind beforehand. Consumers are likely to have a 'ball park' figure only in mind when considering the financial limits on spending prior to departure and at the destination.

Nevertheless, among the respondents who could provide a monetary figure for spending, significant differences occur between the planned budget for, and final trip expenditure on, PEI. Table 8.1 shows that spending increased from an average stated budget of $387 per respondent ($n = 1231$) to $505 ($n = 2105$) for stated spending in the exit survey. A two-sample t-test revealed a significant relationship between the two means. Overall, average reported spending behaviour was 30% higher than planned spending. Since realized spending was significantly greater than planned spending, this finding supports **H₁**.

Planned and Reported Length of Stay

Planned length of stay, expressed in terms of number of overnight stays, was 3.7 nights ($n = 2341$), compared to the reported realized average number of 4.2 ($n = 2138$). A two-sample t-test revealed a significant relationship between the two means (Table 8.2). Expressed as a percentage, the difference between planned and reported length of stay behaviour was 15%. Since realized length of stay was significantly greater than planned length of stay, **H₁** is supported.

Stewart and Vogt (1999) also examined planned versus actual length of stay, although from a different viewpoint. They found that the greatest concordance was in the 7+ day category, in which 90% of respondents who planned to stay seven or more days actually stayed that length of time. They concluded with the following self-evident truth: 'If visitors changed plans, they were more likely to lengthen than shorten their stay'. Travellers can be confronted with a number of compelling rea-

Table 8.1. Means, standard deviations and significance test results for planned and realized spending.

Planned		Done				
M	SD	M	SD	t	df	P
$387	408	$505	576	6.26	3334	0.001

M, mean; SD, standard deviation.

Table 8.2. Means, standard deviations and significance test results for planned and realized length of stay.

Planned		Done				
M	SD	M	SD	df	t	P
3.7 nights	5.53	4.2 nights	4.88	4477	3.542	0.001

M, mean; SD, standard deviation.

sons to shorten their holidays, such as weather, illness, issues at home, or sheer boredom. Any compulsion to stay longer must be accompanied by the capacity to extend a holiday.

Time is much less transferable and substitutable than, for example, money (Leclerc *et al.*, 1995). If a taxi costs $50 more than expected, we can reduce consumption in other areas to cover the loss, but if the taxi ride from the airport takes an hour longer than expected, the hour may be difficult to recoup. Conversely, time saved cannot be stored and used later, and therefore is less attractive than money saved. Individuals will spend substantially more money than planned, but are unwilling or unable to substantially increase the amount of time spent in the destination. One

simple explanation could be that time is less flexible than money, and that consumers are always more likely to engage in more unplanned spending than extend the amount of time allocated to the particular task.

Planned and Reported Attractions

Respondents were asked their intention of visiting one or more of six major attractions located on Prince Edward Island. Figure 8.1 shows the percentage and number of respondents reporting intentions and behaviours for visits to the four major PEI attractions: Cavendish, Green Gables House, Province House and PEI National Park. Cavendish gained a sizeable

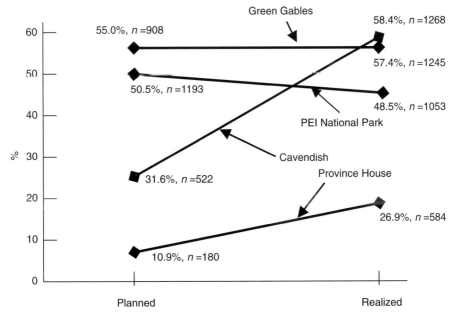

Fig. 8.1. Percentage and number of respondents reporting intentions and behaviours for visits to four major attractions.

increase in visitation when planned and actual behaviours are compared, with 32% of respondents planning to visit Cavendish and 57% reporting having visited the attraction.

Two-sample *t*-tests revealed a significant difference between planned and actual visitation for four attractions, Province House, Cavendish, Fort Amherst and PEI National Park (Table 8.3).

The difference between the average number of attractions respondents reported as planning to visit prior to entry, and the average number of attractions reported as having been visited upon exiting the consumption site, was also calculated. Upon entry, respondents reported that they intended visiting an average of 0.97 attractions; upon leaving, the average number of attractions visited per respondent was reported as 1.97 (an increase of 181.4%). An independent-samples *t*-test run after combining the data from the entry and exit surveys revealed a significant difference ($P < 0.001$) between the two groups. Therefore **H₁** is supported for attractions.

Planned and Reported Destinations

Respondents were asked about their planned and actual main destinations. 'Main destination' is a key decision for visitors to a travel consumption system, and one that is typically made prior to entry. A hierarchy of destinations exists for visitors, with some locales being seen as a primary or main destination, while others are secondary or minor (cf. Leiper, 1989; King and Choi, 1997; McKercher, 2001). For Americans travelling to Australia, for example, the Great Barrier Reef may be a main destination, and Sydney is a secondary destination. Oppermann (1995) suggests that some multi-destination trips, typically touring holidays, may involve main and 'through' destinations, while pure touring trips may have no main destination at all. Travel patterns revealed in the present study indicate that Charlottetown and Cavendish are main destinations, and others are through or secondary destinations.

Table 8.4 summarizes the planned and realized main destinations. Although significant dif-

Table 8.3. Proportions of visitors to main attractions, planned and realized.

	Planned (%) (*n* = 1652)	Realized (%) (*n* = 2170)	Chi-square	*P*
Province House	10.9	26.9	154	0.001
Cavendish	31.6	58.4	297	0.001
Fort Amherst	0.7	4.7	55	0.001
PEI National Park	1.3	48.5	1045	0.001
Ardgowan	0.8	1.4	3	ns
Green Gables	55.0	57.4	3	ns

ns, not significant

Table 8.4. Significance test results for planned and realized main destinations.

Main destination	Planned (%) (*n* = 1751)	Done (%) (*n* = 2155)	Chi-square	*P*
Charlottetown	43.6	41.5	42.240	0.001
Southern Kings	1.9	3.3	17.184	0.001
Summerside	5.8	9.4	46.981	0.001
Brackley/Stanhope/Dalvay	5.1	7.6	30.240	0.001
West Prince	3.2	4.4	14.025	0.001
Cavendish	30.4	24.6	2.832	ns
Eastern Kings	7.1	6.0	1.201	ns
South Shore	2.8	3.2	5.815	0.016

Chi-square values significant at $\alpha < 0.01$, ns, not significant.

ferences ($P < 0.01$) were found for all destinations except Cavendish and Eastern Kings, little can be read into the results. In the entry survey, 31% (551/1799) of respondents reported 'Do not know' in response to the question about their main destination; in other words, it was an unplanned behaviour for almost one in three respondents. In fact, of course, many respondents – wanting to appear rational and goal-oriented – are likely to have stated a main destination without having determined such beforehand.

Planned and Reported Accommodation

Respondents were asked the type of accommodation they intended to, and actually did, spend most of their time in while visiting Prince Edward Island. Accommodation used was the most 'unplanned' behaviour of all examined in this project; interviewed upon arrival, 56% reported not having made reservations. Chi-square tests revealed significant differences in the choice of accommodation between the reporting of planned and realized behaviours (Table 8.5). Three accommodation types – farm vacation home, B&Bs and tourist homes – did not register a significant difference.

Why would so many respondents who required paid accommodation (i.e. were not VFR or did not intend to stay in self-provided accommodation such as caravans) not have made reservations prior to arrival? Either they expected little difficulty in finding accommodation once on the island, or the choice of accommodation was not a critical part of planning the vacation on PEI. Confusing the situation is the response to the entry-survey question, 'What type of accommodation do you intend to spend *most of your time in* while on PEI?'. Only 5.3% of respondents provided an answer. This tends to confirm the view that accommodation, in this consumption system at least, is a predominantly unplanned activity. It may also indicate that large numbers of individuals had no particular main destination in mind, which is exactly what we found in the previous section on planned and realized main destinations.

Only further research can shed light on what could be termed 'indifferent' behaviour exhibited by the visitors towards the choice of accommodation. One possible explanation may lie in the multiple- versus single-item nature of choice tasks. In contrast to many other touristic components, accommodation is a single-item measure, and single-item choice tasks have been shown to require different information search routines than multiple-item tasks (see, for example, McClelland *et al.*, 1987; Abdul-Muhmin, 1999). Whatever the reason, the lesson for researchers and marketers is that, for certain destinations, data on planned accommodation information may strongly misrepresent actual behaviour.

Planned and Realized Activities

Respondents were queried about their intention and consumption of 13 leisure activities. Table 8.6 ranks the planned activities, ranging from the most popular, 'sightseeing' (81% of all respondents stating they intended to do sightseeing), to the least popular, 'nightlife' (5%). (Respondents were asked to name their intended activities in two unaided stages: first, 'What do you intend to do, while on the

Table 8.5. Significance test results for planned and realized accommodation.

	Planned (%) (n = 787)	Done (%) (n = 1818)	Chi-square	P
Campground	5.1	14.5	46.679	0.001
Cabin or cottage	18.8	10.7	11.527	0.001
Hotel/motel	58.8	54.9	7.394	0.007
Farm vacation home	1.0	0.4	3.352	ns
Bed and Breakfast	13.5	16.1	1.863	ns
Tourist home	2.8	3.4	0.459	ns

Chi-square values significant at $\alpha < 0.01$, ns, not significant.

Table 8.6. Proportion of planned activities, first mention and other mentions (sample size, $n = 2131$).

	Planned (unaided, first activity mentioned) (%)	Planned (unaided, other mentions) (%)	% of all activities mentioned
Sightseeing	50	31	81
Go to the beach	21	22	43
Visit museums and historical sites	7	29	36
Lobster supper	5	21	25
General shopping	2	20	21
Shopping for antiques and handcrafts	1	15	16
Live theatre	3	12	14
Water sports	2	9	11
Golfing	4	6	9
Active sports	2	6	8
Land or harbour tour	2	4	6
Nightlife	1	5	5

Island?', and, after naming one activity the respondent is asked 'Anything else?'.)

Table 8.7 compares the differences between the planned and reported activities. Figure 8.2 illustrates these differences for the four main activities. Table 8.8 ranks the activities in order of the magnitude of increase between planned and reported behaviours.

It was hypothesized that vacationers actually engage in a greater number of activities than they plan to, because travellers often find themselves in destination situations that include convenient-to-do and previously unknown attractions/activities. An independent-samples t-test was applied after recoding and combining the data from the entry and exit surveys. The mean for intended attractions in the entry survey was 2.70 (SD = 2.68), compared to a mean of 6.08 (SD = 2.48) in the exit survey. A significant difference ($P = 0.001$) was identified between the two groups. This finding confirms H_1. Table 8.7 lists the results of chi-square significance tests. There were no significant differences between planned and realised behaviours for two activities – water sports and golfing. These results may not be that surprising, since both sports require prior experience in order to participate. Individuals without prior experience can undertake all other activities.

'Activities' is an overwhelmingly unplanned behaviour. This finding may partly be explained by the leisure-oriented nature of Prince Edward Island as a destination. As Table 8.6 shows, the

Table 8.7. Comparison of planned and realized activities

	Planned (%) ($n = 2131$)	Done (%) ($n = 2239$)	Chi-square	P
Sightseeing	81	87	28.215	0.001
Visiting museums and historical sites	36	62	315.827	0.001
Going to the beach	43	63	178.615	0.001
Lobster supper	25	44	174.713	0.001
General shopping	21	58	625.682	0.001
Antiques and handcrafts shopping	16	54	689.105	0.001
Live theatre	14	22	41.913	0.001
Active sports	8	14	36.741	0.001
Land or harbour tour	6	16	108.831	0.001
Nightlife	5	13	70.358	0.001
Water sports	11	15	5.713	0.010
Golfing	9	9	0.400	0.842

Chi-square value is significant at $\alpha < 0.01$.

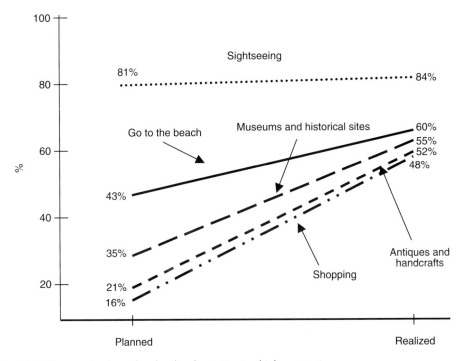

Fig. 8.2. Differences in planned and realized activities (multiple answers).

leisure-oriented activities of 'Sightseeing' and 'Going to the beach' were easily the two most popular activities (indicated in the 'first activity mentioned' column). Put another way, these activities were 'top of mind' pull factors in attracting individuals to the destination.

Another noteworthy finding is the sharp increase for 'General shopping' and 'Shopping for antiques and handcrafts', from 1.6% and 0.9%, to 20% and 15.3%, respectively. This finding reflects a typical pattern of tourist behaviour across most cultures. While shopping tends not to be reported as an intended holiday activity, it is often the main leisure activity cited by individuals at the conclusion of a vacation.

Contingency Influences on Planned and Realized Behaviours

While studies examining the relationships between planned purchases and actual purchase behaviour have generally confirmed a positive relationship (Warshaw, 1980; Manski,

1990; Young *et al.*, 1998), the strength of the relationship has differed from study to study, depending on the contingencies inherent in the research setting. In this study, the effects of three contingency influences are examined: product experience, composition of the travel party and motivation.

Research shows that intentions are affected by past experience (Fazio and Zanna, 1981; Morwitz and Schmittlein, 1992). Product experience is critical when studying the dynamic choice processes of consumers new to a market (Heilman *et al.*, 2000). Experience teaches people how to plan, and the actual behaviour of consumers with product experience will more closely approximate their plans than in the case of consumers with no or little product knowledge (Stewart and Vogt, 1999). Routine and habitual buyer behaviour allows for purposive and intelligent behaviour without deliberation (Katona, 1975). Visitors who vacation at the same place regularly are likely to engage in little pre-arrival planning, relying instead on their accumulated knowledge and experience from previous visits (Fodness and Murray, 1999).

Table 8.8. Ranking of activities, by magnitude of increase between planned and realized behaviours.

Activity	% Planned behaviours	% Done	% Difference
Shopping for antiques and handcrafts	16	54	+235
Shopping in general	21	58	+230
Land or harbour tour	6	16	+171
Nightlife	5	13	+136
Active sports	8	14	+80
Visiting museums and historical sites	36	62	+75
Lobster supper	25	44	+67
Live theatre	14	22	+54
Going to the beach	22	43	+48
Sightseeing	81	87	+7
Water sports	11	10	−6
Golfing	9	9	−2

The social setting (presence or absence of others) that characterizes the consumption of a product or service influences both planned and actual behaviours, as it does other consumer behaviour (Stayman and Deshplande, 1989). Fisher (2001) found that greater collaboration led to higher decision quality and smaller deviations between consumers' planned and actual expenditures. In leisure settings, the behaviour of travellers is heavily influenced by the composition of the travelling party (McIntosh and Goeldner, 1990). Leisure travel is a product that is jointly consumed, and leisure travel activities reflect the influence – direct and indirect – of all those travelling together (Chadwick, 1987). This phenomenon is particularly noticeable when children are present (or absent). It is safe to assume that travelling with children in a tourist destination requires greater planning and forethought than is required by couples or tourists travelling alone. Therefore, groups with children are likely to plan their trip itinerary prior to, rather than after, arrival in the destination (Fodness and Murray, 1999). Also, large travel parties comprising friends will require greater coordination in order to meet differential needs than will couples or individuals travelling alone.

Motivations underlying a leisure trip will have a significant influence on the traveller's behaviour (Morrison, 1996). Travellers visiting friends or relatives (VFR) are more likely to rely on the advice of their hosts, less likely to use product information and therefore more likely

to deviate between planned and eventual behaviours (Gitelson and Crompton, 1983). Leisure travellers are generally more likely to engage in pre-arrival planning by obtaining information, particularly if they are first-time visitors. Excitement and adventure seekers tended to seek more information and undertake more activities (Gitelson and Crompton, 1983). Their planned behaviours are therefore more likely to approximate their eventual behaviours.

These three influences were tested using spending and length of stay as the dependent variable. We would expect 'spending' to perhaps generate richer insights than 'length of stay', which registered no significant difference in analysis earlier in this chapter. 'Experience' was classified into three types: first-timers, moderately experienced (four or fewer previous visits) and 'highly experienced' (five or more previous visits). Four travel party groups were compared: visitors travelling alone, one-couple groups, one-family groups, and groups comprising two or more families. For motivations, we examined two groups: those seeking familiarity and those seeking history and culture.

Table 8.9 shows the planned and realized levels of spending and length of stay for the three levels of experience. Regression analysis was performed after converting each of the 12 cases to Z scores as unweighted values. Planned and realized values were treated as a single variable, called 'strategy'. The equation used to run regression analysis is as follows:

Table 8.9. Planned and realized consumption behaviours by degree of experience.

	Planned			Realized		
	First-timers ($n = 1236$)	Moderately experienced ($n = 489$)	Highly experienced ($n = 637$)	First-timers ($n = 1184$)	Moderately experienced ($n = 397$)	Highly experienced ($n = 524$)
Spending	$394	$432	$352	$518	$532	$453
Length of stay (nights)	3.0	3.8	4.8	3.5	4.6	5.5

Behaviour = a + b1 Strategy + b2 Experience + b3 Strategy by Experience

where for Strategy: 0 = planned and 1 = realized; and for Experience: 0 = none; 1 = moderate; 2 = highly

The hypotheses applied to this analysis are as follows:

Ha1: if b1 is positive, respondents spend significantly more than planned;
Ha2: if b2 is negative, highly experienced respondents spend less;
Ha3: if b3 is significant, the greater the experience, the greater is the difference between planned and realized behaviour.

For spending, regression analysis rendered a P value of 0.692 for the 'Experience by Strategy' variable, indicating that experience did not significantly influence the differences between planned and realized spending and planned and realized length of stay.

A similar finding was found for 'Size of party' variable, where P = 0.701. Table 8.10 indicates the planned and realized behaviours by the four levels of party size. In short, the proposition that higher experience or a smaller travel party would reflect significantly smaller differences between planned and realized consumption behaviours was not confirmed.

Planned and Realized Activities by Length of Stay

Increased length of stay is typically associated with increased number of consumption activities in the consumption system. We would expect, for example, a visitor staying for one night to engage in less consumption behaviour than one staying several nights. To test this proposition, the changes in the number of planned and realized activities by length of stay were compared for the entry and exit surveys. The number of activities listed in both surveys was 15, ranging from going to the beach and water sports, to antique shopping and lobster dinners.

Figure 8.3 illustrates the relationship between length of stay and activities. That is, there seems to be a general trend that the longer the length of stay, the greater the number of activities reported. Moreover, vacationers tend to underestimate the number of activities they eventually engaged in at the entry into the PEI. The figure also lends support to the argument that while people do engage in a greater number of activities when they actually have more time to spend, people who are planning to stay on the island for a longer period of time do not necessarily have

Table 8.10. Planned and realized consumption behaviours by size of travel party.

	Planned				Realized			
	Alone ($n = 157$)	One couple ($n = 1076$)	One family ($n = 502$)	2 or more families ($n = 200$)	Alone ($n = 182$)	One couple ($n = 957$)	One family ($n = 467$)	2 or more families ($n = 139$)
Spending	$263	$370	$474	$390	$343	$475	$638	$520
Length of stay (nights)	5.4	3.5	4.2	3.1	6.0	4.2	4.5	3.8

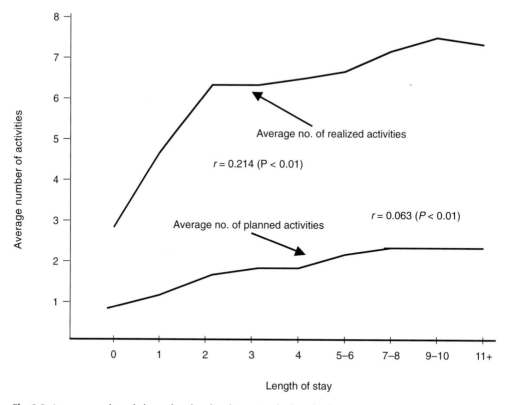

Fig. 8.3. Average number of planned and realized activities by length of stay.

more activities planned. A significance test using the Fisher Z-transformation (Papoulis, 1990) to test for the difference between the two correlation coefficients revealed that they were highly significant ($P < 0.05$).

Multiple regression analysis was used to test whether the gap between the planned and the actual number of activities increases with an increase in the length of stay. A significant amount of variance in the dependent variable was found (F change $= 52.33$, $P = 0.001$). This finding supports H_3.

While individuals planned to engage in a greater number of activities when they had more time, the number of activities they planned to undertake was still relatively small. For example, visitors planning to stay three nights planned to undertake fewer than two activities. In reality, individuals who *did* stay three nights engaged in an average of six activities. One possible explanation is that individuals delay decisions about certain consumption

activities until they enter the consumption system – even when offered choices (in the survey) that they may not have considered or had knowledge of previously. This finding confirms the importance of offering product information to consumers after arrival in the destination.

Summary and Discussion

This chapter detailed research findings and offered preliminary observations with respect to the relationship between planned and reported consumption behaviours across the two samples. A summary relating to H_1 is shown in Table 8.11.

These mixed results raise a number of questions. Why does reported behaviour exceed planned behaviour for some consumption activities and not others? When realized behaviour exceeds planned behaviour, what conclusions can we draw about the nature of the

Table 8.11. Summary of results of testing of Hypothesis 1 for planned versus realized behaviours.

	Supported for	Rejected for
Spending	Planned versus realized spending	–
Length of stay	–	Planned versus realized length of stay
Attractions	Province House	Green Gables
	Cavendish	PEI National Park
		Ardgowan historic site
		Fort Amherst
Destinations	Charlottetown	Cavendish
	Southern Kings	Eastern Kings
	Summerside	South Shore
	Brackley/Stanhope/Dalvay	
	West Prince	
Accommodation	Bed and breakfast	Cabin/cottage
	Campgrounds	Farm vacation home
		Hotel/motel
		Tourist home
Activities	Antique shopping	Golfing
	General shopping	
	Lobster dinner	
	Visiting historical sites	
	Going to the beach	
	Other active sports	
	Enjoying spectator sports	
	Land or harbour tours	
	Sightseeing	
	Attending live theatre	
	Enjoying nightlife	
	Enjoying water sports	

activity or behaviour? And what are the implications for management of these outcomes?

In beginning to address these issues, we should cite a limitation of the study. The survey assumes that respondents have formulated plans for a whole range of trip activities – covering such aspects as accommodation, places to visit and things to do. This view is clearly not the case. While respondents have the option of not answering these questions, they are not explicitly asked whether they indeed had plans to begin with. We can safely assume that not all tourist behaviours investigated in the survey had been considered, formulated, or, in the case of a travel party greater than one, discussed or mentioned before the survey was administered.

The literature offers a number of explanations for differences between planned and realized behaviours. First, studies have found that the strength of the intent–behaviour relationship differs across types of products (Ferber and Piskie, 1965; Kalwani and Silk, 1982;

Bemmaor, 1995; Morwitz et al., 1996). Both Simonson (1993) and Bemmaor (1995) found that while intentions predict behaviour for existing consumer products, they do not predict behaviour for new products and products targeted to business markets. In a similar finding, Morwitz et al. (1996) found a significantly higher correlation between intentions and market performance for existing products than for new products. While other studies provide empirical demonstrations that product type moderates the intent–behaviour relationship, they do not offer much theoretical explanation for it. Also, individuals are likely to acknowledge less *perceived behavioural control* (using the dimension of the theory of planned behaviour) over the choice of tourist services and experiences than other product types where external factors are less important (for example, Notani, 1998).

Consider the figures for planned accommodation. Forty-two per cent of respondents who reported needing paid accommodation reported not having made bookings prior to entry on to PEI. If an essential trip component such as shelter had not been planned, we cannot expect substitutable tourist components, such as activities, to be both planned and enacted (for example visiting a beach could be substituted for visiting a museum under conditions of inclement weather, or vice versa if the children began to complain about visiting a museum).

In the context of leisure travel, some decisions assume more importance than others. The main destination(s) to be visited, the cost of getting there (as opposed to the budget allocated for spending while in the consumption system) and the time available for the trip would be three critical decisions confronting most travellers. These decisions could be regarded as higher-order choices. Less critical decisions, and thus more susceptible to alteration, being forgotten, or abandoned would be such plans as visiting a particular museum, going to a famous sightseeing place, eating at a famous restaurant, and so on.

Put another way, many touristic consumption behaviours are neither essential nor mutually exclusive acts. After the consumer arrives at his or her destination, accommodation and meals are the only essential and unavoidable consumption activity. Every other planned activity is, arguably, expendable. (There are a few exceptions. A family with children who visit Anaheim, California are, barring a severe earthquake, unlikely to forgo a visit to Disneyland.)

The planning process in tourism differs from conventional consumer or even services marketing in the nature of the choice that consumers make. A customer who walks into a supermarket has a number of product categories in mind; for each category the customer makes the purchase decision among competing brands based on brand loyalty, price, attractiveness of the packaging and so on. While the tourist has product categories in mind, such as natural attractions, city tour or meal, he or she is likely to pay little regard to brands (except perhaps for accommodation, if the lodging is commercial). Moreover, in the mind of the tourist, product categories will often compete *against* each other. For example, a typical decision might have to be made

between visiting the local historical museum (the parent's wish) or going on a boat tour of the harbour (the children's wish).

Secondly, time is a critical variable. Buehler *et al.* (1994) found that, in general, people have a systematic tendency to underestimate their own completion times, a phenomenon they label 'planning fallacy'. Applying this argument to a travel setting, it could be argued that consumers plan to do more than they can actually complete within the time constraints of a trip away from home. However, the evidence here refutes this logic. People engage in more activities and visit more attractions than they had planned.

Gross (1994) argues that responses to time pressures are contingent upon the degree of intensity of 'objective' time pressure (clock and calendar time) and 'subjective' time pressure (perceived urgency in response to the objective pressures of clock or calendar deadlines). Another possible explanation for discrepancies between planned and actual behaviours may be that subjective time pressures have an influence on consumers, who are cautious in expressing intentions in an entry survey.

One empirical study does support our findings. Read and Loewenstein (1995) argue that consumers compress future time intervals when making combined choices, and hence overestimate the effect of satiation. It is not until the individual enters the destination does he or she realize that activities will take less time than initially envisaged. This factor could help explain the low levels of intended activity reported prior to entry. While time issues are important factors to consider, it would be naïve to assume – in the absence of further research – that time is a critical factor in the discrepancies between planned and actual behaviours.

Thirdly, situational factors are an obvious explanatory variable. The extent to which unforeseen events will change a person's intention depends on how accurately people can predict how their preferences will change (Simonson, 1990). Using the logic of the theory of reasoned action, intentions would most likely match behaviour the more the purchase behaviour is within the volitional control of the individual.

Fourthly, Shapiro and Krishnan (1999) remind us that consumers often forget intentions. They argue that marketing models used to forecast sales should incorporate memory as a variable to explain why some intentions do not lead to purchases. They also point out the complexity of memory processes (see also Krishnan and Shapiro, 1999). Memory that a person had intended to do *something* is prospective (remembering to remember), whereas memory for the content of the intended action is retrospective (remembering what to remember). They found that increasing the importance of an intention facilitated both prospective and retrospective memory. (Do entry survey questions 'increase' the importance of intentions?)

The distinction has been drawn between event-, time- and activity-based intentions in relation to memory retrieval clues (Kvavilashvili and Ellis, 1996). The authors argue that intentions differ to the extent that external clues are absent (for time-based intentions) or present (for event- and activity-based intentions), as well as to the extent that ongoing behaviour requires interruption (event- and time-based) or not (activity-based). Individuals are likely to more easily remember activity-based intentions because of their contingency on cues and their decoupling from ongoing behaviour (Bagozzi and Dholakia, 1999).

Fifthly, the timing of the intercept survey may have influenced the nature of the responses. Wright and Weitz (1977) found that when the outcomes of a choice were to be experienced in the near future, subjects were more averse to risk than at a more distant point in time. This finding may suggest that respondents were more conservative in their reported intentions in this survey than they would be had they been surveyed some days or weeks prior to entry.

Sixthly, tourists and leisure consumers are confronted with multiple-item – not single-item – decisions for many experiences and services. As such, decision making is more complex, involves higher risk and is more susceptible to change and adaptation. In deciding the composition of a holiday, consumers make multiple choices between the bundle of destinations, bundle of activities and tours, all of which are interlaced with pre-arranged free time. Moreover, the relative importance of each tourism element – from destination, accommo-

dation, length of stay to budget – changes as couples advance through the family life cycle (Cosenza and Davis, 1981). In this study, respondents are unable to foresee or account for the complexity of the cognitive decision tasks that lie ahead when completing the entry survey. Abdul-Muhmin (1999) highlights the difficulty of understanding this complex task environment with his argument that consumers may make multiple-item consumption decisions as a strategy to either diminish cognitive dissonance or to test consumption or experiential alternatives that normally would not be ordinarily selected. The latter consumer strategy has implications for tourism marketers, especially when adopted by consumers lacking experience in the destination.

Seventhly, Weick (1998) suggests that behaviour is not goal-directed but goal-interpreted. People are more comfortable and better able to describe what they did, rather than what they plan to do. If we apply this view of human behaviour to this project, two conclusions can be drawn. First, reports by individuals of their consumption behaviours immediately upon leaving the consumption space are likely to be fuller and more detailed than reports of their intentions immediately prior to entry. Secondly, and as a consequence of the first point, we should not only expect 'gaps' between planned and reported behaviours, but also be extremely cautious in drawing lessons at all about so-called 'planned' behaviours. Many travellers might only be able to report that they plan to 'have fun' in the entry interviews, with no specifics known.

Consider the response in the exit survey to the question regarding actual spending relative to budget, shown in Table 8.12. Only 7.1% of respondents in the exit actually reported spending 'over budget' – despite the large increases in spending we have identified (see Chapter 10) for most demographic variables. At least two equally powerful explanations can be presented for this response. We can accept Weick's view of behaviour and conclude that the great majority of respondents in the entry survey had little idea of their spending strategy for the impending duration on Prince Edward Island – and probably randomly assigned a 'ball park' figure for intended spending when surveyed. On the other hand, we could accept

Table 8.12. Comparison of entry and exit survey responses to budget-related questions.

	Entry (%)	Exit (%)
Over budget		7
No budget	52*	18
On budget		47
Under budget		8
Do not know	37	16
No response	11	4
Total	100	100

*The entry survey question allowed respondents to report their budget, not to respond, or to say 'Don't know'.

the more widely held view of behaviour which states that the low figure of 7.1% reflects the desire of survey respondents to appear rational in their consumption behaviour.

The result for Green Gables House is also noteworthy. Little improvement in visitation rates was found between the entry and exit survey for the island's premier attraction. One possible explanation for this finding is that an inverse correlation exists, whereby the more famous a tourist icon is, the less likely is a significant increase between planned and actualized visitation to occur. From a marketer's perspective, icons may have a ceiling affect, in that an incremental increase in promotional spending on an icon does not yield a significant increase in visitation. If so, this has implications for marketing strategists in the allocation of their scarce marketing funds.

The nature and effect of questioning in the pre-consumption (entry survey) and post-consumption (exit survey) phases also shed light on discrepancies between reported intentions and actual behaviour. Questions asked in the exit survey elicit a cognitive response from respondents. Simple facts derived from very recent memory – such as number of days stayed, places visited, attractions visited and money spent – are requested. Affective reactions are neither requested nor triggered. Compare this situation with the entry survey. Respondents are asked to make a series of choices among, for example, attractions and activities. This forces them to cognize places, objects and experiences, yet the reality is that the 'decisions' (putting aside the doubtful legitimacy of this nomenclature) reported in the survey are much more likely to constitute affective reactions than to be rationally conceived goals. In a sense, there is a psychic gap between the asking of the question and the moment in the consumption system that the decision to consume the 'product' is considered (if in fact that moment does arrive). The magnitude and influence of this psychic gap far exceeds the time lapse between the surveying of intentions and the actualization of behaviours.

Tests of the competing theoretical propositions as to why planned behaviours are often less than realized behaviours need to be examined in future research. This research focuses on probing the extent of the differences between planned and realized, not on providing a 'critical test' as to the efficacy of the multiple rationales found in the literature regarding such differences.

In conclusion, we can only concur with the findings of Young et al. (1998, p. 189):

> [I]ntentions appear to almost always provide biased measures of purchase propensity, sometimes underestimating actual purchasing and other times overestimating actual purchasing.

9 Influence of Product Information on Planned and Realized Consumption Activities

This chapter examines the effects of product information on the planned and realized behaviours for six consumption activities: spending, length of stay, attractions, destinations, accommodation and activities. By 'effects' of product information, we are referring to the situation of respondents who simply *receive* the visitor's information guide (VIG), rather than those who *use* the VIG. A key premise of this research is that consumers underestimate the influence of promotional materials such as product literature. Research has shown that much attention and comprehension processing of product information occurs quickly and automatically with little or no conscious awareness (see, for example, Lynch and Srull, 1982; Kahneman and Treisman, 1984).

Product information plays a critical role in consumer planning, by allowing consumers to evaluate and purchase products. Information is also a recreational activity for many consumers, particularly in a leisure-oriented setting such as vacations. Information assumes critical importance for consumers when making decisions about services, which are harder to evaluate than tangible products (Zeithaml, 1981). Since services are also associated, *ceteris paribus*, with greater perceived risk, service consumers would presumably use more information sources as a risk-coping strategy than would consumers of less risky products (Murray, 1991).

In the case of tourism, information may perform several functions in different stages of the vacation sequence: (i) it can encourage people to think positively about the idea of having a vacation, by raising expectations and creating fantasies; (ii) background information on aspects of the destination may assist choices and heighten appreciation of the destination; and (iii) the information may be used to 'rationalize, justify or legitimize' the vacation decision. Indeed, it may be useful after the vacation by reducing possible cognitive dissonance (Van Raaij and Francken, 1984). Although there exists a reasonable body of literature on the relationship between product information exposure and consumption behaviour, the issue has been little explored in the tourism literature. A notable exception is the study of Woodside *et al.* (1997), which found that linkage-advertising programmes had a substantial influence on changing destination behaviours and increasing the expenditures of visitors.

The consumer's ability to make good decisions can be impeded if excessive amounts of information are offered and/or the information is presented at an inappropriate time (Jacoby *et al.*, 1974; Malhotra, 1982; Bettman *et al.*, 1991). Having particular relevance to the current research, the timing of information has received closer attention in recent years (for a thorough overview of this topic, see Ariely, 2000).

The VIG is provided to visitors either by mail on request prior to the trip, or upon request after arrival at Prince Edward Island (PEI). In 1993, the PEI VIG was a 184-page glossy, soft-covered book in magazine format. For the 1992 marketing campaign, a total of 280,000 VIGs were printed: 250,000 in English and 30,000 in French. A total of 96% of the VIGs were distributed during 1992. Of these, 84% (267,860) were mailed to customers (and potential visitors) who requested the guide in response to the advertised free offer. The remaining 16% were distributed at PEI provincial information centres.

Typically, the VIG is divided into two sections. The introductory first section (39 pages) provides an overall view of PEI, with general information about the island, covering topics such as history, population, geography and seasonal characteristics. Also featured are tourist highlights, such as festivals and events, sightseeing tours, outdoor adventure recommendations, golf and dining. According to the introduction on the Table of Contents page (p. 5): 'The first section is designed as a visual tour of the Island. It offers a taste of our beautiful scenery combined with suggestions for places to go and things to do.'

The second, more substantial section (131 pages), is called the Day Tours section. It introduces each of the six tourist-designated regions, with the recommendation that 1 day be set aside to explore each region. For each region, information is listed under the headings of 'Attractions', 'Dining', and 'Accommodations'. Leisure activities such as sea kayaking, seal watching, trail riding and camping are listed under their own titles rather than under a general title such as 'Activities'.

Testing for Influence of VIG

Before we examine the influence of the VIG on particular consumption behaviours, two questions need to be resolved: (i) What percentages of respondents received and did not received the VIG? (ii) What demographic profiling was possible to identify respondents who received and did not receive the VIG?

To begin with, we determined the use of the VIG prior to and after entry to Prince Edward Island. Upon entry, 22% of respondents (n =

517) reported having received a VIG; this number rose to 58% (n = 1313) at the time of the exit survey. Table 9.1 details the receipt and non-receipt, and use and non-use, of the VIG, *as reported in the entry and exit surveys*.

These data are intriguing. The behaviour of consumers toward product information does not fundamentally change from the period prior to entry into the consumption system, in this case Prince Edward Island, to the period while in the consumption system. (Chi-square tests were run by combining 'Used completely' and 'Used somewhat' as one cell and 'Used very little' and 'Received and not used' as another cell. Although the chi-square coefficient was significant, this result is likely more a function of sample size than an indicator of significant differences between groups.) By eyeballing Table 9.1, we must conclude that consumers' behaviour toward product information changes little, regardless of how geographically or temporally proximate the consumption act may be.

This finding is counter-intuitive. After arrival, a greater proportion of consumers in possession of the VIG might be expected to utilize the product information than those prior to entry. How can we explain this? First, the amount of time between exposure to product information and consumption appears to have virtually no influence on the degree to which information is used. In other words, whether a purchase is the next day or the next week, the proportion of consumers utilizing information does not change. Secondly, if the use of product information does not shift across time, the critical objective of marketing organizations is to get the product information into as many 'hands' as possible.

Table 9.1. Use and non-use of VIG (visitor information guide) reported in entry and exit surveys.

	Entry (%)	Exit (%)
Received VIG	22	65
Did not receive VIG	78	35
VIG use by respondents who received VIG	n = 517	n = 1313
Used completely	27	30
Used somewhat	51	50
Used very little	10	9
Received and not used	10	9

A key proposition of this project is that consumers who receive (and use) product information such as the VIG will report higher levels of consumption than consumers who report not using the VIG. At face value, the PEI tourism authorities appear to have been successful in distributing the VIG to visitors after arrival on the island: while 78% of respondents reported not having acquired a VIG in the entry survey, this figure had been reduced to 35% by the exit survey. (We will explore the extent and effectiveness of VIG distribution later in this chapter.)

Also worth noting is that 2.4% ($n = 53$) of respondents in the exit survey could not answer whether they had received the VIG; see Table 9.2 below. This outcome reminds us of the difficulty that some people have even remembering their exposure to information, let alone being able to estimate how much they used the information and how much they were influenced by the information.

Since respondents were not asked about the extent of their search behaviour for a VIG after arrival, no conclusions can be drawn about the reasons for what appears, at first glance, to be a relatively high number of visitors with no product information. The most obvious reasons would be that either the VIG was not readily accessible and available, or that respondents were not interested in receiving it.

In an attempt to identify the types of respondent who use and do not use the VIG, use of the VIG by motivation was examined. Unfortunately, few insights were generated. The Visiting Friends and Relatives segment reported, not surprisingly, the smallest percentage for use of VIG in both surveys: 9% and 35%, respectively. The motivation segment with the highest percentage was Family Vacation (73% in the exit survey).

We also examined the influence of the VIG depending on whether respondents reported PEI as their main destination. (The assumption we tested was that visitors for whom Prince Edward Island was not the main destination may be less influenced by the VIG than those for whom Prince Edward Island was their only, or main, destination.) However, the findings suggested that there was no significant difference between the two groups for planned behaviours.

Spending and VIG use

Differences between planned and reported spending behaviour according to the use or non-use of the VIG were plotted (Fig. 9.1). Spending increased for all categories, whether the VIG was used or not. Two observations are offered. First, the use of the VIG is associated with increases in planned spending. Respondents who did not receive the VIG stated an average of $224 for planned spending, while those who did use the VIG declared a budget of $360. Secondly, the use of VIG is associated with increases in actual spending. Respondents who did not receive the VIG stated an average of $334 for actual spending, while those who did use the VIG reported spending an average of $603. Two-sample t-tests revealed a significant relationship between spending and use or non-use of VIG for two groups: those who used the map only and those who received but did not use the VIG (Table 9.3). A significant difference was found for planned and realized spending for respondents using the VIG; in contrast, no significant difference was found for planned and realized spending for respondents who did not receive the VIG.

One-way ANOVA was conducted to examine the effect of VIG use on spending, and to determine whether the use of the VIG had led to a greater than expected increase in spending. Participants were categorized into three groups: those who did not receive the VIG; those who had limited information from the VIG (used map only); and those who used the

Table 9.2. Respondents' response to the exit survey question 'Did you receive the Visitors Guide?'

	Frequency	Percentage
Prior to coming	759	35.0
On arrival	524	24.1
Both prior and arriving	30	1.4
Did not receive	804	37.1
Do not know	53	2.4
Total	2170	100.0

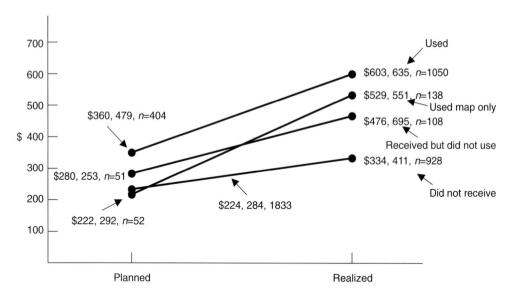

Fig. 9.1. Planned and realized spending by use or non-use of the *Visitor Information Guide* (VIG), standard deviation and number of persons interviewed.

Table 9.3. Planned and realized spending, according to use or non-use of VIG.

	Planned		Realized			
	M	SD	M	SD	t	P
Received VIG	$515 (n = 293)	521	$605 (n = 1261)	638	2.251	0.025
Did not receive	$348 (n = 938)	357	$354 (n = 844)	424	0.488	0.626

M, mean; SD, standard deviation.

VIG. The results show that those who had limited information from the VIG spent more money than those who did not receive the VIG ($F = 18.69, P = 0.001$). In turn, those who used the VIG spent a greater amount of money than those who had limited information from the VIG ($F = 7.42, P = 0.001$). Therefore it can be concluded that the greater the information available to the visitors, the greater their spending.

For all three groups of subjects, the actual spending was greater than the estimated spending ($F = 99.10, P = 0.001$). The increase in spending was greater for those who used the VIG and those who had limited information than those who did not receive

the VIG ($F = 10.28, P = 0.001; F = 17.55, P = 0.001$, respectively). Thus, the increase in the amount of spending depended on whether the vacationers received the VIG. Since realized spending is significantly greater than planned spending, H_6 and H_7 are supported. (H_6: Consumers who use product information are likely to plan and report higher consumption behaviours (such as spending and length of stay) than consumers who do not use product information. H_7: Within a given time period (period the consumer is in the tourism destination), first-time consumers planning and actually doing the trip will use product information more than experienced consumers.)

Length of stay and VIG use

The differences between planned and reported length of stay according to the use or non-use of the VIG were examined. The average number of nights spent on PEI increased for three of the four categories of information availability and use (Fig. 9.2). The average lengths of stay reported in the entry survey for respondents who 'Did not receive the VIG' and those who 'Used the VIG' were 3.59 days and 3.94 days, respectively. This represents a modest increase of 9.8%. Similarly, the average lengths of stay reported in the exit survey for respondents who 'Did not receive the VIG' and those who 'Used the VIG' were 3.99 days and 4.36 days, respectively. This represents an increase of 9.3%. Table 9.4 also shows the results of two-sample t-tests for significance. The relationship between length of stay and use or non-use of VIG was found to be significant only for visitors who did receive the VIG. Therefore, H_6 is only partially supported for length of stay.

Attractions and VIG use

Respondents were asked whether they intended and actually visited one or more of six major attractions. The influence of the VIG on attraction visitation was examined at the individual attraction level, rather than in terms of the average number of attractions visited by the customer segment.

Let us look at the figures for PEI's most famous landmark, Green Gables House. Upon entry, 699 individuals (or 52.7%) who did not use the VIG stated an intention to visit this site; meanwhile, 209 respondents (64.1%) who did use the VIG intended to visit the attraction. A similar trend was found in the exit survey, where 536 individuals (47.9%) who did not use the VIG reported having visited the attraction. In comparison, 709 respondents (67.4%) of visitors using the VIG reported a visit. Chi-square tests confirmed significance, with $P = 0.001$. The results are illustrated in Fig. 9.3.

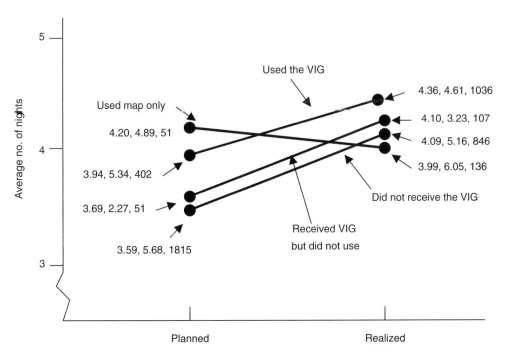

Fig. 9.2. Planned and realized length of stay by use or non-use of the *Visitor Information Guide* (VIG), standard deviation and number of persons interviewed.

Table 9.4. Significance test results for relationship between length of stay and visitor information guide (VIG) use, according to use or non-use of VIG.

	Planned		Realized			
	M	SD	M	SD	t	P
Received VIG	3.9 nights (n = 508)	5.3	4.3 nights (n = 1294)	4.7	0.28	0.78
Did not receive	3.6 nights (n = 1833)	5.7	4.1 nights (n = 844)	5.2	2.17	0.03

M, mean; SD, standard deviation.

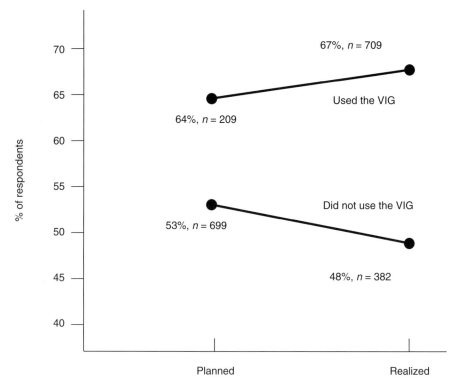

Fig. 9.3. Percentage of visitors to Green Gables House by those who used and did not use the *Visitor Information Guide* (VIG).

In the entry survey, 908 respondents (55% of all respondents) planned to visit Green Gables; of these, 23% used the VIG. In other words, the majority of visitors planned to visit the famous landmark of Prince Edward Island even though they did not receive the VIG. This is hardly surprising given that this is the most famous attraction on the island. In the exit survey, however, the situation is more complex. Of the 1245 visitors (57% of all respondents) to the attraction, 69% used the VIG.

These findings are difficult to interpret. Although chi-square significance was confirmed, we can make no conclusion as to the overall influence of the VIG. This is because a large number of individuals who reported visiting the attraction may have visited it anyway, whether or not they had received a VIG.

Also, while the influence of the VIG was confirmed, there was no significant difference between planned and realized visitation to Green Gables House. This may indicate the presence of a 'ceiling' effect for famous icons, whereby information will have little effect in increasing the number of visitors to a famous tourist site (this concept was also discussed in Chapter 8). Conversely, it may suggest that information is very critical for unknown attractions.

Visitation to Cavendish Beach suggests the opposite phenomenon; namely, the VIG is more influential while people are in the consumption site. Prior to entry, a far greater number of respondents who did not use the VIG planned to visit the site, compared to those who did use the VIG. Yet after entering PEI, the number who used the VIG is greater than the number who did not (Fig. 9.4).

Table 9.5 summarizes the results for all six attractions tested in the surveys. Interestingly, actual visits to PEI National Park were less than intended visits in terms of the use and non-use of the VIG. For example, while 88.1% of respondents who used the VIG in the planning stage intended to visit the Park, this figure dropped to 62.4% in the exit survey. In other words, the VIG was *less* influential while respondents were on PEI. This may indicate

the existence of a moderating variable; perhaps time constraints or the decision to forgo a visit to the Park in order to undertake other consumption behaviours. Yet it does suggest that the relative attractiveness of attractions is influenced by the use of the VIG.

The VIG also had little affect in increasing visits to the two less popular attractions of Ardgowan and Fort Amherst. Therefore, H_8 is not supported: lesser known attractions do not benefit more from the VIG than more popular ones. (H_8: The more unknown an attraction is, the greater will be the influence of product information about that attraction on planning and actual consumption of the experience.)

Main destinations and VIG use

Respondents were asked to cite their main destinations in the entry and exit surveys. The results for the use and non-use of the VIG on main destinations for planned and realized behaviours are summarized in Table 9.6.

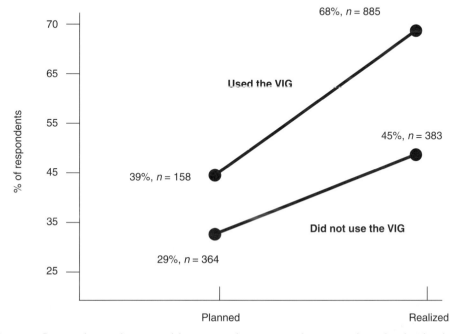

Fig. 9.4. Influence of use and non-use of the *Visitor Information Guide* (VIG) on planned and realized visitation to Cavendish Beach.

Table 9.5. Planned and realized visitation to major attractions by use and non-use of *Visitor Information Guide* (VIG).

	Planned			Realized		
	Did not use VIG (*n* = 1326) (%)	Used VIG (*n* = 326) (%)	Overall (%)	Did not use VIG (*n* = 1118) (%)	Used VIG (*n* = 1052) (%)	Overall (%)
Cavendish Beach	28.9 (*n* = 384)	38.8 (*n* = 138)	31.5 (*n* = 522)	39.9 (*n* = 522)	70.9 (*n* = 736)	58.4 (*n* = 1258)
Green Gables House	52.7 (*n* = 699)	64.1 (*n* = 209)	54.9 (*n* = 908)	47.9 (*n* = 536)	67.4 (*n* = 709)	57.4 (*n* = 1245)
PEI National Park	69.9 (*n* = 927)	88.1 (*n* = 266)	72.2 (*n* = 1193)	35.5 (*n* = 397)	62.4 (*n* = 656)	48.5 (*n* = 1053)
Province House	8.8 (*n* = 117)	19.3 (*n* = 63)	10.9 (*n* = 180)	20.7 (*n* = 231)	33.6 (*n* = 353)	26.9 (*n* = 584)
Ardgowan	0.8 (*n* = 10)	1.2 (*n* = 4)	0.8 (*n* = 14)	0.9 (*n* = 10)	2.0 (*n* = 21)	1.4 (*n* = 31)
Fort Amherst	0.7 (n = 9)	0.6 (*n* = 2)	0.7 (*n* = 11)	3.0 (*n* = 34)	6.6 (*n* = 69)	4.7 (*n* = 103)

Table 9.6. Planned and realized visitation to major destinations by use and non-use of *Visitor Information Guide* (VIG).

	Planned			Realized		
	Did not use VIG (*n* = 80) (%)	Used VIG (*n* = 303) (%)	Overall (*n* = 383) (%)	Did not use VIG (*n* = 188) (%)	Used VIG (*n* = 939) (%)	Overall (*n* = 1127) (%)
Charlottetown	41.3 (*n* = 33)	40.9 (*n* = 124)	41.0 (*n* = 157)	58.0 (*n* = 109)	48.2 (*n* = 453)	49.9 (*n* = 562)
Cavendish	33.8 (*n* = 27)	37.6 (*n* = 114)	36.8 (*n* = 141)	34.0 (*n* = 64)	36.1 (*n* = 339)	35.8 (*n* = 403)
Summerside	3.9 (*n* = 3)	5.3 (*n* = 16)	5.0 (*n* = 19)	7.4 (*n* = 14)	14.3 (*n* = 134)	13.1 (*n* = 148)
Brackley/ Stanhope/ Dalvay	7.5 (*n* = 6)	6.3 (*n* = 19)	6.5 (*n* = 25)	6.9 (*n* = 13)	12.2 (*n* = 115)	11.4 (*n* = 128)
Eastern Kings	2.5 (*n* = 2)	5.0 (*n* = 15)	4.4 (*n* = 17)	4.8 (*n* = 9)	9.3 (*n* = 87)	8.5 (*n* = 96)
West Prince	5 (*n* = 4)	1.3 (*n* = 4)	2.1 (*n* = 8)	2.7 (*n* = 5)	6.7 (*n* = 63)	5.9 (*n* = 66)
Southern Kings	2.5 (*n* = 2)	0.7 (*n* = 2)	1.0 (*n* = 4)	2.7 (*n* = 5)	5.4 (*n* = 51)	5.0 (*n* = 56)
South Shore	2.5 (*n* = 2)	3.0 (*n* = 9)	2.9 (*n* = 11)	3.7 (*n* = 7)	5.0 (*n* = 47)	4.8 (*n* = 54)
Evangeline	1.3 (*n* = 1)	0 (*n* = 0)	0.3 (*n* = 1)	0.5 (*n* = 1)	1.4 (*n* = 13)	1.2 (*n* = 14)

Two observations can be made. First, for planned behaviours, there is little difference whether individuals used or did not use the VIG. For example, 41.3% of respondents who did not use the VIG reported Charlottetown as their main destination, while a smaller percentage, 40.9%, of those who used the VIG intended to make Charlottetown their main destination.

Secondly, the influence of the VIG appears to be greater for less well-known destinations than for the most famous destinations of Charlottetown and Cavendish. Figure 9.5 shows the situation for Summerside. As can be seen, almost twice the percentage of respondents visited Summerside when the VIG was used (14.3% compared to 7.4%). The VIG increased the number of individuals who chose that place as their main destination. In contrast, the percentage of respondents who used the VIG and planned to visit Cavendish (entry survey) was higher than the percentage that used the VIG and stated that Cavendish had been their main destination (exit survey).

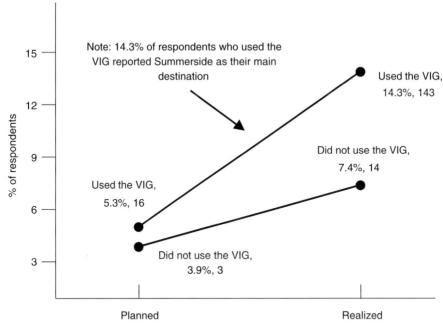

Fig. 9.5. Planned and realized visits to Summerside as main destination, percentages and number of respondents.

Chi-square tests revealed that the VIG had a significant influence on visitation to two destinations: Eastern Kings and West Prince. This finding lends partial support for **H₄**. (**H₄**: Consumers use product information more while in the consumption site than prior to entering the consumption site.)

Accommodation and VIG use

Accommodation was the most unplanned behaviour reported by respondents. Of the 1746 individuals who stated in the entry survey that they required paid accommodation, only 775 (44%) had made reservations.

Table 9.7 shows the choice of the four main accommodation types by respondents who used or did not use the VIG. For example, for respondents who did not use the VIG for planning their accommodation, 10.4% indicated the intention to stay in bed and breakfast accommodation (B&Bs); in contrast, of those respondents who used the VIG, 21.2% intended to stay in B&Bs. As such, the VIG would appear to have a positive affect in influencing potential customers to choose B&Bs as their form of accommodation. (Virtually identical results are seen in the realized behaviours for B&Bs.)

For hotels and motel accommodation, however, the use of the VIG appears to have had a

Table 9.7. Choice of planned and realized accommodation by use or non-use of *Visitor Information Guide* (VIG).

	Planned		Realized	
	Did not use VIG (%) (n = 606)	Used VIG (%) (n = 203)	Did not use VIG (%) (n = 755)	Used VIG (%) (n = 955)
Bed & breakfast	10.4 (n = 63)	21.2 (n = 43)	10.1 (n = 76)	22.6 (n = 216)
Hotel/motel	59.2 (n = 359)	51.1 (n = 104)	65 (n = 491)	53.1 (n = 507)
Cabin or cottage	16.3 (n = 99)	24.1 (n = 49)	12.8 (n = 97)	16.6 (n = 159)
Campground	3.9 (n = 24)	7.9 (n = 16)	12.1 (n = 91)	18.1 (n = 173)

negative influence on consumer's decision making. For both planned and realized behaviours, a greater proportion of respondents who did not use the VIG reported staying in hotels or motels. This suggests that, in the absence of product information, consumers will opt to stay in hotel or motel accommodation. When they are exposed to product information such as the VIG, they decide on other forms of accommodation. Obviously, from a managerial point of view, there is the potential to draw customers away from the hotel and motel-type accommodation by providing product information.

The figures for campground accommodation offer two points of note. First, the use of the VIG generates more consumers than does the absence of product information. Secondly, the exit survey reveals higher proportions of respondents staying in campgrounds than does the entry survey. We may infer that consumers learn about campground facilities during their stay on PEI, whether they use or do not use the VIG.

Chi-square tests revealed significance for all accommodation types. However, as noted above, the influence of the VIG in the choice of hotel/motel was in the reverse direction. Support is therefore found for H_5 for B&Bs, cabin/cottage and campgrounds.

Activities and VIG use

The influence of the VIG on intended and realized activities was tested by examining each activity individually. Table 9.8 details the influence of the VIG on planned and realized behaviours for the six main activities. For example, for the activity of 'Going to the beach', 18.3% of respondents who did not use the VIG stated the intention to undertake that activity; in contrast, 26.0% of respondents who used the VIG expressed the intention to go to the beach. The exit survey revealed that 50.2% of respondents who did not use the VIG visited the beach, while 76.9% of respondents who used the VIG reported a visit to the beach. In other words, a greater percentage of respondents are likely to visit the beach if they use the VIG than if they do not use the VIG.

The results for the other activities show a similar trend. For the activity of 'Go shopping for antiques or handcrafts', there is large increase from planned to realized behaviour for both use and non-use of the VIG. For instance, 45% of respondents who did not use the VIG reported this activity. This suggests that, in addition to the influence of the VIG, other factors existed which prompted individuals to undertake this activity.

For instance, Fig. 9.6 vividly illustrates the influence of the VIG for the category of 'Antique and handcraft shopping'. This is an interesting finding, since such shops are ubiquitous on the island and, given an arguable lack of alternative shopping activities, it is unsurprising that visitors would opt to browse and buy in such outlets. Chi-square significance tests revealed that the use of the VIG triggered a significant increase in the consumption of all activities. More people who use the VIG are likely to undertake the activity than those who do not use the VIG. This finding supports H_5. (H_5: Consumers with product information are more likely to both plan and engage in more tourist consumption behaviours than those without product information).

Table 9.8. Planned and realized behaviours for six main activities by respondents.[a]

	Planned		Realized	
	Did not use VIG (%) ($n = 1955$)	Used VIG (%) ($n = 407$)	Did not use VIG (%) ($n = 1187$)	Used VIG (%) ($n = 1052$)
Antique/handcraft shopping	6.9 ($n = 135$)	19.1 ($n = 78$)	45.0 ($n = 534$)	64.8 ($n = 682$)
Visiting museums/historical sites	30.0 ($n = 587$)	43.5 ($n = 134$)	51.8 ($n = 615$)	74.0 ($n = 251$)
Go to the beach	18.3 ($n = 357$)	26.0 ($n = 209$)	50.2 ($n = 596$)	76.9 ($n = 809$)
Sightseeing	44.5 ($n = 869$)	46.0 ($n = 337$)	78.5 ($n = 932$)	93.8 ($n = 987$)
Attend live theatre	11.1 ($n = 217$)	19.9 ($n = 81$)	19.4 ($n = 230$)	23.8 ($n = 251$)
Eat lobster suppers	21.5 ($n = 420$)	27.8 ($n = 113$)	39.7 ($n = 471$)	49.3 ($n = 519$)

[a] All chi-square values are significant at $\alpha < 0.01$ except for planned sightseeing.

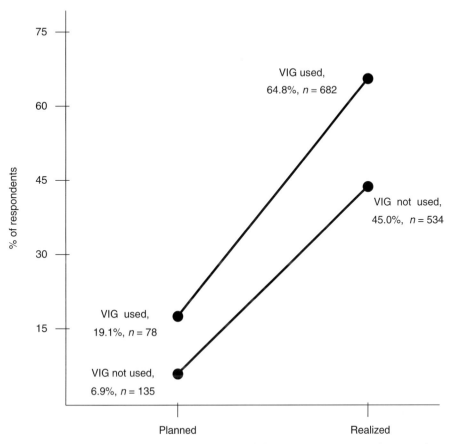

Fig. 9.6. Planned and realized visits to antique and handcraft shops by use or non-use of *Visitor Information Guide* (VIG), % and number.

Product Experience and Use of VIG

The relationship between product experience and VIG acquisition and use is a key exploratory factor in our investigation. [Other variables were worthy of investigation, for instance, the level of education, which has been shown to positively correlate with the amount of information sought (Westbrook and Fornell, 1979).] The most common assumption underlying the influence of information on consumption is that a consumer's familiarity with a product decreases the amount of information required. A study by Bennett and Mandell (1969, cited by Zalatan, 1996) established a negative relationship between the information required to purchase an automobile and past familiarity (and satisfaction) with an automobile brand. In contrast,

Manfredo (1989) suggested that information search serves different functions for consumers with product experience compared with those without product experience. He cautions against assuming that the increased likelihood of consumers seeking and acquiring information correlates with increased consumption activities. For example, experienced seekers of information may pursue information for its 'recreational' value, that is, it is part of the recreation experience in which they are likely to participate.

The relationship between product experience and VIG was examined from two perspectives: in terms of individuals who received the VIG and in terms of the usage of the VIG. Table 9.9 details the respondents who received and did not receive the VIG by visitation, either first-timer or repeater.

Table 9.9. Respondents who received and did not receive the *Visitor Information Guide* (VIG), by experience.

	Planned		Realized	
	First timer (%)	Repeat visitor (%)	First timer (%)	Repeat visitor (%)
Received VIG?				
Yes	175 (68)	342 (53)	468 (49)	839 (66)
No	83 (32)	308 (47)	492 (51)	425 (34)
Total	258 (100)	650 (100)	960 (100)	1264 (100)
	Chi-square = 17.436		Chi-square = 69.959	
	P = 0.001		P = 0.001	

A higher percentage of repeat visitors reported having received the VIG in the exit survey than first-time visitors. This suggests that (i) destination marketers failed to get the VIG into the hands of first-time travellers to Prince Edward Island, who are arguably the most in need of information and more likely to be influenced by information in their consumption behaviours; (ii) a large number of first-time visitors were disinterested in receiving information; or (iii) repeat visitors had retained the VIG obtained on previous visits. Obviously more research is needed in this area. The challenge for marketers is clear: to raise the percentage of visitors who receive destination information.

The same surprising result was found when we look at VIG usage. Table 9.10 lists the use of the VIG reported in the entry and exit surveys by three levels of experience: first-timers, those who have visited once or twice and those that have visited at least three times. (This breakdown was applied in order to gen-erate richer results by differentiating visitors with low and high levels of experience.)

Although first-time customers are thought more likely to acquire and use product infor-mation than customers with experience of the product, our results suggest a more complex reality. While first-time visitors reported the highest usage of the VIG prior to entering Prince Edward Island, visitor behaviour with respect to product information is difficult to interpret beyond this comforting confirmation of accepted logic.

The finding that respondents with 1–2 times the experience reported the highest level of realized use of product information supports Bettman and Park's (1980) proposition that more consumers with medium experience search/use information than novices or highly experienced consumers, because novices are overwhelmed by information and highly experi-enced consumers do not need the information. For respondents of the entry survey, while a high proportion (79%) of first-time visitors reported using the VIG 'completely' or 'to some extent', this finding may reflect an attitude of 'looking in the VIG for possible things to do' that need not manifest itself in heavy use.

A number of inferences can be made from the data displayed in Table 9.10. First, the VIG is used more for planning prior to entry than for planning while the visitor is in the consumption system. Secondly, there is virtually no difference in usage in the planning stage between first-time visitors and the most experienced visitors. Thirdly, in the exit survey, less-experienced visi-tors (1–2 visits) reported having used the VIG more than first-time visitors.

Table 9.10. Number and percentage of respondents who used the *Visitor Information Guide* (VIG) for planned and reported stages, by product experience.

Experience	Planned (%)	Realized (%)
First visit	81.5 (n = 274)	55.3 (n = 694)
1–2 visits	76.1 (n = 54)	59.2 (n = 148)
3 or more visits	76.0 (n = 76)	29.4 (n = 208)

Chi-square test for planned and realized behaviours by use of VIG generated a chi-square of 172.768 with P = 0.001.

Summary and Discussion

The core hypothesis, that consumers who use product information are likely to both plan and engage in more consumption activities than those who do not use product information, was generally well supported; consumers who used the VIG reported significantly greater spending, and a significantly greater number of activities undertaken. As the above results suggest, however, the relationship was less clear for other consumption behaviours, such as attractions visited, main destinations and main accommodation. Likewise, the hypothesis that consumers use product information more while in the consumption site than prior to entering the consumption site was supported for main destinations but rejected for activities.

The hypothesis that first-time visitors will rely on product information more than experienced visitors was not supported. At first glance, this appears a surprising outcome. Numerous studies have found that low product knowledge, unfamiliarity and product category inexperience are associated with information search and acquisition (Bucklin, 1966; Moore and Lehmann, 1980; Reilly and Conover, 1983). Berger and Dibattista (1992, p. 382) offer the following view:

> [I]f plans are already highly specified when they are retrieved, one would not expect persons to seek further information beyond being made aware of the goal ... By contrast, a less specific plan retrieved from memory would require the acquisition of additional information to aid in the process of specifying the plan.

On the other hand, a number of researchers have argued that there may be conditions under which uncertainty actually reduces search behaviour (Bettman, 1979; Bettman and Park, 1980; Alba and Hutchinson, 1987; Wilkie, 1975, cited by Urbany et al., 1989). And as Manfredo (1989) suggested, experienced consumers may seek information for its recreational value, as distinct from a basis on which purchase decisions are made.

The hypothesis that the more unknown an attraction is, the greater the influence of product information about that attraction on planning and actual consumption of the experience, was rejected. In fact, the reverse phenomenon was found. The VIG was shown to have a significant influence on visitation to the more famous places such as Green Gables and Cavendish, and no significant influence on the lesser known and less popular attractions of Ardgowan and Fort Amherst.

An unknown variable in this discussion is the timing of information acquisition and the level of respondents' motivation with regard information acquisition. Visitors to the destination who obtained the VIG prior to arrival are, by definition, more motivated to obtain and receive information than respondents who obtained the VIG after arrival. In addition to stronger motivation, they have more time to plan their activities based on the information. Visitors who receive the VIG after landing on Prince Edward Island are, overall, less motivated and have less time to use the information for planning purposes. Bronner (1982), for example, found that demand for additional information was drastically reduced when a decision was made under time pressure. It appears that individuals rely on available information to make a decision rather than incur the additional (temporal or monetary) cost of gathering more information. The inherent time pressures of a short stay on Prince Edward Island (remembering the majority of visitors stayed 4 nights or less) confirm our view that destination-marketing strategists need to distribute VIGs well in advance of visitors arriving at the destination.

At the same time, our results also challenge this conventional wisdom. Individuals who received the VIG after arrival are more likely to engage in higher consumption behaviours than the latter, many of whom probably obtained the VIG in a passive manner, such as off the counter at a visitor information centre, or tourist facility such as a motel or tourist attraction. Being able to differentiate the consumption behaviours of passive and active seekers of information after arrival in the consumption system would deepen our understanding of the influence and effectiveness of information.

10 Influence of Consumer Characteristics on Planned and Realized Behaviours

This chapter builds upon the findings of the previous chapters by investigating the relationship between planned and actual behaviours through the medium of consumer characteristics. Demographic variables may be a major explanatory factor accounting for discrepancies between the planned and eventual behaviours of individuals. This proposition was certainly the view of US researchers as far back as the 1950s, when government studies concluded that intentions only complement financial, demographic and economic variables for predicting behaviour, but intentions are not an adequate substitute for these data (Tobin, 1959, cited by Morwitz, 1997a).

In this chapter, the influence of consumer characteristics upon planned and realized consumption behaviours is examined through the effect of seven independent variables – geographical origin, income, product experience, motivation, education, travel party composition and age – on each of five dependent variables. Although gender is widely acknowledged as a predictor of unplanned and impulse purchasing (Rook and Hoch, 1985; O'Guinn and Faber, 1989; d'Astous, 1990; Fairmaner and Dittmar, 1993: Dittmar et al., 1995, 1996), we decided that the multi-member composition of travel parties renders analysis at the gender level inappropriate.

Influence of Geographical Origin on Behaviours

The role of national characteristics in the consumption behaviour of tourists has been an area of substantial investigation (see Woodside and Lawrence, 1985; Richardson and Crompton, 1988; Yiannakis et al., 1991; Rao et al., 1992; Pizam and Sussmann, 1995; Nicholls et al., 2001). Schul and Crompton (1983, p. 25) suggest that 'information search [is] likely to be greater for major (that is long-distance travel) rather than minor (short-distance) investments'. Pertinent to this study, studies have shown that levels of unplanned purchases differ significantly according to nationality (Nicholls et al., 2001).

Respondents who reside within a few hours driving distance of PEI are more likely to travel on a smaller budget, have a clearer idea of what they can expect from the visit, and spend less time planning than overseas visitors from, say, Europe, who spend more, plan longer and have less experience with the product. Overall, a trip to PEI for Europeans is likely to be a high-involvement purchase compared to the relative low-involvement act of Canadians and Americans.

This section quantifies the influence of country or regional origin on modifying the influence of planned and realized behaviour on selected planned and realized consumption activities. The usefulness of examining this relationship is limited to certain behaviours, namely, spending, length-of-stay, activities, attractions and destinations.

Spending and country/regional origin

This section examines the influence on spending of country/regional origin. Figure 10.1 shows the planned and realized spending behaviours for three geographical groups: Canada, the USA and overseas markets. Significance results are shown in Table 10.1. Consistent with other results, realized behaviours exceed the level of planned behaviours, thus confirming H_1. (H_1: Realized consumption behaviours are greater than planned for most specific services related to a purchased service system.)

In contrast to the overall spending patterns shown above, Fig. 10.2 shows the average expenditure per day for each of three main regional origins. The overseas market shows the largest increase in spending per day between planned and realized behaviours. (The main nationalities in the overseas market are the Japanese ($n = 96$), British ($n = 23$), followed by smaller numbers of other Europeans ($n \le 20$) and Australians ($n \le 20$).) The illustration suggests that little change occurs between planned and actual spending for the US market, in contrast to the more geographically proximate Canadian regions and the distant overseas markets.

Let us look at these latter two markets in more detail. Figure 10.3 displays the differences for planned and realized behaviours for the five regions of the Canadian market. All regions, with the exception of British Columbia, show a marked increase in per day spending between the entry and exit surveys. For example, the average spending for Ontario citizens, rose 60%, from $58 ($n = 421$) to $93 ($n = 425$). The lowest increase was for Quebec, which increased 24%, from $50 per day ($n = 105$) to $61 ($n = 126$). The only region to record a drop between planned and realized spending was British Columbia. Reported spending of $59 per day ($n = 71$) was 19% lower than the intended budget of $73 per day ($n = 80$).

The overseas market also displayed a tendency to report significantly higher spending than they expressed for the reported planned budget (Fig. 10.4). The critical caveat here, however, is the small sample size for each market. Japan, the largest sample market of non-North American visitors, shows a 47% increase from a budget of $64 per day ($n = 96$) to realized spending of $94 ($n = 150$). The most dramatic increase was reported for the Europeans, whose reported spending of $103 ($n = 18$) was 3.5 times the size of planned budget of $29 ($n = 19$).

Canadian visitors registered the lowest average spending, while average per person spending by American visitors was marginally higher than that by overseas visitors. However, the differentials between planned and realized spending for each of three main markets lend support to H_9 that tests the proposition that the gap between planned and spending is greater the further is distance from the destination: Canadian, $\Delta = 205; USA, $\Delta = 226; and overseas, $\Delta = 429.

Length of stay and country/regional origin

This section examines the differences between planned and realized length of stay by origin of the visitor. All regions within each of the three main geographical source markets – Canada, the USA and overseas – recorded increases between the entry and the exit surveys. As Table 10.2 reveals, the differences between planned and realized length of stay for Canadian and American visitors were statistically significant.

Figure 10.5 shows the differences for the five Canadian regions. A cursory glance reveals strong similarities among the responses of respondents from Quebec, Ontario and Maritime Canada. Visitors from British Columbia registered the sharpest increase: from 3.3 nights ($n = 80$) on average to 7.0 nights ($n = 71$), or a rise of 112%. It is not surprising, therefore, that British Columbia visitors should report spending less per day than they had budgeted for (see previous section); having made the decision to stay extra days, British Columbians cut back on their daily spending. Meanwhile, visitors from the Prairie

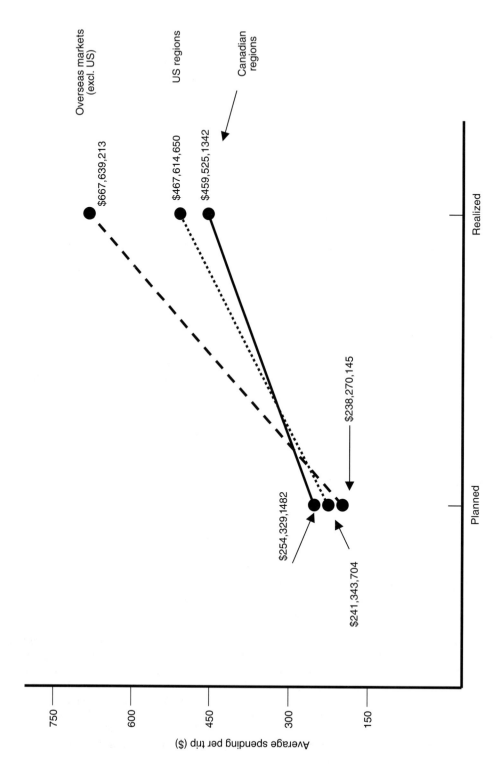

Fig. 10.1. Planned and reported expenditures among Canadian, US and overseas visitors: average budget or spending, standard deviation and number of respondents.

Table 10.1. Planned and realized spending by origin of visitors.

	Planned		Realized			
	Mean	SD	Mean	SD	t	P
Canadian visitors	$254	329	$459	525	12.56	0.001
American visitors	$241	343	$467	614	8.44	0.001
Overseas visitors	$238	270	$667	639	7.63	0.001

SD, standard deviation.

Provinces also displayed strong divergence between planned and reported length of stay: up 58% from 3.6 nights on average to 5.7 nights. Table 10.3 details differences in means for planned and realized length of stay by origin of Canadian visitors.

Figure 10.6 shows the differences in planned and reported length of stay for visitors from the USA. All groups registered significant differences in lengths of stay between the entry and exit surveys. Visitors from the Southeast recorded the largest divergence: from a planned average of 2.9 nights ($n = 134$) to a reported 6.8 nights ($n = 89$), a rise of 134%. The 'smallest' increase was registered by visitors from the Mid Atlantic, whose planned average length of stay of 3.1 nights rose to 4.4 nights, for a 42% increase. Table 10.4 details the differences in means.

Figure 10.7 shows the differences in planned and reported length of stay for overseas visitors. Since the sample size for each group is small, except for the Japanese, these findings must be viewed with caution. All groups show increases in length of stay, except for the Europeans whose average length of stay fell from 5.5 days to 5.0 days. The Japanese, by contrast, showed a significant rise in length of stay: from a planned 4.3 days to a reported 7.8 days, or an increase of 81%. The presence in flexibility in the itinerary of the Japanese respondents suggests the presence of a large proportion of independent tourists (or FITs). Differences in means are outlined in Table 10.5.

Based on these findings, $\mathbf{H_1}$ – realized consumption behaviours are greater than planned for most specific services related to a purchased service system – is only partially supported. Similarly, $\mathbf{H_9}$ – increases in the distance that consumers travel to engage in destination-specific consumption activities increases the differences in expenditures between planned and realized consumption activities – is only partially supported.

Geographical origin and activities

The comparison of the relationship between geographical origin and number of planned and realized activities is summarized in Table 10.6. Student t-tests revealed significant differences between planned and realized number of activities for all markets. In an attempt to generate richer insights, the mean number of planned and realized activities by the broad geographical markets of Canada, the USA and overseas were compared (Table 10.7). Again significant differences were recorded.

The next step was to 'eyeball' the data. Table 10.8 details the planned and realized activities reported by respondents from each of the three broad origin markets. From examining the data we can determine that most of the differences are significant. (The exception is golfing, which we found in Chapter 8 to have no significant difference between planned and realized behaviour.) The overseas group shows strong increases for virtually all activities, and while some reported behaviours of the Canadian group suggested otherwise, significant differences were recorded for all activities.

The American group generated the most interesting results. Chi square tests ($P < 0.01$) revealed no significant differences between planned and realized behaviours for water sports ($P = 0.028$) and lobster dinners ($P = 0.620$). At the same time, weak significance was found for active sports ($P = 0.005$), sightseeing ($P = 0.003$) and live theatre ($P = $

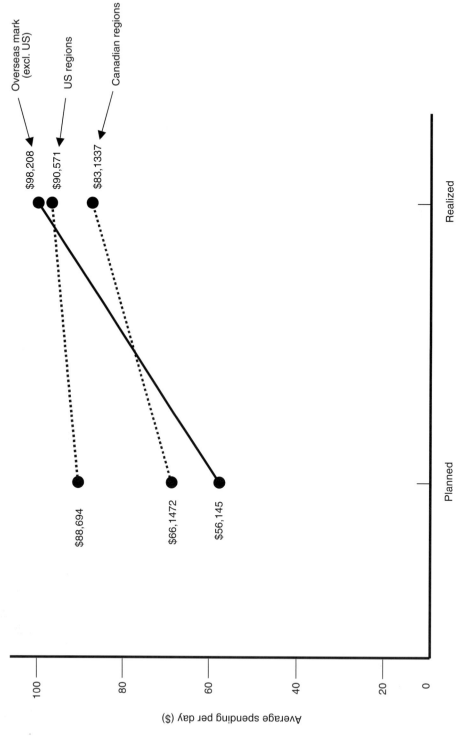

Fig. 10.2. Planned and reported expenditures among Canadian, US and overseas visitors: average budget or spending per night and number of respondents. For example, the average planned spending per night for overseas visitors (excluding the US) was $56 and *n* = 145. The overall planned spending per night for all visitors was $67.90 and average reported spending was $85.46, an increase of 25.9%.

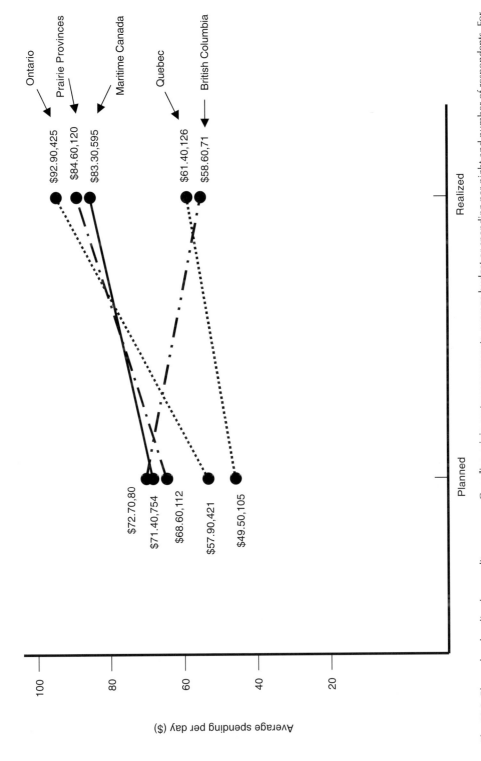

Fig. 10.3. Planned and realized expenditures among Canadian origin customer segments, average budget or spending per night and number of respondents. For example, the average planned spending per night for visito's from Quebec was $49.50 and $n = 105$. The overall planned spending per night was $65.80 and average reported spending per night was $83.10, an increase of 25.7%.

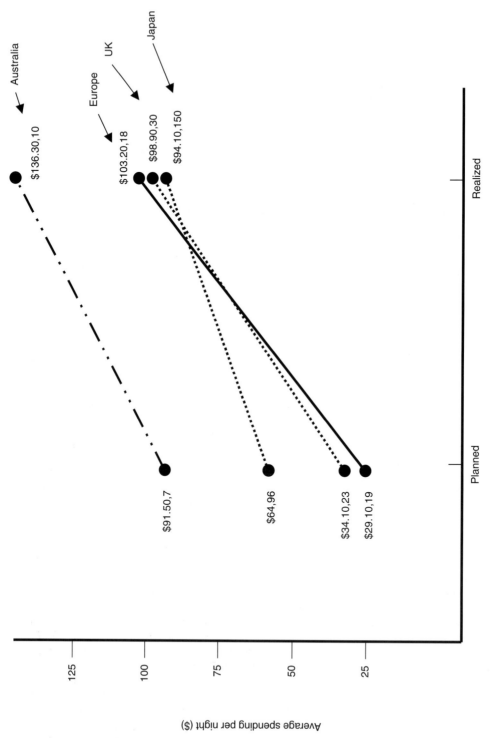

Fig. 10.4. Planned and realized expenditures among overseas origin (excluding US) customer segments, average budget or spending per night and number of respondents. For example, the average planned spending per night for visitors from Europe was $29.10 and n = 19. The overall average planned spending per night for overseas visitors (excluding US residents) was $56 and average reported spending was $97.60, an increase of 74.3%.

Table 10.2. Planned and realized length of stay by origin of visitors.

	Planned		Realized			
	Mean	SD	Mean	SD	t	P
Canadian visitors	3.9	5.6	4.4	4.8	2.684	0.007
American visitors	3.1	4.2	3.8	5.0	3.123	0.002
Overseas visitors	4.4	9.5	4.3	5.6	0.160	0.873

SD, standard deviation.

0.004). A deeper analysis of the data, by examining responses for each US region, would perhaps explain these anomalies.

Accordingly, tests were conducted for water sports and lobster dinners for the six regions of the USA as defined in this study: New England, Mid Atlantic, Southeast, Southwest, Mid West and West. None of the regions showed a significant difference in planned and realized behaviours for water sports. (Chi-squares ranged from 0.094 for West to 3.561 for Mid Atlantic.) In contrast, regions differed for lobster dinners. New England ($P = 0.001$, chi square, 12.471) and Mid Atlantic ($P = 0.001$; chi square, 10.270) registered significant differences.

These findings suggest that Americans, in contrast to respondents from other parts of the world who significantly increased their behaviours between planned and realized activities, display a uniform indifference to water sports on PEI. A strategic implication is that marketing water sports to Americans may be a waste of money (although lack of product awareness may also be a factor). [Another possibility is that Americans have better options closer to home for water sports.]

If we look at the behaviour with regard to lobster dinners, the results are more interesting. American respondents from the Atlantic Coast (New England and Mid Atlantic), where lobsters are plentiful in season, reported increases in consumption. This finding may indicate that those consumers with a high awareness of lobsters are more inclined to undertake the same consumption activity on PEI, in comparison to respondents from the other parts of the country less exposed to lobster cuisine. Again, a lack of awareness may contribute to the low consumption rate for other visitors to Prince Edward Island.

Geographical origin and attractions

A comparison of the relationship between geographical origin and planned and realized attractions reveals significant differences between planned and realized behaviours for all three groups. Table 10.9 shows that the greater the distance between Prince Edward Island and origin market, the higher is the average of realized attractions. This finding may be explained partly by the desire of consumers from distant places to fully 'experience' Prince Edward Island. It would also explain the fact that for planned behaviours, Canadians register the highest average number of planned attraction visits (mean = 1.0), presumably a reflection of the greater knowledge of the Prince Edward Island leisure product offer.

To generate richer insights, the values for planned and realized responses for individual attractions were listed and analysed. Table 10.10 lists the planned and realized behaviours for the main attractions by the three main source markets. Chi-square significance tests reveal no significant increases in the number of Canadian visitors and American visitors to Green Gables in terms of planned and realized behaviours. Visits to Green Gables House by the overseas respondents also shows no significant difference, although this finding may be due to the large percentage of visitors from that market who both planned to visit and actually did visit PEI's most famous landmark (89% and 93%, respectively). No difference was also identified for Canadians visiting Ardgowan also ($P = 0.311$), although the sample size is small.

Why was the Green Gables landmark unable to attract a significant increase in the number of visitors after they arrived on the island? The answer lies most likely in its high

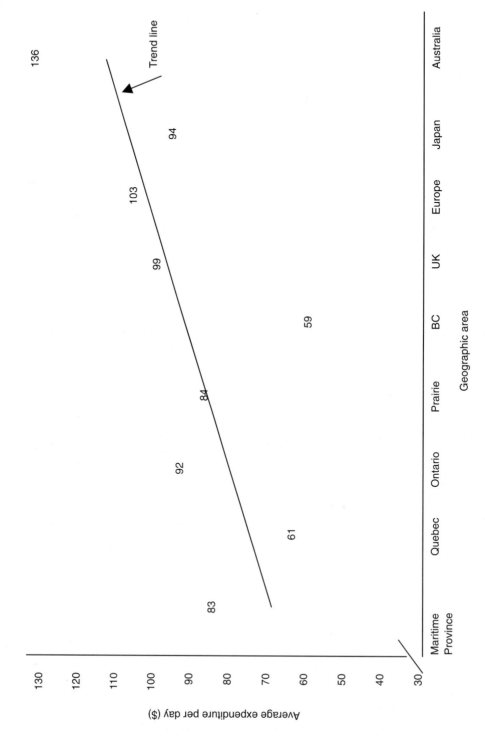

Fig. 10.5. Average expenditures per day by distance from Prince Edward Island. Data for the USA (i.e. $90) not included.

Table 10.3. Planned and realized length of stay by origin of Canadian visitors.

	Planned		Realized			
	Mean (nights)	SD	Mean (nights)	SD	*t*	*P*
Quebec (*n* = 105 and 112)*	5.5	8.5	8.3	18	1.93	0.055
British Columbia (*n* = 80 and 71)	3.3	4.0	7.0	17.0	1.89	0.049
Ontario (*n* = 421 and 425)	4.3	6.8	6.3	12.2	4.80	0.001
Prairie Provinces (*n* = 112 and 120)	3.6	6.3	5.7	9.9	1.91	0.057
Maritime Canada (*n* = 754 and 595)	3.6	4.0	4.3	7.6	2.30	0.021

* Numbers in parentheses refer to sample sizes for entry and exit surveys.
SD, standard deviation.

brand awareness or, put another way, customers' strong 'product' knowledge. All but the most uninformed of visitors would *not* know of the relationship between Prince Edward Island and the novel *Anne of Green Gables*. So the number who would arrive at the island not intending to visit, but in the end actually visiting, would be very small (as the numbers indicate). Such consequences of high brand awareness and strong product knowledge also explain the behaviour of visitors from the USA and Canada. As the critical 'pull' determinant in consumer motivation to travel to PEI, the role of Green Gables is both unquestioned and powerful. However, once visitors arrive on the island, the icon fails to generate a significant increase in numbers; in other words, a major icon has generated little unplanned behaviour.

What lessons are contained here for destination marketing organizations? As we know from our own experiences and our own home towns and cities, icon attractions and activities serve as core attractors for visitors. In the case of Prince Edward Island, the 'pulling power' of its major icon is greatest prior to arrival in the destination. Since the maximization of unplanned behaviour should be a major goal of any destination marketing organization, this result reinforces the need to offer other attractions and experiences to visitors after arrival.

Geographical origin and planned and realized main destinations

This section examines the relationship between planned and realized main destination in terms of geographical origin. The results are mixed and difficult to interpret. Let us examine the results for PEI's two most popular destinations, Charlottetown (Table 10.11) and Cavendish (Table 10.12). For both Charlottetown and Cavendish, there is a significant difference in planned and realized behaviour for the Canadian and overseas markets, but virtually no difference ($P = 0.962$ and $P = 0.845$, respectively) exists for Americans. Does this mean that Americans are less susceptible to altering their plans with regard main destinations than their counterparts elsewhere? We can only conjecture as to the reason.

Three less popular destinations are examined here: Summerside (Table 10.13), Southern Kings (Table 10.14), and West Prince (Table 10.15). The obvious observation is that the overseas market shows no significance between planned and realized behaviour. This result is expected, as it is highly likely that the overseas visitors would have predetermined their destinations to reduce the uncertainty associated with travelling to a distant place for the first time.

Influence of Income on Behaviours

This section will examine the influence of income upon three planned and reported behaviours: spending, length of stay and activities. Incomes were classified into five groups: less than C$20,000, C$20,000–35,000, C$35,000–50,000, C$50,000–75,000 and C$75,000 and over.

The financial situation of a consumer is an inhibiting factor that can explain why he or

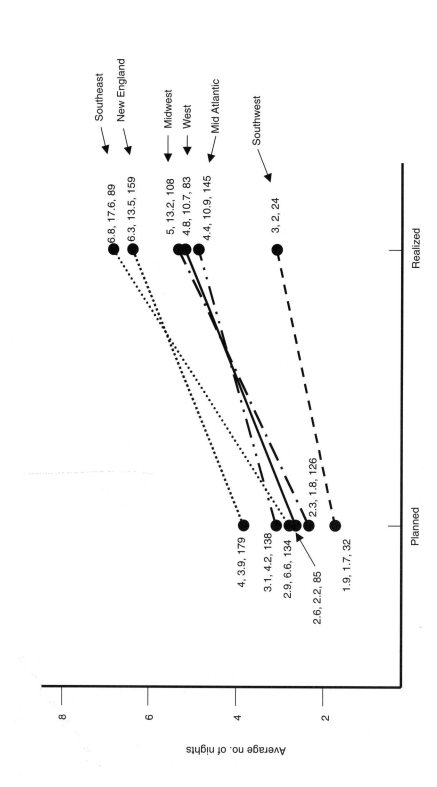

Fig. 10.6. Planned and realized lengths of stay among US origin customer segments, mean, standard deviation and number of persons interviewed. For example, the average planned nights on PEI for visitors from New England, USA was 4.0, SD = 3.9 and n = 179. The overall average increase in number of nights on PEI between the entry and exit surveys was 53%.

Table 10.4. Planned and realized length of stay by origin of American visitors

	Planned		Realized			
	Mean (nights)	SD	Mean (nights)	SD	t	P
Southeast	2.9	6.6	6.8	17.6	2.36	0.019
New England	2.9	3.9	6.8	13.5	2.24	0.026
Midwest	2.3	1.8	5.0	13.2	2.00	0.046
West	2.6	2.2	4.8	10.7	1.88	0.061
Mid Atlantic	3.1	4.2	4.4	10.9	1.32	0.187
Southwest	1.9	1.7	3.0	2.0	2.20	0.032

SD, standard deviation.

she might act contrary to previously formed attitudes or intentions (Howard and Sheth, 1969). Income has been identified as an important indicator of tourist spending (Agarwal and Yochum, 1999). Individuals with higher incomes have a greater propensity to engage in more commercial leisure activities than those with lower incomes. Beatty and Ferrell (1998) suggest that availability of money produces positive feelings and a positive influence on actual impulse or planned purchasing. Some research has found that income was not significantly related to unplanned or impulse purchasing (e.g. Wood, 1998). Van Raaij (1986) argued that individuals from lower-income groups engage in more planning to offset their greater perceived risk. This was supported in a recent tourism study by Fodness and Murray (1999), who found that travellers from lower socio-economic groups relied more heavily on planning than on-site decisions, in inverse contrast to their higher socio-economic group counterparts. Higher-income levels have also been found to be positively associated with greater levels of information search and usage (Gitelson and Crompton, 1983).

Our results show that income influences consumers in significantly increasing their overall spending, the number of nights they spent on Prince Edward Island, the number of attractions visited and the number of activities undertaken. These results run counter to research of unplanned purchases in retail settings (Kollat and Willett, 1967; Prasad, 1975; Agee and Martin, 2001) in which socio-economic variables did not explain consumers' rate of unplanned purchasing.

Income and spending

Average spending per trip was higher for successive income groups, for both planned and realized behaviours, as Fig. 10.8 indicates. The differences were statistically significant for all income groups except 'less than C$20,000' and 'C$35,000–50,000', as Table 10.16 shows. While the result for the lowest income group is intuitive, it is difficult to fathom why the middle-income group should exhibit such remarkable similarity between planned spending (mean = $359.12) and realized spending (mean = $360.79). (Sample sizes were 460 and 379, respectively.) The finding nevertheless supports H_1, whereby realized consumption behaviours were hypothesized to be greater than planned behaviours. Similarly, H_{11} is supported, since the results of the two highest income groups suggest that we can infer that higher income groups have a greater capacity for increased consumption.

Income and length of stay

The actual average number of nights spent on PEI exceeded those of planned number of nights for all income levels. All increases were significant ($P < 0.05$) except for the second highest income bracket ($50,000–75,000) which registered the smallest rise, of just 2.6%. In contrast, the highest income bracket ($75,000+) increased by 7.9%. The lowest income bracket recorded the highest difference: a rise of 13.5% (from 3.7 planned nights to 4.2 reported nights). Differences in means for income and length of stay are shown in Fig. 10.9 and listed in Table 10.17.

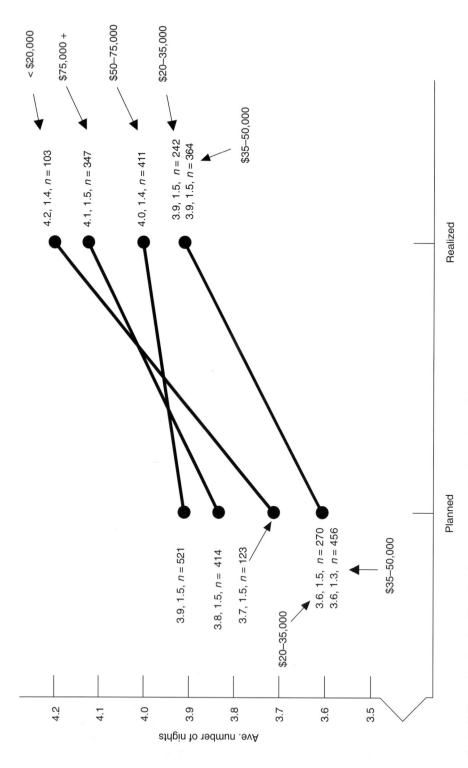

Fig. 10.7. Planned and realized lengths of stay among non-North American origin customer segments, mean, standard deviation and number of persons interviewed. For example, the average planned nights on PEI for visitors from Japan was 4.3, SD = 9.8 and n = 96. The overall average increase in number of nights on PEI from planned to reported behaviour was 53%.

Table 10.5. Significance test results for relationships between planned and realized length of stay by origin of overseas visitors.

| Origin | Planned | | | Realized | | | | |
	Mean (nights)	SD	df	Mean (nights)	SD	df	t	P
Japan	4.3 nights	9.8	95	7.8 nights	20.0	149	1.62	0.107
United Kingdom	4.6 nights	5.1	22	5.5 nights	3.9	29	0.72	0.477
Europe	5.5 nights	13.3	18	5.0 nights	2.8	17	0.15	0.879
Australia	2.0 nights	1.0	6	2.7 nights	1.0	9	1.42	0.176

SD, standard deviation; df, degree of freedom.

Table 10.6. Significance test results for relationship between geographical origin and activities.

| | Planned | | Realized | | |
	Mean	SD	Mean	SD	P
Quebec	2.2	1.5	6.9	2.5	0.001
British Columbia	2.9	1.9	6.8	2.4	0.001
Ontario	2.7	1.7	6.9	2.5	0.001
Prairie Provinces	2.7	1.8	6.6	2.2	0.001
Maritime Canada	2.7	1.9	5.2	2.7	0.001
Southeast	2.7	1.7	5.6	1.9	0.001
New England	2.9	2.0	6.1	2.4	0.001
Midwest	2.5	1.7	6.1	2.4	0.001
West	2.7	1.8	5.5	2.6	0.001
Mid Atlantic	2.8	1.8	6.3	2.2	0.001
Japan	2.3	10.1	7.0	1.5	0.001
United Kingdom	2.8	2.1	6.4	2.3	0.001
Europe	2.6	2.6	6.9	2.7	0.001
Australia	3.3	1.3	7.1	1.5	0.001
Total	2.7	2.7	6.1	2.5	0.001

SD, standard deviation

Table 10.7. Planned and realized number of activities by origin of visitors.

| | Planned | | Realized | | | |
	Mean	SD	Mean	SD	t	P
Canadian visitors (n = 1472 and 1323)*	2.7	1.8	6.1	2.6	41.253	0.001
American visitors (n = 694 and 608)	2.7	1.8	5.9	2.3	29.091	0.001
Overseas visitors (n = 139 and 208)	2.5	8.3	6.9	1.8	7.856	0.001
Total (n = 2311 and 2139)	2.7	2.7	6.1	2.5	44.155	0.001

* Numbers in parentheses refer to sample sizes for entry and exit surveys.
SD, standard deviation.

These results indicate significant relationships between income and length of stay for all income categories other than $50,000–75,000; as such, **H₁** is partially supported. The managerial or conceptual conclusions that can be drawn are limited. Income does not appear to explain increases in length of stay, a finding with strategic marketing

Table 10.8. Planned and realized individual activities by main origins of visitors (percentages, multiple answers).

	Planned				Realized			
	Canada	US	Overseas	Total	Canada	US	Overseas	Total
Go to the beach	46	29	9	39	64	59	66	63
Water sports	12	6	4	10	22	9	6	17
Golfing	11	4	1	8	12	5	4	9
Active sports	8	7	1	7	16	12	8	14
Spectator sports	5	1	1	4	8	3	3	6
Land or harbour tour	3	1	15	5	14	19	17	16
Sightseeing	68	85	70	73	84	90	95	87
Antiques/handcrafts	14	18	5	15	56	50	60	54
General shopping	21	17	5	19	60	51	66	58
Museum/historical sites	30	39	17	32	55	66	93	62
Live theatre	12	14	12	13	18	20	50	22
Lobster supper	229	45	19	29	40	43	74	44
Local cuisine	14	17	8	15	62	58	46	59
Nightlife	6	2	3	5	17	7	5	13
Total respondents	1482	704	138	2324	1324	668	213	2205

Table 10.9. Planned and realized number of attractions by origin of visitors, mean and standard deviation.

	Planned		Realized			
	Mean	SD	Mean	SD	t	P
Canadian visitors	1.0	0.9	1.8	1.5	16.3	0.001
American visitors	0.9	0.8	2.2	1.3	21.2	0.001
Overseas visitors	0.9	0.8	2.8	1.2	16.1	0.001
Total	1.0	0.9	2.0	1.4	14.5	0.001

SD, standard deviation.

Table 10.10. Relationship between planned (P) and realized (R) visits to main attractions by origin of visitors (percentages).

	Canada		US		Overseas		Total	
	P	R	P	R	P	R	P	R
Ardgowan	1	2	1	2	1	1	1	2
Cavendish Beach	34	55	25	63	40	71	32	59
Fort Amherst	1	4	1	6	0	5	1	5
Green Gables	44	48	67	69	89	93	55	58
PEI National Park	48	44	57	54	52	66	51	49
Province House	15	25	6	28	3	41	11	27
Total	1001	1287	501	587	119	206	1621	2080

implications for destination marketing organizations (DMOs). For example, the tourism marketing environment is scattered with well-meaning, but largely doomed, campaigns by DMOs that have attempted to extend the stay of high-yield markets.

Table 10.11. Geographical origin and planned and realized main destination of Charlottetown.

	Planned (n = 1778) (%)	Realized (n = 1649) (%)	Chi-square	P
Canadian	42 (n = 1200)	48 (n = 911)	7.49	0.006
American	51 (n = 448)	51 (n = 540)	0.00	0.962
Overseas	18 (n = 130)	86 (n = 198)	153.15	0.001

Table 10.12. Geographical origin and planned and realized main destination of Cavendish.

	Planned (n = 1778) (%)	Realized (n = 1649) (%)	Chi-square	P
Canadian	27 (n = 1200)	33 (n = 911)	11.40	0.001
American	25 (n = 448)	26 (n = 540)	0.05	0.845
Overseas	73 (n = 130)	40 (n = 198)	33.66	0.001

Table 10.13. Geographical origin and planned and realized main destination of Summerside.

Origin	Planned (n = 1778) (%)	Realized (n = 1649) (%)	Chi-square	P
Canadian	6 (n = 1200)	11 (n = 932)	19.85	0.001
American	7 (n = 448)	15 (n = 552)	18.87	0.001
Overseas	2 (n = 130)	5 (n = 199)	2.72	0.099

Table 10.14. Geographical origin and planned and realized main destination of Southern Kings.

	Planned (n = 1778) (%)	Realized (n = 1649) (%)	Chi-square	P
Canadian	3 (n = 1200)	5 (n = 911)	9.66	0.002
American	0 (n = 448)	4 (n = 540)	13.41	0.001
Overseas	1 (n = 130)	2 (n = 198)	0.82	0.366

Table 10.15. Geographical origin and planned and realized main destination of West Prince.

Origin	Planned (n = 1778) (%)	Realized (n = 1649) (%)	Chi-square	P
Canadian	4 (n = 1200)	6 (n = 932)	4.78	0.029
American	1 (n = 448)	6 (n = 552)	12.56	0.001
Overseas	2 (n = 130)	2 (n = 199)	0.10	0.755

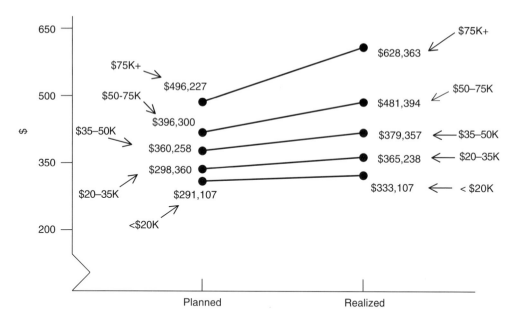

Fig. 10.8. Influence of income on planned and realized spending, by income group ($ amount and number of respondents).

Table 10.16. Differences between planned and realized income and spending, means and standard deviations.

	Planned		Realized			
	Mean	SD	Mean	SD	t	P
<$20K	$293	277	$332	365	−0.819	0.418
$20–35K	$298	252	$376	453	−2.073	0.039
$35–50K	$359	364	$361	361	−0.068	0.946
$50–75K	$401	417	$475	463	−2.176	0.029
$75K +	$503	502	$626	641	−2.467	0.014
Overall	$387	399	$457	495	−3.802	0.001

Significant at P <0.05.
SD, standard deviation.

Income and activities

This section examines the relationship between income and the consumption of leisure activities. The earlier analysis of overall planned and realized activities (see Chapter 8) revealed significant differences in planned and realized behaviours for all activities except golf. Examined through the prism of income groupings, however, the shifts in behaviour are much less clear-cut.

Behaviour relates to activities in two ways: in terms of the average number of planned and realized activities reported by each income group (details in Table 10.18), and by frequency of consumption for each activity type (see Table 10.19).

Two observations can be made about the mean scores. First, individuals underestimate the number of activities they will actually engage in: hence, the significant difference found for all income groups. Secondly, as Table 10.18 shows, no pattern occurs between the average number of planned activities and the income groups: the lowest income group reported the highest

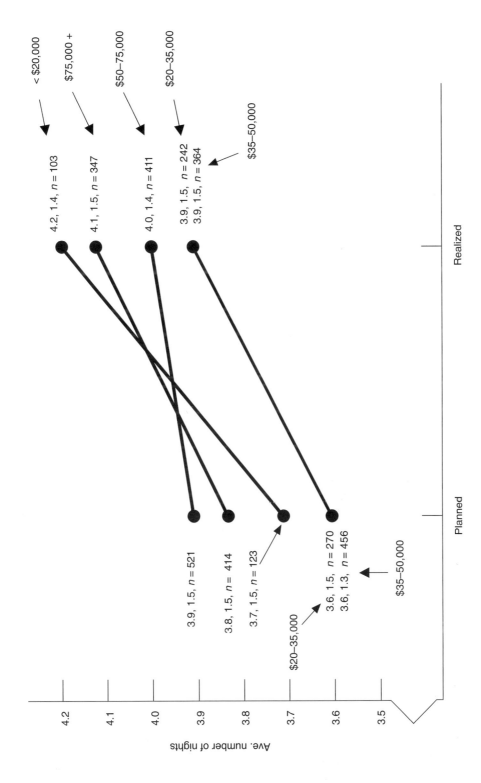

Fig. 10.9. Planned and realized length of stay by income levels, mean, standard deviation and number of respondents.

Table 10.17. Income and length of stay.

	Planned		Realized			
	Mean (nights)	SD	Mean (nights)	SD	t	P
Less than $20,000	3.7	1.5	4.2	1.4	2.69	0.008
$20,000–35,000	3.6	1.5	3.9	1.5	2.13	0.034
$35,000–50,000	3.6	1.3	3.9	1.5	3.09	0.001
$50,000–75,000	3.9	1.5	4.0	1.4	1.11	0.267
Over $75,000	3.8	1.5	4.1	1.5	2.75	0.006
Overall	3.7	5.5	4.2	3.5	3.54	0.001

SD, standard deviation.

Table 10.18. Relationship between income and activities, means and standard deviations.

	Planned		Realized			
	Mean (nights)	SD	Mean (nights)	SD	t	P
Less than $20,000	2.9	2.0	5.0	2.6	7.78	0.001
$20,000–35,000	2.7	1.7	5.9	2.3	17.42	0.001
$35,000–50,000	2.9	4.8	5.7	2.4	10.11	0.001
$50, 000–75,000	2.8	2.0	6.1	2.4	23.57	0.001
Over $75,000	2.8	2.9	6.5	2.5	25.00	0.001
Overall	2.8	2.9	6.0	2.4	33.69	0.001

SD, standard deviation.

Table 10.19. Relationship between planned and realized individual activities by income (percentages; multiple answers).

Activity	Planned activities (%)					Realized activities (%)				
	<20K	20–35K	35–50K	50–75K	>75K	<20K	20–35K	35–50K	50–75K	>75K
Go to the beach	46	42	37	41	43	61	57	61	62	68
Water sports	12	11	9	10	9	18	13	14	20	22
Golfing	12	7	5	10	11	8	6	9	11	10
Active sports	12	5	7	7	10	12	12	12	16	14
Spectator sports	12	5	4	3	2	8	9	8	6	4
Land or harbour tour	5	3	7	5	4	16	13	11	14	15
Sightseeing	68	69	75	74	74	82	49	83	87	89
Antiques/handcrafts	13	15	16	16	15	36	51	53	59	55
General shopping	23	20	21	22	14	57	58	52	58	61
Museum/historical sites	29	32	35	31	31	51	60	58	61	68
Live theatre	11	14	12	14	17	11	21	16	17	26
Lobster supper	16	23	25	24	26	26	44	35	43	51
Local cuisine	19	20	15	15	14	53	54	58	61	67
Nightlife	15	8	6	4	4	22	14	12	14	11
Total respondents	124	272	460	527	416	108	250	379	416	372

planned average and the highest income group reported the second lowest average. This finding contrasts with realized behaviours, in which average scores increase through the income ranges (with one exception).

Let us consider the reported frequencies for each planned and realized activity, as shown in Table 10.19. A number of interesting insights can be offered. First, chi-square tests reveal significant differences across all income groups for 5 of the 14 activities: namely, going to the beach, land or harbour tours, shopping, visiting museums and historical sites, and enjoying local cuisine. This finding suggests that the consumption of these activities may not depend on income as for other activities. Secondly, if we use the lowest income group (less than \$20,000) as the benchmark, income appears to influence the ability of respondents in this group to significantly increase their consumption behaviour for several activities. No statistically significant difference is found between planned and realized behaviours for water sports ($P = 0.173$), lobster dinners ($P = 0.066$), live theatre ($P = 0.966$), nightlife ($P = 0.177$), spectator sports ($P = 0.884$) and golf ($P = 0.884$). In contrast, the highest-income group shows increases in behaviour for all activities except golf. This finding suggests that income may inhibit the ability of lower-income consumers to undertake consumption of these activities, whether they desire them or not.

Thirdly, the behaviour related to the activity of 'Visiting antique and handcraft shops' is worth noting. While 15% of respondents in the \$20–35K income bracket said they intended visiting such stores, 51% reported that they had actually visited such stores. Even people in the highest-income bracket (\$75K+), which could be assumed to have the financial resources and the interest in such leisure pursuits, showed almost identical tendencies; 15% expressed intention to visit, in contrast to 55% reporting having made a visit. We can label 'Visiting antique and handcaft shops' as an emergent strategy in Mintzberg's typology. (Figure 10.10 shows the differences in planned and reported visits to antique and handcraft stores. The gap between reported behaviours for the lowest income group and for all other groups is the largest of any of the main activities examined.)

Overall, these findings tend to confirm H_{11},

that the higher the income the larger would be the discrepancy between planned and realized consumption behaviours. (The jump in realized versus planned visits to antique and handcraft stores may be due to the ubiquitous nature of these outlets in PEI – most of these stores appear, from the viewpoint of this researcher, to be unprofitable attempts to create a net cash flow among the substantial share of low-income families living in PEI.)

Income and attractions

The mean scores for the number of attractions visited between the entry and exit surveys increased significantly, as Table 10.20 shows. The highest income group recorded the highest average number of both planned and realized attractions. The frequency of consumption for each attraction between planned and realized behaviours is shown in Table 10.21. Two interesting observations can be made. First, greater uniformity in the relationship exists between income and consumption for realized rather than planned behaviours; that is, the order of magnitude from low to high visitation for realized behaviours matches that of income groupings, with the lowest-income group recording the smallest number of realized average visits (1.62) and the highest-income group reporting the highest number of average visits (2.10). This suggests that income is a useful indicator of visitation to tourist attractions.

Secondly, the actual number of visits to Prince Edward Island National Park were less than planned for *all* income groups – a highly unusual occurrence. (The characteristics of the product need to better understood before conclusions can be drawn from this finding.)

Income and destinations

The relationship between income groups and planned and realized main destination for four destinations – Cavendish, Charlottetown, Summerside and West Prince – were tested (Tables 10.22–10.25). Respondents in the highest income bracket exhibit the greatest likelihood of altering their plans about the main destination after arriving at the destination:

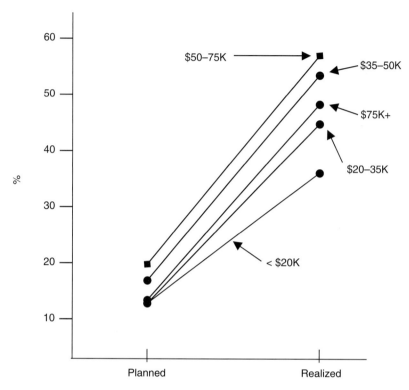

Fig. 10.10. Planned and reported behaviours for visiting antique and handcraft stores, by proportion of respondents for each income bracket.

Table 10.20. Significance values for relationship between income and attractions.

	Planned		Realized			
	Mean	SD	Mean	SD	t	P
Less than $20,000	1.0	0.9	1.6	1.5	3.658	0.001
$20,000–35,000	1.1	1.0	1.8	1.4	6.603	0.001
$35,000–50,000	1.0	0.9	1.8	1.5	10.779	0.001
$50,000–75,000	1.0	0.9	2.0	1.4	14.285	0.001
Over $75,000	1.1	1.0	2.1	1.4	11.904	0.001
Overall	1.0	0.9	1.9	1.4	21.951	0.001

SD, standard deviation.

significant differences between their planned and realized behaviour were identified for all the destinations except Cavendish, the most popular destination on PEI. These findings are difficult to interpret, since no intuitive reason comes to mind as to why income would influence the choice of main destination (other than the perceived cost of accommodation).

Influence of Product Experience on Behaviours

Consumers with previous experience of a tourist destination should have better formed behavioural intentions than consumers with no experience. The influence of prior experience on intentions is well documented (Fazio and

Table 10.21. Relationship between planned and realized visits to main attractions by income (percentages, multiple answers).

| Attractions | Planned activities (%) | | | | |
	<20K	20–35K	35–50K	50–75K	>75K
Green Gables	33	55	56	53	58
Cavendish Beach	33	35	28	33	40
PEI National Park	53	50	50	53	55
Province House	14	11	12	8	16
Fort Amherst	0	2	1	0	0
Ardgowan	0	1	1	1	1
Total respondents	124	272	460	527	416

| Attractions | Realized activities (%) | | | | |
	<20K	20–35K	35–50K	50–75K	>75K
Green Gables	39	49	54	57	62
Cavendish Beach	50	55	55	59	61
PEI National Park	42	48	43	49	548
Province House	23	2	24	26	29
Fort Amherst	6	3	4	5	6
Ardgowan	4	0	2	1	2
Total respondents	108	250	379	416	372

Table 10.22. Influence of income on planned and realized main destination of Cavendish.

	Planned (%)	Realized (%)	Chi-square	P
Less than $20,000	26 ($n = 106$)	26 ($n = 65$)	0.110	0.921
$20,000–35,000	29 ($n = 220$)	37 ($n = 187$)	3.556	0.059
$35,000–50,000	31 ($n = 339$)	30 ($n = 289$)	0.010	0.922
$50, 000–75,000	27 ($n = 412$)	32 ($n = 319$)	2.399	0.123
Over $75,000	31 ($n = 308$)	32 ($n = 291$)	0.041	0.839

Table 10.23. Influence of income on planned and realized main destination of Charlottetown.

	Planned (%)	Realized (%)	Chi-square	P
Less than $20,000	48 ($n = 106$)	51 ($n = 65$)	0.114	0.736
$20,000–35,000	43 ($n = 220$)	54 ($n = 187$)	4.748	0.029
$35,000–50,000	42 ($n = 339$)	47 ($n = 289$)	0.085	0.771
$50,000–75,000	42 ($n = 411$)	45 ($n = 319$)	0.920	0.337
Over $75,000	43 ($n = 308$)	54 ($n = 291$)	6.949	0.008

Zanna, 1981; Kruglanski and Klar, 1985; Morwitz and Schmittlein, 1992). Product experience is critical when studying the dynamic choice processes of consumers new to a market (Heilman et al., 2000). Experience teaches people how to plan, and the actual behaviour of consumers with product experience will more closely approximate their plans than in the case of consumers with no or little product knowledge (Stewart and Vogt, 1999). Routine and habitual buyer behaviour allows for purposive and intelligent behaviour without

Table 10.24. Influence of income on planned and realized main destination of Summerside.

	Planned (%)	Realized (%)	Chi-square	P
Less than $20,000	6 ($n = 106$)	6 ($n = 66$)	0.018	0.894
$20,000–35,000	5 ($n = 220$)	9 ($n = 190$)	2.641	0.104
$35,000–50,000	7 ($n = 339$)	13 ($n = 294$)	5.166	0.023
$50,000–75,000	6 ($n = 412$)	15 ($n = 324$)	15.993	0.001
Over $75,000	5 ($n = 308$)	13 ($n = 301$)	15.441	0.001

Table 10.25. Influence of income on planned and realized main destination of West Prince.

	Planned (%)	Realized (%)	Chi-square	P
Less than $20,000	2 ($n = 106$)	2 ($n = 65$)	0.028	0.966
$20,000–35,000	3 ($n = 220$)	4 ($n = 187$)	0.337	0.561
$35,000–50,000	4 ($n = 339$)	7 ($n = 294$)	2.372	0.123
$50,000–75,000	4 ($n = 412$)	6 ($n = 324$)	2.726	0.099
Over $75,000	7 ($n = 308$)	19 ($n = 301$)	6.529	0.011

deliberation (Katona, 1975). Research into services has confirmed the direct effect of prior behaviour on customer decisions to use services (Biehal, 1983; Murray, 1991). Experienced consumers should be better able to assess the risks associated with engaging in particular behaviours, and to understand the factors that will influence the decision, than less experienced consumers: for example, how long it takes to drive to particular destinations on an island, which route offers the best scenery, which attractions are worth spending time and money on, and what accommodation is value for money. Consequently, hypothesis H_{10} states that experienced consumers differ from inexperienced consumers in two ways: they plan fewer consumption activities and the difference between planned and realized consumption activities will be less for experienced consumers than for inexperienced consumers.

The influence of experience upon consumption behaviour in the travel context is well documented. Studies show that product experience of the destination plays a significant role in various aspects of travel planning and activities, including information use (Etzel and Wahlers, 1985); time spent planning (Zalatan, 1996); risk perception (Roehl and Fesenmaier, 1992); site choice (McFarlane et al., 1998); destination attractiveness (Hu and Ritchie, 1993); and satisfaction with a destination (Mazursky, 1989b).

This section looks at the relationship between product experience (the number of times an individual has visited PEI) and the consumption behaviours of spending, length of stay, activities and attractions.

Product experience and spending

The relationship between product experience (classified into first-timers, 1–2 visits, or 3 or more visits) and planned budget and reported spending is shown in Fig. 10.11. A number of interesting findings are revealed. First, little difference occurs between planned budget, regardless of experience. Secondly, first-time visitors report spending more than visitors who have been to PEI three or more times, yet less than visitors travelling to the island for the second or third time. (This can be explained readily: the second- and third-time visitors are the highest information users and most efficient in completing activities during their stays.) Thirdly, the most experienced visitors report the lowest average spending, as might be expected. This finding is expected in the light of the studies by Menon (1993) and Menon et al. (1997), which found that respondents are

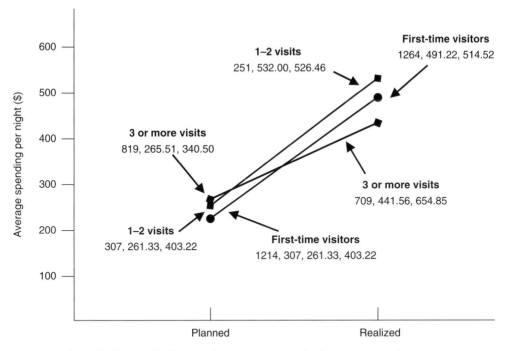

Fig. 10.11. Planned and reported differences in budget and spending by product experience, number, mean and standard deviation.

most accurate in formulating behavioural estimates of consumption and spending for frequent or regular behaviour. The results of two-sample *t*-tests are shown in Table 10.26. These findings confirm H_1, that realized consumption behaviours will exceed planned behaviours.

An important implication for strategic marketing follows. First-time visitors budget to spend less than experienced customers, who are more knowledgeable about the actual costs – and variety – of leisure activities available in the destination. (This view is supported by the finding that 54% of first-time visitors could not, or would not, answer the question of their intended budget in the entry survey; this figure contrasts with 48% for 1–2-time visitors and 39% for visitors with at least 3 visits.) Since somewhat experienced customers spend more than first-time visitors, destination marketing organizations are therefore likely to generate higher yields for local tourism operators by targeting repeat, as well as, first-time visitors. ANOVA tests for the three groups in the entry and exit surveys revealed no significant difference among the groups.

Table 10.26. Planned and realized spending by degree of product experience, means and degrees of difference.

	Planned	Realized			
	Mean ($)	Mean ($)	df	*t*	*P*
First-time visitors	234	491	2481	15.11	0.001
1–2 visits	261	532	487	6.89	0.001
3 or more visits	266	442	1512	6.71	0.001
Overall	388	505	4480	6.26	0.001

Product experience and length of stay

Product experience was found to have a significant influence on the length of stay. Significance tests for the three categories of experience are detailed in Table 10.27.

This confirms H_1 that states that realized behaviours will exceed planned behaviours.

Product experience and activities

An ANOVA test revealed no significant differences across the three groups in the entry survey

but significant differences between '3 or more visits' and the other two categories of experience in the exit survey ($F = 17.418$). In other words, there was an inverse relationship between experience and number of activities (Table 10.28). This finding supports H_{10}. Table 10.29 details the results and significance tests for planned and realized behaviours for each group.

Product experience and attractions

The pattern of behaviour hypothesized earlier in this research is illustrated vividly in Fig. 10.12 for

Table 10.27. Planned and realized length of stay by degree of product experience.

	Planned	Realized			
	Mean ($)	Mean ($)	df	t	P
First-time visitors	3.5	3.9	2563	8.25	0.001
1–2 visits	3.8	4.4	514	4.09	0.001
3 or more visits	4.1	4.3	1495	3.16	0.002
Overall	3.7	4.2	4572	3.54	0.001

Table 10.28. Regression coefficients for influence of product experience on planned and realized activities.

	Coefficient	F	t	P
First-time visitors	0.092*	38.091	6.172	0.001
	0.156	52.978	7.279	0.001
1–2 visits	0.002	0.020	0.140	–
	0.022	1.037	1.019	–
3 or more visits	−0.099	43.834	−6.621	0.001
	−0.181	71.978	−8.484	0.001

*The upper rows are the planned activities results and the lower rows are realized results.

Table 10.29. Planned and realized activities by product experience.

	Planned		Realized			
	Mean	SD	Mean	SD	t	P
First-time visitors	2.7	3.3	6.4	2.2	32.456	0.001
1–2 visits	2.8	1.7	6.2	2.4	19.547	0.001
3 or more visits	2.6	1.9	5.4	2.8	22.500	0.001
Overall	2.7	2.7	6.1	2.5	44.155	0.001

visitation to Green Gables: namely, that realized visits will exceed planned visits and that first-time visitors' planned and actual visits will exceed those of experienced visitors. Considering that Green Gables House is Prince Edward Island's most famous icon and main tourist attractor, this result is intuitively unsurprising. Also logically consistent is the result for Cavendish Beach, shown in Fig. 10.13. Inexperienced visitors are likely to be less aware of generic attractions (such as a beach) than experienced visitors, and therefore fewer first-time visitors than experienced visitors will express an intention to visit such places. Also noteworthy is that Cavendish Beach was

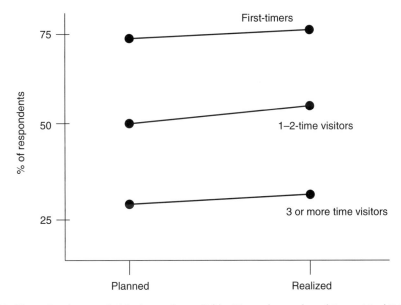

Fig. 10.12. Planned and reported visitation to Green Gables House, by number of times visited Prince Edward Island.

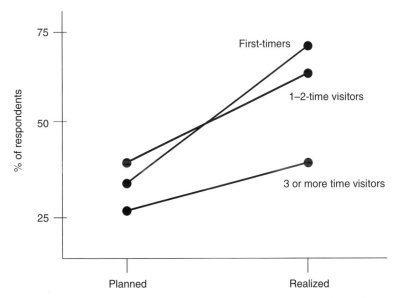

Fig. 10.13. Planned and reported visitation to Cavendish Beach, by number of times visited Prince Edward Island.

also the most popular main attraction for three or more time visitors.

Overall, two effects of product experience on visitation to PEI's major attractions were identified. First, first-time visitors intended to – and actually did – visit attractions more than their more experienced counterparts. Table 10.30 shows the mean number of planned and realized attractions for each of the three experience categories. The same influence is illustrated in Table 10.31, where experience has been recoded into a dichotomous variable – 'first-time' or 'experienced'.

Secondly, regardless of experience, the percentage of realized behaviours exceeded the percentage of planned behaviours. (The one exception was PEI National Park, where 45% of experienced visitors intended to visit the site, while only 35% actually did.) However, little improvement in visitation rates were found for Green Gables House and PEI National Park, a finding that has occurred previously. Underlying this phenomenon may be an inverse correlation, whereby the more famous a tourist icon is, the less likely the occurrence of a significant increase between planned and actualized visitation. If so, the implication for marketing strategists in the allocation of their scarce marketing funds is that the promotion of tourist icons to visitors *after* arrival may lack cost effectiveness.

Since levels of realized behaviour are greater than the level of planned behaviour, these findings confirm support for H_1. The findings also confirm H_{10}, whereby experienced customers plan fewer consumption behaviours and are less likely to engage in unplanned activities than inexperienced customers.

Product experience and main destination

The relationship between product experience and main destination was tested for the selected destinations of Cavendish, Summerside, Charlottetown, West Prince and Southern Kings (Tables 10.32–10.36). The results are more equivocal than those for other consumption activities.

The most interesting observation is that first-timers registered significant differences for all destinations except Cavendish. In direct contrast, the most experienced visitors (three or more times) registered no significant difference for planned and realized main destination except for Cavendish. Second- and third-timers followed a similar pattern: no significant changes between planned and realized choices

Table 10.30. Planned and realized attractions by product experience.

		Planned		Realized			
	n	Mean	SD	Mean	SD	t	P
First-time visitors	916–1205	1	1	3	1	36.000	0.001
1–2 visits	218–239	1	1	2	1	10.597	0.001
3 or more visits	501–700	1	1	1	1	4.363	0.001

Table 10.31. Planned and realized attractions, by experience (%).

	Planned		Realized	
	First time (n = 916)	Experienced (n = 736)	First time (n = 1205)	Experienced (n = 954)
Ardgowan	1	1	2	1
Cavendish Beach	3	29	70	45
Fort Amherst	1	1	6	3
Green Gables	72	34	76	35
PEI National Park	56	45	60	35
Province House	13	9	37	15

Table 10.32. Relationships between product experience and planned and realized main destination of Cavendish.

	Planned (%)	Realized (%)	Chi-square	P
First-timers	37 ($n = 799$)	33 ($n = 1113$)	3.61	0.057
2nd or 3rd timers	34 ($n = 221$)	29 ($n = 203$)	1.38	0.240
Over 3 times	20 ($n = 761$)	29 ($n = 358$)	11.32	0.001

Table 10.33. Relationships between product experience and planned and realized main destination of Charlottetown.

	Planned (%)	Realized (%)	Chi-square	P
First-timers	46 ($n = 799$)	59 ($n = 1113$)	123.69	0.001
2nd or 3rd timers	34 ($n = 221$)	43 ($n = 203$)	3.58	0.058
Over 3 times	40 ($n = 761$)	40 ($n = 358$)	0.00	0.997

Table 10.34. Relationships between product experience and planned and realized main destination of Summerside.

	Planned (%)	Realized (%)	Chi-square	P
First-timers	4 ($n = 799$)	13 ($n = 1113$)	55.55	0.001
2nd or 3rd timers	6 ($n = 221$)	12 ($n = 203$)	3.21	0.073
Over 3 times	7 ($n = 761$)	10 ($n = 358$)	2.39	0.122

Table 10.35. Relationships between product experience and planned and realized main destination of West Prince.

	Planned (%)	Realized (%)	Chi-square	P
First-timers	2 ($n = 799$)	5 ($n = 1137$)	14.27	0.001
2nd or 3rd timers	3 ($n - 221$)	6 ($n - 203$)	3.20	0.074
Over 3 times	5 ($n = 761$)	7 ($n = 364$)	1.90	0.168

Table 10.36. Relationships between product experience and planned and realized main destination of Southern Kings.

	Planned (%)	Realized (%)	Chi-square	P
First-timers	1 ($n = 799$)	4 ($n = 1113$)	21.33	0.001
2nd or 3rd timers	1 ($n = 221$)	6 ($n = 203$)	10.61	0.001
Over 3 times	4 ($n = 761$)	4 ($n = 358$)	0.04	0.843

except for one destination, Southern Kings.

In summarizing, significant effects of product experience on consumption occurred for all the dependent variables except destinations. This finding contradicts that of Manfredo (1989), whose research into the relationship between product experience and information seeking (related to recreation products) found that consumers with product experience have a greater intention to participate in consumption activity than those with no product experience.

Influence of Motivation on Behaviours

Motivations have been shown to influence consumption behaviour in a variety of ways. Excitement and adventure seekers tended to seek more information and undertake more activities (Gitelson and Crompton, 1983), while people looking for more meaningful content in their vacation (such as cultural or historical experiences) will tend to seek longer stays than their hedonistic counterparts (Meyer, 1977, cited in van Raaij and Francken, 1984).

Motivation is a complex construct. The motivations that individuals ascribe to their choice of behaviours can differ significantly between the time the decision is made and after the behaviour is enacted. As Weick argues eloquently in his treatise on 'sensemaking', people reconstruct their goals after the event. Action precedes thought, to the extent that a realistic understanding of human actions can only occur after the behaviour takes place, rather than being represented in plans made beforehand. This is termed retrospective justification. The phenomenon of retrospective justification is, however, not new:

> In place of the view that decisions are made as the occasions require, an alternative formulation needs to be entertained. It consists of the possibility that the person defines retrospectively the decisions that have been made. The outcome comes before the decision ... The rules of decision making in daily life ... may be much

more preoccupied with the problem of assigning outcomes their legitimate history than with the question of deciding before the actual occasion of choice the conditions under which one, among a set of alternative possible courses of action, will be elected. (Garfinkel, 1967, quoted by Weick, 1998, p. 195)

Weick's viewpoint echoes from the behavioural decision research, that suggests that preferences are often constructed, rather than retrieved, when decision makers need to choose one alternative from a set of alternate products, services or courses of action (cf. Fischhoff, 1991; Payne *et al.*, 1992).

Motivation and spending

Significant relationships were identified for planned and realized spending for all eight categories of motivations (Table 10.37). This finding is in line with the relationship between spending and other independent variables examined previously. Consumers, regardless of motivation, tend to spend more than they actually budget for. This occurs for even those seeking to 'Experience nature' and 'Visiting friends and relatives' (VFR) – the two motivational categories that appear least contingent upon financial outlays. This finding reaffirms the view that consumers greatly underestimate the amount of likely spending. Note that the order of magnitude for motivations between planned and realized behaviours does not alter

Table 10.37. Significance of test results for relationships between planned and realized spending and motivation; means, standard deviations (US$).

	Planned		Realized				
	Mean ($)	SD	Mean ($)	SD	t	df	P
Seeking familiar setting	530	496	746	1005	−5.44	90	0.001
Family vacation	523	462	717	675	−1.36	492	0.001
Sports and social activities	471	442	558	450	−5.75	98	0.001
History and culture	356	493	495	515	−0.51	679	0.001
Relaxation	408	376	481	520	−2.62	1241	0.001
Entertainment	385	200	460	423	−2.83	38	0.001
Experience nature	307	279	420	506	−25.11	294	0.001
VFR	282	357	378	522	−1.11	773	0.001
Overall	387	407	502	571	−6.19	3701	0.001

SD, standard deviation.

greatly, that is, VFR and 'Experience nature' are the lowest-spending segments in both surveys, and 'Family vacation' and 'Seeking familiar setting' are the highest-spending segments. This indicates that, from the viewpoint of spending patterns, motivation is not a useful explanatory factor in understanding the difference between planned and realized behaviour.

Figure 10.14 reveals that, in comparative terms, spending levels by motivation change little between the entry and exit surveys. Two observations can be made, however. First, between the entry and exit stages, the gap widens between the two biggest-spending motivation segments of 'Seeking familiar setting' and 'Family vacation' and the other segments. This may indicate that these two segments possess a higher propensity for discretionary spending, an attractive indicator for DMOs when considering target segments for

their overall r
interaction (
'History an'
segments,
high incre...
graphic profile ...
some light on the ma...
the needs of this study). On the
the graph indicates, the issue may ...
characteristics of the 'History and Culture ...
ment, but rather the nature of the 'Relaxation' and 'Entertainment' segments, both of which register relatively small spending increases between the entry and exit surveys.

Motivations and length of stay

Motivations and length of stay are two key variables in which destination marketing orga-

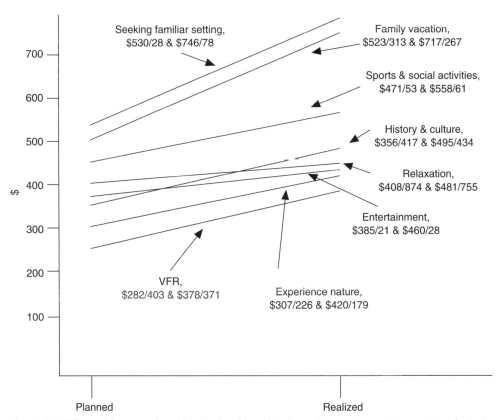

Fig. 10.14. Differences between planned and realized spending, by motivation (average $ amount/sample size).

(DMOs) have a strong interest. ~~~ of stay is a typical performance indica~~~ ~~~r destinations, while motivations are often ~~~d as a psychographic segmentation vari~~~ble. As such, DMOs seek a deeper understanding of the relationship between the two variables.

The differences between planned and realized length of stay for motivation categories were statistically significant except for 'Experience nature and sports' and 'Social activities' (Table 10.38). While planned and realized length of stay for 'Seeking a Familiar Setting' were significantly different, this was due to a negative, rather than positive, increase in the mean. This finding may be explained partly by the small sample sizes: 28 respondents (2.2% of total) cited this motivation in the entry survey and 74 respondents (3.8%) cited it in the exit survey. If the small sample size does not fully explain the negative shift, how else can we explain this anomaly? One obvious implication is that consumers discover that their expectations of the experience on PEI do not match the reality. Using the same logic, we could suggest that the insignificant difference between planned and realized 'Experience nature' motivation – 3.05 planned number of nights versus 3.06 realized number of nights – was also due to the same 'disappointment'.

The case of 'Experience nature' is different, however. A relative large number of respondents named 'Experience nature' as their main motivation: 221 (or 8.0% of the total sample) in the entry survey and 174 (6.1%) in the exit survey. We can therefore reinterpret this behaviour in Mintzberg's model as planned and unrealized.

Interestingly, the VFR segment registered the largest increase between planned and realized length of stay (1.8 nights or 41%), although their spending did not significantly increase, as we learned from the previous discussion.

Motivations and attractions

The kind of attractions that tourists visit is likely to reflect particular travel motivations. For example, we would assume that consumers seeking to experience nature would be unlikely to visit many attractions (other than national parks), while those interested in history and local culture would be expected to visit relatively more attractions.

Analysis of the three main attractions revealed, however, that motivation is not a useful indicator of the shift of attraction preference between the entry and exit surveys. There was a significant increase for most motivations across the three tourist sites (Tables 10.39–10.41).

Table 10.38. Planned and realized length of stay and motivation; means, standard deviations (nights).

	Planned		Realized			
	Mean	SD	Mean	SD	t	P
Family vacation	4.2	4.8	4.5	3.3	−13.5	0.001
Relaxation	3.6	5.2	3.9	4.1	−3.25	0.001
History and culture	2.7	4.4	3.4	3.7	−1.27	0.001
Entertainment[a]	2.6	1.6	3.9	2.4	−2.48	0.001
VFR	4.4	6.6	6.2	8.2	−1.65	0.001
Sports and social activities	3.8	3.1	3.7	2.1	−0.18	0.854
Seeking familiar setting	6.7	9.3	4.5	4.7	−2.55	0.001
Experience nature	3.1	6.4	3.1	2.3	−0.20	0.841
Overall	3.7	5.4	4.2	4.9	−1.12	0.001

[a]Small sample size renders interpretation difficult.
SD, standard deviation.

Table 10.39. Planned and realized visits to Cavendish Beach,

	Planned (%)	Realiz		
Family vacation (96–188)	42			
Relaxation (181–448)	32	ບ.		
History and culture (121–288)	35	70		
VFR (59–114)	25	31		
Sports and social activities (8–26)	22	43	4.7ᴄ	
Seeing familiar setting (3–40)	14	51	9.22	ʋ
Experience nature (45–118)	26	67	59.98	0.00ᴉ
Overall (518–1232)	32	59	267.36	0.001

ᵃCategories with low sample sizes omitted.

Table 10.40. Planned and realized visits to Province House, by motivation.

	Planned (%)	Realized (%)	Chi-square	P
Family vacation (23–55)	10	21	10.72	0.001
Relaxation (53–193)	9	27	64.40	0.001
History and culture (59–172)	17	42	54.49	0.001
VFR (24–42)	10	11	0.25	ns
Experience nature (17–61)	10	35	31.89	0.001
Overall (178–566)	11	27	149.37	0.001

Table 10.41. Planned and realized visits to PEI National Park, by motivation.

	Planned (%)	Realized (%)	Chi-square	P
Family vacation (194–159)	62	60	0.29	ns
Relaxation (466–348)	54	49	4.07	0.044
History and culture (216–262)	52	64	11.85	0.001
VFR (132–84)	33	23	9.54	0.002
Sports and social activities (20–19)	38	32	0.46	ns
Seeing familiar setting (14–48)	50	62	1.13	ns
Experienco nature (127–103)	57	58	0.06	ns
Overall (1179–1028)	51	49	6.88	0.009

ns, not significant.

Two findings are noteworthy. First, visitation by the 'Visiting Friends and Relatives' (VFR) segment did not increase significantly for any attraction, despite the marked increase in length of stay for VFRs that we found above. This view may suggest that marketing strategists may be advised to omit this segment from its targeted marketing communications aimed at visitors during their stay in the destination. It also suggests that the VFR segment is better targeted either prior to arrival or through their hosts already living in the destination. Secondly, there was a large increase in visitation to Province House for the 'History and culture' category. Though not surprising, given the historical nature of this particular attraction, the low intention recorded (17%) indicates a lack of product awareness by visitors and the need for PEI marketers to raise the profile of the attraction among potential visitors.

The overall number of visits to attractions by each motivation category was also considered. The comparison of planned and realized number of visited attractions by motivation is detailed in Table 10.42. A number of observations can be made. First, there is a significant difference for all motivations other than 'Entertainment'. Secondly, the mean score

an doubles from the entry to the exit
s for several motivations: 'History and
re', 'Seeking familiar setting' and
xperience nature'. The dramatic increase for
History and culture' is particularly interesting.
Remember our earlier finding that the realized
spending for this segment represented a significant increase over planned spending compared
to other benefit segments. This offers a possible explanation for that conundrum.

The results for these last two motivation categories are noteworthy, suggesting that attractions have appeal even for consumer segments
for whom the uniqueness of the local
society/community (as manifested in attractions) are not primary attractors in bringing
them to PEI. Thirdly, and perhaps least surprising, the VFR segment, though registering a statistically significant difference in planned and
realized attractions, showed the smallest mean
score for realized behaviours, even though the
segment registered the largest length of stay. At
the same time, product experience may be a
moderating variable for this segment.

Motivations and activities

Activities include such things as going to the
beach, participating in water sports and shopping. Similar to attractions, the number of
activities would likely reflect the type of travel
motivation expressed by respondents. For
example, visitors seeking a relaxing holiday
would have, by definition, little interest in
undertaking a wide variety of activities.

This proposition was tested by examining
planned and realized activities for four motivation categories: 'Relaxation', 'Family vacation',
'Visiting friends and relatives (VFR)', and 'To
learn a new culture' (Tables 10.43–10.45 give
the results for the first three categories).
Expectedly, statistically significant increases
were found in almost all cases. The activity of
'Live theatre', however, did not increase significantly for the motivations of 'Family vacation'
and 'VFR'. 'Historical and cultural' were the
most popular planned *and* realized activities
for all motivation categories, with the exception of 'VFR'.

Table 10.42. Planned and realized attractions visited and motivation;
means, standard deviations (number).

	Mean	SD	Mean	SD	t	P
Family vacation	1.3	1.0	2.3	1.3	−10.66	0.001
Relaxation	1.0	0.9	2.0	1.4	−22.70	0.001
History and culture	1.0	0.9	2.7	1.2	−17.77	0.001
Entertainment	0.8	0.9	0.9	1.2	−1.33	0.520
VFR	0.7	0.8	0.9	1.2	−3.06	0.001
Sports and social activities	0.8	0.9	1.2	1.3	−2.19	0.001
Seeing familiar setting	0.9	0.9	2.4	1.4	−5.21	0.001
Experience nature	0.9	0.8	2.4	1.3	−12.67	0.001
Overall	1.0	0.9	2.0	1.4	−33.00	0.001

SD, standard deviation.

Table 10.43. Planned and realized consumption of selected activities, by 'relaxation' category.

	Planned (n = 874) (%)	Realized (n = 755) (%)	Chi-square	P
Historical and cultural	27	61	190.58	0.001
Live theatre	12	17	8.07	0.001
Lobster dinners	23	45	88.74	0.001
Antiques and handcraft	13	58	368.35	0.001
Organized tours	4	13	45.79	0.001

Table 10.44. Planned and realized consumption of selected activities, by 'Family vacation' category.

	Planned (n = 313) (%)	Realized (n = 267) (%)	Chi-square	P
Historical and cultural	46	74	46.98	0.001
Live theatre	18	24	0.07	ns
Lobster dinners	20	44	38.94	0.001
Antiques and handcraft	19	65	128.68	0.001
Organized tours	3	14	23.80	0.001

Table 10.45. Planned and realized consumption of selected activities, by 'Visiting friends and relatives' category.

	Planned (n = 403) (%)	Realized (n = 371) (%)	Chi-square	P
Historical and cultural	18	35	29.43	0.001
Live theatre	11	13	0.75	ns
Lobster dinners	20	26	4.83	0.028
Antiques and handcraft	14	43	88.59	0.001
Organized tours	1	9	23.14	0.001

Figure 10.15 vividly illustrates the shift in the magnitude of preferences from planned to realized behaviours for the 'Relaxation' motivation category. Four of the five activities increase uniformly from planned to realized; the exception is 'Antiques and handcrafts', which increases significantly. Interestingly, exactly the same pattern is exhibited for the 'Family vacation' motivation segment. The consistency shown by consumers in behaviour between planned and actual consumption is remarkable. It suggests that motivation is a useful indicator of future consumption patterns.

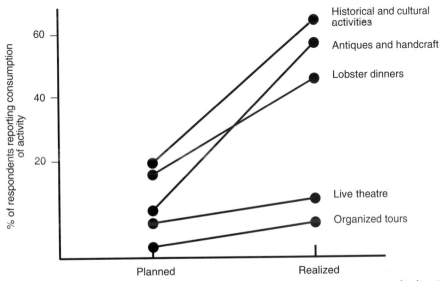

Fig. 10.15. Planned and realized consumption of selected activities by motivation category of 'relaxation'.

The results for the average number of activities for each motivation are shown in Table 10.46. Since all motivations are statistically significant between planned and realized activities, few conclusions can be drawn. A closer look at the mean scores, however, renders more useful insights. First, while there is no surprise in the 'Sports and social activities' segment registering the highest mean score at the planned stage, when realized behaviours are compared this segment registers only the fifth highest mean score. (Again, a relatively small sample size (61 in the entry survey and 58 in the exit survey) may partly explain this phenomenon.) The mean score for the 'Sports and social activities' segment in the exit survey even falls below the average mean score for the entire sample. This failure to convert the customer from intention to purchase (or experience) has implications both for marketing communications and the delivery of the product offering in the destination.

Secondly, 'Family vacation' ranks as the segment with the highest mean score for attractions visited, presumably a reflection of the need for parents to keep their children occupied. Other studies would be worthwhile, to investigate whether the discrepancy between the planned and realized figures is typical of families, who may chronically underestimate the degree of tourist behaviour needed to satisfy the demands of their immediate 'stakeholders'.

Thirdly, the VFR segment records the smallest mean score, which may be the result of numerous previous visits and/or the desire to spend more time 'catching up' with friends and relatives and less time engaged in typical tourist behaviours. Since the behaviour of the VFR segment is of critical interest to destination marketing organizations, this and other insights into this large but poorly researched segment are of potential benefit to them.

Motivation and main destinations

An examination of the relationship between motivation and main destinations produces few insights. This conclusion is explained partly by the small sample sizes for destinations other than Cavendish and Charlottetown. The one constant revealed in this analysis is that the planned and actual main destinations for the 'History and culture' segment are statistically significant different for all destinations detailed here. The anomaly is Cavendish, in which significantly *fewer* respondents citing 'History and culture' as their travel motivation *actually* chose Cavendish as their main destination (Table 10.47). This may have implications for the (in)ability of Cavendish to 'deliver' the benefits desired by consumers seeking a historical and cultural experience. In contrast, Charlottetown 'picked up' a significantly larger number of such visitors, as recorded in the exit survey (Table 10.48).

The findings for Summerside (Table 10.49) and West Prince (Table 10.50) are less

Table 10.46. Planned and realized activities and motivation; means, standard deviations (number).

	Planned		Realized			
	Mean	SD	Mean	SD	t	P
Family vacation	3.1	1.9	7.1	2.2	−22.75	0.001
Relaxation	2.6	1.8	6.1	2.4	−15.96	0.001
History and culture	2.9	5.1	6.3	2.1	−12.61	0.001
Entertainment	2.5	1.7	5.3	2.7	−4.09	0.001
VFR	2.4	1.8	5.1	2.8	−15.41	0.001
Sports and social activities	3.3	1.7	5.9	2.8	−5.83	0.001
Seeing familiar setting	2.2	1.57	6.7	2.0	−10.73	0.001
Experience nature	2.2	1.7	5.9	2.2	−17.04	0.001
Overall	2.7	2.7	6.1	2.4	−43.20	0.001

SD, standard deviation

Table 10.47. Influence of motivation on planned and realized main destination of Cavendish.

	Planned (%)	Realized (%)	Chi-square	P
Family vacation	41 ($n = 260$)	42 ($n = 234$)	0.01	0.946
Relaxation	33 ($n = 623$)	35 ($n = 620$)	0.29	0.589
History and culture	40 ($n = 86$)	26 ($n = 395$)	14.65	0.001
Entertainment	0 ($n = 0$)	30 ($n = 20$)	–	–
VFR	42 ($n = 380$)	44 ($n = 371$)	0.68	0.411
Sports and social activities	18 ($n = 49$)	27 ($n = 51$)	1.16	0.281
Seeing familiar setting	44 ($n = 27$)	42 ($n = 65$)	0.04	0.842
Experience nature	37 ($n = 134$)	28 ($n = 160$)	3.23	0.072

Table 10.48. Influence of motivation on planned and realized main destination of Charlottetown.

	Planned (%)	Realized (%)	Chi-square	P
Family vacation	29 ($n = 260$)	39 ($n = 234$)	4.3	0.038
Relaxation	43 ($n = 623$)	47 ($n = 620$)	1.93	0.165
History and culture	47 ($n = 286$)	68 ($n = 395$)	31.84	0.001
Entertainment	75 ($n = 20$)	65 ($n = 20$)	0.48	0.490
VFR	43 ($n = 380$)	41 ($n = 371$)	2.84	0.092
Sports and social activities	45 ($n = 49$)	45 ($n = 51$)	0.00	0.984
Seeing familiar setting	37 ($n = 27$)	77 ($n = 65$)	13.38	0.001
Experience nature	48 ($n = 134$)	52 ($n = 160$)	0.49	0.482

Table 10.49. Influence of motivation on planned and realized main destination of Summerside.

	Planned (%)	Realized (%)	Chi-square	P
Family vacation	4 ($n = 260$)	10 ($n = 234$)	6.79	0.009
Relaxation	5 ($n = 623$)	14 ($n = 620$)	30.16	0.001
History and culture	4 ($n = 286$)	11 ($n = 395$)	10.60	0.001
Entertainment	0 ($n = 20$)	5 ($n = 20$)	–	–
VFR	11 ($n – 300$)	12 ($n = 371$)	0.04	0.851
Sports/social activities	4 ($n = 49$)	48 ($n = 51$)	–	–
Seeing familiar setting	7 ($n = 27$)	2 ($n = 65$)	–	–
Experience nature	2 ($n = 134$)	16 ($n = 160$)	16.34	0.001

Table 10.50. Influence of motivation on planned and realized main destination of West Prince.

	Planned (%)	Realized (%)	Chi-square	P
Family vacation	4 ($n = 260$)	3 ($n = 237$)	0.69	0.407
Relaxation	2 ($n = 623$)	6 ($n = 628$)	10.95	0.001
History and culture	1 ($n = 286$)	6 ($n = 401$)	9.37	0.002
Entertainment	0 ($n = 20$)	0 ($n = 20$)	–	–
VFR	5 ($n = 380$)	4 ($n = 371$)	0.71	0.399
Sports/social activities	4 ($n = 49$)	16 ($n = 54$)	4.27	0.039
Seeing familiar setting	4 ($n = 27$)	0 ($n = 65$)	–	–
Experience nature	2 ($n = 134$)	6 ($n = 160$)	1.99	0.159
Overall	3 ($n = 1751$)	4 ($n = 2155$)	14.03	0.001

interesting, due mainly to the small sample sizes. Summerside significantly increases the number of visitors citing 'Relaxation' as their main motivation, perhaps indicating a source of untapped appeal. The situation for West Prince reveals a similar trend, although from a small base.

Influence of Education Level on Behaviours

The influence of education level on consumption behaviour is well documented in the tourism literature: educated tourists require more information and more time to reach travel decisions (Francken and van Raaij, 1981; Gitelson and Crompton, 1983; Rao et al., 1992), and a higher level of education is conducive to lower levels of satisfaction (Zalatan, 1996). In his study on unplanned and impulse purchasing, Wood (1998) found education to be useful indicator of impulse buying behaviour, whereby higher levels of impulse purchases were associated with 'some' college educational experience. Wood concluded that since education (and not income, as he found in his study) was associated with high levels of impulse behaviour, cultural and cognitive factors were acting as intervening variables, rather than processes related to material resources that would be confirmed if income had been significant.

This section reveals one very intriguing trend. While planned behaviours are fairly uniform in the sense that the degree of consumption activity is greater the higher the level of education, by contrast, actual behaviours show no such uniformity.

Education and spending

Table 10.51 details planned and realized spending according to education level of the respondents. Due to the strong correlation between income and education, the mean score for spending is greater the higher is the level of education – except for planned spending by 'College or university' respondents. Of the five categories, those reporting 'High school' and 'Technical college' levels show no statistical significance between planned and realized behaviours. This finding is a little surprising, as most other independent variables examined have showed a statistically significant difference between planned and realized spending. The finding that respondents with high school experience reported significant increases in actual over planned spending is supported by Wood's (1998) study in which the highest degree of impulse purchasing was associated with respondents who had college experience but no degree.

Education and length of stay

Significance tests for education and length of stay revealed the same results as above; that is, no statistical significance for 'High school' and 'Technical college' levels (Table 10.52). The two tests differ in one interesting aspect, namely, that for planned behaviours

Table 10.51. Significance test results for relationships between planned and realized spending and education level.

| | Planned | | Realized | | | | |
	Mean	SD	Mean	SD	t	df	P
Some high school	$254	207	$379	443	2.106	160	0.037
High school graduate	$367	388	$398	440	0.939	736	0.348
Technical college	$417	525	$430	593	0.220	365	0.826
College or university	$385	349	$540	607	5.249	1467	0.001
Postgraduate	$436	489	$613	624	3.763	671	0.001

SD, standard deviation.

increased level of education does not equate with a longer length of stay. For realized behaviours, this association is more apparent. Whereas the higher education level respondents planned 3.6 days on average in PEI (placing them the second lowest after 'Some high-school education'), their actual length of stay was the highest at 4.4 days. These results suggest that education is not a useful indicator of length of stay patterns.

Education and activities

An examination of the relationship between level of education and number of activities reveals a more uniform pattern. The pattern seen between education and spending reappears, that is, the higher the level of education the higher is the mean score for planned number of activities planned and done. For realized behaviours this order is virtually unchanged. For all five education levels, realized versus planned activities are statistically significant (see Table 10.53 for details).

Education and attractions

Similar to length of stay, the ranking of consumption levels by education level differs between planned and realized behaviours. For planned behaviour, the higher the education level, the greater the number of attractions planned. For realized behaviour, while the sequence is different, the two highest education levels still report the highest number of attractions visited (Table 10.54).

Education and main destination

In this section, we examine the relationship between education level and choice of main destination. At first glance, education may have little utility as a predictor of this particular behaviour. Yet a number of observations can be made. First, some segments exhibit remarkable consistency of behaviour. The 'Technical college' respondents show no statistically significant change for any of the five main destinations shown below. It also suggests that no destination was able to entice

Table 10.52. Significance test results for relationships between planned and realized length of stay and education level.

	Planned		Realized				
	Mean	SD	Mean	SD	t	df	P
Some high school	3.4	3.2	4.4	4.4	2.049	160	0.042
High school graduate	3.7	6.1	3.8	3.8	0.090	736	0.928
Technical college	3.8	6.9	3.7	3.1	0.220	365	0.826
College or university	3.7	4.7	4.4	6.0	3.065	1467	0.00
Postgraduate	3.6	4.9	4.4	3.6	2.976	671	0.003

SD, standard deviation.

Table 10.53. Significance test results for relationships between planned and realized activities and education level.

	Planned		Realized				
	Mean	SD	Mean	SD	t	df	P
Some high school	2.3	1.5	5.1	2.5	10.769	160	0.001
High school graduate	2.5	4.4	5.7	2.4	13.559	736	0.001
Technical college	2.7	1.8	5.8	2.3	15.979	365	0.001
College or university	2.8	1.9	6.2	2.4	34.000	1467	0.001
Postgraduate	2.9	1.8	6.6	2.5	24.503	671	0.001

SD, standard deviation.

Table 10.54. Significance test results for relationships between planned and realized attractions and education level; means, standard deviations.

	Planned		Realized				
	Mean	SD	Mean	SD	*t*	df	*P*
Some high school	0.7	0.8	1.3	1.5	4.161	160	0.001
High school graduate	0.9	0.8	1.8	1.5	12.297	736	0.001
Technical college	1.0	1.0	1.7	1.4	6.306	365	0.001
College or university	1.0	0.9	2.1	1.4	20.925	1467	0.001
Postgraduate	1.1	0.9	2.1	1.4	12.716	671	0.001

SD, standard deviation.

'Technical college' customers away from their intended main destination (unless, of course, everyone changed their mind in exactly the same proportions, which is unlikely).

Secondly, if we look at the results for the most popular destinations of Cavendish (Table 10.55) and Charlottetown (Table 10.56), 'Some high school' respondents shifted their behaviour between planning and actualization. In other words, these two destinations were successful in attracting a significantly greater number of these visitors than had planned to visit.

Thirdly, the findings for West Prince (Table 10.57) are encouraging. The least visited and most remote destination on Prince Edward Island, West Prince managed to attract a statistically significant increase in postgraduate consumers, who are the highest spending educational segment.

Influence of Travel Party Composition and Size on Behaviours

Early research in the tourism and leisure field flagged the association between social context and the individual's decision process. Burch

Table 10.55. Relationships between education and planned and realized main destination of Cavendish.

	Planned (%)	Realized (%)	Chi-square	*P*
Some high school	21 (*n* = 101)	38 (*n* = 61)	5.50	0.019
High school graduate	34 (*n* = 395)	27 (*n* = 343)	4.06	0.044
Technical college	33 (*n* = 196)	37 (*n* = 171)	0.71	0.400
College or university	32 (*n* = 741)	32 (*n* = 728)	0.03	0.853
Postgraduate	21 (*n* = 334)	32 (*n* = 339)	10.20	0.001

Table 10.56. Relationships between education and planned and realized main destination of Charlottetown.

	Planned (%)	Realized (%)	Chi-square	*P*
Some high school	21 (*n* = 101)	41 (*n* = 61)	7.63	0.006
High school graduate	40 (*n* = 395)	5 (*n* = 343)	26.23	0.001
Technical college	40 (*n* = 196)	44 (*n* = 171)	0.47	0.491
College or university	42 (*n* = 741)	55 (*n* = 728)	24.25	0.001
Postgraduate	48 (*n* = 334)	517 (*n* = 339)	0.54	0.462

Table 10.57. Relationships between education and planned and realized main destination of West Prince.

	Planned (%)	Realized (%)	Chi-square	P
Some high school	4 ($n = 101$)	7 ($n = 62$)	0.51	0.475
High school graduate	3 ($n = 395$)	3 ($n = 351$)	0.25	0.620
Technical college	2 ($n = 196$)	5 ($n = 175$)	2.63	0.105
College or university	4 ($n = 741$)	6 ($n = 740$)	2.33	0.127
Postgraduate	2 ($n = 334$)	7 ($n = 345$)	12.37	0.001

(1969) was one of the earliest to discuss the importance of the social group in relation to recreation and tourist behaviour. His personal community hypothesis suggested that such behaviour is seldom an isolated individual decision. Christensen and Yoesting (1973) confirmed his thesis, and argued that the choice and use of recreational facilities are related to the social context in which the individual is located.

The behaviour of tourists is heavily influenced by the composition of the travel party (McIntosh and Goeldner, 1990). Leisure travel is a product that often is jointly consumed, and tourist activities reflect the influence (both direct and indirect) of all those travelling together (Chadwick, 1987). Travel party size can influence behaviour in several ways. First, a group of travel companions, whether extended family, friends or colleagues, requires greater time for planning than trips of couples or singles (Fesenmairer and Lieber, 1988, cited in Stewart and Vogt, 1999). Secondly, a large group is likely to be more constrained in altering planned behaviours than individual travellers or couples, because of the higher degree of consensus required. Thirdly, Fisher (2001) found that collaboration led to higher decision quality and smaller deviations between consumers' planned and actual expenditures. Fourthly, a respondent travelling alone has more flexibility in changing plans than a respondent travelling with children or with a group of friends. Morwitz (1997b) posits that the intent–behaviour relationship for *durable products* might actually be weaker when the approval of more than one person is required than for products involving a single decision maker. Fifthly, preferences for travel experiences can differ according to travel party composition

(Basala and Klenosky, 2001). Here the role of the family members is highly influential (Moutinho, 1987; Dimanche and Havitz, 1994).

This section examines the relationship between composition and size of the travel party and the consumption behaviours of spending, length of stay, attractions and activities. Travel party sizes were classified as follows: alone ($n = 159$ and 190 in entry and exit surveys), one couple (1089–1000), one family (503–486), two or more couples or families (204–141), group of friends (215–205), or organized tour (94–117). One obvious caveat needs to be stated. One respondent completes a survey but groups often make the final decision. This proposition suggests a weakness in survey methodologies that is often ignored or overlooked. It is axiomatic to state that the larger the number of group members, the greater is the likelihood that a group member can influence the final decision. Against this background, the results detailed below should therefore be treated with a degree of caution.

Travel party size and spending

Significant differences between planned and realized spending were recorded for all categories of travel party, except for organized tours. (This is unsurprising, since an organized tour, by definition, offers the fewest opportunities for discretionary consumption activities other than souvenir and other shopping.) For two categories – two or more couples or families and group of friends – average spending more than doubled. For two other categories – one couple and one family – average spending increased by over

90% (Table 10.58). These results reconfirm findings elsewhere that an apparently high level of discretionary spending is available to most visitors in a leisure or vacation context.

ANOVA analysis was conducted to gain a better understanding of the relationship for planned and realized spending by travel party size. For the entry survey, the *t*-value was 0.028 (*P* = 0.183). For the exit survey, the *t*-value was 0.010 (*P* = 0.652).

Travel party size and length of stay

As we have seen in earlier analyses, few significant differences have been identified for the dependent variable, 'length of stay'. Time constraints are the obvious explanation. Nevertheless, some significant variations in planned and realized behaviours were identified for length of stay by travel party size. As Table 10.59 shows, the two categories exhibit-

ing significant differences were 'one couple' and 'group of friends'.

Again, these findings have useful implications for strategic marketing organizations. Some segments, albeit not the majority, have the capacity to substantially increase their length of stay. And length of stay is the critical consumption variable – along with spending (although the two are inter-related) – that destination marketing organizations are most eager to influence. A focused campaign that targets couples with suggested itineraries, detailing couple-oriented activities, may therefore generate increased length of stay and, concomitantly, increased spending.

ANOVA tests were conducted to gain a better understanding of the relationship for planned and realized spending by travel party size. For the entry survey, the *t*-value was −0.70 with a significance of 0.001. For the exit survey, the *t*-value was −0.110 with significance of 0.001.

Table 10.58. Planned and realized spending by travel party size.

	Planned		Realized				
	Mean	SD	Mean	SD	df	*t*	*P*
Alone	$204	307.0	$326	380.3	345	40.92	0.001
One couple	$230	292.9	$456	560.4	1085	19.33	0.001
One family	$318	367.8	$608	595.1	985	31.38	0.001
Two or more couples/families	$222	258.3	$497	522.9	341	6.45	0.001
Group of friends	$248	291.2	$531	602.5	416	6.15	0.001
Organized tour	$237	592.2	$227	430.0	207	0.14	0.888

SD, standard deviation; df, degrees of freedom.

Table 10.59. Significance test results for planned and realized length of stay by travel party size; means.

	Planned		Realized				
	Mean	SD	Mean	SD	df	*t*	*P*
Alone	5.4	9.9	6.0	8.5	328	0.57	0.569
One couple	3.5	5.5	4.2	5.3	2021	2.85	0.004
One family	4.2	5.0	4.5	3.3	977	0.92	0.358
Two or more couples/families	3.1	5.1	3.8	4.5	335	1.28	0.201
Group of friends	3.1	2.8	3.8	2.8	394	2.57	0.001
Organized tour	2.3	1.7	2.3	1.1	208	0.42	0.675

SD, standard deviation; df, degrees of freedom.

Travel party size and attractions

Analysis of the relationship between travel party size and visitation to PEI's main attractions generated some interesting insights. For instance, little difference was found between planned and realized visitation to arguably the island's most famous attraction, Green Gables House (Fig. 10.16). In contrast, significant increases were recorded for Cavendish. Figure 10.17 indicates that large gaps are apparent for all travel party categories. Even individuals travelling alone, who are least likely to visit an attraction (as the Green Gables results indicate), registered a large increase in actual visitation to Cavendish compared to their planned behaviour (28% stated the intention of visiting Cavendish, whereas 46% actually did). Applying Mintzberg's formulae, visitation to Cavendish is an emergent strategy, that is, unplanned yet realized.

The same trend occurs with planned and realized visitation to a third attraction, Province House. As Fig. 10.18 shows, the results mirror those from Cavendish. All categories exhibited moderate increases between planned and realized behaviours. Overall, while 11% of respondents expressed the intention of visiting Province House, at the time of exit 27% reported having made a visit. This strong increase contrasts with the minimal differences recorded for Green Gables visitation, in which 55% expressed intention to visit and 57% stated having actually visited. This finding may suggest a limit on the degree of increased visitation possible for famous landmarks. Table 10.60 shows changes between planned and realized visits to attractions, along with results of significant tests.

These results indicate that tourism operators of less famous attractions and other products have the capacity to generate visitation after the customer arrives in the destination, even though that individual may have no intention *or knowledge* of the particular product at the time of entry.

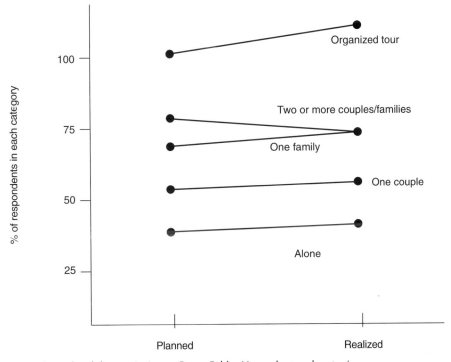

Fig. 10.16. Planned and done visitation to Green Gables House, by travel party size.

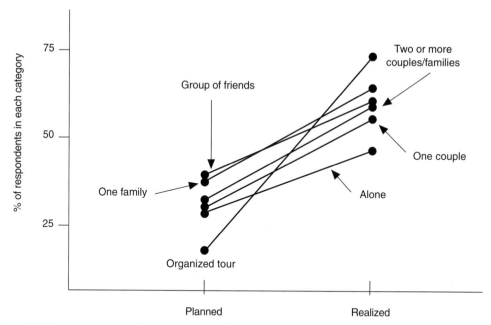

Fig. 10.17. Planned and done visitation to Cavendish, by travel party size.

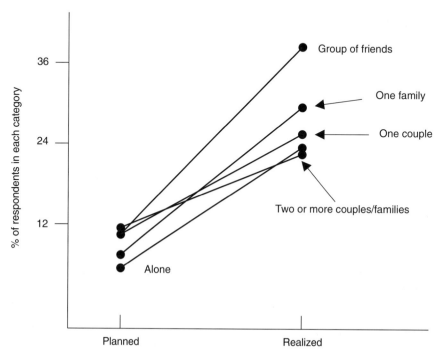

Fig. 10.18. Planned and done visitation to Province House, by travel party size. 'Organized tour' data are omitted: planned = 14%; done = 56%.

Table 10.60. Travel party size and planned and realized attractions.

	Planned		Realized				
	Mean	SD	Mean	SD	df	t	P
Alone	0.8	0.8	1.6	1.5	326	5.735	0.001
One couple	0.9	0.9	1.8	1.4	1999	1.146	0.252
One family	1.2	1.0	2.0	1.4	569	10.526	0.001
Two or more couples/families	1.0	0.9	2.0	1.2	334	6.956	0.001
Group of friends	1.1	0.9	2.2	1.5	392	9.016	0.001
Organized tour	0.9	0.9	2.9	1.1	199	14.598	0.001
Overall	1.0	1.0	2.0	1.5	4249	28.571	0.001

SD, standard deviation.

Travel party size and activities

It was hypothesized that the smaller the travel party size, the less would be the difference between the number of planned and realized activities. The underlying theoretical justification is that the greater the degree of control that an individual possesses over the environment in which decisions are made, the greater is the likelihood that actual behaviours will approximate intentions. The results here reflect the uniformity displayed between consumers' planned and realized consumption activities. Figure 10.19 shows the overall differences in planned and realized activities by travel party size.

Table 10.61 shows changes between planned and realized activities, along with results of significant tests. As indicated, there are significant differences between planned and realized behaviours for travel party types. The type exhibiting the largest increase between planned and realized behaviours was, unsurprisingly, the family group; its mean score increased 122%, from 2.956 planned activities to 6.563 realized activities. This emphasizes the merit for attraction operators in allocating adequate marketing resources to target the family segment after arrival at the destination.

Influence of travel party size on planned and realized main destinations

Four of the main destinations on PEI were examined in terms of planned and realized behaviours by travel party size. In the majority of cases, no significant differences were recorded between the entry and exit surveys (see Tables 10.62, 10.63 and 10.64 for Cavendish, Charlottetown and West Prince, respectively).

Two observations of note are offered. First, there were significant differences in the planned and realized behaviour of the 'One couple' segment for three of the destinations: Cavendish, Summerside and West Prince. (All other segments recorded only one instance of significant difference, except for 'Alone' which recorded two.) Indeed, in the case of West Prince, the 'One couple' segment alone showed a significant increase in visitor numbers. For this customer segment, therefore, West Prince can be termed an unplanned/unrealized strategy by applying our adapted Mintzberg model.

Secondly, we would expect that the choice of main destination is more often made prior to entering the consumption system, in a manner akin to shoppers entering a shopping mall, who will decide beforehand, for example, on the supermarket or greengrocery they will shop in. This would suggest that providing information on destinations *prior to*, rather than *after*, entry to a consumption system is critical in influencing the decision about main destination within the system.

Influence of Age on Behaviours

This section examines the relationship between age and consumption behaviours. Four dependent variables – length of stay, spending, activities and attractions – are tested. Age offers useful insights as an independent variable. Zalatan (1996) identified a positive correlation

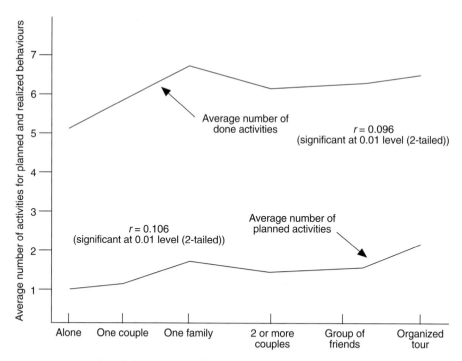

Fig. 10.19. Average number of planned and realized activities by travel party composition.

Table 10.61. Travel party types and planned and realized activities.

	Planned		Realized				
	Mean	SD	Mean	SD	df	t	P
Alone	2.8	7.9	5.2	2.7	335	3.908	0.001
One couple	2.5	1.8	5.9	2.5	2040	36.170	0.001
One family	3.0	1.9	6.6	2.4	964	26.865	0.001
Two or more couples/families	2.6	1.6	6.0	2.3	336	16.585	0.001
Group of friends	2.7	2.0	6.2	2.6	404	15.765	0.001
Organized tour	3.4	1.8	6.5	1.9	193	11.923	0.001
Overall	2.7	2.7	6.1	2.5	4302	43.037	0.001

SD, standard deviation.

between age and planning time. Older persons tend to prefer certainty and will tend to reduce the perceived risk by increasing the search for information.

Age and length of stay

Table 10.65 details the relationships between planned and realized length of stay by age cat-

egory. As indicated, significant differences were found for all categories. The ranking by length of stay does not change from planned to realized behaviour. Notably, the lowest age group registers the highest length of stay in both surveys, and the highest age group registers the lowest each time. Interestingly, the spread between highest and lowest is larger in realized behaviour (1.5 differential) compared to planned behaviour (0.5 differential); also, in

Table 10.62. Influence of travel party size on planned and realized main destination of Cavendish.

	Planned (%)	Realized (%)	Chi-square	P
Alone	19 (n = 151)	29 (n = 87)	5.11	0.024
One couple	22 (n = 723)	31 (n = 767)	13.29	0.001
One family	42 (n = 434)	39 (n = 370)	0.64	0.422
Two or more couples/families	28 (n = 134)	31 (n = 116)	0.10	0.753
Group of friends	485 (n = 181)	39 (n = 149)	2.45	0.117
Organized tour	7% (n = 93)	3 (n = 113)	1.76	0.185

Table 10.63. Influence of travel party size on planned and realized main destination of Charlottetown.

	Planned (%)	Realized (%)	Chi-square	P
Alone	46 (n = 151)	67 (n = 87)	9.75	0.002
One couple	47 (n = 723)	50 (n = 767)	0.94	0.331
One family	28 (n = 434)	40 (n = 370)	12.15	0.001
Two or more couples/families	40 (n = 134)	43 (n = 116)	0.20	0.654
Group of friends	36 (n = 181)	71 (n = 149)	41.89	0.001
Organized tour	82 (n = 93)	95 (n = 113)	8.65	0.003

Table 10.64. Influence of travel party size on planned and realized main destination of West Prince.

	Planned (%)	Realized (%)	Chi-square	P
Alone	3 (n = 151)	2 (n = 87)	0.234	0.626
One couple	4 (n = 723)	8 (n = 767)	12.93	0.001
One family	3 (n = 434)	2 (n = 370)	0.03	0.861
Two or more couples/families	4 (n = 134)	7 (n = 116)	1.82	0.178
Group of friends	2 (n = 181)	4 (n = 149)	0.86	0.355
Organized tour	2 (n = 93)	0 (n = 113)	–	

Table 10.65. Planned and realized length of stay by age category.

	Planned			Realized					
Age	Mean (nights)	n	SD	Mean (nights)	n	SD	df	t	P
Under 20	4.0	24	1.8	5.4	39	6.9	64	−5.601	0.001
20–29	3.8	385	1.4	4.1	367	4.7	761	−23.077	0.001
30–39	3.8	468	1.5	4.5	464	3.5	832	−87.500	0.001
40–54	3.8	667	1.4	4.3	550	4.5	1242	−71.428	0.001
Over 55	3.5	778	1.4	3.9	695	5.7	1545	−57.142	0.001
Total	3.7	2322	1.5	4.2	2115	4.9	–	–	–

A significant relationship was identified between age and planned number of nights ($F = 6.3$, $P = 0.001$, df = 4/2317), while no significant relationship was identified between age and realized number of nights ($F = 1.8$, $P = 0.125$, df = 4/2110).
SD, standard deviation; df, degrees of freedom.

percentage terms, the length of stay for the age 20 group rose 34% while that for the over 55 cohort increased just 11%.

For tourism marketers, these findings suggest that the younger age groups have a propensity to stay longer than planned than older visitors. This finding could be incorporated into marketing campaigns by targeting this customer segment in marketing communications after the visitor arrives at the destination.

realized spending, this result is most likely due to the small sample size). Strong consistency of increase between planned and realized spending was found: the percentage increases in the means for the groups 20–29, 30–39 and 40–49 between planned and realized behaviours were 41%, 41% and 45%, respectively.

Age and spending

Table 10.66 details the relationship between age and planned and realized spending. Significant differences were found for all age categories (although the average planned spending for under 20s was greater than the

Age and activities

Table 10.67 details the difference between planned and realized number of activities according to age category. As shown elsewhere, consumers greatly underestimate the number of activities they will undertake while in the destination. Realized number of activities more than doubled that planned for all categories; unsurprisingly, significant differences

Table 10.66. Planned and realized spending by age category.

Age	Planned			Realized			df	t	P
	Mean $	n	SD	Mean $	n	SD			
Under 20	473	10	775	461	34	574	64	−54.401	0.001
20–29	352	263	326	497	359	485	761	−89.139	0.001
30–39	424	287	415	598	458	556	832	−88.321	0.001
40–54	428	355	449	617	551	653	1242	−111.176	0.001
Over 55	337	308	397	358	688	537	1545	−14.383	0.001
Total	388	1223	409	504	2090	577			

A significant relationship was identified between age and planned spending ($F = 3.235$, $P = 0.012$, df = 4/1218) while no significant relationship was identified between age and realized spending ($F = 20.193$, $P = 0.001$, df = 4/2085).
SD, standard deviation; df, degrees of freedom.

Table 10.67. Planned and realized number of activities by age category.

Age	Planned			Realized			df	t	P
	Mean	n	SD	Mean	n	SD			
Under 20	2.5	24	2.1	6.8	38	2.1	64	−43.877	0.001
20–29	3.0	387	5.3	6.5	364	2.4	761	−233.333	0.001
30–39	2.9	469	1.8	6.7	447	2.5	832	−27.142	0.001
40–54	2.8	670	1.8	6.3	559	2.6	1242	−28.225	0.001
Over 55	2.4	793	1.7	5.3	710	2.3	1545	−27.102	0.001
Total	2.7	2343	2.7	6.1	2118	2.5	–	–	–

A significant relationship was identified between age and planned number of activities ($F = 3.933$, $P = 0.003$, df = 4/2338) and between age and realized number of activities ($F = 30.827$, $P = 0.001$, df = 4/2113).
SD, standard deviation; df, degrees of freedom.

were found for all age categories. Once again, the percentage increase from planned to realized behaviours was similar for all categories.

Age and attractions

A pattern emerged in examining the differences between planned and realized number of attractions visited. The higher the age group, the greater was the percentage increase from planned to realized: for 20–29, 30–39, 40–54 and over 55 the increases were 143%, 178%, 187% and 190%, respectively (Table 10.68). This result accords with the prevailing wisdom that the cultural and historical elements of a destination appeal more to older visitors than their younger counterparts. At the same time, younger travellers also greatly underestimate their likelihood of visiting attractions.

Overall, the over 55 segment is the least attractive segment for destination marketers in this case. They stay fewer nights, spend less and visit the smallest number of attractions. The unanswered question is whether this reflects the nature of Prince Edward Island or is representative of a more generic trend.

Summary and Discussion

This chapter has compared planned and actual consumption behaviours across a wide variety of products and experiences. The findings have extended the work of Morwitz and Schmittlein (1992) who concluded that the impact of demographic (and product use) variables on purchase differs for consumers who intend to purchase versus those who do not intend to purchase.

Understanding consumer demographics and related consumption patterns is essential for all marketers. Such insights allow for the delivery of products and services that better satisfy customer needs. More importantly from a marketing strategy perspective, such insights can underpin segmentation of customers that facilitate the formulation of strategic decisions regarding the relative value and accessibility of those segments.

The study generated useful insights regarding changes that occur from planned to actual behaviour in the value of sub-categories of consumer demographic variables. For example, the changes in the spending levels of the three geographical origin groups between the entry and exit surveys would reveal which, if any, of these three groups are liable to increase their spending while in the destination. Statistically significant differences between the two surveys would indicate elasticity in the customers' demand for particular tourist services or experiences. Where such elasticity exists, opportunities exist for marketers to influence consumption decisions through a variety of marketing communication tools.

Our results indicate the problems that destination marketing organizations face in increasing length of stay, one of the key marketing objectives for destination marketers (Morrissey,

Table 10.68. Planned and realized number of attractions visited by age category.

Age	Planned			Realized			df	t	P
	Mean	n	SD	Mean	n	SD			
Under 20	0.8	24	1.0	2.0	41	1.6	64	−17.91	0.001
20–29	0.9	387	0.9	2.1	375	1.4	761	−315.00	0.001
30–39	0.7	469	0.9	2.0	474	1.5	832	−433.33	0.001
40–54	0.7	670	0.9	2.0	573	1.5	1242	−635.00	0.001
Over 55	0.6	793	0.8	1.7	753	1.5	1545	−560.00	0.001
Total	0.7	2343	0.9	1.9	2216	1.5			

A significant relationship identified between age and planned number of attractions (df = 4/2338, $F = 7.881$, $P = 0.001$). A significant relationship identified between age and realized number of attractions df = 4/2211, $F = 6.701$, $P = 0.001$).
SD, standard deviation; df, degrees of freedom.

1986; Uysal *et al.*, 1994; Tourism New South Wales, 1999). Length of stay relates with higher expenditures by visitors and, by extension, greater benefits to the economies and communities in which visitors undertake their consumption activities. As a performance indicator for destinations, it ranks alongside tourist spending, yet superior to visitation to attractions and other commercial and non-commercial tourist activities. While the overall samples revealed a significant increase in the number of planned versus actual days, deeper analysis revealed discrepancies across the range of segmentation variables. The key independent variables tested in this chapter – geographical origin, income and travel party composition – produced mixed results: not all sub-categories (for example, the five income levels) registered significant differences for planned and realized length of stay.

Some methods of measurement were more useful than others. A key finding from the analysis is that consumers greatly underestimate the number of activities they will undertake and the number of attractions they will visit. With the occasional exception, all sub-categories of all independent variables showed a very large increase from planned to realized consumption behaviours. (The exceptions included 'Entertainment' category of motivations for activities; the 'College or university' category of educational level for activities; and the 'One couple' category of travel party composition for attractions.)

Two implications can be drawn from this trend. First, richer insights are available at the individual product level than at the aggregated level. Secondly, the large increases suggest that visitors set aside substantial amounts of discretionary time – and perhaps discretionary spending, depending on the demographic mix – prior to arriving at the destination. In other words, they engage in planned 'unplanned' behaviours, a consumer's mental construct idea first proposed by Rook and Hoch (1985) in the context of supermarket shopping. Many consumers plan to be impulsive, whether they are tourists on holiday or individuals strolling through the shopping mall.

Spending and length of stay are the two most commonly used indicators of segment or market attractiveness employed by destination

marketing organizations; they are relatively easy to measure, and are useful quantitative indicators of the economic benefits of tourism in general and customer segments in particular. When the size of these two variables increases significantly from planned to actual behaviour for a particular segment, the implications for marketers are thus: the increase indicates that the segment(s) have both discretionary time and spending power beyond what they report at the pre-entry stage.

However, when statistical significance is identified for all categories of an independent variable, the utility of that variable to segment markets is greatly weakened. For example, each category of the 'experience' variable – first-timers, 1–2 visits and three or more visits – showed a significant increase between planned and realized behaviours for spending and length of stay. Since target segments need to be distinguishable from non-target segments, at this level of analysis 'experience' by itself is not a useful segmentation variable. Instead, a two-stage segmentation procedure is required, but such analysis is beyond the scope of this study.

In contrast to 'experience', the 'income' variable allows for differentiation of segments, as Table 10.69 indicates. This finding suggests that segmentation strategies based on income might be more fruitful for destination marketing organizations (although there was no significant increase in length of stay for the $50,000–75,000 income grouping).

In addition to income, education and travel party composition were the other variables that generated strategically useful insights. 'Education' confirms a reasonable assumption: since education and income are highly correlated, consumers with higher education levels

Table 10.69. Significance test results of influence of income on planned versus realized spending and length of stay.

	Spending	Length of stay
<$20K	ns ($n = 79$)	0.008 ($n = 107$)
$20–35K	0.039 ($n = 360$)	0.034 ($n = 238$)
$35–50K	ns ($n = 258$)	0.001 ($n = 357$)
$50–75K	0.029 ($n = 300$)	ns ($n = 394$)
$75K+	0.014 ($n = 222$)	0.006 ($n = 363$)

ns, not significant.

are more likely to possess discretionary spending power than their counterparts from lower education levels. This is confirmed in the results for spending shifts, as seen in Table 10.70. Moreover, the weak results for the other education levels reinforce the strategic importance of the two highest levels.

For travel party composition, only two categories – One couple and Group of friends – registered significant increases in length of stay, as Table 10.71 shows. While 'Group of friends' is a discrete segment arguably difficult for marketers to target successfully, 'One couple' is more readily identifiable and accessible in terms of marketing communication strategies.

Results such as the above offer rare insights into the shifting behaviour of particular demographic segments from planned to actualized consumption patterns. The importance of income and travel party composition has been confirmed. More importantly, the capacity of these segments to significantly alter their plans highlights the strategic importance for destination marketers in targeting particular customer segments during their time in the destination.

Table 10.70. Significance test results of influence of education on planned and realized behaviours.

	Spending	Length of stay
Some high school	0.037 ($n = 101$)	0.042 ($n = 61$)
High school graduate	ns ($n = 95$)	ns ($n = 343$)
Technical college	ns (96)	ns ($n = 171$)
College or university	0.001 ($n = 741$)	0.002 ($n = 28$)
Postgraduate	0.001 ($n = 334$)	0.003 ($n = 339$)

ns, not significant.

Table 10.71. Significance test results of influence of travel party composition on planned versus realized behaviours.

	Spending	Length of stay
Alone	0.001 (n = 151)	ns (n = 87)
One couple	0.001 (n = 723)	0.004 (n = 767)
One family	0.001 (n = 434)	ns (n = 370)
Two or more couples/families	0.001 (n = 134)	ns (n = 116)
Group of friends	0.001 (n = 181)	0.001 (n = 149)
Organized tour	ns (n = 93)	ns (n = 113)

11 Strategic Implications and Discussion

This final chapter discusses the main conceptual and managerial outcomes of the research study and presents the key conclusions. Contributions to our understanding of consumer behaviour in tourism are offered; implications for marketing strategy are discussed; and directions and recommendations for future research are suggested. Limitations of the study are also noted.

Theoretical Implications

Underestimating of likely consumption activities

The study revealed that respondents engaged in significantly higher levels of realized than planned behaviours for a range of products and experiences. Consider the following results:

- average spending was $505 compared to an average budget of $387;
- despite the significant increase in average spending across most demographic variables, only 7% of respondents in the exit survey reported spending 'over budget';
- average length of stay was 4.2 nights, compared with an average planned length of stay of 3.7 nights;
- while only 21% of respondents planned to visit antiques and handcraft shops, 52% eventually did; and

- 56% of respondents in the entry survey who required paid accommodation had, in fact, made no reservations.

What explanations can be considered for respondents underestimating their consumption behaviours? Were they being conservative, in the belief that temporal or financial constraints may prevent them from achieving more ambitious goals? Or maybe they simply had 'no idea' and no plans? Let us consider possible reasons for these differentials.

First, Weick (1998) argues that people are uncomfortable in stating intentions, while finding the reporting of actual behaviour straightforward. The rationale for this view is thus: intentions are cognitive constructs (Gollwitzer, 1993) while reported behaviours are the objective recall of recent and actual events. Tversky et al. (1988) argue that the decision behaviour of consumers does not accord with the principle of *procedural invariance*, which is related to the idea that a decision maker has a set of preferences (values) that are 'read off' from some master list when a person is asked to indicate preferences (see also Payne et al., 1993). Echoing Weick, Tversky and his fellow researchers concluded that these values are constructed in the elicitation process instead of being read off. Observed preferences are likely to reflect both a decision maker's values *and* his/her heuristics used to construct the required response in a particular situation. In a similar

©R. March and A.G. Woodside 2005. *Tourism Behaviour: Travellers' Decisions and Actions* (R. March and A.G. Woodside)

vein, Berger and Dibattista (1993) have argued that people anticipate and prepare for contingencies, rather than assuming that everything will occur as planned. Adapting Mintzberg's work in organizational behaviour (Mintzberg and Waters, 1982), individuals plan not a strategy, but the consequences of it. Individuals may well adopt the same strategy. In this study, for example, travellers may have planned the consequences of spending beyond their budget.

Secondly, the reluctance of respondents to make decisions about tourism services prior to entry (evidenced by, for example, the large proportion who had needed, but not booked, accommodation) may be explained by findings elsewhere that differences exist between service and goods consumers when it comes to information needs and usage. Service scholars have argued that prior evaluation is more difficult for services than goods (Zeithaml, 1981) and that consumers may evaluate them differently than they do goods (Young, 1981). Dorsch et al. (2000) pointed out the complex problem-solving nature of services, particularly when the customer lacks knowledge of the service provider and (except in the case of accommodation) the service category. Murray (1991) found that service consumers were more likely to be deterred from the outright purchase of services than for the purchase of goods because of the higher perceived risk related to services. This last finding, in particular, may go some way to explaining the large discrepancies between plans and behaviours identified in this study. There is a large literature on the role of risk in the consumption of services (e.g. Eiglier and Langeard, 1977; Guseman, 1981; Zeithaml, 1981; Murray and Schlacter, 1990), with both theory and empirical evidence suggesting that services are perceived to be riskier than goods.

Thirdly, personal experience informs us that certain travellers have a psychological or socially acquired predisposition towards not planning. In a major tourism study, Decrop (1999, p. 126) labelled such people 'unplanned tourists', who 'minimize cognitive thinking and planning, either as a strategy or because of time pressures'.

Fourthly, respondents may have underestimated what could be achieved during their stay on Prince Edward Island because they were unsure, and therefore erred on the side of caution. Most studies endorse this view. Gross (1994), for example, identified a 'subjective' time pressure that inhibits individuals in forecasting future consumption activities. One empirical study does support our findings. Read and Loewenstein (1995) argue that consumers compress future time intervals when making combined choices, and hence overestimate the effect of satiation. It is not until the individual enters the destination that he or she realizes that activities will take less time than initially envisaged.

Matching of planned and realized products

Application of Mintzberg's model allowed us to plot the performance of the PEI tourism products and experiences in terms of the shifts that occurred between consumers' stated intentions and reported consumption acts. The study revealed that the majority of products tended to locate either in the 'realized/planned' or 'unplanned/undone' quadrants. Respondents displayed, in most cases, a high degree of consistency between their planned and actualized behaviours, and between unplanned and not done behaviours. Even though consumers greatly underestimate the number of attractions and activities they will consume, the increases identified between the entry and exit surveys occur mainly in the more popular planned behaviours. In other words, a significant increase in the actualized consumption of a relatively unplanned product or experience occurs infrequently. This finding supports the earlier conclusion that the positive influence of product information is not uniform.

Influence of product information

The study found that the influences of product information on consumption were not uniform across all products, experiences or customer segments. On the one hand, the proposition that consumers who use product information are likely to both plan and engage in more consumption activities than those who do not use product information was supported for spending and number of activities undertaken.

However, the influence of information was less clear-cut for other consumption behaviours, such as attractions visited, main destinations and main accommodation.

The study also indicated, contrary to our hypothesis, that product information had no significant influence on visitation to 'unknown' attractions. Intriguingly, the VIG was shown to have a significant influence on visitation to the more famous places such as Green Gables and Cavendish yet no significant influence on the lesser known and less popular attractions of Ardgowan and Fort Amherst. Clearly, more research is needed into the factors that moderate influences of information.

Use of product information

The study revealed no increase in the usage of product information after arrival in the destination; that is, there was no significant difference between the percentage of respondents who possessed a VIG but did not use it prior to entry and the percentage of respondents who reported possessing a VIG upon leaving Prince Edward Island and not having used it. This finding is counter-intuitive. After arrival, a greater proportion of consumers in possession of the VIG might be expected to utilize the product information than those prior to entry. The amount of time between exposure to product information and consumption appears to have virtually nil influence on the degree to which information is used. In other words, whether a purchase is the next day or the next week, the proportion of consumers utilizing information does not change.

This finding may support the work Bronner (1982), who found that the demand for additional information was drastically reduced when a decision was made under time pressure. It appears that individuals rely on available information to make a decision rather than incur the additional (temporal or monetary) cost of gathering more information.

Role of experience

The study confirmed the complexity of the interaction between experience and consump-

tion. There were two key findings related to experience: first, no differences in spending increases were identified between first-time and very experienced visitors; and secondly, no differences were found in usage of information between first-time and very experienced visitors. Experienced visitors should, all else being equal, have clearer goals, be more aware of the available alternatives, and have more information about each alternative than their inexperienced counterparts (see, for example, Barsalou, 1991). We would therefore expect the actual behaviours of experienced consumers to more closely approximate their intentions. Yet this axiom has been repeatedly challenged in this study. No significant difference was identified in the increase between budget and actual spending for very experienced visitors (five or more visits) and first-time visitors; and a significant increase was registered in length of stay, number of activities and number of attractions for both experienced visitors and first-time visitors.

Two phenomena may be in evidence here. Kardes (1994), for instance, contends that a decision that is effective in one situation (for example, in previous visits to Prince Edward Island) may be quite ineffective in another (for example, the most recent visit), thereby forcing decision makers to treat each situation as if it were unique. Another possible explanation comes from the field of social psychology into individuals' perceptions of knowledge and the subsequent impact on decision making behaviour. Research in developmental psychology has examined how individuals' perceptions of what they know change as a function of age (e.g. Wimmer et al., 1988; Ruffman and Olson, 1989) while research in the cognitive domain has focused on the illusion of knowing (Glenberg et al., 1982). These phenomena suggest, respectively, that absence of information in memory concerning a particular fact is interpreted as evidence that the fact is false, and that individuals often believe they gained knowledge when, in fact, they have not (Radecki and Jaccard, 1995). In this study, visitors to Prince Edward Island may have formed intentions about future activities and consumption behaviour based on knowledge which, once they were exposed to the choices available and constraints on those choices, was found to be deficient. A hypothesis to be tested in the future is whether plans will more likely match actual behaviours the more recent is the last visit to the destination. Experience, *per se*, reveals little unless destination marketing organizations understand the recency of the last visit.

The study also found that first-time visitors did not rely more on product information than their more experienced counterparts. At first glance, this appears a surprising outcome. Numerous studies have found that low product knowledge, unfamiliarity and product category inexperience are associated with information search and acquisition (Bucklin, 1966; Moore and Lehmann, 1980, Reilly and Conover, 1983). On the other hand, a number of researchers have argued that there may be conditions under which uncertainty actually reduces search behaviour (Wilkie, 1975, cited by Urbany *et al.*, 1989; Bettman, 1979; Bettman and Park, 1980; Alba and Hutchinson, 1987). And as Manfredo (1989) suggested, experienced consumers may seek information for its recreational value, as distinct from using information to make decisions. On the basis of this study, experience as a moderating variable on consumption needs to be re-examined, at least in the tourism/services context.

Spontaneous nature of the tourism experience

The study has highlighted the spontaneous nature of the tourism experience. Nowhere was this better illustrated than in the unplanned consumption of tourism activities on Prince Edward Island (Table 8.11); of the 13 major activities available on the island, all but golf registered significant increases between planned and realized behaviours. The large degree of unplanned behaviour identified confirms and extends the preliminary findings of an earlier study (Hyde, 2000). The hedonistic nature of the travel experience suggests that decision processes for tourism services do not revolve around seeking to solve any problems (as in conventional decision making) but rather that the consumer's goal would be to provoke feelings and emotions (Holbrook and

Hirschman, 1982; Ryan, 1991). According to Hyde (2000, p. 188), 'the [independent] tourist avoids vacation planning because flexibility of action and experiencing the unknown are key amongst the hedonic experiences they seeking'.

Such reasoning helps explain the large discrepancies between consumer plans and actions. The study found, for instance, that planned consumption of less popular attractions and activities did not accurately predict behaviour, whereas the tourist icons of the destination, such as Green Gables House, revealed both high intentions and equally high consumption rates (with no significant increases recorded between the two).

A Richer Model of Intentions and Behaviours

A secondary aim of this research study was the development of a new model that better captures the complexity of the consumer's plans–behaviour dichotomy. The conventional model incorporates three stages in the process between intention formation and action: planning, implementation and post-action (Gollwitzer, 1993).

First, a planning stage is regarded as preliminary to the forming of intentions. The first stage is a motivational one and largely echoes Ajzen's (1996) definition. Plans are formed about how to ensure that one's intention is acted upon. These plans are referred to as implementation intentions and specify what one will do, and where one will do it, in order to achieve the goal intention (i.e. 'I intend to initiate the goal-directed Behaviour X when Situation Y is encountered'). Implementation intentions commit the individual to a specific course of action when certain environmental conditions are met. In this way they translate goal intentions into action. The second, cognitive stage is a volitional or implemental stage. The third, postactional stage is where the individual compares what has been achieved with what was desired. The individual attempts to either evaluate the worth of the action or to determine whether further attempts at realizing the intention are worthwhile or necessary.

We believe that our new model, shown in Fig. 11.1, offers a more realistic interpretation of the relationship between consumer plans (or intentions) and eventual behaviours, and the influences that play upon each. It provides a richer picture of the complexity of influences and variables that act upon the consumer in the 'journey' from intention formation to post-behaviour interpreting. While based upon the traditional five-stage consumer decision process model, it has four additional concepts that derive principally from the findings of this study. They are, in order of execution by the consumer:

1. The complexity and frequent failure of memory and its influence on plans and actual behaviours is acknowledged. Shapiro and Krishnan (1999) remind us that consumers forget intentions and suggest that marketing models used to forecast sales should incorporate memory as a variable, to explain why some intentions do not lead to purchases.
2. The influence of situational influences at multiple stages in the decision–consumption process is acknowledged.
3. A distinction is made between higher- and lesser-order plans (particularly relevant in tourism where basic needs such as accommodation, transport and food can be distinguished from lower-order wants such as attractions, shopping and so on). Phillips and Bradshaw (1993), for example, argue that customers are in a constant state of interaction with their environment. In their words: '[I]ntent to purchase is far from fixed and can continue to be modified right up to the point of purchase' (Phillips and Bradshaw, 1993, p. 52). They draw the conclusion that: '[T]o assume that the creation of a predisposition to buy is a sufficient explanation of buyer behaviour seems untenable. Creating predisposition is merely one side of the equation. For actual purchasing to occur, in many cases, requires the intervention of the point of sale' (Phillips and Bradshaw, 1993, p. 55).
4. A post-consumption/purchase story-telling process, an acknowledgement of the work of Weick (1998) that informs much of this study, is included.

The model offers two advantages over existing interpretations. First, by incorporating the concept of sense-making (Weick, 1998), it acknowledges the absence of an objective reality in the reconstruction of individuals' actions. The notion of sense-making, as defined by Weick, refers to the way that individuals construct meaning and comprehend information, essentially by shuffling it around within their memory systems until it is understandable to them. The current research sheds light on the relationship between sense-making and plans. As Cohen and March (1974, cited in Weick, 1998) first pointed out, plans are symbols, advertisements, games and excuses for interaction (between individuals in organizations) and, in the context of consumer behaviour, action or non-action. Some consumers plan and some do not. Interpreting Weick, consumer plans – when they do exist – become excuses for action in the sense that they induce awareness among consumers of products and services that hitherto they were either unaware of or had forgotten. In the process of undertaking marketing research, the cognitive process of planning by an individual can be triggered by the asking of questions using brand names attached to products or services that the individual had previously no attention of consuming.

The second advantage of the model is the – unsurprising – acknowledgement that consumers adjust their behaviours after intention formation. Research into this aspect of consumer behaviour has been neglected. As the model illustrates, situational influences play the key moderating influence – whether the consumption system is an island destination or the local supermarket. (Situational influences occur in two stages, with the second 'intervention', marked by the consumer's arrival in the consumption system, being the more influential.) This research study has contributed to an improved understanding of this phase by identifying the characteristics of consumers whose actions reflect and diverge from their intended actions.

Managerial Implications

This study has clear implications for the marketing of tourism destinations and other products. A number of marketing strategy propositions are discussed: the opportunities arising from visitors' tendency towards large

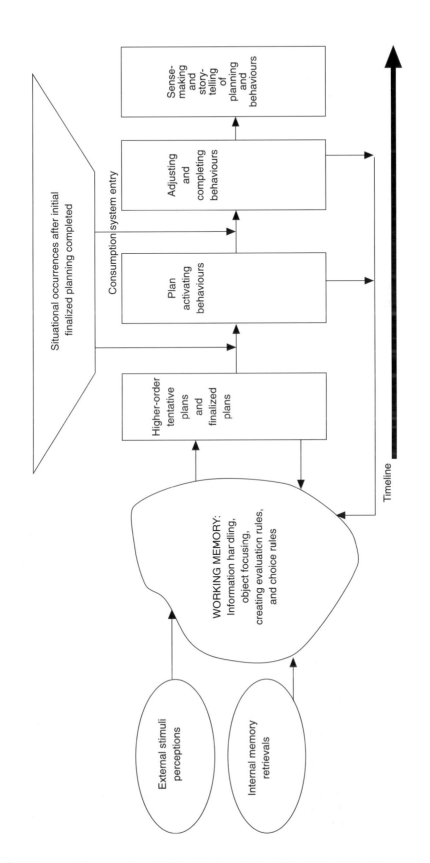

Fig. 11.1. Planning, plans (intentions), situational influences and behaviours through time.

degrees of unplanned behaviour application; application of the Mintzberg grid; the dangers facing marketing researchers in attempting to measure intentions; the provision and timing of product information; and the strategic rethink required regarding the behaviour and information needs of experienced versus inexperienced customers.

Marketing strategy proposition 1: tapping into unplanned consumption behaviour

The hedonistic and spontaneous nature of tourism consumption offers challenges and opportunities for tourism strategists – challenges because such behaviours are often random and subjective, but also opportunities because of the large degree of unplanned consumption of tourism services that the study has revealed.

Visitors to Prince Edward Island engaged in a range of unplanned behaviours to varying degrees. Rook and Hoch's (1985, p. 25) observation, that consumers 'plan on being impulsive', probably has particular relevance to the consumption system of a holiday destination. If we accept the view that the core emotional objective of holidays is, for most individuals, about the collection of experiences and memories (Ryan, 1991), rather than the accumulation of tangible memories, then planned impulsiveness becomes an important ingredient of the overall holiday. From a marketing strategy view then, rather than ask visitors to add to their plans, the marketer must find ways to insert product/service experiences into the paths taken by visitors; as well as suggest paths for visitors to explore that include the opportunity to experience (buy) the marketed product-service.

The application of the Mintzberg grid generated a key insight regarding the levels of planned and unplanned consumption of products and experiences on Prince Edward Island. Using an exit survey requiring recall of original intentions and reporting of actual behaviours would generate a Mintzberg grid for destination tourism marketers. While this would create obvious methodological problems, the indicative nature of the instrument may suffice for the immediate needs of management. A more focused research approach,

to confirm the initial findings and identify possible solutions, could be implemented after 'problem' products or services are identified.

Marketing strategy proposition 2: marketing research into done, not planned, behaviour

A key outcome of the study is that the measurement of intentions may be as meaningless for marketers as they appear to be for many consumers. Destination marketing organizations that undertake consumer research studies prior to departure or upon arrival in the destination must be aware that travellers' plans are likely to change significantly for the range of tourism products and experiences on offer. Research that targets travellers during their stay as well as at the end of their stay will yield richer insights.

Marketing strategy proposition 3: provision and timing of information

The study found that exposure to product information plays a critical role in raising consumption levels both before *and* after arrival in the destination. In other words, any marketing communications strategy should allocate equal weight to ensuring visitors receive information prior to and immediately upon entry.

The important question is at what point in time in the complex task environment of the vacation traveller – from planning, evaluation, decision to implementation – will provision of information be most effective? For instance, information provided well in advance of planned consumption may be ignored, forgotten or lost. Conversely, information provided temporally proximate to planned consumption might, in order to reduce the cognitive strain of integrating information, lead to the discounting or ignoring of information already stored in memory (Slovic, 1972). The inherent time pressures of a short-stay on Prince Edward Island (remembering the majority of visitors stayed four nights or less) confirm our view that destination-marketing strategists need to distribute VIGs well in advance of visitors arriving at the destination. The marketing communication prepared by destination marketers and other tourism operators needs to inform travellers about the time required to consume a particular product or experience. In Hornick's (1982) study of the influence of personal and situational variables on time behaviour, he concluded:

> Differences in consumers' perceptions of the impact of time allocation decisions on personal needs satisfaction have obvious implications for the suppliers of time products ... These differences are particularly important in the case of leisure activities, where greater freedom exists to make such decisions. (Hornick, 1982, p. 53)

The study also indicated, contrary to our hypothesis, that product information had no significant influence on visitation to 'unknown' attractions. Intriguingly, the VIG was shown to have a significant influence on visitation to the more famous places such as Green Gables and Cavendish, yet no significant influence on the lesser known and less popular attractions of Ardgowan and Fort Amherst.

Although the influence of product information has not been found to be universal across all measures, even in these days of increasing Internet usage, the role and influence of visitor information guides should not be underestimated. This conclusion is particularly pertinent in the current climate faced by destination marketing organizations, which may be inclined or obliged – for cost-saving and other reasons – to shift the provision of destination and product information to a web-based environment.

Marketing strategy proposition 4: market segmentation strategies

The study's examination of the interaction between customer demographics and planned/unplanned behaviours has implications for tourism marketing strategists. Income, education and travel party composition were the independent variables that generated the most useful results in terms of significant increases between planned and realized length of stay and spending. While the confirmed influence of income and education comes as no surprise, the findings for travel party composition suggest that destination marketers should considering targeting this customer segment on arrival in their tourism destination.

Marketing strategy proposition 5: re-evaluating the influence of experience on consumption

The study provides tourism-marketing practitioners with clear lessons regarding the targeting of both experienced and first-time visitors. It is widely assumed that experienced consumers require and use less information, and are less risk-adverse than their inexperienced counterparts. The research study generated a number of surprising insights that challenge these assumptions. For instance, respondents were asked in the entry survey whether they had booked accommodation. It might be assumed that first-time visitors, due to their lack of first-hand experience of the availability of accommodation, would be more likely to book accommodation in advance. However, the results show that 41% of first-time visitors who needed accommodation, had made no bookings, compared to 37% for 1–2-time visitors and 55% for three or more time visitors. In other words, despite their previous experience, a greater proportion of respondents in the three or more times experience category booked more accommodation than first-time visitors. The reasons for this finding obviously warrant further investigation. One plausible explanation is that some (perhaps many) experienced visitors are not necessarily less risk-adverse than first-time visitors.

A further surprising finding was that experienced visitors used the VIG only marginally less than their first-time counterparts. As counter-intuitive as this outcome is, it may warrant a rethink by destination marketing organizations about their advertising and other promotional strategies. We could also infer, perhaps, that consumers evaluate previous experiences more than first thought. Why would they use information other than to consider new purchases or new experiences? Of course, many experienced consumers may use existing information to avoid cognitive dissonance. However, in the absence of contradictory evidence, we could equally argue that experienced consumers seek information for the purpose of purchasing new products or engaging in new tourist experiences.

Limitations of Study

Several limitations in the present study need to be cited. First, situational influences were not examined, even though they represent one major set of conditions that account for the poor relationship between intentions and behaviour (see, for example, Warshaw, 1980; Blackwell *et al.*, 1999). As Belk (1974, p. 161) argued, this influence is 'a pervasive factor in consumer behavior' and an 'unfortunate source of noise' (Belk, 1974, p. 156). In findings relevant to this research, Umesh and Cote (1988) and Stanton and Bonner (1980) suggested that experienced consumers, even more so than their inexperienced counterparts, are influenced by situational factors.

Belk (1974, p. 157) defines situation as 'all those factors particular to a time and place of observation that do not follow from a knowledge of personal (intra-individual) and stimulus (choice alternative) attributes, and that have a demonstrable and systematic effect on current behavior'. Later, Belk (1975) divided the situational component into five dimensions. Given the broader spatial and temporal dimensions of the tourism and leisure environments compared to consumer purchasing situations for tangible products, the importance of these dimensions for the present research setting is particularly acute. These situational dimensions are: (i) physical surroundings (e.g. ease of access to certain tourism products and sites; distance between them); (ii) social surroundings (e.g. other members of travel party; number of visitors to the destination; and characteristics of local people gained through service and other interactions); (iii) temporal perspective (e.g. if repeat visitor, the time since the last visit; time constraints while in the destination); (iv) task definition (e.g. intent to purchase or experience a specified tourist product; and intent to obtain product information about a specific purchase prior to purchase); and (v) antecedent states (e.g. tiredness, sense of the unknown, excitation). These factors need to be incorporated into future tourism and leisure research.

The second major limitation relates to concerns over replicability and generalizability. It will be extremely difficult to replicate the remarkable social laboratory of Prince Edward Island that provided a general population sample in both entry and exit surveys. The great majority of respondents travelled by car and coach, not the typical transport mode for travellers, especially those from overseas. Doubts may arise that the insights gained from this research are limited in their generalizability. After all, the environment of a tourist consumption system (whether it be Prince Edward Island, a metropolis like Paris, or a mountain resort) and, say, a retail space such as a shopping mall or supermarket, appear markedly different. Yet in both systems the individual moves through a physical space (with differing degrees of volition and control) and is exposed to external stimuli, such as marketing communications, other individuals, and elements of the physical or man-made environment.

Thirdly, the data were collected in the days before consumers used the Internet widely. The role and influence of printed information has undoubtedly been diluted to some extent by the rise and diffusion of web-based destination and product information. The influence of the Internet would need to be incorporated into any future research carried out by tourism organizations.

Directions and Recommendations for Future Research

This research study has generated a number of research topics worthy of future research. First, the influence of product information should be tested in different tourism settings and on different customer groups. While our study revealed the powerful influence of information on behaviours, generalizability is an issue. Stabler (1988) concluded that the role of locally supplied tourist information as a demand generator in the French region of Languedoc-Roussillon was 'minor'. The extension of length of stay in a destination by certain visitor groups can be interpreted as a form of 'browsing', an antecedent of impulse and unplanned purchasing. Browsing has been examined in the marketing literature (Bloch *et al.*, 1986, 1989; Jarboe and McDaniel, 1987; Beatty and Ferrell, 1998) but needs to be better understood in a tourism setting in order for the provision and timing of product information to be optimized.

Secondly, tests of competing theoretical propositions as to why planned behaviours are often less than realized behaviours need to be examined in future research. Planned purchases do not match actual purchases for a combination of two reasons: consumers do not enact planned purchase intentions and they engage in unplanned purchase behaviour. While the latter phenomenon has been well researched, the former has not. Consumers have been asked why they bought what they had not planned. Rarely have they been asked why they did not purchase what they had planned. Yet does an understanding of unplanned purchases only tell us half the story? Pickering (1977) was one of the few researchers who posed the question, Why did consumers fail to purchase what they had planned to? This is an important question marketers must ask of themselves and also of marketing scholars. This research study has revisited this question, not by asking 'why?', but by asking 'who?'

Thirdly, marketers need to differentiate the consumption behaviours of passive and active seekers of information after arrival in the consumption system. Such research could feed into marketing strategies related to the timing and placement of information provision. We found that individuals who received the VIG before arrival are more likely to engage in higher consumption behaviours than those who received information after arrival, many of whom probably obtained the VIG in a passive manner, such as off the counter at a visitor information centre or tourist facility such as a motel or tourist attraction. Radecki and Jaccard (1995) have highlighted a neglected area of information search behaviour that may shed light on the planned–unplanned conundrum. In a conceptual paper, they developed a theoretical model illustrating the relationships between perceived knowledge and actual knowledge, and how those perceptions impinge on the decision making processes. This is an exciting breakthrough that should be examined in the tourism context, where a range of assumptions exists about the influence of experience on behaviours.

Fourthly, the nature of the consumption system influences the consumers' implementation of behavioural plans and how they compare and choose between alternatives (Felcher et al., 2001). Weick (1998) argues that consumers can only quantify and justify their intended behaviours once they have entered and interacted with the behavioural implementation space. If we apply the insights that Weick offers into organizational theory to a consumption system with specific geographical boundaries (just as organizations have psychological and physical boundaries), useful lessons may be generated into the ways that individuals adapt to existing planned behaviours and/or adopt new behaviours in response to the stimuli of that space.

Fifthly, we need to generate richer insights into how consumers categorize services and experiences available in a destination. Typically tourists choose among competing types of accommodation and different types of restaurant cuisine; these we regard as within-category choices. But the tourism experience involves across-category choices as well, as in the choice between a visit to an amusement park and a family stroll through a national park. While taxonomic product categories are useful when applied to basic needs of travellers (lodging and food services), goal-derived categories in a tourism setting may be more useful in order to understand how consumers make choices. For example, destination marketers could adopt a 'share-of-time' measure to compare how well man-made attractions such as a museums compete with experiential activities such as 'going to the beach' or 'touring through a national park'.

To repeat the axiom, a holiday is a bundle of activities and experiences. It is perhaps the very complexity of such services that explains the lack of research into consumer decision making of multi-item tourist services and experiences. The multiple-item nature of many tourism services and experiences, and the unique characteristics of destination consumption systems, represents major challenges for tourism researchers. The area of single-item choice tasks has been the main focus of investigation in consumer decision processes, dating back to the famous Fishbein model (Fishbein and Ajzen, 1975). According to Simonson (1990, p. 161), 'in making multiple purchases ... consumers' decision strategies are not mere extensions of those used in selecting a single item'.

The idea that tourists use the tourist consumption space as a 'shopping list', by relying on visual clues to determine purchase or experiential consumption is worthy of exploration. The interchangeability of man-made (e.g. museum) and natural attractions (e.g. national park), and of commercial (e.g. organized tour) and natural (e.g. going to the beach) activities may explain the high degree of unplanned behaviour associated with them.

Sixthly, the role of situational and environmental factors in tourism consumption is poorly understood. Indeed, Foxall (1997) has criticized the failure of traditional consumer behaviour scholars to acknowledge the importance of situational context in consumer behaviour models. Phillips *et al.* (1995, p. 280) point out that traditional decision making models are relatively irrelevant for describing choices 'for which consumers have little experience, or where the problem is less well-defined, or where emotional considerations play an important role' – in a task environment very much like a tourist destination in other words. Woodside and MacDonald (1993, p. 32) also recognize that 'while useful, such models fail to capture the rich interactions of decisions and behaviors of the travel party and the destination environment experienced by the travel party'.

The influence of the environment (i.e. the consumption site) on purchase has long been acknowledged in the field of psychology, where the work of Skinner (1953) and the behavioural psychologists half a century ago suggested that the marketer's mantra of understanding the customer's needs and wants may not constitute the sum total of knowledge required to create and implement marketing activities. 'Behaviour is the result of a continuous interaction between personal and environmental variables … [P]ersons and situations influence each other reciprocally. To predict behaviour, we need to know how the characteristics of the individual interact with the characteristics of the situation' (Atkinson *et al.*, 1990, p. 518, cited by Phillips and Bradshaw, 1993, p. 61).

A further study provides more evidence for importance of better understanding situational influences in a tourist setting. Hornik (1982), in his study of situational effects of time on consumption, concluded that 'the greater the degree of obligation imposed by an activity, the less important are situational influences' (p. 54). Consider reversing this finding and applying it to a tourist or leisure setting: the activities and attractions on offer to tourists as they pass through a tourist consumption space like Prince Edward Island are unlikely to embody high degrees of obligation, in particular for tourists citing relaxation as their main visit motivation. Applying Hornik's finding, we might conjecture that situational influences (such as visual clues like signage and product information like the VIG) will play a large role in triggering consumption.

Finally, the multi-dimensional nature of the time construct, particularly in the vacation setting, deserves closer examination from consumer behaviour researchers. In our study, increases in length of stay were associated with increases in unplanned behaviours. We could assume that the greater the exposure that a traveller has to the tourist products, services and experiences, the more likely is s/he to engage in unplanned behaviour. The parallel in consumer research is the finding that unplanned purchases in supermarkets increase as the number of aisles visited increase (Inman and Winer, 1998). However, we know that time is expended differently in a tourist setting. If time is spent with friends or relatives or in an all-inclusive resort, for example, unplanned behaviours may be few in number. Nevertheless, in the tourism context, visitors who visit more destinations are, *ceteris paribus*, more likely to engage in unplanned behaviour. It would be useful to test this proposition.

Also, the amount of time in possession of product information may moderate the impact upon behaviour and the amount of time spent planning may influence eventual activities. Remember the hypothesis that the VIG would be used less after arrival than before was not supported. Can we assume, therefore, that time pressure (while on Prince Edward Island) did not affect the time spent accessing the VIG? Perhaps. On the other hand, the immediacy of a plan being implemented may have 'driven' consumers to access and utilize the product information in their possession.

References

Aarts, H., Verplanken, B. and van Knippenberg, A. (1998) Predicting behaviour from actions in the past: Repeated decision making or a matter of habit. *Journal of Applied Social Psychology* 28, 1355–1374.

Abdul-Muhmin, A.G. (1999) Contingent decision behavior: Effect of number of alternatives to be selected on consumers' decision processes. *Journal of Consumer Psychology* 8(1), 91–111.

Abratt, R. and Goodey, S.D. (1990) Unplanned buying and in-store stimuli in supermarkets. *Managerial and Decision Economics* 11, 111–121.

Adaval, R. and Wyer, R.S. (1998) The role of narratives in consumer information processing. *Journal of Consumer Research* 7(3), 207–245.

Agarwal, V.B. and Yochum, G.R. (1999) Tourist spending and race of visitors. *Journal of Travel Research* 38, 173–176.

Agee, T. and Martin, B.A.S. (2001) Planned or impulse purchases? How to create effective infomercials. *Journal of Advertising Research* December, 35–42.

Ajzen, I. (1985) From intentions to actions: A theory of planned behaviour. In: Kuhl, J. and Beckmann, J. (eds) *Action Control: From Cognition to Behaviour*. Springer-Verlag, Berlin.

Ajzen, I. (1991) The theory of planned behavior. *Organizational Behavior and Human Decision Processes* 50, 179–211.

Ajzen, I. (1996) The social psychology of decision making. In: Higgins, E.T. and Kruglanski, A.W. (eds) *Social Psychology: Handbook of Basic Principles*. Guilford, New York.

Ajzen, I. and Driver, B.L. (1992) Application of the theory of planned behavior to leisure choice. *Journal of Leisure Research* 24(3), 207–224.

Ajzen, I. and Fishbein, M. (eds) (1980) *Understanding Attitudes and Predicting Social Behavior*. Prentice-Hall, Englewood Cliffs, New Jersey.

Alba, J.W. and Hutchinson, J.W. (1987) Dimensions of consumer expertise. *Journal of Consumer Research* 13, 411–454.

Alford, P. (1998) Positioning the destination product – can regional tourist boards learn from private sector practice? *Journal of Travel and Tourism Marketing* 7(2), 53–68.

Ariely, D. (2000) Controlling the information flow: effects on consumers' decision making and preferences. *Journal of Consumer Research* 27, 233–248.

Armstrong, J.S., Brodie, R.J. and Parsons, A.G. (2001) Hypotheses in marketing science: review and publication audit. *Marketing Letters* 12(2), 171–187.

Arnould, E.J. and Price, L.L. (1993) River magic: extraordinary experience and the extended service encounter. *Journal of Consumer Research* 20, 1–23.

Bagozzi, R.P. and Dholakia, U. (1999) Goal setting and goal striving in consumer behavior. *Journal of Marketing* 63 (Special Issue), 19–32.

Bagozzi, R.P. and Nataraajan, R. (2000) The year 2000: Looking forward. *Psychology and Marketing* 17(1), 1–11.

Bargh, J.A. (2002) Losing consciousness: Automatic influences on consumer judgment, behavior, and motivation. *Journal of Consumer Research* 29, 280–285.

Barsalou, L.W. (1991) Deriving categories to achieve goals. *The Psychology of Learning and Motivation*, 27, 1–66.

Basala, S.L. and Klenosky, D.B. (2001) Travel-style preferences for visiting a novel destination: A conjoint investigation across the novelty–familiarity continuum. *Journal of Travel Research* November, 172–182.

Bass, F.M., Tigert, D.J. and Lonsdale, D.T. (1968) Market segmentation: Group versus individual behaviour. *Journal of Marketing Research* 5, 264–270.

Bayley, G. and Nancarrow, C. (1998) Impulse purchasing: a qualitative exploration of the phenomenon. *Qualitative Market Research: An International Journal* 1(2), 99–114.

Beatty, S.E. and Ferrell, M.E. (1998) Impulse buying: modeling its precursors. *Journal of Retailing* 74(2), 169–191.

Beatty, S.E. and Smith, S.M. (1987) External search effort: An investigation across several product categories. *Journal of Consumer Research* 14, 83–95.

Beatty, J.E. and Torbert, W.R. (2003) The false duality of work and leisure. *Journal of Management Inquiry* 12(3), 239–252.

Becker, H.S. (1998) *Tricks of the trade*. The University of Chicago Press, Chicago, Illinois.

Beckman, J. and Kuhl, J. (1984) Altering information to gain action control: functional aspects of human information-processing in decision making. *Journal of Research in Personality* 18, 224–237.

Belk, R.W. (1974) An exploratory assessment of situational effects in buyer behaviour. *Journal of Marketing Research* 11, 156–163.

Belk, R.W. (1975) Situational variables and consumer behaviour. *Journal of Consumer Research* 2, 157–163.

Belk, R.W. and Costa, J.A. (1998) The mountain man myth: A contemporary consuming fantasy. *Journal of Consumer Research*,25, 218–240.

Bellenger, D.N., Robertson, D.H. and Hirschman, E.C. (1978) Impulse buying varies by product. *Journal of Advertising Research* 18, 15–18.

Bemmaor, A.C. (1995) Predicting behavior from intention-to-buy measures: the parametric case. *Journal of Marketing Research* 32, 176–191.

Bergadaà, M. (1990) The role of time in the action of the consumer. *Journal of Consumer Research* 17(4), 289–302.

Berger, C.R. and DiBattista, P. (1992) Information seeking and plan elaboration: what do you need to know to know what to do? *Communication Monographs* 59, 368–387.

Berger, C.R. and DiBattista, P. (1993) Communication failure and plan adaptation: If at first you don't succeed, say it louder and slower. *Communication Monographs* 60, 220–238.

Berger, C.R. and DiBattista, P. (1999) Information seeking and plan elaboration: What do you need to know to know what to do? *Communication Monographs* 59, 368–387.

Bettman, J.R. (1979) Memory factors in consumer choice: A review. *Journal of Marketing* 43, 37–53.

Bettman, J.R. and Park, C.W. (1980) Effects of prior knowledge and experience and phase of the choice process on consumer decision processes: A protocol analysis. *Journal of Consumer Research* 7, 234–248.

Bettman, J.R., Johnson, E.J. and Payne, J.W. (1991) Consumer decision making. In: Robertson, T.S. and Kassarjian, H.H. (eds) *Handbook of Consumer Behavior*. Prentice-Hall, Englewood Cliffs, New Jersey, pp. 50–84.

Bettman, J.R., Luce, M.F. and Payne, J.W. (1998) Constructive consumer choice processes. *Journal of Consumer Marketing* 25(3), 187–217.

Biehal, L.L. (1983) Customers prior experiences and perceptions in auto repair choice. *Journal of Marketing* 47, 82–91.

Bishop, D.W. and Witt, P.A. (1970) Sources of behavioural variance during leisure time. *Journal of Personality and Social Psychology* 16, 352–360.

Blackwell, S.A., Szeinbach, S.L., Barnes, J.H., Garner, D.W. and Bush, V. (1999) The antecedents of customer loyalty: an empirical investigation of the role of personal and situational aspects on repurchase decisions. *Journal of Service Research* 1(4), 362–375.

Bloch, P.H., Sherrell, D.L. and Ridgway, N.M. (1986) Consumer search: An extended framework. *Journal of Consumer Research* 13, 119–126.

Bloch, P.H., Ridgway, N.M., and Sherrell, D.L. (1989) Extending the concept of shopping: an investigation of browsing activity. *Journal of Academy of Marketing Science* 17, 13–21.

Brennan, D.G. and Woodside, A.G. (1982) Cooperative national advertising. *Journal of Travel Research* 20, 30–34.

Bronfenbrenner, U. (1986) Recent advances in research on the ecology of human development. In: Silbereisen, R.K., Eyferth, K. and Rudinger, G. (eds) *Development as Action in Context: Problem Behavior and Normal Youth Development*. Springer, New York, pp. 287–309.

Bronfenbrenner, U. (1992) Ecological systems theory. In: Vasta, R. (ed.) *Six Theories of Child Development: Revised Formulations and Current Ideas*. Jessica Kingsley, London, pp. 187–249.

Bronner, R. (1982) *Decision Making under Time Pressure*. D.C. Heath, Lexington, Massachusetts.

Bruce, V. and Green, P.R. (1991) *Visual Perception*. Lawrence Erlbaum Associates, London.

Bucklin, L.P. (1966) Testing propensities to shop. *Journal of Marketing* 30, 22–27.

Buehler, R., Griffin, D. and Ross, M. (1994) Exploring the planning fallacy: Why people underestimate their task completion times. *Journal of Personality and Social Psychology* 67, 366–381.

Burch, W.R. (1969) The social circles of leisure: Competing explanations. *Journal of Leisure Research* 1, 125–147.

Bureau of Tourism Research (2000) *International Visitors Survey, 1999*. BTR, Canberra.

Chadwick, R.A. (1987) Concepts, definitions, and measures used in travel and tourism research. In: Brent Ritchie, J.R. and Goeldner, C.R. (eds) *Travel, Tourism and Hospitality Research*. John Wiley, New York.

Christensen, J.E. and Yoesting, D.R. (1973) Social and attitudinal variants in high and low use of outdoor recreational facilities. *Journal of Leisure Research* 5, 6–15.

Clawson, C. J. (1971) How useful are 90-day purchase probabilities? *Journal of Marketing* 35, 43–47.

Clover, V.T. (1950) Relative importance of impulse buying in retail stores. *Journal of Marketing* 25, 66–70.

Cobb, C.J. and Hoyer, W.D. (1986) Planned versus impulse purchase behaviour. *Journal of Retailing* 62, 384–409.

Cohen, E. (1972) Towards a sociology of international research. *Social Research* 39,164–182.

Conner, M. and Armitage, C.J. (1998) Extending the theory of planned behavior: a review and avenues for further research. *Journal of Applied Social Psychology* 28(15), 1429–1464.

Corfman, K.P. (1991) Comparability and comparison levels used in choices among consumer products. *Journal of Marketing Research* 28(3), 368–374.

Cosenza, R.M. and Davis, D.L. (1981) Family vacation decision making over the family life cycle: a decision and influence structure analysis. *Journal of Travel Research* Autumn, 17–23.

Cotte, J. and Ratneshwar, S. (2001) Timestyle and leisure decisions. *Journal of Leisure Research* 33(4), 396–409.

Cotte, J., Ratneshwar, S. and Mick, D.G. (2004) The times of their lives: phenomenological and metaphysical characteristics of consumer timestyles. *Journal of Consumer Research* 31(3), 333–345.

Coupey, E., Irwin, J.R. and Payne, J.W. (1996) *Product Category Familiarity and Preference Evaluation*. Working Paper. Stern School of Business, New York University.

Cox, K. (1964) The responsiveness of food sales to shelf space changes in supermarkets. *Journal of Marketing* May, 63–67.

Crompton, J. (1979) Motivations for pleasure vacation. *Journal of Leisure Research* 6, 408–424.

Crotts, J.C. and Reid, L.J. (1993) Segmenting the visitor market by the timing of their activity decisions. *Visions in Leisure and Business* 12, 4–7.

Dann, G.M.S. (1981) Tourist motivation: an appraisal. *Annals of Tourism Research* 8, 187–219.

d'Astous, A. (1990) An inquiry into the compulsive side of 'normal' customers. *Journal of Consumer Policy* 13, 15–31.

Decrop, A. (1999) Tourists' decision-making and behavior processes. In: Pizam, A. and Mansfeld, Y. (eds) *Consumer Behavior in Travel and Tourism*. Haworth Hospitality Press, New York.

Deshpande, R. and Krishnan, S. (1980) Consumer impulse purchase and credit card usage: An empirical examination using the log linear model. *Advances in Consumer Research* 7, 792–795.

Dimanche, F. and Havitz, M.E. (1994) Consumer behavior and tourism: Review and extension of four study areas. *Economic Psychology of Travel and Tourism* 3(3), 37–57.

Dittmar, H. and Drury, J. (2000) Self-image – is it in the bag? A qualitative comparison between 'ordinary' and 'excessive' consumers. *Journal of Economic Psychology* 21(2), 109–142.

Dittmar, H., Beattie, J. and Friese, S. (1995) Objects, decision considerations and self-image in men's and women's purchases. *Acta Psychologica* 93, 187–206.

Dittmar, H., Beattie, J. and Friese, S. (1996) Gender identity and material symbols: Objects and decision considerations in impulse purchases. *Journal of Economic Psychology* 15, 391–511.

Dorsch, M.J., Grove, S.J. and Darden, W.R. (2000) Consumer intentions to use a service category. *Journal of Services Marketing* 14(2), 92–117.

Drucker, P.F. (2001) *The Essential Drucker: Selections from the Management Works of Peter F. Drucker*. HarperBusiness, New York.

Earl, P.E. and Potts, J. (2000) Latent demand and the browsing shopper. *Managerial and Decision Economics* 21, 111–122.

East, R. (1997) *Consumer Behaviour: Advances and Applications in Marketing*. Prentice Hall, London.

Eiglier, P. and Langeard, E. (1977) A new approach to service marketing. In: Eiglier, P., Langeard, E., Lovelock, C.H., Bateson, J.E.G. and Young, R.F. (eds) *Marketing Consumer Services: New Insights*. Marketing Science Institute, Cambridge, Massachusetts, pp. 33–58.

Engel, J.F., Blackwell, R.D. and Miniard, R.W. (1993) *Consumer Behavior*, 7th edn. Dryden Press, New York.

Etzel, M.J. and Wahlers, R.G. (1985) The use of requested promotional material by pleasure travelers. *Journal of Travel Research* 12, 2–6l.

Faber, R.J. and O'Guinn, T.C. (1989) Classifying compulsive consumers: Advances in the development of a diagnostic tool. In: Srull, T.K. (ed.) *Advances in Consumer Research* 16, 738–744.

Fairmaner, W. and Dittmar, H. (1993) The Role of Gender in the Choice of Objects and Experiences of Compulsive Buyers. Working paper, School of Social Sciences, University of Sussex, UK.

Fazio, R.H. and Zanna, M.P. (1981) Direct experience and attitude behaviour consistency. *Advances in Experimental Social Psychology* 14, 161–202.

Felcher, E.M., Malaviya, P. and McGill, A.L. (2001) The role of taxonomic and goal-derived product categorization in, within, and across category judgments. *Psychology and Marketing* 18(8), 865–887.

Feldman, J.M. and Lynch, J.G. Jr (1988) Self-generated validity and other effects of measurement on belief, attitude, intention and behaviour. *Applied Psychology* 37(3), 421–435.

Feldman, L.P. and Hornik, J. (1981) The use of time: An Integrated conceptual model. *Journal of Consumer Research* 7, 407–419.

Ferber, R. and Piskie, R.A. (1965) Subjective probabilities and buying intentions. *Review of Economics and Statistics* 47, 322–325.

Fesenmaier, D.R. and Johnson, B. (1989) Involvement-based segmentation. *Journal of Tourism Research* December, 293–300.

Fesenmaier, D.R., Vogt, C.A. and Stewart, W.P. (1993) Investigating the influence of Welcome Center Information on travel behaviour. *Journal of Travel Research* 34, 47–52.

Filiatrault, P. and Ritchie, J.R.B. (1988) The impact of situational factors on the evaluation of hospitality services. *Journal of Travel Research* 26(1), 29–37.

Fischhoff, B. (1991) Value elicitation: Is there anything in here? *American Psychologist* 46, 835–847.

Fishbein, M. and Ajzen, I. (1975) *Belief, Attitude, Intention and Behaviour*. Addison-Wesley, Reading, Massachusetts.

Fisher, R.J. (2001) The role of collaboration in consumers' in-store decisions. *Advances in Consumer Research* 28, 251.

Fitzsimons, G.J. and Morwitz, V. (1996) The effect of measuring intent on brand level purchase behavior. *Journal of Consumer Research* 23, 1–11.

Floyd, M.F., Shinew, K.J., McGuire, M.A. and Noe, F.P. (1994) Race, class, and leisure activity preferences: marginality and ethnicity revisited. *Journal of Leisure Research* 26(2), 158–173.

Fodness, D. and Murray, B. (1999) A model of tourist information search behavior. *Journal of Travel Research* 37(3), 220–230.

Foxall, G.R. (1983) Consumers' intentions and behaviour. *Journal of Market Research Society* 26(3), 231–241.

Foxall, G. (1997), *Marketing Psychology*. Macmillan, London.

Foxall, G.R. (2000) The behavioural economics of consumption: introduction to the special issue. *Managerial and Decision Economics* 21, 93–94.

Francken, D. and van Raaij, W. (1981). Satisfaction with leisure time activities. *Journal of Leisure Research* 13, 337–352.

Frazer, K. (1991) *Bad Trips*. Doubleday, New York.

Gardner, M.P. and Rook, D.W. (1988) Effects of impulse purchases on consumers' affective states. In: Houston, M.J. (ed.) *Advances in Consumer Research*, volume 15. Association for Consumer Research, Provo, Utah.

Geertz, C. (1973) *The Interpretation of Cultures*. Basic Books, New York.

Getzels, J.W. (1982) The problem of the problem. In: Hogarth, R. (ed.) *Question Framing and Response Consistency*. Jossey-Bass, San Francisco, California.

Gholson, B.D., Smither, A., Buhrman, A., Duncan, M.K. and Pierce, K.A. (1996) The sources of children's reasoning errors during analogical problem solving. *Applied Cognitive Psychology* 10(5), S85–S97.

Gibbs, B.J. (1997) Predisposing the decision maker versus framing the decision. *Marketing Letters* 8(1), 71–83.

Gitelson, R.J. and Crompton, J.L. (1983) The planning horizons and sources of information used by pleasure vacationers. *Journal of Travel Research* Winter, 2–7.

Gitelson, R.J. and Kerstetter, D.L. (1990) The relationship between sociodemographic variables, benefits sought and subsequent vacation behavior: a case study. *Journal of Travel Research* 11, 24–29.

Gladwell, M. (2000) *The Tipping Point: How Little Things Can Make a Big Difference*. Little, Brown, Boston.

Glazer, B.G. and Strauss, A.L. (1967) *The Discovery of Grounded Theory*. Aldine, Chicago, Illinois.

Glenberg, A.M., Wilkinson, A.C. and Epstein, W. (1982) The illusion of knowing: Failure in the self-assessment of comprehension. *Memory and Cognition* 10, 597–602.

Godbey, G. and Graefe, A. (1991) Repeat tourism, play and monetary spending. *Annals of Tourism Research* 18, 213–225.

Gollwitzer, P.M. (1990) Action phases and mind-sets. In: Higgins, E.T. and Sorrentino, R.M. (eds) *Handbook of Motivation and Cognition: Foundations of Social Behaviour*. Guilford, New York, pp. 53–92.

Gollwitzer, P.M. (1993) Goal achievement: The role of intentions. *European Review of Social Psychology* 4, 141–185.

Graburn, N.H.H. (1977) Tourism: The sacred journey. In: Smith, V. (ed.) *Hosts and Guests: The Anthropology of Tourism*. University of Pennsylvania, Philadelphia, Pennsylvania.

Granbois, D.H. (1968) Improving the study of customer in-store behavior. *Journal of Marketing* 32, 28–33.

Gregory, R., Lichenstein, S. and Slovic, P. (1993) Valuing environmental resources: a constructive approach. *Journal of Risk and Uncertainty* 7, 177–197.

Gross, B.L. (1994) Consumer responses to time pressure: A qualitative study with homeowners in foreclosure. *Advances in Consumer Research* 21, 121–125.

Guseman, D.S. (1981) Risk perception and risk reduction in consumer services. In: Donnelly, J.H. and George, W.R. (eds) *Marketing of Services*. American Marketing Association, Chicago, Illinois, pp. 200–204.

Hall, E.T. (1983) *The Dance of Life*. Anchor Press-Doubleday, New York.

Hawkins, S.A. and Hoch, S.J. (1992) Low-involvement learning: Memory without evaluation. *Journal of Consumer Research* 19, 212–225.

Heckhausen, H. (1991) *Motivation and Action*. Springer, Berlin.

Heider, F. (1958) *The Psychology of Interpersonal Relations*. Wiley, New York.

Heilman, C.M., Bowman, D. and Wright, G.P. (2000) The evolution of brand preferences and choice behaviors of consumers new to a market. *Journal of Marketing Research* May, 139–155.

Hendrick, C., Mills, J. and Kiesler, C. (1968) Decision time as a function of the number and complexity of equally attractive alternatives. *Journal of Personality and Social Psychology* 8(3), 313–318.

Hirschman, E.C. (1987) Theoretical perspectives of time use: Implications for consumer research. *Research in Consumer Behavior* 2, 55–81.

Holbrook, M.B. and Hirschman, E.C. (1982) The experiential aspects of consumption: Consumer fantasies, feelings, and fun. *Journal of Consumer Research* 9, 132–140.

Hornik, J. (1982) Situational effects on the consumption of time. *Journal of Marketing* Fall, 44–55.

Howard, J.A. and Sheth, J.N. (1969) *The Theory of Buyer Behavior*. John Wiley & Sons, New York.

Howard, J.A. and Sheth, J.N. (1973) A theory of buyer behavior. In: Kassarjian, H.H. and Robertson, T.S. (eds) *Perspectives in Consumer Behavior*. Scott, Foresman and Company, Glenview, Illinois.

Hu, Y. and Ritchie, J.R.B. (1993) Measuring destination attractiveness: A contextual approach. *Journal of Travel Research* Fall, 25–34.

Hyde, K.F. (2000) A hedonic perspective on independent vacation planning, decision-making and behaviour. In: Woodside, A.G., Crouch, G.I., Mazanec, J.A., Oppermann, M. and Sakai, M.Y. (eds) *Consumer Psychology of Tourism, Hospitality and Leisure*. CAB International, Wallingford, UK.

Infosino, W. J. (1986) Forecasting new product sales from likelihood of purchase ratings. *Marketing Science* 5(4), 372–384.

Inman, J.J. and Winer, R.S. (1998) *Where the Rubber Hits the Road: A Model of In-store Consumer Decision Making*. Marketing Science Institute, Report 98–122. Marketing Science Institute, Cambridge, Massachusetts.

Iyer, E.S. (1989) Unplanned purchasing: Knowledge of shopping environment and time pressure. *Journal of Retailing* 65(1), 40–57.

Jackson, E.L. (1997) In the Eye of the Beholder: A Comment on Samdahl and Jekubovich (1997), 'A Critique of Leisure Constraints: Comparative Analysis and Understandings'. *Journal of Leisure Research* 29(4), 458–468.

Jacoby, J., Speller, D.E. and Berning, C.K. (1974) Brand choice behavior as a function of information load. *Journal of Consumer Research* 1(1), 33–42.

Jacoby, J., Szybillo, G.J. and Berning, C.K. (1976) Time and consumer behavior: An interdisciplinary overview. *Journal of Consumer Research* 2, 320–339.

Jarboe, G. and McDaniel, C. (1987) A profile of browsers at regional shopping malls. *Journal of the Academy of Marketing Science* 15, 46–53.

Jeng, J. (1997) Facets of the complex trip decision making process. Paper presented at the Travel and Tourism Research Association's 28th Annual Conference, June 1997, Norfolk, Virginia.

Johnson, H.M. and Seifert, C. (1992) The role of predictive features in retrieving analogical cases. *Journal of Memory and Language* 31(4), 648–667.

Johnson, M. (1984) Consumer choice strategies for comparing noncomparable alternatives. *Journal of Consumer Research* 16, 300–309.

Johnson, M. (1988) Comparability and hierarchical processing in multialternative choice. *Journal of Consumer Research* 15, 303–314.

Johnson, M. (1989) The differential processing of product category and noncomparable choice alternatives. *Journal of Consumer Research* 16, 303–314.

Juster, F.T. (1964) *Anticipations and Purchases: An Analysis of Consumer Behavior*. Princeton University Press, Princeton, New Jersey.

Juster, F.T. (1966) *Consumer Buying Intentions and Purchase Probability*. Occasional Paper 99, National Bureau of Economic Research, Colombia University Press, New York.

Kahneman, D. and Treisman, A. (1984) Changing views of attention and automaticity. In: Parasuraman, R. and Davies, D.R. (eds) *Varieties of Attention*. Academic Press, New York.

Kahneman, D., Slovic, P. and Tversky, A. (1982) *Judgment Under Uncertainty: Heuristics and Biases*. Cambridge University Press, Cambridge, UK.

Kalwani, M.U. and Silk, A.J. (1982) On the relationship and predictive ability of purchase intention measures. *Marketing Science* 1, 243–286.

Kardes, F.R. (1994) Consumer judgment and decision processes. In: Wyer, R.S. and Srull, T.K. (eds) *Handbook of Social Recognition*, 2nd edn. Lawrence Erlbaum Associates, Hove, UK.

Katona, G. (1975) *Psychological Economics*. Elsevier, New York.

Kelly, R. (1965) An evaluation of selected variables of end display effectiveness. Doctoral dissertation, Harvard University, Cambridge, Massachusetts.

Kendzierski, D. (1990) Exercise self-schemata: Cognitive and behavioral correlates. *Health Psychology* 9(1), 69–82.

King, B. and Choi, H.J. (1997) The attributes and potential of secondary Australian destinations through the eyes of Korean travel industry executives. *Journal of Vacation Marketing* 3(4), 314–326.

Klenosky, D.B. and Rethans, A.J. (1988) The formation of consumer choice sets: A longitudinal investigation at the product class level. In: Houston, M.J. (ed.) *Advances in Consumer Research*, volume 15. Association of Consumer Research, Provo, Utah, pp. 13–18.

Kollat, D.T. and Willett, R.P. (1967) Customer impulse purchasing behaviour. *Journal of Marketing* 6, 21–31.

Krishnan, H.S. and Shapiro, S. (1999) Prospective and retrospective memory for intentions: A two-component approach. *Journal of Consumer Psychology* 8(2), 141–166.

Kruglanski, A.W. and Klar, Y. (1985) Knowing what to do: On the epistemology of actions. In: Kuhl, J. and Blackman, J. (eds) *Action Control: From Cognition to Behavior*. Springer-Verlag, Berlin.

Kvaviliashvili, L. and Ellis, J. (1996) Varieties of intention: Some distinctions and classifications. In: Brandimonte, M., Einstein, G.O. and McDaniel, M.A. (eds) *Prospective Memory: Theory and Applications*. Lawrence Eribaum Associates, Mahwahy, pp. 23–51.

Langley, A. (1999) Strategies for theorizing from process data. *Academy of Management Review* 24(4), 691–710.

Lazarsfeld, P.F. and Rosenberg, M. (1965) *The Language of Social Research/A Reader in the Methodology of Social Research*. Free Press, New York.

Leclerc, F., Schmitt, B.H. and Dube, L. (1995) Foreign branding and its effects on product perceptions and attitudes. *Journal Of Marketing Research* May 31, 263–270.

Leiper, N. (1989) Main destination ratios: Analyses of tourist flows. *Annals of Tourism Research* 16(4), 530–541.

Lewin, K. (1951) *Field Theory in Social Science*. Harper, New York.

Lewis, D. and Weigert, D.J. (1981) The structures and meanings of social time. *Social Forces* 60, 432–457.

Lilien, G.L., Kotler, P. and Moorthy, K.S. (1992) *Marketing Models*. Prentice Hall, Englewood Cliffs, New Jersey.

Lynch, J.G. Jr and Srull, T.K. (1982) Memory and attention factors in consumer choice: Concepts and research methods. *Journal of Consumer Research* September, 18–37.

Malhotra, N.K. (1982) Information load and consumer decision making. *Journal of Consumer Research* 8, 419–430.

Manfredo, M.J. (1989) An investigation of the basis for external information search in recreation and tourism. *Leisure Science* 11, 29–45.

Manski, C. (1990) The use of intentions data to predict behavior: A best-case analysis. *Journal of American Statistical Association* 85, 934–940.

March, R. and Woodside, A. (2005) Testing theory of planned versus realized tourism behavior. *Annals of Tourism Research*, 35 (in press).

Marketing Agency (1993) Available at: http://www.tiapei.pe.ca/TourismResources/News.htm (accessed 1 January 2005).

Mazursky, D. (1989a) Past experience and future tourism decisions. *Annals of Tourism Research* 16, 333–344.

Mazursky, D. (1989b) Temporal decay in the satisfaction-purchase intention relationship. *Psychology and Marketing* 6(3), 211–322.

Mazursky, D. and Geva, A. (1989) Temporal decay in satisfaction–intention relationship. *Psychology and Marketing* 6(3), 211–227.

McClelland, G.H., Stewart, B.E., Judd, C.M. and Bourne, L.E. Jr (1987) Effects of choice task on attribute memory. *Organizational Behavior and Human Performance* 24, 300–316.

McCracken, G. (1988) *The Long Interview*. Sage, Newbury Park, California.

McFarlane, B., Boxall, P. and Watson, D. (1998) Past experience and behavioural choice among wildnerness users. *Journal of Leisure Research* 30, 195–213.

McGoldrick, P.J. (1982) How unplanned are impulse purchases? *Retail and Distribution Management* Jan/Feb, 27–30.

McGrath, J.E. and Kelly, J.R. (1986) *Time and Human Interaction: Toward a Social Psychology of Time.* Guilford Publications, New York.

McIntosh, R.W. and Goeldner, C.R. (1990) *Tourism: Principles, Practices, Philosophies.* John Wiley, New York.

McKercher, B. (2001) A comparison of main-destination visitors and through travelers at a dual-purpose destination. *Journal of Travel Research* 39, 433–441.

Menon, G. (1993) The effects of accessibility of information in memory on judgements of behavioral frequencies. *Journal of Consumer Research* 20, 431–440.

Menon, G., Raghubir, P. and Schwarz, N. (1997) How much will I spend? Factors affecting consumers' estimates of future expense. *Journal of Consumer Psychology* 6(2), 141–164.

Messmer, D.J. and Johnson, R.R. (1993) Inquiry Conversion and travel advertising effectiveness. *Journal of Travel Research* 14, 14–21.

Mintzberg, H. (1973) Strategy-making in three modes. *California Management Review* 16(2), 44–53.

Mintzberg, H. (1978) Patterns in strategy formation. *Management Science* 24(9), 934–948.

Mintzberg, H. (1987) The strategy concept I: five Ps for strategy. *California Management Review* (Fall), 11–24.

Mintzberg, H. (1994) *The Rise and Fall of Strategic Planning: Reconceiving Roles For Planning, Plans, Planners.* The Free Press, New York.

Mintzberg, H. and Waters, J.A. (1982) Tracking strategy in an entrepreneurial firm. *Academy of Management Journal* 25(3), 465–499.

Mintzberg, H. and Waters, J.A. (1985) Of strategies, deliberate and emergent. *Strategic Management Journal* 6, 257–272.

Mitra, A. (1995) Advertising and the stability of consideration sets over multiple purchase considerations. *International Journal of Research in Marketing* 12, 81–94.

Mittal, V., Kumar, P. and Tsiros, M. (1999) Attribute-level performance, satisfaction, and behavioral intentions over time: A consumption-system approach. *Journal of Marketing* 63 (April), 88–101.

Mo, C., Howard, D.R. and Havitz, M.E. (1993) Testing an international tourist role typology. *Annals of Tourism Research* 20, 319–335.

Moore, W.L. and Lehmann, D.R. (1980) Individual differences in search behavior for a non-durable. *Journal of Consumer Research* 7, 296–307.

Morrison, A.M. (1996) *Hospitality and Travel Marketing*. Delmar, Albany, New York.

Morrissey J. (1986) Tourism and the public sector. *Planner* 72(6), 17–18.

Morwitz, V.G. (1997a) Why consumers don't always accurately predict their own future behaviour. *Marketing Letters* 8(1), 57–70.

Morwitz, V.G. (1997b) It seems like only yesterday: The nature and consequences of telescoping errors in marketing research. *Journal of Consumer Psychology* 6(1), 1–29.

Morwitz, V.G. and Schmittlein, D.C. (1992) Using segmentation to improve sales forecasts based on purchase intent: Which 'intenders' actually buy? *Journal of Marketing Research* 29, 391–405.

Morwitz, V.G., Johnson, E. and Schmittlein, D. (1993) Does measuring intent change behaviour? *Journal of Consumer Research* 20, 46–53.

Morwitz, V.G., Stekel, J. and Gupta, A. (1996) *When Do Purchase Intentions Predict Sales?* Working paper, Stern School of Business, New York University, New York.

Moutinho, L. (1987) Consumer behavior in tourism. *European Journal of Marketing* 21(10), 5–44.

Mullen, P.D., Hersey, J.C. and Iverson, D.C. (1987) Health behavior models compared. *Social Science and Medicine* 24, 973–983.

Murray, K.B. (1991) A test of services marketing theory: Consumer information acquisition activities. *Journal of Marketing* 55, 10–25.

Murray, K.B. and Schlacter, J.L. (1990) The impact of services versus goods on consumers' assessments of risk and variability. *Journal of the Academy of Marketing Science* 18(1), 51–65.

Newman, J.W. and Staelin, R. (1972) Prepurchase information seeking for new cars and major household appliances. *Journal of Marketing* 9, 249–257.

Nicholls, J.A.F., Li, F., Roslow, S., Kranendonk, C.J. and Mandakovic, T. (2001) Inter-American perspectives from mall shoppers: Chile–United States. *Journal of Global Marketing* 15(1), 87–103.

Notani, A.S. (1998) Moderators of perceived behavioral control's predictiveness in the theory of planned behavior: A meta-analysis. *Journal of Consumer Psychology* 7(3), 247–271.

O'Guinn, T.C. and Faber, R.J. (1989) Compulsive buying: A phenomenological exploration. *Journal of Consumer Research* 16, 147–157.

Oppermann, M. (1995) A model of travel itineraries. *Journal of Travel Research* 33(4), 57–61.

Otto, J.E. and Ritchie, J.R.B. (1996) The service experience in tourism. *Tourism Management* 17, 165–174.

Papoulis, A. (1990) *Probability and Statistics.* Prentice-Hall International Editions, New York.

Park, C.W. and Lutz, R.J. (1982) Decision plans and consumer choice dynamics. *Journal of Marketing Research* February, 108–115.

Park, C.W., Hughes, R.W., Thukral, V. and Friedmann, R. (1981) Consumers' decision plans and subsequent behavior. *Journal of Marketing* 45, 33–47.

Parr, D. (1989) Free independent travellers. MSc Thesis, Lincoln College, University of Canterbury, UK.

Payne, J.W. (1982) Contingent consumer behavior. *Psychological Bulletin* 92(2), 382–402.

Payne, J.W., Bettman, J.R. and Johnson, E.J. (1992) Behavioral decision research: A constructive processing perspective. *Annual Review of Psychology* 43, 87–131.

Payne, J.W., Bettman, J.R. and Johnson, E.J. (1993) *The Adaptive Decision Maker.* Cambridge University Press, Cambridge, UK.

Pearce, P.L. and Caltabiano, M. (1983) Inferring travel motivations from travelers' experiences. *Journal of Travel Research* 22, 25–30.

Perdue, R.R. (1986) The influence of unplanned attraction visits on expenditures by travel-through visitors. *Journal of Travel Research* 25, 14–19.

Peter, J.P. and Olson, J.C. (1999) *Consumer Behavior and Marketing Strategy*, 5th edn. Irwin McGraw-Hill, Boston, Massachusetts.

Phillip, S. F. (1998) Race and gender differences in adolescent peer group approval of leisure activities. *Journal of Leisure Research* 30(2), 214–232.

Phillips, D.M., Olson, J.C. and Baumgartner, H. (1995) Consumption visions in consumer decision making. In: Kardes, F. and Sujan, M. (eds) *Advances in Consumer Research*, vol. 22. Association for Consumer Research, Provo, Utah, pp. 280–284.

Phillips, H. and Bradshaw, R. (1993) How customers actually shop: customer interaction with the point of sale. *Journal of the Market Research Society* 35(1), 51–62.

Pickering, J.F. (1977) *The Acquisition of Consumer Durables: A Cross-sectional Investigation.* Associated Business Programmes, London.

Pizam, A. and Sussmann, S. (1995) Does nationality affect tourist behavior? *Annals of Tourism Research* 22(4), 901–917.

Plog, S. (1974) Why destinations areas rise and fall in popularity. *Cornell Hotel Restaurant and Administration Quarterly*, 14, 55–58.

Prasad, V.K. (1975) Unplanned buying in two retail settings. *Journal of Retailing* 51(3), 3–12.

Radecki, C.M. and Jaccard, J. (1995) Perceptions of knowledge, actual knowledge, and information search behavior. *Journal of Experimental Social Psychology* 31, 107–138.

Ragin, C.C. (1987) *The Comparative Method: Moving Beyond Qualitative and Quantitative Strategies.* University of California Press, Berkeley, California.

Raju, P.S. (1980) Optimum stimulation level: Its relationship to personality, demographics, and exploratory behavior. *Journal of Consumer Research* 7, 272–282.

Ransome, P. (1996) *The Work Paradigm*. Avebury, Aldershot, UK.

Rao, S.R., Thomas, E.G. and Javalgi, R.G. (1992) Activity preferences and trip planning behavior of the US outbound pleasure travel market. *Journal of Travel Research* 30, 3–13.

Raymore, L. (2002) Facilitators to leisure. *Journal of Leisure Research* 34 (1), 37–51.

Read, D. and Loewenstein, G. (1995) Diversification bias: Explaining the discrepancy in variety seeking between combined and separated choices. *Journal of Experimental Psychology: Applied* 1, 34–39.

Reilly, M.D. and Conover, J.N. (1983) Meta-analysis: Integrating results from consumer research studies. In: Bagozzi, R.P. and Tybout, A.M. (eds).*Advances in Consumer Research*. Association for Consumer Research, Ann Arbor, pp. 509–513.

Rhoads, C. (2002) Short work hours undercut Europe in economic drive. *Wall Street Journal*, CCXL (28), A1, A6.

Richardson, S.L. and Crompton, J. (1988) Vacation patterns of French and English Canadians. *Annals of Tourism Research* 15, 430–448.

Ritchie, J.R.B. (1994) Research on leisure behavior and tourism – state of the art. In: Gasser, R.V. and Weiermair, K. (eds) *Spoilt for Choice: Decision Making Processes and Preference Changes of Tourists – Intertemporal and Intercountry Perspectives*. Kulturverl, Germany.

Roehl, W. and Fesenmaier, D. (1992) Risk perception and pleasure travel: an exploratory analysis. *Journal of Travel Research* 30(4), 17–26.

Rook, D.W. (1987) The buying impulse. *Journal of Consumer Research* 14, 189–199.

Rook, D.W. and Fisher, R.J. (1995) Normative influences on impulsive buying behaviour. *Journal of Consumer Research* 22, 305–313.

Rook, D.W. and Gardner, M.P. (1993) In the mood: Impulse buyings' affective antecedents. In: Arnold-Costa, J. and Belk, R.W. (eds) *Research in Consumer Behaviour*, volume 6. JAI Press, Greenwich, Connecticut.

Rook, D.W. and Hoch, S.J. (1985) Consuming impulses. In: Holbrook, M.B. and Hirschman, E.C. (eds) *Advances in Consumer Research*, volume 12. Association for Consumer Research, Provo, Utah, pp. 23–27.

Ruffman, T.K. and Olson, D.R. (1989) Children's ascriptions of knowledge to others. *Developmental Psychology* 25, 601–606.

Ryan, C. (1991) Tourism and marketing – a symbiotic relationship. *Tourism Management* 12, 113–124.

Schor, J. B. (1991) *The Overworked American*. Basic Books, New York.

Schul, P. and Crompton, J.L. (1983) Search behavior of international vacationers: Travel-specific lifestyle and socio-demographic variables. *Journal of Travel Research* Fall, 25–30.

Scitovsky, T. (1992) *The Joyless Economy*. Oxford University Press, Oxford, UK.

Scrull, T.K. (1982) The representation of consumer information in memory. *Advances in Consumer Research* 9, 499–511.

Senge, P. (1990) *The Fifth Discipline*. Doubleday, New York.

Shank, R.C. (1999) *Dynamic Memory Revisited*. Cambridge University Press, Cambridge, UK.

Shapiro, S. and Krishnan, H.S. (1999) Consumer memory for intentions: A prospective memory perspective. *Journal of Experimental Psychology* 5(2), 169–189.

Sheppard, B.H., Hartwick, J. and Warshaw, P.R. (1988) The theory of reasoned action: A meta-analysis of past research with recommendations for modifications and future research. *Journal of Consumer Research* 15, 325–343.

Shoemaker, S. (1994) Segmenting the US travel market according to benefits realized. *Journal of Travel Research* 33(3), 8–21.

Simonson, I. (1990) The effect of purchase quantity and timing on variety-seeking behavior. *Journal of Marketing Research* 27, 150–162.

Simonson, I. (1993) Get closer to your customers by understanding how they make choices. *California Management Review* 35(4), 68–84.

Skinner, B.F. (1953) *Science and Human Behavior*. Free Press, New York.

Snepenger, D. (1987) Segmenting the vacation market by novelty seeking role. *Journal of Travel Research* 26(2), 8–14.

Solomon, M.R. (1983) The role of products as social stimuli: A symbolic interactionism perspective. *Journal of Consumer Research* 10, 319–329.

Solomon, M.R. and Assael, H. (1988) The forest or the trees? A gestalt approach to symbolic consumption. In: Umiker-Sebeok, J. (ed.) *Marketing and Semiotics: New Directions in the Study of Signs for Sale*. Mouton de Gruyter, Berlin, pp. 189–218.

Stabler, M.J. (1988) The image of destination regions: Theoretical and empirical aspects. In: Goodall, B. and Ashworth, G. (eds) *Marketing in the Tourism Industry*. Croom Helm, London.

Stanton, J.L. and Bonner, P.G. (1980) An investigation of the differential impact of purchase situation on levels of consumer choice behaviour. *Advances in Consumer Research* 8, 639–643.

Stayman, D.M. and Deshplande, R. (1989) Situational ethnicity and consumer behavior. *Journal of Consumer Research* 16, 361–371.

Stebbins, R.A. (1992) *Amateurs, Professionals, and Serious Leisure.* McGill-Queens University Press, Montreal, Canada.

Stebbins, R.A. (1997) Serious leisure and well being. In: Haworth, J.T. (ed.) *Work, Leisure, and Well-Being.* Routledge, London, pp. 117–130.

Stern, E. (1962) The significance of impulse buying today. *Journal of Marketing* 26(2), 59–62.

Stewart, S.I. and Vogt, C.A. (1999) A case-based approach to understanding vacation planning. *Leisure Sciences* 21, 79–95.

Stigler, G.J. (1961) The Economics of Information. *Journal of Political Economy* 59, 213–225.

Sutton, S. (1998) Predicting and explaining intentions and behaviour: How well are we doing? *Journal of Applied Social Psychology* 28, 1317–1338.

Tauber, E. (1975) Predictive validity in consumer research. *Journal of Advertising Research* 15, 59–64.

Tobin, J. (1959) On the predictive value of consumer intentions and attitudes. *Review of Economics and Statistics* 41, 1–11.

Tourism New South Wales (1999) *Five-Year Strategic Plan.* TNSW, Sydney, Australia.

Tsang, G.K.Y. (1993) Visitor Information Network Study: Visitors' information seeking behaviour for on-site travel-related sub-decision making and evaluation of service performance. MCom Thesis, University of Otago, Dunedin, New Zealand.

Tufte, E. (2003) *The Visual Display of Quantitative Information.* Graphic Press, Cheshire, Connecticut.

Tversky, A. and Kahneman, D. (1984) Extensional versus intuitive reasoning: The conjunction fallacy and probability judgment. *Psychological Review* 91, 293–315.

Tversky, A., Sattath, S. and Slovic, P. (1988) Contingent weighting in judgment and choice. *Psychological Review* 95, 371–384.

Um, S. and Crompton, J.L. (1990) Attitude determinants in tourism destination choice. *Annals of Tourism Research* 17, 432–448.

Umesh, U.N. and Cote, J.A. (1988) Influence of situational variables on brand-choice models. *Journal of Business Research* 16, 91–99.

Urbany, J.E., Dickson, P.R. and Wilkie, W.L. (1989) Buyer uncertainty and information search. *Journal of Consumer Research* 16, 208–215.

Uysal, M., Fesenmaier, D.R. and O'Leary, J.T. (1994) Geographic and seasonal variation in the concentration of travel in the United States. *Journal of Travel Research* 32(3), 61–64.

Van Maanen, J. (1988) *Tales of the Field.* University of Chicago Press, Chicago, Illinois.

van Raaij, W.F. (1986) Consumer research on tourism: Mental and behavioral constructs. *Annals of Tourism Research* 13, 1–9.

van Raaij, W.F. and Francken, D.A. (1984) Vacation decisions, activities, and satisfactions. *Annals of Tourism Research* 11, 101–112.

Vernplanken, B., Aarts, H. and van Knippenberg, A. (1997) Habit, information acquisition, and the process of making travel mode choices. *European Journal of Social Psychology* 27, 539–560.

Wallendorf, M. and Brucks, M. (1993) Introspection in consumer research: Implementation and implications. *Journal of Consumer Research* 20, 339–359.

Warshaw, P.R. (1980) Predicting purchase and other behaviors from general and contextually specific intentions. *Journal of Marketing Research* 17, 26–33.

Warshaw, P.R., Sheppard, B.H. and Hartwick, J. (1986) A general theory of intention and behavioral self-prediction. In: Bagozzi, R.P. (ed.) *Advances in Marketing Communication.* JAI Press, Greenwich, Connecticut.

Wegner, D.M. (2002) *The Illusion of Conscious Will.* Bradford Books, MIT Press, Cambridge, Massachusetts.

Weick, K.E. (1995) *Sensemaking in Organizations.* Sage, Thousand Oaks, California.

Weick, K.E. (1998) *The Social Psychology of Organizing.* McGraw-Hill, New York.

Westbrook, R.A. and Fornell, C. (1979) Patterns of information source usage among durable goods buyers. *Journal of Marketing Research* 16, 303–312.

Weun, S., Jones, M.A. and Beatty, S.E. (1998) The development and validation of the impulse buying tendency scale. *Psychological Reports* 82, 1123–1133.

Wicks, B. and Schuett, M. (1991) Examining the role of tourism promotion through the use of brochures. *Tourism Management* 12, 301–313.

Williams, J. and Dardis, R. (1972) Shopping behavior for soft goods and marketing strategies. *Journal of Retailing* 48(3), 32–41 and 126.

Wilson, T.D. (2002) *Strangers to Ourselves: Discovering Adaptive Unconscious.* Belknap Press, Cambridge, Massachusetts.

Wimmer, H., Hogrefe, J. and Perner, J. (1988) Children's understanding of informational access as a source of knowledge. *Child Development* 59, 386–396.

Wood, M. (1998) Socio-economic status, delay of gratification, and impulse buying. *Journal of Economic Psychology* 19, 295–320.

Woodside, A.G. (1990) Measuring advertising effectiveness in destination marketing strategies. *Journal of Travel Research* 29, 3–8.

Woodside, A.G. (2004) Advancing means-end chains by incorporating Heider's balance theory and Fournier's consumer-brand relationship typology. *Psychology and Marketing* 21(4), 279–294.

Woodside, A.G. (2005) *Market-Driven Thinking.* Elsevier, Amsterdam.

Woodside, A.G. and Bearden, W.O. (1978) Field theory applied to consumer behavior. *Research in Marketing,* volume 1. JAI Press, Stamford, Connecticut.

Woodside, A.G. and Chebat, J.-C. (2001) Updating Heider's balance theory in consumer behavior. *Psychology and Marketing* 18(11), 475–496.

Woodside, A.G. and Dubelaar, C. (2002) A general theory of tourism consumption systems: A conceptual framework and an empirical exploration. *Journal of Travel Research* 41, 120–132.

Woodside, A.G. and Dubelaar, C. (2003) Increasing quality in measuring advertising effectiveness: A meta-analysis of question framing in conversion studies. *Journal of Advertising Research* 43(1), 78–85.

Woodside, A.G. and Jacobs, L.W. (1985) Step two in benefit segmentation: Learning the benefits realized by major travel markets. *Journal of Travel Research* 24(1), 7–14.

Woodside, A.G. and King, R. (2001) Tourism consumption systems: Theory and empirical research. *Journal of Travel and Tourism Research* 10(1), 3–27.

Woodside, A.G. and Lawrence, J. (1985) Step two in benefit segmentation: learning the benefits realized by major travel markets. *Journal of Travel Research* 24(1), 7–13.

Woodside, A.G. and MacDonald, R. (1993) General system framework of customer choice processes of tourism services. In: Gasser, R.V. and Weiermair, K. (eds) *Spoilt for Choice: Decision Making Processes and Preference Changes of Tourists – Intertemporal and Intercountry Perspectives,* Proceedings of the International Conference at the University of Innsbruck, November 1993, Kultur.

Woodside, A.G. and Wilson, E.J. (1995) Applying the long interview in direct marketing research. *Journal of Direct Marketing* 9(1), 37–55.

Woodside, A.G., MacDonald, R. and Trappey, R.J. (1997) Measuring linkage-advertising effects on customer behaviour and net revenue: Using quasi-experiments of advertising treatments with novice and experienced product-service users. *Canadian Journal of Administrative Sciences* 14(2), 214–228.

Wright, P.L. (1974) The harrassed decision maker: Time pressure, distraction, and the use of evidence. *Journal of Applied Psychology* 59, 555–561.

Wright, P. (1975) Consumer choice strategies: Simplifying vs. optimizing. *Journal of Marketing Research* 12(1), 60–67.

Wright, P.L. and Kriewall, M.A. (1980) State-of-mind effects on the accuracy with which utility functions predict marketplace choice. *Journal of Marketing Research* 17, 277–293.

Wright, P.L. and Weitz, B. (1977) Time horizon effects on product evaluation strategies. *Journal of Marketing Research* 14, 429–443.

Yiannakis, A. and Gibson, H. (1992) Roles tourists play. *Annals of Tourism Research* 19, 287–303.

Yiannakis, A., Levadi, S. and Apostolopoulos, Y. (1991) Some cross-cultural patterns in tourist role preference: A study of Greek and American tourist behaviors. *World Leisure and Recreation* 33(2), 33–37.

Yin, R.K. (1994) *Case Study Research, Design and Methods,* 2nd edn. Sage Publications, Newbury Park, California.

Young, M.R., DeSarbo, W.S. and Morwitz, V.G. (1998) The stochastic modeling of purchase intentions and behavior. *Management Science* 44(2), 188–202.

Young, R.A. and Kent, A.T. (1985) Using the theory of reasoned action to improve the understanding of recreation behavior. *Journal of Leisure Research* 17(2), 90–106.

Young, R.F. (1981) The advertising of consumer services and the hierarchy of effects. In: Donnelly, J.H. and George, W.R. (eds) *Marketing of Services.* American Marketing Association, Chicago, Illinois, pp. 196–199.

Zajonc, R.B. and Markus, H. (1982) Affective and cognitive factors in preferences. *Journal of Consumer Research* 9, 123–131.

Zalatan, A. (1996) The determinants of planning time in vacation travel. *Tourism Management* 17(2),
    123–131.
Zaltman, G. (1997) Rethinking market research: Putting people back in. *Journal of Marketing Research* 34(4),
    55–67.
Zaltman, G. (2003) *How Consumers Think*. Harvard Business School Press, Cambridge, Massachusetts.
Zeithaml, V.A. (1981) How consumer evaluation processes differ between goods and services. In: Donnelly,
    J.H. and George, W.R. (eds) *Marketing of Services*. American Marketing Association, Chicago, Illinois,
    pp. 186–190.
Zerubavel, E. (1981) *Hidden Rhythms: Schedules and Calendars in Social Life*. University of Chicago Press,
    Chicago, Illinois.

Index

Note: page numbers in *italics* refer to figures, tables and exhibits